W9-AUT-692

GOVERNING JAPAN

GOVERNING JAPAN

Divided Politics in a Resurgent Economy

Fourth Edition

J. A. A. Stockwin

Blackwell Publishing

© 1975, 1982, 1999, 2008 by J. A. A. Stockwin

BLACKWELL PUBLISHING
350 Main Street, Malden, MA 02148-5020, USA
9600 Garsington Road, Oxford OX4 2DQ, UK
550 Swanston Street, Carlton, Victoria 3053, Australia

The right of J. A. A. Stockwin to be identified as the author of this work has been asserted in accordance with the UK Copyright, Designs, and Patents Act 1988.

All rights reserved. No part of this publication may be reproduced, stored in a retrieval system, or transmitted, in any form or by any means, electronic, mechanical, photocopying, recording or otherwise, except as permitted by the UK Copyright, Designs, and Patents Act 1988, without the prior permission of the publisher.

Designations used by companies to distinguish their products are often claimed as trademarks. All brand names and product names used in this book are trade names, service marks, trademarks, or registered trademarks of their respective owners. The publisher is not associated with any product or vendor mentioned in this book.

This publication is designed to provide accurate and authoritative information in regard to the subject matter covered. It is sold on the understanding that the publisher is not engaged in rendering professional services. If professional advice or other expert assistance is required, the services of a competent professional should be sought.

First published by Weidenfeld and Nicholson 1975
Second edition published 1982
Third edition published 1999
Fourth edition published 2008 by Blackwell Publishing Ltd

1   2008

Library of Congress Cataloging-in-Publication Data

Stockwin, J. A. A. (James Arthur Ainscow)
   Governing Japan : divided politics in a resurgent economy / J. A. A. Stockwin. – 4th ed.
      p. cm.
   Includes bibliographical references and index.
   ISBN 978-1-4051-5415-4 (hardcover : alk. paper) – ISBN 978-1-4051-5416-1 (pbk. : alk. paper)
1. Japan–Politics and government–1945– 2. Japan–Economic policy–1945– I. Title.

   JQ1631.S76 2008
   320.952–dc22

                                      2007048801

A catalogue record for this title is available from the British Library.

Set in 10.5/12.5pt Sabon
by SPi Publisher Services, Pondicherry, India
Printed and bound in Singapore
by Utopia Press Pte Ltd

The publisher's policy is to use permanent paper from mills that operate a sustainable forestry policy, and which has been manufactured from pulp processed using acid-free and elementary chlorine-free practices. Furthermore, the publisher ensures that the text paper and cover board used have met acceptable environmental accreditation standards.

For further information on
Blackwell Publishing, visit our website at
www.blackwellpublishing.com

In memory of David Sissons

who showed me how to study Japanese politics

Contents

General Editor's Introduction

This book is a distinguished and well-established part of a series of studies in comparative government. The original goal of the series was to provide clear and comprehensive analyses of the governmental systems of individual countries selected either for their intrinsic importance or because their pattern of government was of special interest to the students of political science. Although the series is aimed at students and teachers in higher education, it has always been an important part of the series' mission that the volumes should be accessible and attractive to the general reader.

This fourth edition of Arthur Stockwin's *Governing Japan* exemplifies that approach: it offers a comprehensive and lucidly argued analysis of the Japanese political system which meets the needs of those who seek to understand this important country both for practical and for academic purposes. Since its first appearance in 1975 Professor Stockwin's text (originally published as *Japan: Divided Politics in a Growth Economy*) has provided authoritative guidance in unravelling the complexities of Japan's democratic institutions. Although this new edition is as insistent as previous volumes on the importance of history in shaping modern Japanese politics, it focuses especially on the important structural developments that have occurred in the early twenty-first century. In particular, it analyses the profound changes that have brought much-needed modernization to the faltering Japanese economy, and the administrative and political reforms introduced under Koizumi that were designed to strengthen the capacity both of the Prime Minister and of the political system more generally. Even so, as Professor Stockwin convincingly argues, Japan still faces a number of daunting challenges relating to its political life, its demographic composition and its international status. How Japan meets those challenges is a question of crucial importance not just for Japan itself but for the whole international community. Professor Stockwin's timely book provides us with an invaluable tool for understanding that process of adjustment and for interpreting a political system which has too often seemed remote and culturally idiosyncratic. I am delighted to have this new edition in the series and anticipate that it will command a wide and appreciative audience.

Gillian Peele
Series Editor

List of Tables

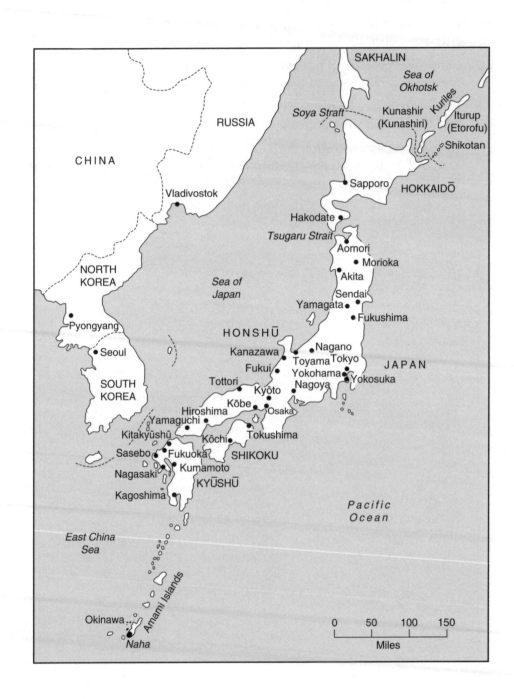

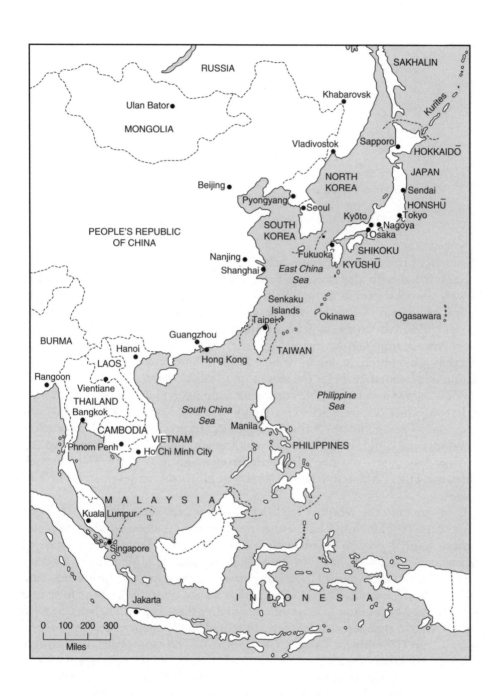

Conventions

Throughout this book, Japanese, Chinese and Korean names are given in their correct order, with the surname first and the personal name second. When, however, works written in English by Japanese writers are cited in footnotes, the order natural to English is preserved. Macrons are used over vowels that are lengthened in Japanese pronunciation, in order to distinguish them from short vowels; thus *fukoku* but *kyōhei*. For Tokyo, Osaka and Kyoto, however, macrons are omitted. It should be noted that a 'long' vowel is given in pronunciation approximately twice the length of a 'short' vowel. Another useful pronunciation hint is that a double consonant is doubled in length when spoken, as in Italian. Thus *Nikkei* is spoken roughly as 'Nick Kaye', not 'Nick eh' (BBC newsreaders please note!). While on the subject of pronunciation, Japanese long vowels are not diphthongs, as so often in English. Thus *rōdō* (labour) is spoken as 'raw door', not 'roe doe'. Japanese pronunciation is not heavily stressed. Thus, not HiROshima, nor HiroSHIma, but Hi ro shi ma (even stress on each syllable).

In my opinion the accepted English translations for some Japanese terms are unsatisfactory. Therefore I have either retained the Japanese word or employed a more normal English word in the following cases: *Tennō* (not 'emperor'), Parliament (not 'Diet'), *han* (not 'clan', 'fief' or 'domain'), *Meiji ishin* (not Meiji Restoration). The names of political parties create particular problems, since some of them have official English titles that do not mean the same as their titles in Japanese. My solution in this edition is to give the accepted English title when a party is first encountered, followed by initials and Japanese title in brackets. Thus: Clean Government Party (CGP, *Kōmeitō*). The same order (English title, followed by Japanese title) is applied at first usage to government ministries (especially the 'super-ministries' created in January 2001, where the English title sometimes differs wildly from the Japanese title. For instance, what is in English the Ministry of Public Management, Home Affairs, Posts and Telecommunications is in Japanese simply *Sōmushō* ('Ministry of General Affairs').

Acknowledgements

This edition of *Governing Japan* is dedicated to the memory of David Sissons, who was my doctoral thesis supervisor in the early 1960s at the Australian National University in Canberra when I first began to study the politics of Japan. He imposed much-needed discipline upon a disorganized graduate student and taught me how to study this subject area, which has continued to intrigue me over four decades. I owe to him more than I can say.

Several of those who have helped and inspired me over the years are sadly no longer with us. These include Hayashi Shigeru, who was my thesis supervisor in Japan during fieldwork in 1962–3, and subsequently mentor and friend. He graciously bequeathed much of his collection of books on modern Japanese political history to the Bodleian Japanese Library at the Nissan Institute of Japanese Studies in Oxford. With Frank Langdon, of the University of British Columbia in Vancouver, I conducted a correspondence lasting over 40 years, and although we met rather rarely (usually in Japan), when we did it was like resuming a conversation only recently interrupted. Among other things he taught me scepticism and a distrust of jargon. Araki Toshio introduced me to local politicians in Hokkaidō, and shared his political insights. Okamoto Tomotaka did the same for me in the Tōhoku region of northern Honshū, and told me of his experiences as a twelve-year old on an island within sight of Hiroshima in August 1945. The fine *Asahi* journalist Ishikawa Masumi stayed in Oxford in the early 1990s and was intrigued by the phenomenon of 'Essex man'.[1] I must also mention Dorothie Storry, who for more than twenty years with her quiet good sense supported all of us in Japanese studies at Oxford.

---

[1] A term used to describe habitual Labour Party voters who moved out of working-class areas of London into suburban counties such as Essex, then shifting their allegiance to the Conservative Party because of Margaret Thatcher's policies of lower taxation, inflation control and, in particular, the sale of council housing stock at subsidized rates.

There are many others, very much alive, to whom I am grateful. Directly or indirectly (in some cases just through inspiration) the book owes much to colleagues and friends in several countries. I should single out Banno Junji, a wonderful friend and lateral thinker about politics, as well as his delightful wife Kazuko. For the rest I have no space to do more than list them, and there are many others that I could mention as well.

In Japan I am particularly indebted to Abe Shirō, Aiuchi Toshikazu, Robert Aspinall, Hatashin Ōmi, Hori Harumi, Inoguchi Takashi and Kuniko, Ishida Takeshi and his son Hiroshi, Itō Daiichi, Miyaoka Isao, David Morris, Muramatsu Michio, Nagai Fumio, Nakamura Kenichi, Nakano Kōichi, Nishida Yoshiaki, Nonaka Naoto, Roger Smith, Watanabe Akio, Watanabe Osamu, John Welfield, Noel Williams, Yamaguchi Jirō and Yamamoto Mari; in Australia to Christopher Braddick, Donald Calman, Sydney Crawcour, Peter Drysdale, James Horne, Purnendra Jain, Rikki Kersten, Hayden Lesbirel, Gavan McCormack, Richard Mason, Aurelia George Mulgan, Alan Rix and Sandra Wilson; In the UK (Oxford) to Jenny Corbett, Roger Goodman, Joy Hendry, Sharon Kinsella, James McMullen, Ian Neary, Brian Powell, Mark Rebick and Ann Waswo, as well as to Izumi Tytler and the staff of the Bodleian Japanese Library, and (elsewhere) to Kweku Ampiah, Lesley Connors, Marie Conte-Helm, Ronald Dore, Reinhard Drifte, Glenn Hook, Christopher Hughes, Janet Hunter, Sarah Hyde, Stephen Johnson, Stephen Large, Ian Nish, John Swenson-Wright and David Williams; in the United States to David Asher, Michael Beeman, Lawrence Beer, Kent Calder, John Campbell, Gerald Curtis, Chalmers Johnson, Ellis Krauss, Oka Takashi, Daniel Okimoto, T. J. Pempel, Susan Pharr, Bradley Richardson and Leonard Schoppa and Ezra Vogel; in Hong Kong to Mito Takamichi; in Denmark to Inge Engel-Christensen; in the Netherlands to Christopher Goto-Jones; in Israel to Ehud Harari and Ben-Ami Shillony; in Italy to Peter Dale and in Germany to Park Sung-Jo and Philipp Schuller.

I am grateful to the Japan Foundation, the British Council and the Institute of Social Science (*Shaken*), University of Tokyo, for funding periods of study in Japan at various times, and also to the Daiwa Foundation in London for many wonderful intellectual occasions. Over many years I have had much useful and stimulating contact with *Shaken*, and also with the International House of Japan (*Kokusai Bunka Kaikan*), both in Tokyo. I have received enormous insight from my graduate students, not to mention undergraduates. Students are in the business of looking at phenomena with fresh eyes. To the two universities in which I was privileged to spend my academic career – the Australian National University and the University of Oxford (in particular, the Nissan Institute of Japanese Studies and St Antony's College) I give unreserved thanks. Finally, to my wife Audrey and to the rest of my family, I thank you for helping me to see that there are also worlds of surprising interest beyond the mesmeric arena of Japanese politics.

Chapter 1 | Introduction: Why Japan and its Politics Matter

In 1979 the Harvard Professor Ezra Vogel wrote *Japan as Number One: Lessons for America*.[1] This book was widely read (especially in Japan) in the early 1980s, when the US economy was in difficulties while Japan seemed to be steaming ahead. How things changed in the 1990s, when it was the turn of the Japanese economy to stagnate and the US appeared for a while to be the sole superpower and, for some, the only model worth following!

With the new millennium, things have changed once more. The growth economies of Asia are those of China and India, and these have attracted enormous international attention. The 'Japan-bashing' of the 1980s was replaced by the 'Japan-passing' of the 1990s. But less attention than it deserves is given to the fact that Japan has been undergoing a quiet revolution in its political economy. This is bearing fruit in the form of steady if unspectacular economic growth and remarkable, if patchy, dynamism. In GDP terms, the Japanese economy remains over twice the size of the Chinese economy, and its focus is on high technology and service industries. The workforce enjoys a high average standard of living, though income and wealth distribution is less equal than it used to be. Japanese foreign policy initiatives remain low-key, but Japan has become a weighty factor in the affairs of East and South-East Asia in particular. Social patterns have been evolving in more open and outward-looking directions.

Many generalizations that used to be made about Japanese society are looking increasingly obsolete, while, as we shall see, patterns of political interaction have also been evolving significantly. Japan, moreover, is a mature democracy in most senses of the word, even though serious problems persist in the practice of democratic government, particularly in certain areas of human rights. We would

---

[1] Ezra Vogel, *Japan as Number One: Lessons for America*. Cambridge, MA and London, Harvard University Press, 1979.

argue that the political system of Japan is an excellent model to compare with other mature democracies, particularly those of Europe, Australasia and North America.[2]

Japan, in two words, is back.

On 11 September 2005 – just four years after the terrorist attacks on the Twin Towers in New York and the Pentagon in Washington DC – Japan held general elections for its main parliamentary house, the House of Representatives. In these elections the long-ruling coalition of the Liberal Democratic Party (LDP, *Jiyūminshutō* or *Jimintō*) and the much smaller Clean Government Party (CGP, *Kōmeitō*) won a sweeping victory, increasing its combined total of seats from 246 to 327, in a house consisting of 480 seats in all.[3] Conversely, the principal opposition party, the Democratic Party (DPJ, *Minshutō*), which in previous elections at various levels had been steadily gaining ground on the coalition, saw its vote total slashed from 177 to 113 – a crushing defeat that prompted its leader to resign.

It is curiously symbolic that the government's electoral victory should have taken place exactly four years after 9/11. The span of time between the two events also covers the most significant years as Prime Minister of Koizumi Junichirō, who arrived in the post in April 2001 and stepped down in September 2006. If 9/11 changed the course of world history, Koizumi during his period in office made a concerted effort to change the established patterns of politics in Japan. When he took up his post, the Japanese economy had been underperforming for a decade, the banking system was in serious trouble, with a huge overhang of non-performing loans, attempts by previous governments to spend their way out of economic crisis had been unsuccessful, deflation had become endemic, investment was down, unemployment was rising and economic growth was chronically low or negative. The national debt had also soared to worrying levels.

Koizumi and his Economics Minister, Takenaka Heizō, single-mindedly pursued policies directed to rescuing the beleaguered banking system and to creating the conditions for economic recovery. The eventual success of these policies was not entirely down to government policies, since private sector firms had been going through a long-drawn-out process of restructuring, but the Koizumi government strove to create a favourable climate for structural reform. Koizumi's flagship policy was privatization of postal services, with the aim of eliminating the ample slush funds, derived mainly from postal savings accounts, that had enabled governments in the past to protect myriad vested interests against the chill wind of domestic and international competition. In retrospect, Koizumi's economic policies were aimed at restoring the economy to health by moving it out of a protectionist ghetto and embracing the free market forces that underlay globalization.

---

[2]   See J. A. A. Stockwin, 'Why Japan still Matters', *Japan Forum*, vol. 15, no. 3 (2003), pp. 345–60.

[3]   LDP seats increased from 212 to 296, while those won by the CGP fell slightly, from 34 to 31. At dissolution, however, some weeks earlier, the LDP had held 249 seats. The discrepancy is accounted for by the Prime Minister's expulsion of those LDP parliamentarians who had voted against his bill to privatize postal services.

A few weeks before the September 2005 general elections, Koizumi's postal services privatization bills had been defeated in the House of Councillors (upper house of Parliament) after having narrowly passed the House of Representatives (lower house). He responded dramatically by dissolving the lower house, declaring new elections, expelling the postal privatization rebels from the LDP and choosing new candidates (dubbed 'Koizumi's children') to stand against them in the elections. His bold moves struck a chord with the electorate, particularly with younger age groups in big cities who had previously been least favourably disposed to the LDP, and in many cases abstained from voting altogether. Koizumi, who had spoken publicly about 'smashing' (*bukkowasu*) the LDP, had led it to a spectacular victory, but he had remoulded it in his own image, at least temporarily.

Koizumi's international policies stirred up fervent controversy, particularly his periodic visits to the Yasukuni Shrine in Tokyo, sacred to the war dead.[4] He also authorized the despatch of a contingent of the Self-Defence Forces to Iraq in January 2004, as part of the US-led 'coalition of the willing'. Even though they performed entirely non-military tasks, this was controversial under the terms of the 1946 'Peace Constitution'. Military–strategic cooperation between Japan and the United States had also been steadily improving since the 1990s. The two countries' military systems were becoming steadily more 'interoperable', while constitutional inhibitions on Japanese projection of military force were being worn more and more lightly.[5]

When Koizumi made way for Abe Shinzō to become Prime Minister in September 2006, even though both these men came from the same right-wing faction of the LDP, priorities shifted. Whereas Koizumi had directed the bulk of his energies towards the task of making the economy fit for globalization, Abe showed much less enthusiasm for economic policy and concentrated rather on such traditional rightist concerns as revising the Basic Law on Education (which in his view had been too liberal and did not sufficiently promote patriotism), and seeking to revise the Constitution. His decision to re-admit the postal privatization rebels into the party was highly controversial, and marked a sharp departure from the tough stand Koizumi had developed against vested interests. On the other hand, at the outset of his rule Abe made his peace with the Chinese and the Koreans, who had been protesting vigorously against prime ministerial visits to the Yasukuni Shrine. (See Chapter 6 for detailed discussion of these issues.)

The present book is written in an attempt to make at least partly comprehensible what to the outside observer (and indeed to many Japanese themselves) often appears to be the great muddle of Japanese politics. Despite the fact that the Japanese economy remains the second largest in the world in GDP terms, the economic growth of China and India, coupled with Japanese economic

---

[4] Fourteen Class A war criminals – so designated by the Tokyo war crimes trials after the war – had been enshrined at Yasukuni in 1978.

[5] Christopher W. Hughes, *Japan's Re-emergence as a 'Normal' Military Power*, Abingdon and New York, Routledge for International Institute for Strategic Studies, 2005 (Adelphi Paper 368–9).

difficulties, has diverted attention away from Japan, so that Japanese political and economic reporting receives less attention from the international media than it did a decade and more ago.

If this book manages to provide some guidelines towards such understanding, it will have succeeded in its aim. The fundamental premise on which the book is based is that Japanese politics – much like other aspects of Japanese life – is susceptible to the same kinds of analysis as are regularly applied to the politics of other countries, which may be more familiar, for geographical and cultural reasons, to the reader. Obvious as this proposition may appear to some, it is subject to attack from two diametrically opposite positions. On the one hand is to be found the view that Japan is *sui generis*, or unique, and can be understood only in its own terms. On the other hand, there is the view that any cultural differences are irrelevant to the study of Japanese politics and should be eliminated from the discussion. In the present writer's view, the fact that for most of its history Japan developed outside the ambit of Judaeo-Christian civilization should suggest that cultural differences may have some relevance for politics. On the other hand, analysis based on the idea that there is an unbridgeable gap between Japan and the rest of the world seems equally unacceptable.[6] Japan is indeed unique, as is France, or Mexico or Vietnam; but there is assuredly no reason for believing that it is *uniquely* unique.[7]

This book is now in its fourth edition. It first appeared as *Japan: Divided Politics in a Growth Economy* in 1975, and then in a second, revised edition in 1982.[8] The third edition appeared in 1999, much updated and revised, and with a new title: *Governing Japan: Divided Politics in a Major Economy*.[9] It may be useful to recall the basis of the approach taken in the previous editions in order to understand the philosophy underlying the present volume. The original book (like the present edition) was one of a series on modern governments, the series having a definite institutional bias. In the words of the introduction to the first and second editions by the series editor, the late Max Beloff: 'our authors have kept in mind that while the nature of a country's formal institutions may be explained as the product of its political culture, the informal aspects of politics can only be understood if the legal and institutional framework is kept in mind.'[10] The present writer paid due regard to this intention of the series in writing the first edition. At the same time, an attempt to understand the dynamics of Japanese

---

[6] 'East is east and west is west, and never the twain shall meet' (from Rudyard Kipling, 'The Ballad of East and West'). This line is widely quoted; less well known are Kipling's later lines: 'But there is neither East nor West, Border, nor Breed, nor Birth, / When two strong men stand face to face, tho' they come from the ends of the earth.'

[7] The idea that the Japanese are not *uniquely* unique has also been used by another writer: Patrick Smith, *Japan: A Reinterpretation*, New York, Random House, 1997, p. 204. We arrived at this formulation quite independently.

[8] J. A. A. Stockwin, *Japan: Divided Politics in a Growth Economy*, London, Weidenfeld & Nicolson, 1975, 1982.

[9] J. A. A. Stockwin, *Governing Japan: Divided Politics in a Major Economy*, Oxford and Malden, MA, Blackwell, 3rd edn, 1999.

[10] Stockwin, *Japan*, 1st and 2nd edns, p. xii.

politics in the early 1970s (the first edition was substantially completed by the end of 1973) led to the ideas embodied in the title: *Japan: Divided Politics in a Growth Economy*.

The phrase 'divided politics' was intended to reflect the political turbulence of the late 1960s and early 1970s. Since the Allied Occupation (1945–52) the political arena had been sharply divided over foreign and defence policy, industrial relations, education policy and, most importantly, the Constitution. The economy had grown spectacularly throughout the 1960s, but growth was about to be temporarily halted by the first oil crisis of 1973–4. The LDP had lost votes at every lower house general election between 1958 and 1972, though the opposition parties had fragmented and proliferated over the same period. It seemed reasonable to predict the ending of the LDP monopoly on power in the foreseeable future. In retrospect, we know that the political 'shocks' of the early 1970s were to lead to a more conservative period, as the electorate took stock and voted for continuity and for the consolidation of material gains. But the signs of that decision did not emerge until the middle of the decade.

In 1970 the American futurologist Herman Kahn had published *The Emerging Japanese Superstate*,[11] a rather early (but not the first) attempt to extrapolate from the spectacular growth of the Japanese economy during the 1960s on to a future where Japan would exercise major political as well as economic power.[12] Kahn's book combined a realist approach to international relations with heavy reliance on Ruth Benedict's wartime anthropological study of Japanese society, with its emphasis on mutual obligations having to be 'repaid ten thousand times'.[13] Kahn believed that before too long constitutional and other constraints on the projection of military power by Japan would largely disappear and the country would become a formidable force to be reckoned with on the world stage.[14] The approach taken by Kahn was in vogue in the early 1970s, but it greatly underestimated the divisions within the Japanese system, as well as serious elements of fragility that were to emerge later.

In that period the notion of 'consensus', as a key to understanding the way the economy, society and polity worked in practice, became widespread. The present writer devised the concept of 'divided politics' in part to throw doubt on the consensus model. Whereas 'consensus' implied the relative absence of Western-style adversarial politics, 'divided politics' suggested not only that political outcomes resulted from the working out of clashes of interests and opinions, but that divisions, in some areas of policy at least, ran deep.

The second edition was published in 1982, under the same title. The LDP had won a convincing electoral victory in June 1980 and the system seemed to have settled down into a conservative mould, with the LDP firmly in the saddle, and

---

[11] Herman Kahn, *The Emerging Japanese Superstate: Challenge and Response*, Englewood Cliffs, NJ, Prentice Hall, 1970.
[12] The honour of being the first should perhaps go to Norman McRae of the *Economist*. See The Economist, *Consider Japan*, London, Duckworth, 1963.
[13] Ruth Benedict, *The Chrysanthemum and the Sword: Patterns of Japanese Culture*, Boston, Houghton Mifflin, 1946, pp. 114–44.
[14] Kahn, *The Emerging Japanese Superstate*, pp. 186–213.

social welfare spending being cut back in the interests of balanced budgets. Some observers were arguing that divisive political issues were exhausted, and that consensus politics was the order of the day.[15]

The present writer maintained his opposition to that approach in preparing the second edition. It had to be conceded that the steam had gone out of some earlier controversial issues. The LDP had regained its position of dominance and the opposition was weak and demoralized. Many interest groups were less inclined to confront the holders of power than to become their clients. On the other hand, major divisions had appeared within the LDP itself, leading to a serious political crisis in 1979–80. (See Chapter 4 below.) Moreover, new controversial issues were emerging, and some of the old ones had not been satisfactorily resolved.

To call Japan a 'growth economy' seemed uncontroversial in 1973, even though the first oil crisis was about to stop the economy in its tracks. The country had just experienced a decade and a half of economic growth running at an average of around 10 per cent per annum. In global terms this was unprecedented, and arguably brought about the most profound social and economic transformation of Japan in its history. Even though there were problems of distributing the new-found national wealth, there was no denying the significance of economic growth. By the early 1980s the economy had overcome two oil crises and was growing at 4 or 5 per cent most years, which by the international standards of the day was more than respectable.

Under the rubric of his chosen title, the present writer sought, in the first two editions of the book, to strike a balance between a positive appraisal of Japan's remarkable economic growth and a cautious or sceptical analysis of the capacities of the political system to deal with serious and recurring divisions. Such caution may perhaps be regarded as prescient of the politics of the late 1980s and 1990s.

What, then, of those two decades that formed the principal focus for the third edition, published with a modified title in 1999?

The first point to be made is that by the end of the 1980s, with Japan clearly established as the world's second largest economy, writing about the country increased in quantity and improved in quality of analysis. This continued into the 1990s, although later in that decade attention began to fade to some extent. It was now possible to draw on a respectable corpus of good-quality research on nearly all aspects of the politico-economic system. The bulk of this research was being conducted by Japanese and American scholars, but much useful writing also came out of Australia, Britain, Canada, Germany, India, Israel, the Republic of Korea, New Zealand, Singapore and elsewhere. The tendency evident in the past for Japanese and non-Japanese scholars to operate in separate spheres and virtually to talk past each other was now much less of a problem, and collaborative projects involving Japanese and non-Japanese political scientists became commonplace. Indeed, theoretical or ideological orientation irrespective of

---

[15] For instance, T. J. Pempel, *Policy and Politics in Japan: Creative Conservatism*, Philadelphia, Temple University Press, 1982, pp. 25–6. Pempel links consensus to the social 'homogeneity' of the Japanese people, though he argues for qualified homogeneity.

nationality, rather than nationality itself, came to be the most accurate predictor of conclusions to a particular piece of writing.

Secondly, with the benefit of hindsight, we can see that Japan between the early 1950s and the mid-1980s was relatively insulated from international pressures, so that both the ruling elite and the general population could devote most of their energies to economic recovery and growth. The United States generally tolerated a highly regulated Japanese economy, and provided security for a militarily weak Japan under the Japan–US Mutual Security Treaty. That treaty created serious difficulties in domestic politics, the resolution of which tested the ingenuity of governments, but it allowed military spending to be kept within bounds while ensuring that any external threats could be deterred. The fact that no Japanese servicemen were killed in combat over four decades and more from 1952 symbolized how easy it was for governments to concentrate on non-military matters.

By the 1980s, however, the sand had begun to shift a little underfoot. The economy was now so large and powerful that the US (along with some other states) was no longer willing to tolerate what it saw as protectionist policies by Japan. Foreign pressure was applied to get rid of both overt and covert measures of industrial and commercial protection, and in particular to deregulate the financial system. Large corporate firms were now able to raise finance on international money markets, so that they were more independent from government control through the banking system than they had been.

While the feisty Nakasone Yasuhiro was Prime Minister, between 1982 and 1987, several public sector enterprises were privatized, most significantly the National Railways. Domestic industries (including agriculture to a limited extent) began to experience some reduction in government protection, and attempts were made to restructure the fiscal system away from direct taxes and towards indirect taxes. These reforms, however, attracted fierce opposition from interested groups, and were at the centre of a political crisis at the end of the 1980s. The labour union movement also underwent drastic reorganization at this period.

Very few observers predicted that Japan's economic difficulties of the 1990s, following the collapse of an unsustainable asset bubble at the end of the 1980s, would prove so difficult to remedy, nor that they would persist for more than a decade. But even though the economic problems had economic causes, they were also compounded by persistent political disarray. Serious attempts were made to refashion the way politics worked in practice, starting in the early 1990s. The LDP lost power for a period of about nine months in 1993–4, but the reformist coalition government that replaced it got into difficulties and the LDP was able to claw its way back into power. Governments remained fragile, however, for the rest of the decade, with the LDP no longer able to govern on its own but needing to attract small parties to enter into coalition with it. For much of the decade party loyalties were uncertain; party-hopping became a common pastime among parliamentarians, and many new parties were formed and disappeared. By the end of the decade, however, party stability had been more or less re-established.

The political process in the 1990s was thus extremely messy and difficult to follow, resulting in widespread political apathy and disillusion with parties as a whole. Reform was in the air, but there was much disagreement over what aspects of the system needed to be reformed. The one really crucial reform put in place during the decade was a radical refashioning of the electoral system for the House of Representatives (see Chapters 6 and 8 below). As the third edition of this book was being prepared (1996–8), it was fairly clear that the political system was in transition between an established but outmoded pattern and a new pattern that had yet to emerge. So much transformation, at so many levels, had taken place in Japanese politics and economic management since 1945 that structure and practice had lagged behind. It also seemed evident that necessary reform would not be accomplished simply by juggling with political alliances, changing the electoral system and effecting marginal measures of deregulation and decentralization. Something more radical and carefully thought through was needed.

A central task of this fourth edition is to assess the important changes that have taken place in the way Japan is governed since the start of the new millennium. One individual has dominated the politics of this new period: Koizumi Junichirō, Prime Minister from April 2001 to September 2006. That the Koizumi era was one of concerted reform is beyond doubt. It is, however, often the fate of reformist politicians to confront new issues that emerge, requiring attention and to an extent distorting the initial intentions of reform. For Koizumi, these came largely in the area of foreign and defence policy. The 'war on terror' became a major issue after the Twin Towers attacks of 11 September 2001, and the US-led invasion of Iraq required Japanese participation in some form. Relations with China and the two Koreas entered a period of difficulty. Nevertheless, he had considerable success in deregulating the economy and putting the banking system, which had been near to collapse, on a healthier footing. The economy moved into a phase of sustained, if unspectacular, growth after many years of stagnation. Reforms that had already been implemented before he became Prime Minister enabled him to exert more effective power from the centre than most of his predecessors had been able to do. His own strategic brilliance in the summer of 2005, when challenged by rebels against postal privatization within the LDP, allowed him to consolidate his dominance of the political process.

Nevertheless, Japan still faces a formidable set of challenges that will test political leaders in the years to come. Some of these are external, relating to developments in the wider world. Some are domestic, relating to social change and demographic imbalances. Some concern the structure and practice of the political system. And others are by-products of recent policies, whereby strengthening of central authority has been achieved at the expense of democratic accountability and human rights.

In concluding this chapter, we identify six broad areas of crisis that seem likely to remain central to the political agenda over a number of years.

1   A crisis of political power and democratic accountability   The location of political power in Japan presents us with some perplexing problems, of which two stand out. One is the dominant role of the LDP, and the difficulty for opposition parties of replacing it in power. Until it becomes normal for parties to alternate in power following general elections,[16] Japan will be something less than a truly democratic system.[17] The second is the weakness of Cabinet,[18] and the power of unelected civil servants in decision-making. The government bureaucracy has to some extent had its wings clipped since the early 1990s, though the extent of this restraint has varied from ministry to ministry. For instance, the Ministries of Finance and of Foreign Affairs have been notably politicized, though others have been rather less affected. The rule that ministers decide and civil servants implement has yet to be firmly established, but in some instances there is concern about ministries becoming too politicized.[19] A proper balance, of course, also requires that both politicians and civil servants act in the interests of the whole and not in the interests of narrow pressure groups to which they are beholden.

2   A crisis of political participation and non-involvement in politics   Until the 1990s, voting turnout rates in Japan were relatively high, often averaging over 70 per cent in lower house general elections. Perhaps reflecting the political confusion of the mid- to late 1990s, rates then declined, and have since stabilized at lower levels than before. Political participation other than voting has long been rather limited, and radical groups on the left (including labour unions and left-wing parties) that used to challenge government policies have become much weaker. The bundle of activities referred to as 'civil society' showed few signs of life until participation in non-profit organizations (NPOs) increased after the experience of helping victims of the Kobe earthquake of the mid-1990s. Part of the reason for weak civil society participation is that governments have been chronically suspicious of NPOs and sought to control them, though regulations are now somewhat more relaxed (see Chapters 3 and 11).

3   A crisis of the Constitution and political fundamentals   After his election by Parliament as Prime Minister in September 2006, Abe Shinzō indicated that revising the 1946 Constitution would be one of his main priorities. Constitutional inhibitions on the projection, or use anywhere, of military force have been a matter of controversy for the whole period since the Occupation, and the issue has been handled over the years through a series of subtle and often ingenious compromises. The peace clause (article 9) which purports to ban armed forces has become ever more remote from reality, even though it has inhibited projection of military force overseas, as well as export of armaments. But other articles of the Constitution are also under discussion by revisionists. The real, as well as

[16]   Not necessarily at any election, but frequently enough to make a change of party or parties in office normal and expected.
[17]   That the electorate continues to elect the same party to office is not of itself undemocratic, but for a party to remain semi-permanently in power often leads to undemocratic tendencies among politicians and their advisers.
[18]   Anecdotal evidence about meetings of Cabinet suggest that much of their time is given over to signing documents.
[19]   I am grateful to an anonymous reader of my original manuscript for emphasizing this last point.

the symbolic, value of the Constitution is so great that this emotive and divisive set of issues will continue to stir up controversy for several years yet.

4   A crisis of liberal versus illiberal ideas   There has long been a division in Japanese politics and public opinion between liberal and democratic ideas, resting on the primacy of the individual as the fundamental political unit, and collectivist ideas, centred on the family, the quasi-family group and the state. This of course reflects the juxtaposition of the collectivist policies, prescribed by the state, that were dominant in the period up to 1945, and the liberalizing reforms of the Occupation between 1945 and 1952. An argument often mobilized by the collectivists is that since liberal ideas were introduced by the Americans, they are not indigenous and should be modified in favour of ideas originating in Japan itself. The last three prime ministers have belonged to the most right-wing of the LDP factions, and in some policy areas (notably education) their policy preferences have been decidedly illiberal. Those who might be inclined to oppose these policies in the interests of liberal and democratic values have suffered from pervasive political apathy, political weakness, or both.

5   A crisis of ageing society and diverging life-chances   In 2006 the Japanese population peaked at around 127 million, and demographic projections suggest that numbers will decline quite sharply. Since expectation of life at birth is higher in Japan for both sexes than in any other country in the world, Japanese society is faced with the twin problems of a declining workforce and an increasing number of old people. This conjunction is causing acute problems for the financial health of pension schemes, and brings with it difficult problems of intergenerational equity. A different problem of equity is the widening income and wealth gap that has been appearing in Japan over the past decade and more. Income differentials used to be relatively narrow, but they have been sharply widening. The potential for these differences to take the form of political division is considerable.

6   A crisis of national status and role   Japan remains the second largest economy in the world. In the 1980s it seemed set to become the second most powerful country in political terms as well. The changes since then – internal and external, though most significantly external – have been dramatic, but the most conspicuous development affecting the international status of Japan is the economic rise of China since the 1990s. The average standard of living in China is far lower than that in Japan, economic growth is spread most unevenly between different parts of the country and China faces huge problems of governance, which may affect economic performance in the future. But at the same time the population of the People's Republic of China is more than ten times that of Japan, the Chinese state lacks Japanese-style inhibitions about projection of military force, and the regime actively disputes sections of the maritime boundary between the two countries. Since the early 1990s Japan has been seeking permanent membership of the United Nations Security Council. If this were to be realized, Japan would receive a welcome boost to its international status. But in fact this could take place only in the context of a fundamental restructuring of the world body, the chances of which appear rather small in the foreseeable future. In these circumstances, successive Japanese governments have sought to consolidate Japan's relationship of alliance with the United States under the Mutual Security Treaty. This has its advantages, but also risks pulling Japan into international conflicts that would do it little good in terms of its national interests.

The six crises outlined above are all relatively serious, actually or potentially; but we ought not to lose sight of the fact that Japan remains a major and dynamic economic power, with a basically democratic structure of government and liberal values. Difficulties and pitfalls lie ahead, but the political system has repeatedly demonstrated its capacity to overcome crises and achieve reasonably satisfactory solutions to problems. Sophistication and experience, as well as resourcefulness and ingenuity, lie embedded in the Japanese system.

Chapter 2 | Historical Background: Japan's Emergence as a Modern State and the Politics of War, 1853–1945

The idea that you cannot understand the contemporary politics of a nation-state without a good understanding of its history is today hardly controversial, even though much contemporary political science appears to take history for granted. This may be reasonable enough where the general historical context is familiar, for instance in analysing the politics of a European country where analyst and target audience are firmly embedded in the Judaeo-Christian tradition.

With Japan, on the other hand, there is a case for saying that the need to come to grips with the historical background of the nation-state assumes a rather special significance. It is important here not to go too far and imply that Japanese politics is simply and solely the inevitable product of Japanese history. There is nothing inevitable about political outcomes, in Japan or elsewhere, since human beings have the quality of free will, and politicians calculate advantage without necessarily referring to precedent.

Nevertheless, the course of Japanese history is sufficiently distinct from that of Western Europe or North America that political analysts carrying with them the unconscious intellectual assumptions derived from life in those areas have an acute need to be sensitive to the historical experiences of the Japanese people. Over the past century and a half we may find many instances of distorted analysis stemming from a failure to understand that the Japanese historical legacy includes certain features that are greatly at variance with those of Western countries.[1]

To understand politics requires sensitivity to history essentially for two reasons, whether we are talking of Japan or elsewhere.

---

[1] The same may well apply in the case of analysts from non-Western countries, including those elsewhere in Asia, even though the actual assumptions made may be different from Western ones. For instance, contemporary Chinese assumptions about the politics of Japan incline to emphasize the danger of a resurgent Japanese militarism for reasons that reflect Chinese – not Western – historical experience in relation to Japan.

First, it is reasonable to expect that history will have determined the boundaries of the nation-state, moulded the fundamental shape of the polity, shaped attitudes – positive or negative – to government, made citizens aware (or unaware) that they may be capable of affecting policy, created certain assumptions about the economy, including the role of government in economic matters, influenced attitudes to war, feelings about neighbouring nation-states, and many other matters. Moreover, the legacy of catastrophic events, such as defeat in war, may stay in the national consciousness and affect political outcomes over many decades.

Second, history is not merely an objective set of data to which citizens all have equal access. The historical legacy of the nation-state is interpreted, and at times manipulated. History is constantly re-interpreted, not only by professional historians, but by the mass media,[2] and in some cases by governments or politicians seeking political goals.[3]

Japan's historical legacy is, of course, cumulative. Formative periods include the impact of China from the seventh century, the influence of Spanish and Portuguese missionaries in the sixteenth century (whereby substantial numbers of Japanese became Christian), over two and a half centuries of self-imposed isolation under the Tokugawa Shogunate (roughly 1600 to 1868), the modernizing and expansionist impetus of the Meiji regime (established 1868), a semi-liberal period in the 1920s, and the expansionist militarism that emerged during the years 1931–45. Developments since 1945 now cover more than six decades. Much of what happened in those years may now be considered as history, and we shall consider this in Chapters 4–6.

It is possible to discover rough parallels between some of what happened in Japan and some of what happened in Europe. Mediaeval European feudalism looked somewhat like Japan's 'feudalism' of the Tokugawa period, while Weber's 'Protestant Ethic' was not wholly removed from the ethical systems of the *samurai*, who were both warriors and administrators. Nevertheless, it is best to treat Japanese history as sufficiently distinct from that of Europe (or indeed of China) to merit analysis paying rigorous attention to the singularities of the Japanese case. This in no way rules out sensible historical comparison between Japan and elsewhere, but we should carefully guard against mechanically applying inappropriate external models to the Japanese case.

The impact of China upon Japan over several centuries can hardly be overestimated. Not only did Japan assimilate the main elements of the Chinese writing system to its own, very different, language, but China exerted an inestimable impact upon Japanese religious concepts, political organization, literary creation

---

[2]   In Japan this includes television *samurai* dramas and historical episodes portrayed in widely read *manga* (cartoon story) magazines and books.

[3]   For instance, official visits to the Yasukuni Shrine in Tokyo by Koizumi Junichirō (Prime Minister 2001–6), despite intense protests from Beijing and Seoul, implied a positive reckoning of Japan's war in Asia from 1937 to 1945. Koizumi's motivations were no doubt complex, but in visiting a shrine sacred to the memory, among many others, of fourteen men designated Class A war criminals by the Tokyo trials after the war, he was certainly catering to a domestic constituency that was pressing for a more nationalistic assessment of the war. This issue will be discussed in detail in Chapter 6.

and even city planning.[4] Not only did Confucianism come to Japan from China, but Buddhism arrived via China (and Korea), contributing to the complex mixture of beliefs and practices (including the native *Shintō*) with which the nation came to be endowed. The view is common in the Chinese-speaking world that Japanese culture is unoriginal, because it derived from China. Though not without a grain of truth, this view is much exaggerated, since in the area of political values, for instance, at least one crucial departure from Chinese Confucianism emerged after that set of doctrines entered Japan. Whereas the Chinese version held that an unjust or tyrannous sovereign could morally be overthrown, this element largely dropped out of sight in Japanese Confucianism.[5]

Again, during the Tokugawa period, at a time when intense leader–follower relations prevailed between local lords and their retainers, much argument took place about whether in the case of a clash of loyalties, it was loyalty to one's lord, or loyalty to one's family, that ought to prevail. In Japan, the predominant answer was that one's lord had a prior claim on one's loyalty, and one's family came second. Generally speaking, in China the reverse was the case.[6] Nevertheless, the legacy of Chinese Confucianism enshrined the values of an ordered society, the importance of form, hierarchy, deference to superiors and paternalistic government – values which remain politically relevant even in the first decade of the twenty-first century.

The late sixteenth and early seventeenth centuries – known, in a famous phrase, as 'Japan's Christian century'[7] – was a period of warlordism, which was gradually moving towards the national Tokugawa settlement of the early seventeenth century. The arrival of mainly Spanish and Portuguese missionaries was the nation's first substantial encounter with European civilization. Although large numbers of converts were made, particularly in south-western Japan, the missionary period ended, in the first half of the seventeenth century, with savage repression, including the expulsion of missionaries and persecution of converts.[8] Even though small numbers of converts survived and remained loyal to the faith, the main impact of this period of Western contact was negative. The success of the missionaries in propagating their message led to a vicious and durable nationalist reaction on the part of the authorities.

The historical legacy of the Tokugawa period is enormously important. There is one negative reason for this: namely, that strict policies of national isolation

[4]   William Coaldrake, *Architecture and Authority in Japan*, London, Routledge, 1996, p. 12.
[5]   W. G. Beasley, *The Meiji Restoration*, Stanford, CA, Stanford University Press, 1972, pp. 38–9.
[6]   I. J. McMullen, 'Rulers or Fathers? A Casuistical Problem in Early Modern Japanese Thought', *Past and Present*, no. 16 (August 1987), pp. 56–97. It may not be coincidental that firms consisting of family members are deeper-rooted in the Chinese commercial world than in Japan.
[7]   Charles Boxer, *The Christian Century in Japan, 1549–1650*, Berkeley and Los Angeles, University of California Press, 1967.
[8]   For a fictionalized account of the extirpation of Christian influence from Japan, see Shusaku Endo, *Silence*, London, Quartet, 1978.

meant that Japan, which during the sixteenth century was subject to extensive European influence, largely missed out on European developments occurring between the early seventeenth and mid-nineteenth centuries. This was a period of crucial economic, political and social change in Europe, including the early stages of the industrial revolution, the French Revolution, the emergence of a middle class and an industrial proletariat, the Napoleonic wars and gradualist political evolution in Britain and elsewhere.

The omission of these influences was to have a profound effect on Japan. When, finally, in the latter half of the nineteenth century, Japan became open to the outside world, there followed a desperate struggle to catch up with Europe and America, and what Ronald Dore has called the 'late development effect'.[9] But what is truly extraordinary about the Tokugawa period is that this era of near-complete isolation was in practice far from being a time of social and economic stagnation: indigenous developments produced results that remain important in understanding contemporary Japan. Indeed, historians now generally refer to it as the 'early modern' period of Japanese history.

The Tokugawa settlement, effected in the early seventeenth century, was based not so much on a principle of absolutism as on that of balance between centres of power, none of which was to be allowed to become overwhelmingly powerful.[10] Even though the means by which these compromises were maintained were specific to the period, in a sense they foreshadowed much more recent political arrangements based on complex balancing of forces inhibiting bold or wilful leadership from the centre.

The principal power centre of Tokugawa Japan, and nearest approximation to a central government, was the *bakufu* ('military camp government'), based at Edo (now Tokyo), headed by the *shōgun* ('generalissimo'). Although shogunal territories existed in various parts of the country, the principal power base of the Shogunate was a coalition of various self-governing and self-supporting *han* (fiefs), situated largely in the northern and eastern parts of the country. Other *han*, principally in the southern and western regions, were regarded by the *bakufu* as potentially less loyal, but were kept in check by a comprehensive set of restrictions designed to reduce to a minimum their physical capacity to challenge the *bakufu*.

---

[9] Ronald Dore, *British Factory, Japanese Factory*, London, Allen & Unwin, 1973.

[10] Inoguchi, following Brown and Kasaya, argues that the feudal lords Oda Nobunaga and his successor Toyotomi Hideyoshi, in the late sixteenth century, both aimed in vain to create an absolutist state, and though Hideyoshi finally succeeded in unifying the country, he did so only by entering into extensive compromises with other centres of power. The ultimate founder of the Tokugawa peace, Tokugawa Ieyasu, was relatively weak in terms of his own political power, but through his shrewdness was able to establish a political system that lasted two and a half centuries. See Inoguchi Takashi, 'The Programmatic Development of Japanese Democratic Politics', in Michèle Schmiegelow (ed.), *Democracy in Asia*, Frankfurt, Campus-Verlag, 1997; Philip Brown, *Central Authority and Local Autonomy in Early Modern Japan*, Stanford, CA, Stanford University Press, 1993; Kasaya Kazuhiko, *Shi no shisō* (The Idea of Being a Warrior), Tokyo, Nihon Shuppan, 1993.

This was a regime for which the stability of the existing order was a paramount consideration. What today would seem extraordinary measures were put into effect to ensure that the political order remained intact. The Japanese people were, by deliberate policy of the *bakufu*, virtually isolated from contact with the outside world – a policy that began with the expulsion of Christian missionaries and persecution of indigenous Christian converts, but was extended to the virtual closing of Japan to international trade and banning of travel into or out of Japan.[11] The population was divided into five principal, rigidly defined, social strata: *samurai* (warrior-administrators), farmers, artisans, merchants and outcasts (*eta/hinin*), in that hierarchical order of priority. In practice, the boundaries between these categories (except the last) were somewhat permeable, but in principle (and to a large extent in practice) each stratum had its own allotted and unchangeable place in the established order.

The Tokugawa period, which brought peace after centuries of recurrent civil war, was founded in the perception that social, economic and political change, as well as foreign influences, were likely to be destabilizing. Therefore, ingenious and at times draconian measures were devised to avoid such destabilization.[12]

Ironically, the final collapse of the regime in the 1860s bore out the apprehension of its rulers about the destabilizing character of piecemeal relaxation of controls. Once foreigners had been allowed limited access to Japan and some of the controls over the southern and western *han* had been lifted, the overthrow of the *bakufu* and the collapse of the stable order it had cherished came swiftly. This is not to say, however, that had the controls been retained, things would have continued indefinitely as before.

Many of the conditions for change had been maturing over the long Tokugawa peace. The rigid hierarchy of social strata bore less and less relationship to economic reality. Despite the fact that the merchants had the lowest formal status of any except the outcast groups,[13] they had accumulated wealth and were creditors of many of the *samurai*. Many *samurai* had, for a variety of reasons, become disgruntled and impoverished. Moreover, peace had brought a degree of national prosperity, which happened to favour the 'outer' (southern and western) *han* rather than the *bakufu*, whose finances were in poor shape, thus upsetting the delicate balance of power. There was also a slow but steady spread of education,[14]

[11]   The main exception to this was the Dutch trading post at Deshima, an island in Nagasaki harbour. Some contact was also maintained with China, and a little with Korea. Through these 'windows on the world', some external developments became known to well-placed intellectuals. For instance, the invention of smallpox vaccine was known about in Japan by the 1840s.

[12]   For instance, the *sankin kōtai* system required that feudal lords travel to Edo every other year with their retinue, and in the intervening years leave close relatives in Edo as hostages to their good behaviour.

[13]   Below the merchants were various categories of 'outcast' (*eta*) or 'non-people' (*hinin*), who are basically the ancestors of the low-status category known in contemporary Japan as *burakumin* ('village people').

[14]   Ronald Dore, *Education in Tokugawa Japan*, London, Routledge & Kegan Paul, 1965; 2nd edn, London, Athlone, 1984.

and of commercial institutions, during the Tokugawa period, so that the country was not entirely unprepared for modernizing and innovating once the old regime was overthrown.

A key feature of the Tokugawa era was that for two and a half centuries Japan was almost entirely at peace – in great contrast to the three-quarters of a century that was to follow (1868–1945). The legacy of the Tokugawa peace was important in various ways, but we emphasize two. First, it furnished material for those wishing to embed in the national consciousness the notion that Japan did not have to be constantly at war. Second, and more specifically, it furnished a model of bureaucracy, crucial elements of which remained imprinted in the habits of mind of government officials right up to the present. This point is important and requires some exploration. As mentioned above, the *samurai* were (apart from the *daimyō*, or feudal lords) the highest of the social orders. Their fundamental function was that of a warrior class, but a consequence of the Tokugawa 'peace dividend' was that their military function was no longer much required, and in large part they became administrators of the various *han*. For reasons we do not need to go into, many of them were administering *han* other than those in which they originated. In Inoguchi's formulation, as elite administrators with limited inherent power they developed habits of self-discipline and devotion to duty, careful cultivation of as wide a segment of local interests as possible, and continuous monitoring of local conditions, with due sensitivity to change.[15] It is possible to trace these elements through into the history of Japan's modern government bureaucracy, right up to the present, though bureaucratic dominance is now facing serious challenges (see Chapter 7).

The 1850s and 1860s were a time of increasing instability, precipitated by the pressures which several Western nations were bringing to bear with a view to opening up Japan to commercial interaction with the outside world. Whether internal change or external pressure was the more crucial cause of the eventual change of regime is hard to say because of the extent to which the various trends and events overlapped.[16] What is striking is that once the old Tokugawa regime was overthrown (in 1868), and after rearguard action by supporters of the Shogunate had been defeated, the politics of the status quo was swiftly replaced by the politics of radical innovation. The new rulers had little compunction about discarding most of the shibboleths of the former regime, even though in many ways their ideological assumptions were similar. It may be noted in passing that nothing of the sort happened in China until much later (1911), and that as a consequence China found it considerably harder than Japan to lay the foundations of a modern state.

What is termed in Japanese the *Meiji ishin* of 1868 was the event that obviously marks the transition from the old regime to the new. The usual English

[15] Inoguchi, 'The Programmatic Development of Japanese Democratic Politics'.
[16] For a readable account of the events leading up to the Meiji Restoration, see W. G. Beasley, *The Rise of Modern Japan*, London, Weidenfeld & Nicolson, 1990 (rev. version of *The Modern History of Japan*, London, Weidenfeld & Nicolson, 1963 and later editions). See also Marius Jansen, *The Making of Modern Japan*, Cambridge, MA and London, Harvard University Press, 2002.

translation of *ishin* is 'restoration', but 'renovation' is more accurate. Given the root and branch character of the changes that the Japanese people subsequently underwent, the sum total of those changes may well be regarded as revolutionary. Nevertheless, the events of 1868 themselves seem to have had a more limited aim. The new leaders were concerned, in overthrowing the Shogunate, to place the *Tennō*, and the imperial institution, at the centre of the political system that they were about to create. This was in great part a matter of legitimizing the new regime, although the ideological drive behind the movement to bring back the *Tennō* (Emperor), based on Neo-Confucianist principles, should not be ignored.[17] The *Tennō*, though quite powerless, had continued to reside in Kyoto, any real power having been 'usurped' by the shoguns many centuries earlier. The imperial line was said never to have been broken, and the Shogunate had continued to acknowledge that its own legitimacy ultimately derived from him. This apparent example of 'indirect' rule, where nominal power is separated from effective power, occurs repeatedly throughout Japanese history.

It was only comparatively late in the process of turmoil and agitation that culminated in the *Meiji ishin* that the imperial institution came to be championed seriously as a substitute for the *bakufu*. Previously many of the revolutionary leaders had been seeking ways of strengthening the *shōgun* and his government in their struggle to ward off the danger of foreign penetration.

Once, however, the *bakufu* had been overthrown,[18] the newly 'restored' Emperor proved to be a powerful weapon in the hands of the revolutionary leaders. As a symbol of the legitimacy of their newly established regime, the *Tennō* was a powerful support for them in the enactment of a range of bold and adventurous reforms. As the most recent in an ancient and unbroken line of sovereigns, he could be manipulated into the supreme symbol of nationhood, and in practical terms could be used as an instrument of the centralizing and modernizing enterprise that the new leaders proceeded to take upon themselves.

As a revolution, which it undoubtedly was, the *Meiji ishin* has some surprising features from the perspective of revolutions that have occurred in Western countries. Indeed, theories of revolution derived from Western experience make rather little sense when applied to the Meiji revolution. Japanese Marxists were later to engage in convoluted argument in trying to fit the Japanese revolutionary experience into standard Marxist categories.

What, then, were its salient characteristics? First of all, most of the revolutionary leaders came from the ranks of the *samurai* administrators who had held effective power at the local level in the old regime. It was not, in Marxist terms, a 'bourgeois-democratic' revolution, since the merchants, no doubt because of their low formal status, seem to have taken no active part. Essentially it was a revolution carried out by dissident elements of the old ruling class: a revolution from above, not below. Geographically speaking, however, the status quo was

---

[17]   See Marius B. Jansen, 'The Meiji Restoration', in Marius B. Jansen (ed.), *The Cambridge History of Japan*, vol. 5: *The Nineteenth Century*, Cambridge, Cambridge University Press, 1989, pp. 313–14.

[18]   With the overthrow of the *bakufu*, the emperor's court was moved from Kyoto to Edo (where the shogun had previously resided), and the name Edo was changed to Tokyo (Eastern Capital).

overturned. Apart from a handful of court nobles from Kyoto, the rulers of the new Japan hailed largely from the southern and western *han* of Satsuma, Chōshū, Tosa and Hizen, which had always been regarded with suspicion by the *bakufu*. Despite the fact that the *han* were abolished as administrative units in 1871, Japan's key political and military leaders were still being identified with these four areas (especially Satsuma and Chōshū) for another forty years.[19]

The second remarkable feature of the *Meiji ishin* and its aftermath was the essential ambivalence of the new leadership towards change. We must remember here that the leaders did not always agree among themselves, and different strands of thinking were to appear. But they all faced a common dilemma, namely how to modernize Japan, which for the survival of state and nation they knew they had to do, while preserving the spiritual essence (as they saw it) of the Japanese people. What is amazing in retrospect is the sheer scope and ambition of the modernizing and Westernizing reforms embarked upon over the two or three decades following the *Meiji ishin*. But when such reforms threatened to dilute the essential qualities of what it meant to be Japanese, a reaction would take place in favour of the reassertion of national values. A pattern of alternation between modernizing reforms and reassertion of national essence came to be established in the years between the *Meiji ishin* and the end of the Second World War.

The rationale of this process is easy to discern in the character and background of the Meiji leaders themselves. If one phrase is to be chosen to characterize them, they were, for the most part, ardent nationalists. Initially, from the 1850s, incensed by the failure of the *bakufu* to withstand foreign pressures, they took the extreme nationalist stance enshrined in the slogan 'expel the barbarian'. Later, when it became apparent to them that it was futile to attempt to rid the country of foreign influences without the material means to do so, they had the foresight and flexibility of mind to embrace the very enemy they had sought to expel. A new slogan, 'prosperous nation and powerful army' (*fukoku kyōhei*) became the order of the day, and even if the long-term consequences of making Japan both prosperous and powerful were not universally appreciated, the programme itself achieved rapid and impressive success.

The sweeping reforms of the early Meiji period (1868–1912) included abolition of the *han* in 1871 and their replacement by prefectures (*ken*), which formed the principal local units in an increasingly centralized system of local government. A system of universal conscription removed the old *samurai* monopoly on the right to bear arms and formed the base for the creation of an army with truly national loyalties. It proved itself early by defeating the serious rebellion of disgruntled *samurai* led by Saigo Takamori, one of the original Meiji leaders but a fierce traditionalist, in 1877. Universal primary education was introduced as a matter of priority, and a number of universities and other secondary and tertiary educational institutions were set up. The first steps were taken towards industrialization, with the government in several cases setting up an industry on its own

---

[19]   It may be noted that two post-war prime ministers, Kishi Nobusuke and Satō Eisaku (who, despite having different surnames, were brothers) came from Yamaguchi Prefecture, the area of the former Chōshū *han*.

initiative and later handing it over to private entrepreneurs. The taxation system was completely restructured, and the government proceeded to obtain much of its revenue from a land tax, the effect of which was to produce a surplus for industrialization at the expense of rural interests. Reforms to the legal system were also initiated, although these did not come to full fruition until much later, when the government was determined to abolish the principle of extraterritoriality, whereby foreigners could be tried in their national courts for offences committed on Japanese soil.

The question may be posed: why did the governments of the Meiji period manage to carry out such drastic reforms with comparatively little effective protest from those adversely affected by them? Answers in terms of a culture of deference are hardly convincing in view of the events leading to the *Meiji ishin* itself, but a more satisfying explanation in terms of interests is provided by Stephen Vlastos. He emphasizes the benefits obtained by the better-off sections of the community, both agricultural and commercial, as a result of the Meiji reforms, and the willingness of government ruthlessly to sacrifice the interests of strata marginalized by the reforms. These included traditional *samurai* and small-scale subsistence farmers who for various reasons lacked the social or political structures to revolt effectively. Even so, a number of rebellions did break out, the most dangerous of which was that of Saigo Takamori, referred to above.[20]

So far as central government was concerned, the Meiji leaders were content to work for some twenty years on the basis of temporary and ad hoc administrative arrangements. Meanwhile, pressures for the wider sharing of political power were building up in some quarters, and embryo political parties made their appearance during the 1870s. A movement seeking to introduce Western notions of popular rights was an important feature of politics at this time. Government leaders reacted for and against these developments, which caused dissension and splits within their ranks. When a constitution was finally introduced, after a long period of gestation, in 1889 (effective from 1890), it was found to contain severe restrictions upon effective sharing of political power.

Nevertheless, the Meiji Constitution is a landmark in Japan's modern political development. In part, it represented a policy of the dominant Meiji leaders that Japan should have at least the forms of a modern Western-type state. Significantly, they were most attracted by the constitutional practices of Bismarck's Prussia. Although their motives here were by no means uniform, there is little reason to believe that they saw the Constitution other than as formalizing and thus perpetuating substantially the same sort of regime as had obtained hitherto. That is, the *Tennō* (meaning in practice his advisers) should retain effective power, the newly created popular assembly should have only a consultative role, and the political parties should be an impotent opposition rather than a potential alternative government. In practice, as we shall see, things did not quite work out like that, and the government leaders, to an extent at least, found themselves imprisoned by constitutional forms of their own making. It has been argued that their later reluctance, despite these difficulties, to suspend or blatantly override the

[20]   Stephen Vlastos, 'Opposition Movements in Early Meiji, 1868–1885', in Jansen (ed.), *The Cambridge History of Japan*, vol. 5: *The Nineteenth Century*, pp. 367–431.

Constitution derived from the same determination to be seen as an equal of the Western powers that had inspired so many of the reforms from 1868 onwards.[21]

The Meiji Constitution established a parliament, known in English as the Imperial Diet, consisting of two houses: a House of Peers, composed of members of the imperial family, nobles created after the *Meiji ishin* and imperial nominees, and an elective House of Representatives (articles 33–4). The House of Representatives was not designed as the more effective house, since each had equal powers of initiating legislation (article 38),[22] and the House of Peers had the right of veto over legislation initiated in the House of Representatives, as was also the case in reverse (article 39).[23]

The position of the Parliament as a whole, however, was severely limited by the superior status and powers of the *Tennō*, although these were not always easy to pin down in practice. Thus the *Tennō* was 'sacred and inviolable' (article 3). In him (not, or course, in the people) resided sovereignty, although he was to exercise it in accordance with the Constitution (article 4). It was the *Tennō* who exercised the legislative power, albeit with the consent of the Imperial Diet (article 5), who gave sanction to laws (article 6), had considerable powers over the duration of Diet sessions (articles 7, 42 and 43) and dissolved the House of Representatives, this leading to new elections (articles 7, 45).

Moreover, the *Tennō* was able to issue imperial ordinances for a wide range of purposes when the Parliament was not sitting (articles 8, 9), although they were to be submitted for its approval subsequently, at its next session. Since the Parliament was expected to sit for only three months in any year (although prolongations of a session, and also extraordinary sessions, could be held by imperial order), the scope for exercise of the imperial ordinance power was obviously considerable. Ex post facto review of such ordinances by Parliament was unlikely to be very effective.

The powers attributed to the *Tennō* by the Constitution were not expected to be exercised by him as a personal ruler.[24] The preamble stated that the ministers of state, on behalf of the *Tennō*, should be held responsible for implementing the Constitution (Preamble, para. 6). They were also specified as imperial advisers who were 'responsible' for their advice, while the counter-signature of a minister of state was required on '[a]ll Laws, Imperial Ordinances and Imperial Rescripts of whatever kind' (article 55). The ministers of state, however, were not alone in tendering their 'advice' to the *Tennō*. He could also consult a separate body, the

---

[21]   George Akita, *Foundations of Constitutional Government in Modern Japan, 1868–1900*, Cambridge, MA, Harvard University Press, 1967.
[22]   Article 38: 'Both Houses shall vote upon projects of law submitted to it by the Government, and may respectively initiate projects of law.'
[23]   Article 39: 'A bill, which has been rejected by either the one or the other of the two Houses, shall not be again brought in during the same session.'
[24]   It is possible to find occasions where a *Tennō* took some kind of personal initiative, and controversy continues about how far the Shōwa *Tennō* (Hirohito) influenced political decisions between 1926 and 1945. For contrasting analyses, see Stephen Large, *Emperor Hirohito and Shōwa Japan: A Political Biography*, London, Routledge, 1992; Herbert P. Bix, *Hirohito and the Making of Modern Japan*, London, Duckworth, 2000.

Privy Council (*Sūmitsuin*), which was then required to 'deliberate on important matters of state' (article 56). Moreover, an extra-constitutional body called the *genrō* (Elders) – of which more will be said later – occupied a key position of power at certain periods, while the chiefs of staff of the armed services enjoyed what was termed 'independent access' to the *Tennō* on purely military matters, and certain members of the Imperial Household Ministry occupied positions of great influence at certain times.

The situation of the ministers of state, as well as their relationship with the Imperial Diet, contained a number of uncertainties and anomalies. The Constitution deliberately contained no reference to the term 'Cabinet', and Itō Hirobumi, the principal author of the Constitution, in his *Commentaries on the Constitution of the Empire of Japan*, specifically rejected the doctrine of collective Cabinet responsibility as derogating from imperial sovereignty.[25] Moreover, there was no provision in the Constitution stating that ministers had to be members of Parliament, or that they needed to be answerable to Parliament.

On both of these issues there was much subsequent controversy, which the extreme ambiguity of the Constitution did little to help solve. The traditionalists continued to support the principle of what were termed 'transcendental cabinets' (*chōzen naikaku*), whose members were neither members of Parliament nor dependent upon a parliamentary majority, while those more progressively inclined wanted 'responsible cabinets' (*sekinin naikaku*), which among other things would have to resign if defeated on the floor of the House of Representatives. Something like a British-style relationship between Cabinet and Parliament had been established by the 1920s, but such a fundamental liberal principle enjoyed only a brief flowering at that time.

The working of the Meiji Constitution in practice did not entirely bear out the expectations of the Meiji leaders. The House of Representatives proved anything but docile, and the political parties, which despite their recent origin had already accumulated some experience in regional assemblies, fought hard against the principle of transcendental cabinets. Successive governments applied a variety of weapons, constitutional and otherwise, in an attempt to confine the parties to an advisory role. These included frequent dissolution of the House of Representatives, large-scale bribery at elections and the use of article 71 of the Constitution to override opposition by the parties to governmental budgetary policies.

This last issue is of particular importance. Article 71 reads: 'When the Imperial Diet has not voted on the Budget, or when the Budget has not been brought into actual existence, the Government shall carry out the Budget of the preceding year.' On the face of it, this presented any government with a cast-iron method of nullifying party objections to government proposals in the crucial area of budgetary policy. However, this would have been the case only where the size of the budget did not substantially change from year to year. In a period of rapidly rising government expenditure, such as occurred from the outset of the Sino-Japanese war in 1894, the parties had in their possession a weapon of considerable effectiveness.[26]

---

[25]   Marquis Hirobumi Ito, *Commentaries on the Constitution of the Empire of Japan*, trans. Baron Miyoji Ito, Westport CT, Greenwood Press, 1978 (repr. of 1906 edn).

[26]   Akita, *Foundations*, pp. 76–89.

The use they actually made of this weapon provides us with a fascinating test of party–government relationships at this period. It also illuminates a much longer-term characteristic of Japanese politics, namely the equivocal nature of both conflict and compromise between governments and oppositions.

In the 1890s the electoral franchise was confined to about 1 per cent of the population of Japan. This meant in effect that a high proportion of the parliamentarians elected in the early general elections represented the landlord interest upon which fell most heavily the burden of the land tax, used by the government as the main means of financing its 'prosperous nation and powerful army' policies. This undoubtedly accounts for the vehemence with which parliamentarians in the mid-1890s called on the government to retrench its spending; and the threat of forcing the government to carry on with the budget of the previous year was a powerful one. It is therefore doubly interesting that by the end of the decade the government leaders had succeeded in breaking the deadlock by a series of deals with Diet members and leading party men, which gave the latter an entrée into the councils of government while allowing the government to maintain its fiscal policies more or less intact.[27]

The Meiji 'oligarchs' – the powerful and creative political leaders of pre-Constitution days, who continued to dominate governments throughout the 1890s – were ultimately forced to step down into the arena of party politics themselves. When Marquis Itō founded the *Seiyūkai* party in 1900 with a membership largely of established party politicians, he was pointing the way to a new style of politics, different indeed from what he himself had envisaged in his *Commentaries on the Constitution*. By going along with this and subsequent arrangements, however, the parties were gaining a limited right of participation in decision-making at the expense of their ability to present forthright and effective opposition. Henceforth, the line between government bureaucrats and party politicians was a thin one, and elements of this situation remain to this day.

One weakness that political parties continued to manifest to their very great cost was the frequent corruption of party politicians. Their willingness to enter into advantageous deals with outsiders, and their consequent propensity to be 'bought', made it particularly difficult for the parties to maintain cohesion or internal unity of purpose. There is a sociological dimension to this tendency which will be discussed in Chapter 3, section A3. At the same time it was also undoubtedly related to the ambiguities inherent in the Constitution itself. According to that document, sovereignty resided in the *Tennō*, but the *Tennō* did not rule personally (with occasional exceptions) and it was not at all clear who *was* supposed to. The enthusiasm with which the authors of the Constitution sought to ensure a strong executive and a weak legislature led them to downgrade even the position of the Cabinet, by providing rival centres of power and attacking the principle of collective Cabinet responsibility. The *Tennō* 'cult', which they

---

[27]   Banno Junji, *Meiji kenpō taisei no kakuritsu* (The Establishment of the Meiji Constitutional System), Tokyo, Tokyo Daigaku Shuppankai, 1971; trans. into English by J. A. A. Stockwin as *The Establishment of the Japanese Constitutional System*, London, Routledge, 1992.

assiduously promoted as a means to national discipline, also tended to force overt criticism and opposition under the surface, where it was more likely to become immersed in factional intrigue.[28]

Japanese politics during the first two decades of the twentieth century involved a complex and shifting process of balancing elites. Cabinets, political parties, senior government bureaucrats, the House of Peers, the Privy Council, the *Tennō*'s personal advisers in the Imperial Household Ministry, the chiefs of staff of the armed forces and directors of certain big business combines were all jockeying for power in a situation where it was unclear where power really lay. Indeed, there were frequent power plays within elites as well as between them.[29] For a time, the ultimate direction of key decisions was in the hands of *genrō*. This group, never more than seven in number, furnished senior Cabinet ministers from among its own ranks until the turn of the century, when it retired more into the background. Even after that, however, the *genrō* continued to make important decisions, particularly when the choice of a new prime minister, or a matter of war and peace, was at stake. The influence of the *genrō* had much declined by the end of the First World War, when few of them were left and younger politicians resented their 'meddling in politics'.[30]

The *genrō*, though anachronistic, had at least functioned as ultimate political coordinators and setters of guidelines. By the 1920s the base of political participation had significantly broadened, but the locus of power at the top remained unstable. The suffrage was increased by stages, and by 1925 encompassed all males over 25 . The period from 1924 to 1932 saw a succession of party cabinets, so that transcendental cabinets appeared to be a thing of the past. Mitani identifies six factors accounting for this change: (1) the establishment of the superiority of the House of Representatives over the House of Peers; (2) the emergence of Minobe's constitutional theory (see below) as orthodox; (3) the political neutralization of the Privy Council; (4) party penetration of the civil bureaucracy; (5) party accommodation with the judiciary; and (6) party *rapprochement* with the military.[31]

It soon became clear, however, that this arrangement was unstable, and in the early 1930s several of the above conditions for party ascendancy had ceased to apply. Indeed, it was fragile even during the 1920s, as indicated by the fact that the same Cabinet that introduced universal male suffrage in 1925 also introduced a 'peace preservation law' designed to increase the power of the police against manifestations of political dissent.

---

[28]   For a detailed examination of the ambiguities inherent in the Meiji Constitution and the political consequences of these, see Taichiro Mitani, 'The Establishment of Party Cabinets, 1898–1932', trans. Peter Duus, in Peter Duus (ed.), *The Cambridge History of Japan*, vol. 6: *The Twentieth Century*, Cambridge, Cambridge University Press, 1988, pp. 55–96.

[29]   John K. Fairbank, Edwin O. Reischauer and Albert M. Craig, *East Asia, The Modern Transformation*, Cambridge, MA, Harvard University Press, 1965, pp. 554–63.

[30]   Roger F. Hackett, 'Political Modernization and the Meiji Genro', in Robert E. Ward (ed.), *Political Development in Modern Japan*, Princeton, NJ, Princeton University Press, 1968, pp. 65–97.

[31]   Mitani, 'The Establishment of Party Cabinets', pp. 76–96.

During the 1930s the power of the political parties ebbed rapidly as the armed forces came to play an increasingly commanding role in the affairs of state. In the Manchurian Incident of September 1931 a gross act of insubordination by the Kwantung Army stationed in Manchuria – connived at, apparently, by the army high command in Tokyo – went unpunished and uncorrected by the civilian government. Japan proceeded to take over the whole of Manchuria and set up the puppet state of Manchukuo.[32]

A series of political assassinations and attempted coups followed, the most serious of which occurred on 26 February 1936, resulting in the deaths of several members of the Cabinet. Although those directly responsible for these crimes were not admitted to positions of power and some of them were severely punished, their actions helped elements in the army high command increasingly to take over the reins of government.[33]

The reasons for this reversal of previous trends are extremely complicated and can only be briefly summarized here. Five main factors command attention. The first is social and economic. The world depression bore particularly hard on the Japanese peasantry, and provided fertile soil for right-wing radicalism. Since the army recruited a high proportion of its younger officers from farming areas, ultra-nationalist agitation spread easily within the armed forces and, given the delicate balance of power in government, exerted a pervasive political effect.

The second is international. This was the age of economic protectionism and a fascist example in Europe. Both politically and economically the international situation was very fluid, and this seems to have affected the views of some political leaders. Some others, basically liberal, were eliminated by assassination.

The third relates to ideology and indoctrination. Since the Imperial Rescript on Education in 1890, *Tennō*-worship had been officially sanctioned as the keystone of a national ideology, thus blurring in people's minds the true location of decision-making. There was a tradition, not confined to the far right, of appealing to the *Tennō* against corrupt, tyrannical or remote officials, so that it was easy for ultra-nationalists in a period of national crisis to gain wide support for acts of insubordination and of revolution taken in the name of loyalty to the *Tennō*.[34] It was not difficult for them to pillory members of the existing establishment as corrupt and disloyal.

Fourth, as we have seen already, the constitutional arrangements that had prevailed since the Meiji period contained an unsettling element of ambiguity. The attempts by the Meiji oligarchs to prevent the legislature gaining supremacy by a series of checks and balances had merely served to obscure the effective location of sovereignty. Nevertheless, a rather liberal interpretation of the Constitution had taken root by the 1920s. According to the 'organ theory' of Minobe Tatsukichi, Professor of Constitutional Law at Tokyo Imperial University,

[32]   Sadako N. Ogata, *Defiance in Manchuria: The Making of Japanese Foreign Policy, 1931–1932*, Berkeley and Los Angeles, University of California Press, 1964.

[33]   Richard Storry, *The Double Patriots*, London, Chatto & Windus, 1957.

[34]   Indeed, fanatical loyalty to the emperor sometimes went along with advocacy of his replacement by somebody more favourable to the national chauvinist cause. Stephen Large identifies this threat as a factor that inhibited the Shōwa Emperor from taking a more active line against extremism: Large, *Emperor Hirohito and Shōwa Japan*, pp. 46–75.

the *Tennō* was not an absolute ruler but was dependent on the other 'organs of state', much as a human head cannot live without the body to which it is attached. This did not constitute a Western-style liberal democratic interpretation, and Minobe publicly opposed the new Constitution introduced in 1946–7, during the Allied Occupation. But in the context of the times, it could be used to justify relatively liberal political arrangements. However, when ultra-nationalist thinking gained the upper hand in the early 1930s, the organ theory was rejected as heresy, Minobe was dismissed from his university post, and an absolutist school maintaining that the emperor was above the state, not accountable to other 'organs', became the new orthodoxy.

Finally, the special position of the armed forces calls for comment. Ever since the leaders of the *Meiji ishin* had invented the slogan 'a prosperous country and a strong army', priority had been given to military preparedness. Japan had defeated China in 1895 and Russia in 1905. Reference has already been made to the independent access to the *Tennō* enjoyed by the chiefs of staff of the armed services. Although this was officially restricted to 'purely military' matters, it could prove a useful means of bypassing Cabinet on sensitive issues. Another convention (introduced by the *genrō* Yamagata Aritomo at the turn of the century) held that the war and navy ministers in any cabinet should be serving officers of the highest rank in their respective services. A serving officer is of course subject to military orders, and therefore as a member of a cabinet would have divided loyalties. In the 1930s this brought about the collapse of several cabinets that were reluctant to let the armed forces have their own way. The resignation of a service minister would be followed by the refusal of the service concerned to provide a replacement, and thus the Cabinet would fall.

For these principal reasons, Japan experienced what is sometimes termed 'dual government' in the early to mid-1930s, with the civilian and military establishments pursuing uncoordinated, though not always unrelated, strategies. From the outbreak of war in China in 1937, the character of Japanese politics had undergone a profound transformation. Nearly all parts of the system had assimilated a militant nationalist ethic, even though the young army officers who participated in the attempted coup of February 1936 (known in Japan as the 'two-twenty-six incident') and similar instances of bloodletting were little more than a catalyst. It is quite misleading to regard the parties as defeated defenders of the 'liberal' norms of the 1920s and the armed forces and other 'reactionary' groups as the victors. With some rather minor exceptions, party politicians were enthusiastic about many of the developments taking place. Even after June and July 1940, when all political parties were merged into the monolithic Imperial Rule Assistance Association (*taisei yokusankai*), sponsored by Prince Konoe, party politicians continued to play an important role in the political structure, and indeed they went on politicking in ways that were familiar to them.[35] In April 1942, with war raging in the Pacific, the Tōjō government even held general elections for the House of Representatives. The vast bulk of successful candidates

[35]   Gordon M. Berger, *Parties out of Power in Japan 1931–1941*, Princeton, NJ, Princeton University Press, 1977.

were from a list of those 'sponsored' by the government, but a small number of unsponsored candidates were elected.[36]

Politics during the Pacific and East Asian war have been described as 'totalitarian'. Whether or not the term is appropriate, the regime bent its energies to the task of mobilizing the population for total war. Functional groups (business organizations, labour unions and the like) were made organs of state, a network of 'neighbourhood associations' did the government's bidding at the local level, and the *kenpeitai* (thought police) were pervasive. Under wartime pressures, the involvement of the state in most areas of the life of the people became entrenched. Multiple linkages between government and industry, encompassing habits of regular and close consultation, were a legacy of the 1930s and the early 1940s that was transmitted through the time of the Allied Occupation to the Japan of the 1950s and 1960s.[37]

[36] See Ben-Ami Shillony, *Politics and Culture in Wartime Japan*, Oxford, Clarendon Press, 1981.

[37] Gary D. Allinson, *Japanese Urbanism: Industry and Politics in Kariya, 1872–1972*, Berkeley, Los Angeles and London, University of California Press, 1975.

Chapter 3 | Social Background: How far Social Norms and Behaviour Influence Politics

The idea that politics may be studied without reference to social and cultural norms may be attractive to some hard-nosed political scientists who believe that political analysis alone can explain political outcomes. For the present writer, however, it is much too simplistic, both in relation to Japan and in relation to anywhere else. On the other hand, we equally reject the notion that Japanese social norms and behaviour are so different from those found elsewhere that Japanese politics is incapable of being compared with the politics of other countries. Both are self-evidently extreme positions, but it is surprising how often one encounters opinions close to one or other of the two poles. In this book, a middle view is taken, regarding Japanese society and politics as open-ended – that is, capable of encompassing a variety of behaviour – but at the same time bounded by social norms, as well as habits of social and political interaction, that have their roots in history. If this argument appears trite (since much the same could be said about most countries), we should remember that the image of Japanese society as 'different' remains embedded both within Japan and outside it, while by contrast it has become fashionable in some circles to regard Japan as just another bit of the global village.

Crucially also, to regard social and cultural norms of behaviour as important is not to make the assumption that they are immutable. Indeed, change is built into most social models constructed by social anthropologists.[1] Change and development, driven by economic, political, social, international and indeed ecological factors, are central to modern societies. Japan since 1945 has been transformed in many of its aspects through unprecedented economic growth, whereby it has become one of the most advanced nations of the world. It would be indeed surprising if that had not affected values as well. Change of this kind is relevant to our understanding of politics also, in the sense that political leaders who promote policies based on atavistic ideas about the traditional essence of the society

---

[1] Joy Hendry, seminar intervention, Oxford Brookes University, 27 March 2006.

may find their efforts contested by major elements of the population who have grown away from such old-fashioned social norms and values. On the other hand, a political leader who ignores tradition may also encounter difficulties in securing support.[2]

In analysing politics it is often difficult to know what weight to give to sociological factors. We encounter the problem of ambiguity, since possible alternative explanations dangle before our eyes. We shall try to illustrate this through a number of politically relevant vignettes, some taken from the author's personal experience, others from elsewhere or from the public record.

1   Some time in the 1980s I contacted a conservative member of Parliament in Tokyo and requested an interview. The parliamentarian generously invited me to his house in a Tokyo suburb and agreed to meet me in his car at the nearest railway station. On the way from the station to his home we passed a house which had a wreath prominently displayed outside, indicating that somebody living there had died. My host stopped the car, went to the house and spent about ten minutes paying his respects. Naturally the house was in his constituency.

2   I was interviewing another member of Parliament, this time at his office opposite the Parliament building in Tokyo. Almost from the start of the meeting we were interrupted by parties of visitors calling in, as well as by constant telephone calls. Most of the callers were from his constituency, some with particular grievances that needed attending to, others just to pay their respects. Towards the end of the interview the parliamentarian said to me, in some exasperation: 'You see what life is like for parliamentarians in this country.'

3   I had the task of allocating work rooms, some of them accommodating two people, to Japanese visitors at an academic institute in England. One older visitor took me aside and said that whatever I did I must not put Japanese whose rank was substantially different in the same room. Later, however, when I checked this out with younger visitors, they laughed at the advice I had been given.

4   In the early 1990s I was able to observe a session of the prefectural assembly in the principal city of a prefecture distant from Tokyo. The prefectural governor was to be questioned on policy matters by elected members of the assembly. Before entering the assembly hall, I was introduced to a number of officials, and was lent a transcript of both the questions and the answers that were expected. The course of the discussion, as it turned out, had been anticipated with almost verbatim accuracy by the transcript, which was hardly surprising, since both the assembly members and the governor had copies of the same transcript, and were, for the most part, reading from it.

5   A young Japanese woman was accused of an offence by a compatriot. The police were brought in and she was able to establish her innocence. But during

---

[2]   This discussion impinges upon the question of convergence between different societies, concerning which there is a voluminous literature.

the period of investigation her parents attempted to contact the family of the alleged victim in order to apologize.

6   A minister in the Japanese government resigned in order to take responsibility for a failure of policy implementation by officials in his ministry. The failure was not something he could readily have prevented, especially given that (like most ministers) he had not been long in the job and that officials in practice had a large degree of autonomy in their actions. At the next Cabinet reshuffle (or perhaps the one after that) he was given another portfolio in government.

7   In November 2000 the moderate LDP faction leader Katō Kōichi, objecting to certain right-wing policies of the Prime Minister, Mori Yoshirō, supported a no-confidence motion in the government brought by opposition parties. He attempted to persuade his faction to follow him out of the party, but few of his followers were prepared to do so, and the revolt collapsed. Katō had been a credible future candidate for Prime Minister, but this episode virtually finished his career. (See Chapter 6.)

8   In April 2004 three young Japanese voluntary workers were kidnapped in Iraq, but were released some two weeks later. On their return to Japan they were widely criticized for causing a nuisance, and received little credit for their voluntary work on behalf of distressed Iraqis (See Chapter 6.)

9   An island some hundreds of metres offshore from mainland Japan was home to about 500 inhabitants, but the only way of travelling to the mainland was by boat. Political pressure had been exerted for a bridge to be built between the mainland and the island. Finally it was determined that a bridge was needed. At this point two separate and rival agencies of the central government became active on the issue, and two separate bridges were built.

10   In June 2004 the Democratic Party and the Social Democratic Party boycotted the final session of the House of Councillors, charged with voting on a revised pensions bill, on the grounds that the chairman of one of that house's committees had cut off debate prematurely (see Chapter 6). This was merely the latest example of what had been the common practice of opposition parties absenting themselves en masse from parliamentary debate, and then, when the legislation they were objecting to was passed in their absence, accusing the government parties of perpetrating the 'tyranny of the majority'.

Let us examine these ten vignettes, and see what they tell us.

The first story illustrates the importance of personal constituency service on the part of parliamentarians. For a member of Parliament, the purpose of paying his respects to a bereaved family is not simply humanitarian. It is part of the process of building up a network of obligation in his constituency. To do the 'done thing' is also to build up personal support. Of course, this kind of activity can lead to various forms of corruption, though we must take care with the definition of that word.

The second story relates closely to the first. Members of Parliament are expected to be at the beck and call of their constituents to an extent that would amaze, for instance, the average British or Australian member. Often the demands on them seem to make little sense in terms of a rational allocation of their time, since many constituents come simply to pay their respects. But again, it is important in terms of networking, and without networking the member may find that his seat is in peril.

Story number three simply illustrates the importance given to hierarchy of position in Japanese organizations. Distinctions of rank are often precisely defined in a generally recognized hierarchical system. But the reaction of the younger visitors might suggest that consciousness of hierarchy is diminishing. On the other hand, it is possible that when the young grow older, a sense of hierarchy grows with their advancing years.

So far as the fourth story is concerned, it suggests a preference within politics and other walks of life for setting up arrangements behind the scenes, and presenting a common front once the public arena is involved. Lest this seem too much like a copy of the system operative in the former Soviet Union, we should note that probably a great deal of fierce bargaining had gone into the process of writing the transcript in the first place. It seems possible to consider this story as an example of a commonly made distinction about Japanese society, namely that between *uchi* (that which is within) and *soto* (that which is without). That which appertains to the *uchi* is frank, intimate, internally contested, whereas that which appertains to the *soto* is formal, superficial and unanimous. In the *uchi* you may find *ura* (behind the scenes reality), whereas in the *soto* you will discover only the *omote* (surface appearance). Strangely, though, both *uchi/ura* and *soto/omote* are functional, the first to hammer out real solutions and the second to present them to the outside world. Having put this case, however, we have to admit that the example presented in this story is by no means the universal norm of local assembly procedures in the new century. Things change.

Story number five illustrates the role of apology. Whereas, generally speaking, in Western societies, the function of an apology is to mitigate a wrong for which the person apologizing is responsible, in Japan this condition does not necessarily apply. Rather, it performs a kind of lightning conductor function, whereby to apologize is to dissipate tension and satisfy the other party rather than actually admit guilt. The practice whereby those accused of crimes, under police pressure, sign confessions to let themselves off the hook (not always with desired results) may be connected with the role of apology in Japanese society. Today, however, this practice, like others in the criminal justice system, is under attack from human rights activists.[3]

The sixth story is a composite of many similar episodes. Here again the lightning conductor analogy is relevant. By resigning, the minister makes a dramatic statement of contrition, even though he personally was not to blame, knowing that this act of contrition is likely to be of limited duration. There is a sense, however, in which the lightning conductor has the function of diverting the

---

[3] See for instance the film, released in January 2007, entitled in Japanese *Sore demo boku wa yatte inai*, and in English *I just didn't do it*, directed by Suo Masayuki.

blame away from the unelected officials who were personally responsible for the failure, and this tendency too has been coming under critical scrutiny as the idea of bureaucratic immunity has been unravelling.[4]

The seventh story illustrates the importance of loyalty to the group in Japanese party politics. But loyalty in this context is not just an abstract ideal: for so long as the LDP remains in power, membership of it brings patronage, and apostasy is a leap in the dark. The particular situation described was complicated (see Chapter 6), but Katō could be accused of bad judgement, both in relation to the chances of mustering the necessary numbers to take power in some combination of current opposition parties, and in relation to his understanding of the needs and aspirations of his factional followers. Evidence from the mid-1990s, when party politics became very unstable and some members of Parliament were changing parties much in the way they changed their socks, suggests that party loyalty is to a high degree instrumental, and should not be conceptually reduced to essentialist notions of group belonging (see Chapter 9).

Story number eight no doubt illustrates the relative weakness of a 'voluntary sector' mentality in Japan, though in this respect things seem to be changing (see Chapter 11). But more fundamentally, it imparts a sense of ready acceptance of official policy in preference to unstructured activity that is not part of that official policy. Of course, voluntary workers who have endangered not only their own lives but also those of putative rescuers in the murderous conditions of Iraq are not popular in other countries such as the United Kingdom.[5] Whatever the qualifications that need to be made about this particular story, it indicates a sense of conformity that tends to pervade political attitudes at many levels.[6]

The ninth story has entered into the folklore of Japanese bureaucracy. What it illustrates is sectionalism. Now, inter-departmental rivalry is a feature of bureaucracies the world over, but in the Japanese case it has sometimes gone to extremes. The amalgamation and restructuring of ministries and agencies of the government that was put in place in January 2001 was in part an attempt to curb such absurdities as the story illustrates, and to bring about greater bureaucratic coordination, or what is sometimes called 'joined-up government'.

The final story illustrates the theme of consensus. We must emphasize that consensus is not something that occurs naturally, but is a mechanism for creating order between competing entities. Moreover, the practice of parliamentary

[4]   There are recent examples in British politics (such as Mandelson and Blunkett) of ministers resigning (or being dismissed), then being admitted back into Cabinet some time later, though one resignation seems to be the limit, a second not forgiven so easily. But in Britain a resigning matter normally involves a substantial degree of personal responsibility for failure *by the Minister*. Since the Crichel Down affair in the 1950s, very few ministers have resigned as the result of a misdemeanour, by officials of their department, which they could not reasonably have prevented.

[5]   For instance, the British peace activist Norman Kember was kidnapped and had to be rescued by a contingent of British forces in Iraq in 2005. This occasioned scathing public comment from a leading British general that he had endangered not just his own life, but the lives of his rescuers.

[6]   One hears the statement *kuni ga kimeta* (the state has decided it), as a resigned reaction to some irksome regulation.

boycott also has a highly instrumental purpose, namely to show up any government that pushes ahead with a vote on legislation in the face of a boycott as riding roughshod over the views of the minority. Decision-making by consensus is a quite different mechanism from decisions made by majority vote. The phenomenon of a boycott followed by a 'forced vote' represents an attempt, by a minority that cannot get its own way through the majoritarian system that currently operates, to refer to the norms of a different system, in order to shame the majority.

Reflecting on these ten cases, care needs to be taken if a sociological explanation is being offered. Apart from the fact that we should not generalize from single, anecdotal cases, some of them may be explicable by other factors, such as institutional constraints or rational calculation of advantage. Explanation is not a simple task, since most situations require multi-factor explanations. Even so, it is worth looking for what can be generalized about Japanese society, as models to hold up against reality. Needless to say, we are concentrating on social aspects that are particularly relevant to politics.

Here we need to take into account the ways in which the society has been evolving, and avoid an approach that might suggest that it is static. We first of all present five well-recognized propositions about the nature of social interaction. Second, later in the chapter, we shall put forward another five propositions suggestive of current reality, or a reality towards which the society is moving. In putting the two sets of propositions together, we shall endeavour to throw light on how society and politics interact in the first decade of the third millennium.

The first set of propositions (A1–5) are as follows.

A1   Japanese society is especially group-oriented   This implies, first of all, that Japanese people experience a more or less intense identification with the group to which they belong and, second, that group loyalty brings with it a degree of exclusivity: relationships between people in different groups are sharply distinguishable from those between people within the same group. As we have seen (story 4, above), this has been linked with the distinction between *uchi* (inside) and *soto* (outside). This distinction has itself been linked by social anthropologists with the transition that takes place in a Japanese house when you move from outside, via the *genkan* (threshold), into the house itself. The change from *soto* to *uchi* is symbolized by the removal of shoes at the *genkan* – a virtually universal practice. You have moved from the unclean, polluting *soto* into the clean, welcoming and cosy environment of the *uchi*.[7]

A2   Japanese social relations are essentially based on hierarchy   According to this proposition, Japanese generally find relationships based on strict personal equality of status difficult to manage. Aspects of the Japanese language appear to bear this out. Japanese contains a complex set of distinctions collectively known as *keigo* (respect language), whereby quite different forms of expression

[7]   Emiko Ohnuki-Tierney, *Illness and Culture in Contemporary Japan: An Anthropological View*, Cambridge, Cambridge University Press, 1984, pp. 39–46; Joy Hendry, *Understanding Japanese Society*, London and New York, RoutledgeCurzon, 3rd edn, 2003, pp. 47–9.

(for instance common verbs, such as 'see', 'do', 'eat', 'go') are used depending on the hierarchical relationship of the people conversing. Even though the system has now been modified so that by using *keigo* one is often simply expressing politeness rather than responding to a situation of hierarchy, *keigo* remains a central and integral, not a marginal, part of the language, as anyone who has tried to learn Japanese will be aware.[8]

A3   Japanese society attributes great importance to norms of mutual obligation
A sense of mutual obligation appears to serve both as a motivating mechanism and as a binding mechanism. By common observation, Japan is a gift-giving society, gifts from one person, family or group to another symbolizing both the fulfilment of an obligation that should stimulate further action, and a means of cementing a relationship. The first to recognize the significance of mutual obligation for Japanese social dynamics was the American social anthropologist Ruth Benedict, writing towards the end of the Second World War. Benedict concentrated on the concepts of *on* and *giri*, which she likened to Western-style debt repayment conventions, except that they covered a far broader range of activity and relationships than the purely financial. According to her analysis, *on* could best be translated as 'love' and 'devotion', generally to a hierarchical superior. She speaks of *on* as a set of obligations passively incurred, since every Japanese thinks of himself as a 'debtor to the ages and the world'. *On* can be received from the *Tennō*, one's parents, one's lord, one's teacher, and from all the contacts in the course of one's life.[9]

A4   Japanese prefer to reach decisions by consensus   We have already touched on the distinction between decision-making by consensus and decision-making by majority-take-all, systems radically different as methods and in their effects. The formal institutions of politics (parliaments, local assemblies) vote according to the majority principle. But not infrequently the actual vote is a formal endorsement of a decision reached by consensus behind the scenes. An argument heard in Japan against real majority vote-taking is that it leaves some members of the group dissatisfied and is therefore potentially disruptive. Another is that it may expose the individual to an uncomfortable assertion of his or her actual view, whereas the final responsibility for a decision should be collective. Decision-making by consensus, on the other hand, involves adjusting initially differing views, so that everyone having a part in the decision can in the end subscribe to it knowing that his or her views have been taken into account.[10] It takes time, but it is worth it in the end. If, however, consensus proves impossible to attain,

---

[8]   For instance, 'do you see it' turns into *sore, miru no* (to a child); *sore wa, mimasu ka* (to a friend); *sore wa, goran ni narimasu ka* (to a hierarchical superior, or any person to whom one is being super-polite for whatever reason). We should note that English is not wholly free from such distinctions. For instance, we may say 'got it?' (to a child); 'do you understand?' (to a friend); 'has your Grace taken the point?' (to an archbishop). In both languages, in principle, the more polite an expression, the longer it is.
[9]   Ruth Benedict, *The Chrysanthemum and the Sword*, Boston, Houghton Mifflin, 1946.
[10]   See story number 4 above. The pre-scripted debate in the local assembly avoided the kind of unpredictability that might expose individuals to public criticism.

the consequences may be serious, and may include extreme expressions of hostility and frustration on the part of those who feel that their views have been ignored or rejected.

A5   Japanese tend to accept values based on subservience to authority   Central to Western democratic theory is the notion that the autonomous individual citizen has the freedom, and indeed the duty, to criticize government where necessary and to hold it to account. By contrast, according to this view, Japanese are much more inclined to regard government as something that is there by right, that almost by definition will govern in the best interests of the people; and to believe that even if it doesn't, there is not much point in contesting what it does, since this risks unduly disturbing the natural order of things. Some people vote for opposition parties, but these have little chance of replacing the government in power, so that voting for the opposition is more of a demonstrative act than a true act of citizenship. Similarly, protest movements have at times developed intense energy, but they have little staying power, as people tend to drift away after they have made their point (which is usually ignored, or deflected by the device of apology or resignation).

These five propositions taken together suggest that Japanese society is group-oriented, hierarchical, based on mutual obligation and inclined to making decisions by consensus. But is this an accurate or adequate description of how Japanese behave in social situations, especially those that impinge on politics?

Before seeking to answer this question, we need to explore further the intellectual underpinning of a model of Japanese society based on these five factors. Central to the model is the concept of the 'household', or in Japanese *ie*. We are talking here of an ideal-type, traditional *ie*, from which most contemporary households no doubt differ greatly. It is crucial to realize that this is an idealized model, not a description of reality on the ground. But the *ie* in this sense is not entirely irrelevant to an understanding of contemporary households in their infinite variety, or indeed for an understanding of other kinds of organization, such as small companies or political factions.

The *ie* in this idealized sense may be seen as a corporate body, with the whole more important than the sum of its parts, that is, its individual members. Vertical relations, between generations, were more important than horizontal ones, for instance between husband and wife. It was male-oriented and paternalistic, though female members had effective power in their allotted spheres. Perpetuation of the family, and reverence for ancestors, were a supreme duty. Equality between members was not recognized; nevertheless, the obligations between the head of the household and other members were not simply one-way, but contained a strong element of mutuality and paternalism. By extension, relations between student and teacher, or craftsman and master craftsman, took on similar characteristics of hierarchy combined with mutual affective regard.[11]

---

[11]   The words *sensei* and *onshi* – both roughly meaning 'teacher' but implying respect combined with affect – are widely used today. This is especially true of *sensei*, which is a term of address used to those who are not necessarily 'teachers' as understood in Western countries. For instance, medical doctors are regularly addressed as *sensei*.

In the model of a traditional *ie*, blood ties were of course important, but did not necessarily override the more basic consideration of perpetuating the family line. The practice of adult adoption, whereby a young male from another family was brought in to marry a daughter of the *ie*, and would accept the family name as his own, was relatively common in the pre-war period and even persists today to some extent.

What was once an influential analysis of the *ie* system and its implications was put forward in the 1970s by the social anthropologist Nakane Chie, who argued that the nature of the system greatly inhibited social pluralism. Her analysis is interesting and suggestive, but it is also highly essentialist, and needs to be taken with extreme care as a guide to family and social relations in contemporary Japan. Nakane's model emphasizes the strength of vertical relationships and the weakness of horizontal ones. Three particular aspects of her model are significant. The first is the ready extension of patterns of behaviour within the family to non-family groups; the second is its emphasis on vertical ties and de-emphasis of horizontal ones, implying that cohesion between vertically structured groups is difficult to obtain; the third is the assertion that Japanese have a more acute consciousness of belonging to a group (family, company, political faction, sect, craft tradition, etc.) than of belonging to a profession or occupation (doctor, engineer, plumber etc.).

If this characterization is accurate, it has important implications for the conduct of politics, as well as for the economy. If political and economic behaviour is conducted by small vertical groups with weak horizontal ties between them, then we would expect to find both the political and economic worlds badly fragmented. To some extent, this is indeed the case. To take an example from industrial relations, trade unions are typically organized on the basis of the firm in which their members are employed, not on the basis of a craft or an industry. Indeed, 'trade union' in the Japanese case is a misnomer, and we prefer the usage 'labour union', or more specifically 'enterprise union'. In political parties, especially if we examine the three or four decades following the 1945 defeat, it often seemed to be the case that the principal focus of loyalty was the faction rather than the party of which it was a part. If members of a union regard the company for which they work as the most important thing in their lives, then they are unlikely to agree to industrial action that would seriously harm that company. If members of a political faction find the set of personal relationships encompassed by their factional membership as absolutely crucial to their political lives, then under pressure they are likely to follow the decision of their faction, even if that decision involves disloyalty to the party of which it is a part.

Historians have examined clashes that occurred among *samurai* between loyalty to family and loyalty to feudal lord, and concluded that loyalty to one's lord often overrode loyalty to one's father.[12] This was, generally speaking, the opposite of patterns in China, where loyalty to family was seen as more important than loyalty to a corporate group outside the family, and many firms, for instance, were (and are) quite literally family firms.

[12]   See Chapter 2, note 6.

The question we need to ask, however, is an empirical one. If we seek to apply the 'vertical society' model to contemporary reality, to what extent does it enable us to predict actual outcomes? Let us take, first of all, the question of fragmentation.

In the case of the union movement, it is indeed true that the basic unit is the enterprise union. But enterprise unions have long been affiliated to industrial unions, and these are affiliated to a very small number of national union federations. Overwhelmingly the largest union in the first decade of the twenty-first century is the Japanese Trade Union Confederation (*Rengō*). It is true that much industrial bargaining is done at the enterprise level, but since 1954 a mechanism has existed for coordinating settlements over wages and conditions, namely the Spring Struggle (*Shuntō*). The Spring Struggle provides a template to which management of firms and enterprise unions refer in reaching agreement.

In our second case, that of political factions, the Nakane model would lead us to expect a highly fragmented party system. There have been periods of fragmentation, for instance 1945–55, and also from 1992 to 1998 and beyond. In the post-war Socialist movement, mostly out of office and lacking the discipline of power, factional fragmentation was particularly marked, so much so that some tight factional groups could boast a longer life than the parties of which they were at times members.[13] What the Nakane model fails to predict, however, is that mechanisms would readily emerge to channel factionalism into a larger and far more powerful institution, namely a dominant political party, the LDP. (In other parties, to a lesser extent and with various qualifications, a similar thing happened: see Chapter 9).

Without wishing to underestimate the importance of factions (some with long pedigrees) within the LDP, two points need to be made about them. The first is that over the history of that party, they came to play roles that were functional for the smooth operation of the party itself, as they channelled factional energies into the business of power-broking, fund-raising and securing of leadership succession. In much Western literature on political parties, factions are seen as self-seeking and disruptive entities, and this is not entirely inapposite to the Japanese case; but at the same time they became a key functional part of the larger system. The second point is that with the radical reform of the electoral system for the House of Representatives that became law in 1994, a key electoral motivation for factional division (multi-member constituencies) was removed. The result has been that over the most recent decade the salience of factions within the LDP has declined, and their nature and function have also been substantially modified (see Chapters 8 and 9).

Our argument then, is that the 'vertical society' model gives only a very incomplete idea of reality, and one, moreover, that fails to account for the effect of institutional change. In addition to these reservations, there is the problem of perceptions. Societies work in certain ways, but they are also perceived to work in certain ways; and it is sometimes possible for the perception to be substituted for reality. In its time, Nakane's model exerted considerable influence on how Japanese society operated, both among Japanese and, especially, among foreign

---

[13] J. A. A. Stockwin, *The Japanese Socialist Party and Neutralism*, Melbourne, Melbourne University Press, 1968.

observers. Although too much, perhaps, should not be made of this argument, there is a sense in which the model was both conservative in its implications and suggested that Japan behaved on the basis of different rules from other societies, thus justifying behaviour that did not follow international rules.[14]

Even so, the idea of a 'vertical society' does retain some relevance for an understanding of Japanese reality, provided that it is heavily qualified by multiple factors of adaptation and change over time. Let us examine, in turn, a number of the implications of the model.

One, already mentioned, is Nakane's belief that 'vertical society' patterns, modelled on the traditional *ie*, inhibited social pluralism. A particular aspect of this contention relates to the apparent slowness of civil society to emerge in Japan by comparison with other economically advanced countries. With horizontal ties weak, the argument goes, motives leading people to organize on behalf of disadvantaged groups or individuals with whom they are not connected by ties of family or work place are unlikely to show firm development. No doubt there is some force in this argument, but two factors should be considered on the other side. One is that the institutional barriers to the development of civil society have been formidable, though to some extent they have now been relaxed. Charity law and its administration has been a big obstacle to the formation of NPOs, especially those that would be national in scope and potentially critical of government.[15] The second factor in relation to civil society is that after the Kobe earthquake of January 1995, voluntary groups filled the vacuum caused by a poorly organized and slow official response. This led to an upsurge of voluntary movements, attracting much interest especially among younger age groups, and eventually to a partial relaxation of the legal obstacles inhibiting the formation of NPOs.

In other words, 'vertical society', and the traditional *ie*, as an explanatory framework need to be supplemented by both institutional factors and social change leading to institutional change.

A second implication of the 'vertical society' model is that it leads to exploitation of the weak by the strong. Relationships, rather than being contractual, are based on loyalty to the one exclusive group you happen to belong to, and within which your relationship with others is hierarchical. Therefore, since group aims predominate and relationships within the group are based on personal obligation and human feeling (*giri-ninjō*), rather than on contract, those at the top have

---

[14]   In the 1970s, an abbreviated version of Nakane's *Japanese Society* was distributed by Japanese embassies abroad. For an attack on the alleged political use of a perceived model of social norms and rules, see Yoshio Sugimoto, 'The Manipulative Bases of "Consensus" in Japan', in Gavan McCormack and Yoshio Sugimoto (eds), *Democracy in Contemporary Japan*, Sydney, Hale & Iremonger, 1986, pp. 65–75.

[15]   Robert Pekkanen, 'Molding Japanese Civil Society: State-Structured Incentives and the Patterning of Civil Society', in Frank J. Schwartz and Susan J. Pharr (eds), *The State of Civil Society in Japan*, Cambridge and New York, Cambridge University Press, 2003, pp. 116–34. The most difficult problem is that registration of NPOs is subject to administrative guidance, and those seen as presenting a line contrary to the official one are disfavoured. On the other hand, officially favoured organizations benefit from various financial and other advantages.

little to stop them from ruthlessly exploiting those below. On the other hand, built into *giri-ninjō* is a notion of obligation and loyalty that is mutual, and this is supposed to mitigate exploitation of those lower in the hierarchy by those at the higher levels. Indeed, for permanently employed workers, who are the 'shock troops' of the larger firms, the system, which requires great commitment from them, also gives them attractive material and psychological rewards. In a real sense they have been incorporated into the system, which rewards them for their loyalty.[16]

Once again, however, circumstances do not remain static. The travails through which the economy has passed since the early 1990s have required substantial adjustments to the employment system, once seen as the cockpit of the 'vertical society'. We do not have space to discuss these changes here, but one specialist concludes that much greater employment flexibility has emerged in response to economic stagnation and the need for firms to be much more efficient to survive. He nevertheless qualifies this by arguing that 'many of the features of Japanese employment institutions will remain intact'. He also argues: 'Despite the emergence of greater individualism, Japanese will continue to identify strongly with their company, rather than their occupational specialization.'[17]

This takes us on, however, to the third implication of the 'vertical society' model, namely marginalization. Whatever the advantages economic and political leaders may see in fostering a society based on vertical linkages that cement group loyalties and foster commitment, not everybody can enter the charmed circle. Temporary or casual workers in large firms, workers in small firms doing subcontracting work for large firms, members of social or ethnic minorities and such disadvantaged groups as day labourers are examples of such marginalization. While it is not correct to assert that women as a whole are marginalized, there are disproportionate numbers of women among the ranks of those who may be regarded as marginalized. Social and political protest movements in recent Japanese history may in many cases be explained in terms of the difficult choices faced by those who see themselves as marginalized. One route to improvement of status is by organizing protest, but what may ultimately work better is to 'join the system': that is, to establish themselves in a working relationship with those groups that exercise power in the relevant context. This naturally is preferred and encouraged by the authorities in most circumstances. Recent changes in the workforce include more widespread use of temporary and casual workers, some of whom are then given training to enable them to rise in status within the organization concerned.[18]

When we turn to politics, the dominance of politics by a single party, the LDP, creates a problem of marginalization for parties in opposition. In a sense,

[16]   A Marxist would no doubt argue that they are being rewarded for betraying their class loyalties.

[17]   Marcus Rebick, *The Japanese Employment System: Adapting to a New Economic Environment*, Oxford and New York, Oxford University Press, 2005, p. 174.

[18]   '[T]he distinctions between regular and non-regular workers may become more blurred as firms try to develop the skills of their non-regular employees': Rebick, *The Japanese Employment System*, p. 174.

therefore, an opposition party with apparently little chance of assuming governmental power faces a choice between two possible solutions. One, the most obvious, is to seek by all means to pick up enough votes to be elected to office. This requires attacking the policies and record of the party or parties in power and attempting to demonstrate that one's own party is a better bet than the incumbent party or parties . But another, less obvious, is to appease the holders of government office, who may be grateful for extra parliamentary support and throw out a few crumbs of patronage for the opposition party or parties to pick up. The dilemma may be expressed in terms of a choice whether to oppose or to appease.[19] Whether in the field of employment or the field of political parties, it pays to belong. It is uncomfortable to remain at the margin – except, perhaps, for persons of exceptional individualism and strength of purpose, who are happily far from rare in Japan, and may well be increasing in number and significance.

A fourth implication of 'vertical society', with its *ie* overtones, is what has been termed 'situational ethics'. The point here is that behaviour within cohesive, vertically structured groups is supposed to differ from behaviour between members and outsiders. There may be some truth in this, but it is crucial not to overgeneralize. Here we come up against a fundamental weakness in the 'vertical society' model itself: namely, that both internal and external relationships are far more complicated and situation-dependent than the model allows. Within political factions, for instance, there is often a clear distinction between core and peripheral members, with core members much more committed to the integrity of the faction than those on its periphery, who are often inclined to shop around. But members of factions within political parties also, of necessity, are involved with the wider political environment in many of its aspects. The behavioural implications of these multifarious relationships are complex and not to be restricted to the logic of single in-group membership. Probably, all that can be said about the hypothesis that the Japanese are particularly prone to exhibit situational ethics is that group membership may be one factor affecting ethical attitudes and behaviour, among many others.

A fifth implication of 'vertical society' is that Japanese politics – and indeed many other areas of activity – are particularly subject to corruption. In any society there are likely to be cases of corruption, particularly between officials (elected or otherwise) in public life, and private sector entrepreneurs. Japanese politics has a deserved reputation for corruption, and there have been many well-documented examples where staggering sums of money are exchanged. A relationship between collectivism and corruption is widely recognized in Japan. The 'cashing in' of close personal ties and group relationships to set up corrupt behind-the-scenes deals appears to be widespread, though not all instances of corruption involve such ties. Many have argued that the individual citizen is weak in the face of the arrogance implied by corrupt dealings, whether by politicians, public servants or businessmen.[20]

---

[19]   For a fuller treatment, see J. A. A. Stockwin, 'To Oppose or to Appease? Parties out of Power and the Need for Real Politics in Japan', *Japan Forum*, vol. 18, no. 1 (March 2006), pp. 115–32.
[20]   See e.g. Gavan McCormack, *The Emptiness of Japanese Affluence*, New York and London, M. E. Sharpe, 1996, pp. 33–8 and elsewhere.

On the other hand, a series of measures have been put in place since the 1990s to curb corrupt dealings, following the massive corruption scandals of the late 1980s and early 1990s. How far these measures have been successful is debatable, but the tightening of legal sanctions on electoral fraud, for instance, appears to have had a beneficial effect. Such has been the public concern about corruption that government has been forced to act, to some good effect. Aspects of 'vertical society' may continue to exist, but not all of its consequences are as readily tolerated as they once were.

The final implication of 'vertical society' relates to incentives and achievement. The model posits an ethic, not of achievement for the individual, but of achievement on behalf of the group. Another way of putting this is to say that incentives are group incentives rather than individual incentives. Few would dispute that Japan in the course of its remarkable economic development since the Meiji period, and especially since 1945, has been an achievement-oriented society. What appears surprising from a Western perspective is that a strong collectivist impulse appears to underlie this engine of achievement.[21]

Today, it seems necessary to be extremely careful with this argument. The idea that all Japanese employees exhibit a single-minded devotion to their companies, and will normally sacrifice their own interests to promote the company interest, is far from the truth. In a society with almost universally high educational standards, material incentives oriented to individuals play a central role in maintaining the work ethic. If we consider that a major part of the workforce has a long-term employment arrangement with a company, the interests of the employee and the interests of the company coincide to a great extent because of material incentives. With the firm being the provider of many important welfare services and bonuses for its employees, it is in the employee's interest not to sabotage the capacity of the company to provide those services. Moreover, to leave the firm and seek employment elsewhere may both jeopardize benefits and entail a reduction in rank and salary. At the same time, while there are instrumental reasons for the employee to act in the interests of the collectivity, it is also true that individualism has made considerable inroads into the collectivist ethic. The values of car, home and leisure are certainly not ignored, and are most often treasured, by the average Japanese family.[22]

We now return to our five basic propositions (A1–5), and present five contrasting propositions (B1–5) that appear to reflect important aspects of Japanese society and its interaction with politics early in the twenty-first century.

B1 Japanese society values individual autonomy and the contribution the individual makes to the whole   In relation to individualism, the Japanese language uses a number of words with rather differing connotations. *Wagamama*

---

[21]   An early exponent of a connection between collectivism and achievement in the Japanese case was Ezra Vogel. See his *Japan's New Middle Class: The Salary Man and his Family in a Tokyo Suburb*, Berkeley and Los Angeles, University of California Press, 1963.
[22]   The terms 'my home-ism' and 'my car-ism' were common in discussions about social change from at least the 1960s.

means egotism, or selfishness, though it also means waywardness, which in certain contexts can attract mild admiration. *Kojinshugi* is normally translated as 'individualism', though the connotation is more negative than positive, and suggests reluctance to cooperate with others. The most positive word is *kosei*, which may be translated as 'individuality' and has a much more positive meaning. A person who has *kosei* is a person with an interesting personality, someone worth listening to, a person of substance and probably also of originality. In other words, to describe somebody as having *kosei* is to praise that person for being something more than a member of a group (though not necessarily not a member of a group). This suggests an optimistic attitude to human difference, and attitudes much more open to an individual-centred view of the world than is implied by models of Japanese society based on the traditional model of the *ie*.

Common observation of Japanese people in different walks of life a little over halfway through the first decade of the new millennium strongly suggests that individualism and individuality are valued even if selfishness and lack of concern for others (the main connotation of *wagamama*) are disliked. In Japan the media are full of stories of episodes exhibiting selfish behaviour (and suggesting that the social fabric is fraying as a result) – but so are the media in Britain and elsewhere.

B2 Japanese contemporary social norms value fairness and equality   It became something of a cliché from the 1980s (perhaps before) to suggest that Japan is a classless society. This idea was supported by the demonstration of relatively narrow income and wealth differentials across the various sections of the population, and also by the apparent fact that people exhibited little consciousness of class differences, with the bulk of the population declaring that they were 'middle class'. There were always problems with this idea of Japanese classlessness, and arguments from the left that it represented a kind of false consciousness had a certain amount of credibility. Nevertheless, Japanese modernization was managed in such a way that its benefits were distributed with greater fairness than in many other developing societies, however disruptive the necessary changes were for much of the population.

Income and wealth divisions appear to have grown over the past two decades,[23] but the idea that the healthiest kind of society is one that is fair and equal has persisted. One may perhaps perceive a paradox concerning a society that believes in hierarchy but also in equality. But these are concepts on different planes. Hierarchical relations affect personal relations, where vertical linkages are important, whereas belief in equality is a reflection on society as a whole. Since the war Japan has lacked an aristocracy, and Japanese visitors to the United Kingdom tend to be amazed at stately homes and similar manifestations of an old aristocracy. Similarly, the flaunting of wealth is not widely popular, except

---

[23] See e.g. Mari Osawa, 'The Livelihood Security System and Social Exclusion: The "Male Breadwinner" Model Revisited', paper delivered at a conference entitled 'Negotiating the "Boundaries" of Postwar Japan', University of Sheffield, March 2007.

perhaps in relation to pop stars. But by the same token, Japanese do not expect to find serious poverty in their own society, even if pockets of it exist.[24]

B3   Japanese society values security, stability and a 'normal life'   In a broad sense, Japanese society may be regarded as conservative, though of course not all Japanese are conservative in their social and political attitudes. There are several reasons why the essentially conservative Liberal Democratic Party has been so regularly elected back into office, but one of them is that that party reflects a dominant conservative sentiment in the electorate. When, however, we seek to break down the concept 'conservative' into its constituent elements, we find that a desire for security and stability seems to be particularly important. This is not to say that Japanese people in general are risk-averse, but rather that they are prepared to take risks provided that they enjoy the broad security of a society that is safe. When a terrorist attack occurs in another country, large numbers of Japanese cancel planned trips to that country.[25] The citizens of other countries no doubt also react cautiously in similar circumstances, but the Japanese response appears somewhat extreme.

Attitudes to war appear to reflect a similar set of concerns. It has long appeared rather paradoxical that support for the peace clause of the 1946 Constitution for many years remained high (and though now reduced, is still substantial), while at the same time there is overwhelming support for the Self Defence Forces and widespread support for security arrangements with the United States. But we may discover a resolution of this apparent contradiction in the reflection that whereas between the 1890s and 1945 Japan was at war in almost every decade, since 1945 the country and its citizens have been virtually war-free. It is true that events in East Asia since the ending of the Cold War have moved public opinion some distance in favour of constitutional revision, but given the much-publicized nuclear threat from North Korea and the rising economic power of China, it might seem surprising that a firm bedrock of support for the existing provisions still remains.[26]

[24]   The latest in a regular series of national surveys by the Institute of Statistical Mathematics in Tokyo shows that 'a good salary' ranked low in people's priorities to do with their work. In 2003 choices among four criteria for job satisfaction were as follows: a good salary, 8%; a safe job with no risk of closing down or unemployment, 19%; working with people you like, 26%; doing an important job, 45%. The same question asked in 1978, 1983, 1988, 1993 and 1998 gave roughly similar results. See Research Committee on the Study of the Japanese National Character, *A Study of the Japanese National Character: The Eleventh Nationwide Survey (2003)*, Tokyo, Institute of Statistical Mathematics, January 2007, p. 107.
[25]   For instance, following the terrorist attacks in New York and Washington on 11 September 2001, at least one Japanese university cancelled all foreign travel for staff for several months. The attacks on the London underground on 7 July 2005 led substantial numbers of students to cancel planned study in Britain, as well as substantially reducing the number of tourists from Japan.
[26]   In 1983, 1998 and 2003, the Institute of Statistical Mathematics asked how anxious respondents were about war, under the headings: (1) 'very much', (2) 'pretty much', (3) 'slightly' and (4) 'not at all'. In 1983 the results were: (1) 34%; (2) 19%; (3) 31%; (4) 13%. In 1998 the results were: (1) 26%; (2) 16%; (3) 34%; (4) 23%. In 2003 the results were: (1) 28%; (2) 23%; (3) 3%; (4) 15%: See Research Committee on the Study of the Japanese National Character, *A Study of the Japanese National Character: The Eleventh Nationwide Survey (2003)*, p. 46.

B4   Japanese are critical of those in power, but reluctant to jeopardize political stability   Japanese popular political attitudes are surprisingly ambivalent. On the one hand people generally hold established politicians in low esteem and can be enthused by outsiders with radical messages; but support for radicals (whether of the left or of the right) is often soft support that readily evaporates. The electorate as a whole seems reluctant to jeopardize political stability, so that it will return to office the same politicians as before, but seek to balance their power in various ways.[27] How far this is deliberate or planned is difficult to say, but electoral outcomes show sophistication on the part of the electorate.

The implications of this are not particularly encouraging for those who seek radical reform of the Japanese political economy, and problematic in periods (such as the 1990s and early 2000s) when structural reform is plainly needed. Prevailing electoral attitudes are not always effective in countering illiberal policies on the part of the government and government agencies.[28] Even so, elections matter, and play a crucial checking function over abuse of power.

B5   Japanese society manifests a strong sense of nation and pride in being Japanese, though internationalist values have made some progress   It is commonly observed that Japanese people have a strong sense of nation, though that is not the same thing as saying that they are nationalistic. It is important to distinguish the state-sponsored nationalism that prevailed in the years up to 1945 from the acute consciousness of being Japanese that prevails today. It is also no longer as appropriate as it was in the 1970s and 1980s to subsume Japanese consciousness of nation under the rubric of *nihonjinron*, usually translated as 'what it means to be Japanese'. This refers to a body of literature – some of it popular, some of it quasi-academic – that sought to show that Japanese people, values and culture were in some fundamental sense qualitatively different from those in other countries, particularly those of the Western world. Many of the arguments of the *nihonjinron* writers were exaggerated, unscientific, derivative and repetitious, and they not surprisingly attracted a polemical counter-literature.[29]

Contemporary writing today by Japanese dealing with national identity is generally much more sophisticated, discussing specific issues of social importance, such as crime, youth culture or war memory, rather than resorting to the broad generalizations typical of the *nihonjinron* genre. This no doubt

[27]   The desire to check LDP power without actually replacing that party by an untried opposition may account in part for the fact that the LDP has lacked a majority in the upper house (which can block most legislative proposals coming to it from the lower house) since 1989.

[28]   Koichi Nakano, 'Nationalist Basis of Globalization: A View from Japan', paper delivered to a symposium on globalization, Sophia University, Tokyo, January 2007.

[29]   See e.g. Ross Mouer and Yoshio Sugimoto, *Images of Japanese Society: A Study in the Structure of Japanese Reality*, London, New York, Sydney and Henley, KPI, 1986; Peter N. Dale, *The Myth of Japanese Uniqueness*, London and New York, Routledge, 1986 and later editions.

reflects the differing political realities of the 1980s and the 2000s. In the earlier period, Japan was on a roll, marking up spectacular economic advances at a time when North American and West European economies were in difficulties, so that Japan was attracting much critical comment from the US and elsewhere for allegedly following non-standard rules in relation to trade, investment and economic regulation. The *nihonjinron* writers were therefore in a sense defending Japanese difference and Japanese success against an international orthodoxy inspired by older powers that could be portrayed as decadent. By the 2000s, however, the situation had changed radically. Japan was now recovering from a long period of economic stagnation, Western economies had recovered, and Japan was being ignored by Western countries rather than criticized by them.

In these new circumstances the imperative was not polemical defence of difference, but rather propagation of a sophisticated and dynamic cultural image, suitable for a major, mature economy and a society capable of the kind of inventiveness and creativity that would be attractive to the outside world. Japanese *manga* cartoon stories, *animé* animation films and fashion designs were now in vogue throughout East and South-East Asia, and more broadly throughout the world. Interchange and cooperation between Japanese scientists and their counterparts overseas were now routine on a very large scale indeed. Rather than 'gross national product', the need was to project Japan as the cockpit of 'greater national cool' and 'the knowledge society'.

Also, between the two periods, there had been an enormous increase in the numbers of Japanese (especially young people) venturing abroad and interacting with their overseas counterparts in all kinds of activities. Between the two periods the internet had been invented, hugely increasing the opportunities for unstructured and unregulated interaction between people of different nationality and background. Foreign-owned businesses were now more common in Japan than they had been, although foreign investment in Japan remains low by international standards, and obstacles to a major foreign presence in Japanese industry and commerce remain strong.[30] However this may be, Tokyo and other major Japanese centres were much more international in outlook than they had been two decades earlier. Numbers of foreigners living in Japanese cities had greatly increased, though they were still low by comparison with cosmopolitan cities such as London. International marriages were also much less unusual, and fairly unproblematic, at least in urban centres. What is interesting is that through all this the sense of separate national identity and difference remained strong, though not in an especially exclusive or dogmatic fashion.

---

[30]   Early in 2007 a plan to facilitate foreign takeovers of Japanese firms met with fierce resistance from business interests in Tokyo. The London-based *Financial Times* commented in an editorial: 'The battle has exposed a deep vein of protectionism in Japan's business establishment, which still seems to see globalisation as a one-way street': *Financial Times*, 2 February 2007.

Conclusions

Let us return briefly to the ten vignettes that opened this chapter. Taken as a whole, the stories tell us that Japanese society (in its political and other aspects) places emphasis on personal connections, hierarchy, surface harmony masking concealed division, apology as a diversion ('lightning conductor' function), loyalty, subservience to authority, sectionalism and consensus.

This, however, is only the beginning of our attempt to understand what is happening in the society of contemporary Japan. There is no fixed and immutable way in which that society works (as there is not in the societies of Britain, Italy or Malaysia, for instance). The 127 million citizens of Japan are all different individuals, doing their own thing and thinking their own thoughts. Nevertheless, certain broad patterns of value and behaviour exist and we need to ask whence these patterns derive. Some, no doubt, issue from 'pure' cultural influences. Simply by being brought up in a Japanese family and interacting principally or exclusively with other Japanese people, it becomes second nature to bow to other people as a greeting, or to remove one's shoes when entering a house. But even such 'pure' influences have a history if one cares to trace it back. A preference for collective action may derive from the need for cooperation by whole villages in rice cultivation, to take a well-known example. Moreover, institutions propagate cultural norms. Instruction in the correct etiquette of bowing, for instance is taught meticulously to the employees of some companies. Educational establishments (schools, universities) play a central role in promoting cultural continuities (and not only in Japan). But in Japan, education has been a highly contested field between traditionalists favouring collectivist, nation-centred values, and progressives privileging more individualistic values (The revised Basic Law on Education of December 2006 was an example of the traditionalists triumphing over the progressives: see Chapter 6).

Some aspects of society, such as gender differences and gender relations, have undergone comprehensive change over the past half-century. One manifestation of this is late marriage and a declining birth rate, which now threatens Japan with serious demographic problems (see Chapter 11). Another, related to the first, is the gradually changing status of women in the workforce, consistent with the very high levels of education that many women now achieve. The grandmothers and especially great-grandmothers of the present generation of young people typically had basic education, worked briefly for low wages, married early, had several children, were considered subordinate first to their fathers and then to their husbands, and often were under the firm thumb of their mothers-in-law. A typical contemporary woman attains high educational standards, goes into the workforce with expectation of rising in a hierarchy, marries late (if at all), has one child or at most two children, and is back in the workforce full-time by her forties. Increasing numbers of women enter politics, though the proportion remains low by north European standards. Unlike the UK, New Zealand, Pakistan, India, Bangladesh, Norway, Germany, Latvia, Liberia, Sri Lanka and elsewhere, Japan has yet to produce a prime minister who is a woman. It has at last become the norm, however, for between two and four women to find a place in Cabinet.

Japan is a society at once dynamic and conservative. This may be said of other societies as well, but the coexistence of these two traits seems most conspicuous in the Japanese case. The forces of dynamism and change compete with the forces of conservatism and reaction. The outcome of this contest often gives a frustrating sense of stifling bureaucratic forces inhibiting progress. But the underlying conservatism also has the capacity to provide a stable underpinning for dynamic progress, filtering it into productive channels. Perhaps the biggest problem arises where conservatives become so concerned about social change that they attempt to revert to atavistic models in order to promote a vision of national progress that is both collectivist and anti-democratic.

Chapter 4 | Political Reconstruction and Development, 1945–1989

The late Louis Allen once told how he had taken the surrender of a Japanese officer in Burma around the end of the war in 1945. The officer was starving, emaciated and in rags, having barely survived after weeks isolated in the jungle. Some 30 years later the two men met again in Tokyo. Allen was ushered into the magnificent presidential office on the top floor of one of Japan's leading conglomerate companies, with windows overlooking the Imperial Palace. The starving officer of 1945 had risen to the very top of the Japanese industrial elite.[1]

This story may be used to symbolize the astonishing rise of Japan from the ashes of military defeat into a rich and powerful country. The period covered by this chapter – almost half a century – saw a country that was physically and psychologically on its knees transformed into the second largest economy on the planet. Moreover, Japan was the first *Asian* country in modern times to rank as a leading economic power. Though the focus of international attention may now have shifted from Japan to China, it was Japan that pioneered the way, and China that is following along a similar trail.

In 1945 most Japanese industrial plant and infrastructure had been put out of action. The armed forces were being disbanded and the country's home territory was being occupied by the victorious Americans and their allies. Two of its cities, Hiroshima and Nagasaki, had been atom-bombed. American incendiary raids on Tokyo in March 1945 may well have killed more people in the capital than were killed by the Hiroshima bomb (leaving subsequent radiation-related deaths out of account). The ideological underpinning of the pre-war and wartime regime had been fatally undermined, creating what came to be called a 'spiritual vacuum', though most people in the late 1940s were simply concentrating on physical survival.

After a slow start, economic recovery developed quickly, and by the mid-1950s the standard of living was comparable with what it had been in the late

---

[1] Lecture at the Nissan Institute of Japanese Studies, University of Oxford, 2 March 1982.

1930s. By 1968 Japanese GNP was overtaking that of West Germany, making Japan the third largest economy in the world after the US and USSR. By the early 1990s it was unquestionably the world's second economy, with some commentators, even earlier than this, predicting that Japan was set to overtake the United States.[2] Not all Japanese citizens had profited to the same degree from such rapid economic development, but income distribution remained comparatively even, and rising incomes dampened expressions of discontent. Nevertheless, most sections of the population were expected to work long hours and show intense commitment to the companies, or other organizations, that had hired them.

The Allied Occupation

Between September 1945 and April 1952 Japan was under the control of the Allied Occupation. Principally, this was an American show, although there was also a British Commonwealth presence that had some degree of influence. The larger-than-life figure of the Supreme Commander, Allied Powers (SCAP), General Douglas MacArthur, dominated Occupation decision-making and helped give credibility to the policies being developed. While the Occupation continued, the sovereignty of the Japanese state was suspended, and although governments in Tokyo continued to perform their functions, the ultimate arbiter of policy was the occupying authority (often known by the SCAP acronym).

To evaluate the Occupation's achievements is no easy task. Some, including the Supreme Commander himself, were inclined to overstate the impact of Occupation reforms,[3] while others have emphasized the importance of what the Japanese themselves achieved in the context of a reformed environment.[4] In any case, the exercise did not always run according to plan. Political and economic factors led to inconsistencies in the forming and execution of policy, so that the thrust of policy in the later years was rather different from that in the earlier years. Arguably, some reforms the Americans failed to carry out, as well as some that they initiated but stopped halfway, were as significant as some they actually accomplished. Some reforms that were implemented had later consequences that differed from those originally intended. This is not to say that the Occupation was unimportant. It was of enormous importance. But its impact needs to be placed alongside the influence of several other factors that also helped determine how Japan's political economy would be shaped once the Occupation had ended.

In order to understand the role of the Allied Occupation in the political history of Japan since 1945, it is helpful to distinguish five categories of elements influencing the total picture:

[2] Ezra Vogel, *Japan as Number One: Lessons for America*, Cambridge, MA and London, Harvard University Press, 1979.
[3] MacArthur is said to have expressed the view publicly that 'the Occupation of Japan is an unprecedented revolution in the social history of the world'.
[4] Vogel, *Japan as Number One*. Vogel's book has only three index references under 'Allied Occupation'.

1   Those Occupation reforms having the effect of simplifying and centraliz-
     ing the location of sovereignty and of power.
2   Those Occupation reforms having the effect of broadening participation
     in the political arena.
3   Persistent influences deriving from Japanese social traditions and long his-
     torical experience.
4   More recent historical influences, deriving largely from political develop-
     ments in the 1930s and early 1940s – the period of militarization and war.
5   Political innovation in the post-war and post-Occupation period, in particu-
     lar the establishment of conservative single-party dominance from 1955.

What emerged from the Occupation was a relatively stable politico-economic
system, which we shall seek to describe in this and later chapters of this book.
Often it has been described as the '1955 political system', a term that of course
emphasizes post-Occupation developments, notably the formation of the Liberal
Democratic Party (LDP) in 1955. As a broad descriptive term, we accept this designation, and hold that it lasted until early in the 1990s (hence the end date of this
chapter). The system was far from static. Its path was strewn with controversy
and was the product of many different hands and minds. But it constituted the
political underpinning for the Japanese economic 'miracle'. Its achievement
required a great effort of political, economic and social engineering, and this in
turn required some clear thinking and enlightened leadership as well as a certain
amount of good luck, though there were a number of mistakes and false trails. But
in the end something quite extraordinary was created. Much the same – though
the parameters were radically different – could be said of the Meiji period.
    Let us then examine in more detail our five categories.

*1   Those Occupation reforms having the effect of simplifying and centralizing
the location of sovereignty and power*   The underlying philosophy of the
Occupation was liberal and democratic, 'democratization' being one of the two
great slogans of the occupiers.[5] Strangely, however, no attempt was made to introduce an American-style system based on the separation of powers between the
executive and legislative branches. Such features derived from US practice as were
introduced did not greatly affect the central structure. The formal institutional
framework inherited from the pre-war period was closer to the British model than
to the American, even though the working of the Japanese system had differed
radically from either. In any case, the Occupation reforms ensured that formal
relations between the executive and the legislature were close to the 'Westminster
model', in which Prime Minister and Cabinet are chosen by Parliament (essentially
from within its ranks), and the Cabinet applies executive power.[6]

[5]   The other was demilitarization. The armed forces were demobilized with remarkable
speed, and the attempt was made to prevent Japan re-arming by introducing a 'no-war'
clause into the Constitution. See esp. Chapter 10.
[6]   In practice, the way executive power is used by the Japanese Cabinet has differed from
the case of the British Cabinet in the sense that Japanese government ministries have had
a greater degree of independence in the exercise of their functions than do departments
of the British government.

The Meiji Constitution, as seen in Chapter 2, was vague and ambiguous about where sovereignty lay. Sovereignty rested with the *Tennō*, but since the *Tennō* in practice rarely made political choices, the effective location of sovereignty was a shifting thing, depending on the balance of power at any one time between the various elites. What was termed dual (or multiple) government, whereby the armed forces in particular could exercise uncontrolled power by virtue of their independent access to the *Tennō*, went against the principle of a clear location of sovereignty. This the occupying authorities were determined to clarify.

A number of the main reforms may be grouped under this heading. Their main purpose was to clarify that sovereignty belonged to the people (not the *Tennō*), through a popularly elected National Parliament (*Kokkai*),[7] and that Cabinet was directly responsible to it.

The *Tennō*'s position was downgraded. In a New Year's broadcast in 1946 he renounced his divinity, which had a psychological impact on the people, though perhaps less than the Americans imagined.[8] No longer 'head of state', he became 'symbol of the state and of the unity of the people, deriving his position from the will of the people, with whom resides sovereign power'.[9] The word for 'symbol' (*shōchō*) was unfamiliar to many Japanese at the time, but the 'symbolic' status of the *Tennō* has since gained widespread acceptance.[10] All his special powers (which had normally been exercised by his advisers) were removed, including those that could be used in time of emergency. His functions as listed in the new Constitution were purely ceremonial.[11]

The peerage – a Meiji period legacy – was abolished except for the immediate imperial family, and with it the House of Peers was eliminated. Although SCAP seems originally to have intended a unicameral parliament, the House of Peers was replaced by a 'House of Councillors' (*Sangiin*), elected by a different method from the House of Representatives (*Shūgiin*). Although weaker than the latter, its power to block legislation could be important (see Chapters 5 and 8).

The armed forces were disbanded, and therefore could no longer be a factor in politics. Article 9 (the 'peace clause') of the new Constitution was designed to

[7]   'National Parliament' is preferred to the commonly used 'National Diet', a term derived from German models which now seems dated.

[8]   A *kami* (god) in *Shintō* had a status much closer to that of a human being than is the case with the God–man distinction in Christianity.

[9]   1946 Constitution, article 1.

[10]   The authoritative source on early period Occupation policy commented: 'The Emperor is now no more than the crowning pinnacle of the structure, bearing no functional relation to the frame itself'. Supreme Commander for the Allied Powers, *Political Reorientation of Japan, September 1945 to September 1948*, 2 vols, Westport, CT, Greenwood Press, 1970 (repr. of original, published by US Government Printing Office, 1949), vol. 1, p. 14.

[11]   The *Tennō* does not even enjoy the power, attributed by some authorities to the British monarch, of choosing the Prime Minister in circumstances where there is no clear party majority in Parliament. In the Japanese case, Parliament votes on who shall become prime minister. For assessments of the *Tennō*'s role, see Stephen S. Large, *Emperor Hirohito and Shōwa Japan: A Political Biography*, London and New York, Routledge, 1992; Ben-Ami Shillony, *Enigma of the Emperors: Sacred Subservience in Japanese History*, Folkestone, Kent, Global Oriental, 2005.

make this situation permanent, though it has not prevented the development from the 1950s of the Self-Defence Forces (SDF, *jieitai*).[12] These are substantial and possess sophisticated defence equipment (see Chapters 10 and 12). Perhaps anticipating this, SCAP made sure that the principle of civilian control was strongly emphasized. The Constitution (article 66) also provided that '[t]he Prime Minister and other Ministers of State must be civilians' – an apparently superfluous article if there were to be no armed forces of any kind.[13]

The Privy Council, the *genrō* and the *jūshin* (senior statesmen: in a sense, successors to the *genrō*) were also abolished, while the Imperial Household Ministry was reduced in status and role to an Imperial Household *Agency (kunaichō)*. This was done in the belief that these bodies had weakened the legislative and executive authority of Parliament and Cabinet.

The Constitution, in its article 68, stipulated that the Prime Minister and a majority of his ministers should be members of Parliament. In practice very few ministers have not held a seat in Parliament. Moreover, the Prime Minister was to be chosen by Parliament from among its own members (article 67). Thus a convincing victory was won over the old principle of 'transcendental cabinets'.

Article 66 established the principle of collective Cabinet responsibility to Parliament, absent from the Meiji Constitution (which used the term 'ministers of state', but not 'Cabinet'). The same article clearly vested executive power in Cabinet, stipulating that it should be collectively responsible to Parliament.

Similar clarity in the location of sovereignty was aimed at in the famous article 41, which states: 'The Diet [Parliament] shall be the highest organ of state power, and shall be the sole law-making organ of state'. The various articles relating to Parliament sought to reinforce this supreme position. Thus its power over the budget was assured (article 60), as well as over finance (articles 83–91), and the Meiji Constitution's provision that if the government's budget were rejected by Parliament the budget of the previous year could come into force was dropped.

What these constitutional reforms had in common was the intention to produce a Parliament/Cabinet system, essentially on the British model, with clear lines of responsibility and an unambiguous statement of where sovereignty actually lay. In practice, however, it did not quite work out like this. Although there was no reversion to the system under the Meiji Constitution, neither Cabinet nor Parliament turned out to be in a position to exercise as much effective power as the reforms had anticipated. Why things developed like this, and whether the norms of the 'Westminster model' might be restored, will be discussed in later chapters.[14]

---

[12]   This is the accepted translation of *jieitai*, but possibly 'Self-Defence Corps' would have been more accurate.

[13]   This was interpreted to mean 'civilians at the present time', and therefore not excluding those who had served in the armed forces during or before the war.

[14]   See Aurelia George Mulgan, *Japan's Failed Revolution: Koizumi and the Politics of Economic Reform*, Canberra, Asia Pacific Press, 2002, for the argument that the Japanese political system differs fundamentally from the norms of the Westminster model. In Chapter 6 we shall discuss whether and to what extent Prime Minister Koizumi (2001–6) was able to bring the system back in line with Westminster norms.

2 *Those Occupation reforms having the effect of broadening participation in the political arena* The following reforms may be regarded as largely or in part intended to broaden the base of independent participation in politics.

The suffrage was increased to include women, who had never been enfranchised before, and the minimum age for voting was lowered from 25 to 20.

Labour unions and other independent groups were given official sanction and were encouraged to put forward their views and exert pressure on the government without being required to express their views in terms of the interests of the state, as had tended to be the case before the war.[15]

Left-wing political parties, which had existed precariously since the 1920s, were granted full freedom to organize, and were encouraged actively by some sections of SCAP, as the potential nucleus of an alternative government to the various conservative parties. Communist leaders were released from prison, where some had languished since the late 1920s, and a vigorous Communist Party was formed quite legally (by contrast to the illegal party founded in 1922). A Socialist Party also emerged, combining various pre-war strands, and came to perform much better at the polls than its Communist rival.

A wide range of civil liberties was written into the Constitution, in order to ensure, among other things, that citizens had proper redress against unjust or illegal actions by government. This helped ensure far greater freedom for the mass media than had existed before the war, and the press in particular came to be often critical of government action.

Partly in order to enable 'new blood' to flow freely through the political arteries, a large number of politicians were excluded for the time being from all participation in public life. The purge edict extended broadly through the ranks of politicians, former military men, businessmen and bureaucrats, and although there was some rough justice in implementing it, it cleared the way, for instance, for Yoshida Shigeru, a former Foreign Ministry official with no previous political experience, to become a forceful and successful prime minister over much of the ten years following Japan's defeat.[16]

Following on article 62 of the Constitution, 'Each House may conduct investigations in relation to government, and may demand the presence and testimony of witnesses, and the production of records,' a system of parliamentary committees was set up, and has become in effect the main forum for parliamentary debate. This was perhaps the most significant departure from the British model of parliamentary procedure and the closest point of adherence to the American, since US congressional committees were the model upon which it was based.[17] Here again, the aim seems to have been to avoid narrow cliquishness in decision-making, and throw open the decision-making process to wider scrutiny.

[15] Unions before the war were subject to police surveillance and harassment, as well as closure by the authorities. See Stephen S. Large, *Organized Workers and Socialist Politics in Interwar Japan*, Cambridge, Cambridge University Press, 1981.
[16] Hans H. Baerwald, *The Purge of Japanese Leaders under the Occupation*, Berkeley, University of California Press, 1959.
[17] Interestingly enough, the British House of Commons now has a more substantial system of committees than was the case in the 1940s.

to destroy what were regarded as excessive concentrations of ower, legislation was introduced to split up the *zaibatsu*, or family-ines, which formed an important element in the Japanese economy)s and 1930s. Although this reform had only limited success, it was s a measure of economic democratization, in that economic power (and so, to an extent, political power) was to be distributed more broadly and evenly.[18]

Parallel to the programme of economic deconcentration was a measure designed to bring democracy to the countryside, namely the land reform. Landlord–tenant relations, and especially absentee landlords, had caused much discontent during the rural economic recession of the 1930s. The land reform placed a ceiling of about one hectare (four hectares in Hokkaidō) on individual land holdings, so as to create a relatively egalitarian peasantry of small farmers. These reforms have been widely praised, and did indeed 'democratize' rural Japan. In the long term, however, the small size of farms created an enduring problem for agricultural efficiency. Politically, small farmers became a solid base of support for LDP (and some Socialist) politicians who, made more numerous by electoral malapportionment, lobbied to maintain far higher levels of agricultural protection than was justified in terms of the national economy.[19]

Another area of reform whereby the Occupation authorities sought to broaden the base of political participation (rather on the American model) was in local administration. Whereas previously local government had been firmly in the hands of the Home Ministry, and most important positions were appointive, not elective, the Occupation abolished the Home Ministry and set up in its place the Local Autonomy Agency (later Ministry) with greatly truncated powers. Substantial powers were placed in the hands of local authorities, and most of the relevant positions were made elective.[20]

In the functional areas of policing and education, SCAP initiated drastic decentralization, with the aim of transferring responsibility from central government to the newly elected local authorities. Decentralizing the police did not work well, and the reform was soon reversed once the Occupation was over. In education, decentralization was only one aspect of the democratizing mission. Syllabuses were revised to remove nationalist mythology and to introduce progressive and internationalist themes. The pre-war ethics courses were abolished. The structure of education was revamped and the number of universities increased. But here too decentralization did not long survive the end of the Occupation.

It is difficult to argue that the decentralizing reforms attempted during the Occupation were a success, given that they were subject to wholesale reversal later on. Without adequate funding or tax-raising ability, local authorities were

[18] Eleanor M. Hadley, *Antitrust in Japan*, Princeton, NJ, Princeton University Press, 1970; Michael L. Beeman, *Public Policy and Economic Competition in Japan: Change and Continuity in Antimonopoly Policy, 1973–1975*, London and New York, Routledge, 2002.

[19] The classic work on the land reform is Ronald Dore, *Land Reform in Japan*, London, Oxford University Press, 1959.

[20] Kurt Steiner, *Local Government in Japan*, Stanford, CA, Stanford University Press, 1965.

hard put to contest matters with central government. Nevertheless, the ideal of local autonomy has stayed alive, has been fostered through the habit of democratic elections at local level, and became an important part of the reformist agenda, both in the 1970s and from the 1990s.

Finally, substantial reforms of the judicial system were introduced. These included an attempt to reduce the influence of the Ministry of Justice over the courts and to increase that of the Supreme Court, as well as a revision of the civil code.[21]

Another important reform of the judiciary was that the Supreme Court was given the power of judicial review of the constitutionality of legislative and executive acts. This may be seen as another 'American-style' reform (based on a desire for checks and balances) potentially conflicting with the 'British-style' principle of a single locus of sovereignty. Significantly, however, the power has been most sparingly used.

We may now usefully summarize the relationship between what have here been singled out as two conceptually separate sets of reforms. Essentially, the relationship lay in the desire of SCAP to establish a political system in which the political interests and views of the broad mass of the population should be represented through a government whose lines of responsibility were clear. This desired situation was in turn contrasted with the state of affairs under the Meiji Constitution, where the political voice of the population at large was circumscribed in a number of ways, such as restricted suffrage, officially sanctioned social norms inculcating submissiveness to the state as enshrined in a semi-divine *Tennō*, and police suppression of 'dangerous thoughts', but the power relationships existing among the political elite (or elites) were fluid, ill-defined and, as it turned out in the 1940s, dangerously unstable.

It is possible to take different views about the wisdom or appropriateness of the course of reform undertaken in Japan by the Occupation. In terms, however, of the two broad aims we have identified, success was at best partial. Even though most of the pre-war reasons why lines of responsibility became confused were removed, other factors intervened that complicated the maintenance of accountability. While many pre-war restrictions on political participation were eliminated, obstacles of a political, social and psychological kind to establishing a free society, where citizens can make a real political contribution, remained for a long time (and still remain to some extent).[22]

On the other hand, seizing the opportunity for change provided by the defeat and a reformist Occupation, Japan created a system which for many years was spectacularly successful in terms of different, but not unrelated, aims, namely those of building the nation into a major economic power.[23] In the 1990s,

[21] A further related reform, which has remained something of a curiosity, was the provision for periodic popular referenda on the suitability of Supreme Court judges. The referenda coincide with general elections. In practice they have always resulted in heavy votes of approval for the judges.

[22] One aspect of this much discussed since the 1990s is the relative weakness of civil society in Japan. This will be discussed in Chapter 11.

[23] Thus the Meiji period slogan 'prosperous nation and powerful army' (*fukoku kyōhei*) was now achieved at least in terms of its first element, the creation of a 'prosperous nation'.

however, the lustre came off the economic miracle, and the rickety nature both of accountable government and of participatory politics became all too evident as causal factors in economic failure.

3 Persistent influences deriving from Japanese social traditions and long historical experience

We suggested above an analogy between the changes that took place from 1945 and the reforms of the Meiji period. One obvious difference, however, is that while the Meiji reforms were devised and implemented by Japanese in control of their nation's destiny, the reforms of the Allied Occupation were devised and directed by foreigners. In both cases, however, while there was root and branch reform using foreign models, there was also much referring back to a body of national experience going back over several centuries. We have described in Chapter 3 some of the sociological and ideological aspects of this tradition, but history and historical tradition also played an important role.

A particular example is the fact that the *Tennō*, after the 1945 defeat, used the principles of the Charter Oath of 1868. The Charter Oath had been a formulation devised shortly after the *Meiji ishin* to justify opening the country to foreign influences, breaking with past customs, and recognizing the need for wide consultation. The deliberate re-use of a historical document such as the Charter Oath is a fascinating example of an aspect of a long historical tradition being used as a key reference point. In this case participants in radical political and social transition were drawing continuities with a previous experience of discontinuity.

Another example is the dominance of the bureaucratic element in the politics of post-war Japan. The country has a tradition of bureaucratic rule that goes back at least to the Tokugawa period. The tradition was strengthened by contingent factors after 1945. First, the Occupation, lacking administrators and interpreters in sufficient numbers, needed to rely upon existing bureaucratic structures in order to carry out its reforms. Second, the main pre-war rivals to the civilian bureaucracy – most notably the armed forces – had been removed. Third, the purge of party politicians implicated in wartime policies created a power vacuum which bureaucrats were able to fill. Thus, from the late 1940s the bureaucracy was able to 'infiltrate' the conservative political parties and the corporate sector, so that by the 1960s they were an enormously powerful political force. For these reasons, structures embedded in the long historical experience of the nation-state emerged from the first post-war decade with their power greatly strengthened.

The land reform succeeded in its aims (whatever its later consequences) because it was sensitively designed and competently implemented, but also because it fitted in with the priorities of the bureaucracy (or significant parts of it). There had been bureaucratic plans for more or less similar radical land reform before the war, and the ideal of a conservative, productive and small farmer class had deep roots.

By contrast, administrative decentralization was less successful because it ran counter to the entrenched centralist aims of government policy, and arguably because it was based on an inappropriate model, namely the American tradition that saw elective local government as a vital element in grass-roots democracy. Unfortunately, this thinking wrongly equated American and Japanese conditions in the post-war period. The geographical dispersion of centres of population in the US lent itself to genuine local autonomy, whereas in Japan the mass of the population was concentrated along a narrow strip of coast, and thus more receptive to centralized administration. Historically, too, the Japanese and American experiences could not have been more different. Whereas the constant extension of the 'frontier' by independent-minded citizens was a key part of the American experience (even though by now a historical memory), progress in Japan since the Tokugawa era had been linked with the centralizing of most aspects of administration. In many ways the centre could be regarded as more progressive and modern than the periphery, even though the extension of rule from the centre might well be felt by many as oppressive.

The introduction of local responsibility for education and the police fell foul of inadequate provision of finance, and in any case, a tradition of local autonomy could not be created overnight. Local populations had no tradition of participating in educational decisions, so that most of those elected to newly established boards of education turned out to be teachers. Decentralizing the police was both unworkable with limited finance and against long established tradition. Thus, these reforms were soon reversed by post-Occupation governments. Although their undoing was resisted by the opposition parties on the grounds that they were part of an intended full-scale 'reverse course', it is arguable that they were reversed principally because they were incompatible with long indigenous historical experience.

Here, however, we need to introduce an important caveat, namely that even long historical traditions are not necessarily immutable. One aspect of local government reforms that has survived is the introduction of a great many elective positions. Passin's argument that this reform led to a 'cancerlike growth of elective positions, ... a kind of overloading of the political communication circuits',[24] is questionable in the light of developments in local government and politics from the late 1960s. Rather, the local political structures set up during the Occupation may have ultimately facilitated the vigorous expression of local interests and points of view, and thus provided a crucial counterweight to the centralizing tendencies of Tokyo (see Chapter 11).

Let us then examine further the implications of the basic political structure that emerged from the Occupation. The determination of SCAP to eliminate 'dual government', whereby the military arrogated substantial power to itself, has already been mentioned. In order to do this it proved easier to reconcile a single line of authority and responsibility with a British-type fusion-of-powers theory than with American-style notions of the separation of powers. When Parliament is elected by the people, Cabinet is chosen from among the members of Parliament (in practice by a majority party or parties), the Prime Minister leads the Cabinet, each government department (ministry) has a member of the Cabinet at its head as minister, and legislation is introduced by the government

[24] Herbert Passin, *The Legacy of the Occupation of Japan*, New York, Columbia University Press, 1968 (Occasional Papers of the East Asian Institute, Columbia University), p. 27.

(broadly defined) into Parliament (which it can normally control because of its majority), then the lines of authority and responsibility are fairly clear.

It was probably a correct assessment that this style of government was more likely to solve the problems raised by Japan's ambiguous constitutional traditions than any system based primarily upon a separation of powers. The party-based cabinets of the 1920s (an era of relative liberalism) approximated to the British model, even though their status was uncertain and their powers very incomplete. Conversely, the 'transcendental' cabinets that predominated between 1890 and 1924, and again between 1932 and the war, looked rather more like the American President in his relations with Congress, although Congress has always commanded far more independent influence than did the Japanese parliaments of the 'transcendental' eras.[25]

In choosing a system for Japanese government based on the fusion of powers, therefore, the Occupation authorities ultimately had the effect of further directing Japan along the centralizing path pursued by governments since the mid-nineteenth century. The effect, though not necessarily the intention,[26] of the reforms was thus consonant with long historical experience.

4   More recent historical influences, deriving largely from political developments in the 1930s and early 1940s   We have distinguished between long historical influences, discussed in the previous section, and more recent influences from the militarist period, in part because it is tempting to see historical influences as all of a piece, whereas certain periods can have a disproportionate influence. This is particularly true for the period of the 1930s and early 1940s.

As Japan became more and more entangled in the affairs of continental Asia in the 1930s, so its need for efficient and flexible military production increased. This gradually led to industrial mobilization, and by the time of the attack on Pearl Harbor state direction of industry was pervasive. The habits of interaction between government and industry engendered during this period carried over

---

[25]   SCAP's *The Political Reorientation of Japan* glosses over the differences between the two systems. See the following comment: 'The device of parliamentary responsibility procures the answerability of the executive branch of government to the people through their duly elected representatives. In the United States the responsibility is enforced through direct election of the President and Vice President. In England and the European democracies, the pattern is similar to that of Japan. In either case, the result is the same. The executive branch of government has no legal authority, excuse or justification for acting in defiance of the mandate of the people. Every public officer, every public employee is the agent and servant of the people.' SCAP, *The Political Reorientation of Japan*, pp. 115–16.

[26]   Some Occupation officials do not seem entirely to have appreciated the implications of the reforms they were introducing. Thus some of them seem to have expected Parliament to act more independently of Cabinet than a familiarity with British or British Commonwealth patterns would have led them to expect. They thought, for instance, that Parliament and not Cabinet would have the final say on when Parliament would be dissolved, whereas practice (and an ambiguity in the Constitution) dictated the opposite. See D. C. S. Sissons (ed.), *Papers on Modern Japan 1968*, Canberra, Australian National University, 1968, pp. 91–137.

into post-war Japan, and were important in moulding the kinds of relationship between the two that prevailed in the 1950s and 1960s. During the late 1930s the structure of industry changed substantially, with the so-called 'new *zaibatsu*' emerging to prominence. The power and industrial experience of these companies, forged during the particular conditions of war and preparation for war, also had an impact on the shape of the economy in the post-war period.[27]

Also significant was the development from the 1920s of what has come to be seen as a typically Japanese system of industrial relations, in which firms maintain a permanent workforce of well-paid and highly skilled labour which is led to develop close identification with the firm. Although it was not until after the end of the war that this system became the norm in large firms (and some smaller ones), the influence of the 1920s and 1930s is certainly important in explaining its rise to normality.[28]

Aspects of the post-war banking system – which the Occupation conspicuously failed to reform – may also be derived from the inter-war period. Close linkages between the banks and the government were maintained, and free competition between banks on the American model was generally absent. The Bank Law of 1942, for instance, had confirmed the subservience of the banks to the control of the military, and after the war was over the central government continued to exercise a similar kind of control.[29]

5 Political innovation in the post-war and post-Occupation period, in particular the establishment of conservative single-party dominance from 1955   In November 1955 the Liberal Democratic Party was formed out of various competing conservative parties. It is common to regard this as a turning point, marking the establishment of what is often termed the '1955 political system', which survived until the LDP lost office in August 1993. In reality, however, this interpretation masks a complex and evolving reality. Taking the Occupation period together with the decade that followed its ending in 1952, it is evident that the political elite showed a remarkable ability to innovate. Seminal and innovative changes took place in five inter-related areas:

- The formation of the LDP in 1955.
- The relative marginalization of left-wing parties and the labour union movement from about 1960.
- The infiltration by government ministries of political parties and parts of the corporate sector, from the Occupation period onwards.

[27]   See Richard J. Samuels, *The Business of the Japanese State: Energy Markets in Comparative and Historical Perspective*, Ithaca and London, Cornell University Press, 1987.
[28]   Sheldon Garon, *The State and Labor in Modern Japan*, Berkeley, Los Angeles and London, University of California Press, 1987.
[29]   William M. Tsutsui, *Banking Policy in Japan: American Efforts at Reform during the Occupation*, London and New York, Routledge, 1988, p. 15.

- The realization that US security guarantees provided desirable freedom of manoeuvre in many policy areas, but especially in the pursuit of economic growth.
- The tacit abandonment, from the early 1960s, of attempts at wholesale reversal of the Occupation reforms in favour of directing attention towards economic policies.

Let us expand on each of these areas in turn.

The formation of the LDP was a *tour de force*, precipitated by the unification of the Socialist movement into a single Japan Socialist Party (JSP, *Nihon shakaitō*) a month before, in October 1955, and abetted by leading business representatives anxious at the prospect of a Socialist government. Given a history of internecine strife among the parties that came together to form the LDP and among their leaders, the prospects for the LDP becoming a 'ruling party', or even surviving intact, appeared poor. Its fortunes turned, however, following a major political crisis in 1960, after which the habit of simply being in power took hold.

The second key development, foreshadowed by the 1960s crisis, but not wholly evident at the time it took place, was the relative marginalization of left-wing parties and the union movement. The term 'relative' is used advisedly, because the Socialists were still a force in the land during the 1960s, but the prospects for a change of government bringing them closer to the centre of power receded during that decade. This was, of course, the reverse side of the coin of LDP dominance, but in addition rapid economic growth was taking the edge off radical protest.

The third innovation was the infiltration of political parties and corporate firms, as well as some other organizations, by government ministries. During the 1960s there were cabinets fully half of whose members had served in the bureaucracy, while many corporate firms had former bureaucrats on their boards of management. Thus government, politics and the business world were developing a strongly bureaucratic colouring, contributing to a single-mindedness on matters of policy which was a characteristic of the period.

This brings us to the fourth innovative development of the post-Occupation period, namely the dawning realization that US security guarantees provided desirable freedom of manoeuvre in many policy areas, but particularly in the pursuit of economic growth. The so-called 'Yoshida Doctrine', named after the post-war Prime Minister Yoshida Shigeru, was based essentially on this perception. This involved developing the minimum military capacity to keep the Americans happy, providing them with military bases on Japanese soil, but resisting pressure to take international responsibilities of a military nature. Here, of course, the peace clause of the Constitution proved a most useful bulwark against importunate demands.

The fifth innovation, which is of enormous significance in retrospect, was the abandonment, from the early 1960s, of radical attempts to reverse the Occupation reforms, in favour of concentration on economic priorities. The consequences of this change of approach in moving from the 1950s to the 1960s were to be long-lasting and far-reaching.

The Course of Domestic Politics

Domestic politics during the Occupation was a turbulent affair.[30] All governments in this period were answerable to SCAP, but also to a newly empowered
electorate. They were charged with implementing Occupation-sponsored
reforms, but could not ignore disaffected constituents at a time of economic
disruption and poverty. Government still functioned under the Meiji Constitution
until the new Constitution came into force on 3 May 1947. The first post-war
elections for the all-important House of Representatives, held in April 1946,
were seriously affected by the purge. Although the Liberal Party (LP, *Jiyūtō*)
emerged as the largest party in the house, its leader, the veteran politician
Hatoyama Ichirō, was purged by SCAP straight after the elections. Needing to
find a new leader in a hurry, the party chose Yoshida Shigeru, a former career
diplomat, who had been Foreign Minister for the previous few months, but had
no previous connections with a political party.[31]

This was a fateful decision. Yoshida at the time was 67 years old, and was to
remain Prime Minister, with one break of about seventeen months, for the next
eight and a half years. At least until the purge restrictions were lifted on his
potential rivals towards the end of the Occupation, he dominated his own party
and the Japanese political world to an extent that few politicians have managed
to do before or since.[32] He provided strong and individualistic leadership at a
time when a Prime Minister, sandwiched between the Occupation authorities
and a complex political environment, was in a position of great delicacy. He also
nurtured a small band of younger politicians, similarly of bureaucratic origin,
who were to play a leading role in politics for many years after his retirement.
Although it was not until the January 1949 general elections to the lower house
that former central government bureaucrats became numerically significant in
the conservative parties,[33] the unexpected elevation of Yoshida in 1946, like the
forming of the *Seiyūkai* party in 1900, facilitated that partial fusion of government ministries and ruling party that has been so characteristic of Japanese
politics in the post-war period.

New lower house elections were held in April 1947 under a revised electoral
system that survived, in essence, until 1994 (see Chapter 8). The Japan Socialist
Party, formed less than eighteen months earlier, became the largest party and

[30]   The best book on the Occupation in all its aspects is John Dower, *Embracing Defeat:
Japan in the Aftermath of World War II*, London and New York, Allen Lane/Penguin,
1999.
[31]   His immediate predecessor (Prime Minister from October 1946) was Shidehara Kijūrō,
also a career diplomat.
[32]   John Dower, *Empire and Aftermath: Yoshida Shigeru and the Japanese Experience,
1878–1954*, Cambridge, MA, and London, Harvard University Press, 1979.
[33]   About 15% of conservative members of Parliament in the 1949 elections had entered
Parliament as former bureaucrats. Later, the percentage was to stabilize at about 25%.
See Haruhiro Fukui, *Party in Power: The Japanese Liberal-Democrats and Policy-
Making*, Canberra, Australian National University Press, 1970, pp. 40–1.

was the first party of the left ever to enter government. It did so in a three-party coalition with the essentially conservative Democratic Party (DP, *Minshutō*) and another small party. The new Prime Minister was a Socialist, Katayama Tetsu. This government was beset by factional and ideological divisions, including divisions between left and right within the JSP, and fell in February 1948 over an abortive attempt to nationalize the coal mines. It was succeeded by a government of almost identical composition, led by the DP leader, Ashida Hitoshi, but this in turn fell in October 1948 as the result of the Shōwa Denkō corruption scandal.[34] The JSP was not to hold power again until the mid-1990s.

The 'opening to the left' had ended in fiasco, and as a result Yoshida's Democratic Liberal Party (DLP, *Minshujiyūtō*) came to power, consolidating its position in lower house general elections held in January 1949, which gave it an absolute majority of seats.

Apart from the divided nature of the coalition cabinets, they suffered from the coincidence of their formation with a gradual change in the priorities of the Occupation. With the emergence of the Cold War, the Americans were beginning to see Japan less as a conquered enemy to be reformed, and more as a potential ally in the struggle against 'International Communism'. Other factors were also beginning to affect US policy. Japan was coming to be seen as a burden on the US taxpayer, and economic recovery became a priority. Plans to break up the industrial combines (*zaibatsu*) were suspended; SCAP banned a general strike planned for 1 February 1947 and in 1948 imposed restrictions on the right of public sector workers to organize and strike. In 1949 a stringent economic stabilization programme, known as the 'Dodge Line' (named after the Detroit banker Joseph Dodge, who visited Japan and prescribed unpalatable medicine), was imposed. This stabilized the economy and halted inflation, but left a legacy of bitterness against the Americans on the part of much of the political left.

In October 1951 the San Francisco Peace Treaty was signed; on its becoming effective in April 1952, Japan was once more formally an independent state. Not all the powers that had fought against Japan signed the treaty, so what emerged was a 'partial' peace.[35] Largely at American insistence, the peace treaty was a favourable one for Japan. Although it renounced her claims to its former imperial territories, no restrictions were placed on the development of its economy or trade, nor was it obliged to retain any of the Occupation reforms.

On the same day that the peace treaty was signed, the US and Japan signed a bilateral security pact that was to permit a continued US military presence on Japanese soil after independence. Acute domestic controversy swirled around this issue and the closely related one of Japanese re-armament. In 1951 Yoshida had been able to resist US pressure to undertake large-scale re-armament.

---

[34]   The scandal concerned contributions to politicians from construction companies. The JSP Secretary-General Nishio Suehiro was implicated and forced out of active politics for several years.

[35]   The Soviet Union, Poland, Czechoslovakia, India, Burma and Yugoslavia did not sign, though the last three signed peace treaties with Japan later. Neither the People's Republic of China (PRC) nor the Republic of China (ROC, Taiwan) was invited to the peace conference, but Japan soon signed a separate peace treaty with the ROC.

The chief US negotiator, John Foster Dulles, pressed him to create a force of 350,000 men. Yoshida understood the likely economic, domestic political and international consequences, and refused. The Security Treaty nevertheless contained a clause expecting Japan to take increasing responsibility for its own defence.[36] Subsequent negotiations led to the formation of the Self-Defence Forces (SDF, *jieitai*) in 1954, at a very much lower strength than had been envisaged by Dulles.

Politics after the Occupation

Once the Occupation ended, Yoshida's power within the conservative camp waned as party politicians who had been purged returned to political life. Intense rivalry developed between Yoshida, trying to hang on to power, and the de-purged Hatoyama, working to replace him. Hatoyama succeeded in December 1954, while conservative politics remained split between several parties and splinter groups.

On the left, the JSP split over the peace settlement in 1951, but the two halves of the party together made steady electoral progress until well after their reunification in 1955. The Japan Communist Party (JCP, *Nihon kyōsantō*) had a brief flowering during the Occupation, but turned militant on Moscow orders in 1950, saw its leaders purged by SCAP, and became a negligible political force in the 1950s.

October and November of 1955 saw first the Socialists, and then various conservative groups, unite into single parties. From then on the JSP on the left and the LDP on the right constituted a two-party system, though they did not alternate in power, and the LDP proved more resilient than its Socialist rivals. The mid- to late 1950s saw acute polarization of opinion between the two sides. In February 1957 Kishi Nobusuke took over as Prime Minister. Kishi for a number of reasons was a divisive figure, and his period in office culminated in the Security Treaty revision crisis of 1960, which led to his fall from office.[37]

LDP governments (and their conservative predecessors) were critical of Occupation reforms, and sought to amend or emasculate those they found most objectionable. The opposition (the Socialists, labour unions, many academics and much of the mass media) feared that each new piece of government legislation was part of a planned programme of reversion to the pre-war militaristic regime.

The main areas in which reform was pursued by LDP governments were police administration and powers; labour union rights; educational administration and the content of courses; re-armament and the Japan–US Security Treaty; and perhaps most significantly, the Constitution, in particular the peace clause, article 9.

---

[36] Security Treaty between the United States and Japan, 8 September 1951, preamble. The peace treaty also reaffirmed Japan's right of defence.
[37] Kishi had been a member of General Tōjō's War Cabinet, and was designated a Class A war criminal by the Occupation, though later released from prison. He was an intelligent and innovative politician, but the right-wing radicalism of his approach, combined with his background, alienated much articulate opinion.

During the 1950s the police were recentralized and their powers strength-ened, though Kishi's 1958 Police Duties Amendment Bill, designed to help the police control demonstrations, met a barrage of criticism within and outside Parliament, and was allowed to lapse. Successive governments regarded labour unions with hostility, and passed laws to control them and blunt their impact. Communist influence with the unions was much weakened by 1950, and the Sōhyō Federation formed in that year was initially anti-Communist. It moved rapidly to the left, however, and in 1954 split into a radical wing (still called Sōhyō) and a smaller moderate wing (Zenrō, later Dōmei). Relations between the unions and the Socialists remained close.

Education policy was highly contentious. In 1956 the Hatoyama government recentralized educational administration. The local boards of education ceased to be elective and came to be appointed. The Ministry of Education (MOE, Monbushō) also acquired powers of vetting and authorizing school textbooks – something that remains controversial past the millennium. Teacher evaluation, and the re-introduction into schools of ethics courses (abolished by the Occupation) were widely opposed. Relations between the MOE and the Japan Teachers Union (JTU, Nikkyōso) became strained to say the least.[38]

Re-armament and the Japan–US Security Treaty were the best-known arena of political conflict. Despite the Constitution's peace clause, the SDF were formed in 1954. Even though Yoshida had made sure that these were at the minimum level needed to satisfy the US, they were still hugely controversial in the 1950s. Anti-war feeling had increased during the 1950s, and the JSP from 1955 was campaigning on a platform of 'unarmed neutralism'. Any attempt by the government to enhance national defence capacity or to consolidate its defence relationship with the US was bitterly resisted by the left.

There were many campaigns against US military bases, and the Japan Council against Atomic and Hydrogen Bombs (Gensuikyō), founded after a Japanese fishing boat was showered with radioactive ash from an American test at Bikini atoll in 1954, tapped a vast reservoir of anti-nuclear sentiment – for readily comprehensible reasons.

The 1946 Constitution was a major field of contention. In August 1957, by which time Kishi, an enthusiast for constitutional revision, was Prime Minister, a Cabinet Commission on the Constitution (Kenpō chōsakai) began work. The Socialists and their allies refused to participate in the Commission, which despite this proved not to be the solidly revisionist body that many had feared. It was not until 1964 that it reported (at great length, but without unanimity), but by that time pressure for revision had receded and no action was taken.

The Security Treaty revision crisis of May–June 1960 was the most serious political fracas since the end of the Occupation. It produced mass demonstrations

[38]   The JTU at that period was Marxist-influenced, and the MOE largely refused to negotiate with it. Difficult relations persisted until the late 1980s, when the JTU moved to a much more moderate position, though it suffered major defections as a result. See Robert W. Aspinall, *Teachers' Unions and the Politics of Education in Japan*, New York, State University of New York Press, 2001.

of unprecedented magnitude, led to the cancellation of a state visit by President Eisenhower, precipitated the fall from office of a prime minister (but not his party), and seriously strained Japan–US relations. On the other hand, the Mutual Security Treaty that emerged from the episode was for Japan arguably an improvement on the 1951 treaty. Democracy was tested and strained, but did not collapse. Following the crisis, political stability was greater, and the temperature of politics lower, than in the 1950s.

Briefly, what happened was this. In 1958 Kishi began negotiations with the US to revise the existing Security Treaty so that it would be more acceptable to Japan. He wanted to increase Japan's independence of action under the treaty, without reducing the American defence commitment or committing Japan to excessive defence responsibilities. To a large extent, he succeeded in those aims.[39]

The Socialists and other left-of-centre groups for the most part objected to the continuation of the treaty as such, and saw revision as perpetuating a dangerous 'military alliance'. Their morale was boosted by the March 1959 verdict in the Sunakawa case, which held that the presence of US troops in Japan violated article 9 of the Constitution, even though the verdict of the lower court was reversed by the Supreme Court in December 1959 (see Chapter 10).

In its early stages, the movement against the treaty was fairly limited in scope and numbers. The principal activists were the Socialist and Communist Parties, the Sōhyō labour federation and the radical student movement Zengakuren,[40] with much support from academics and the media.[41] However, developments in May and June 1960 broadened the base of the movement to include previously uncommitted people. As the parliamentary debates on treaty ratification were nearing completion, international tension rose dramatically with the U2 incident and the cancellation of the planned summit meeting between Eisenhower and Khrushchev.[42] Many Japanese now worried that their country could be dragged into an international conflict through its security links with the US. In a change with symbolic impact, Eisenhower's world trip would include anti-Communist capitals but not, as had been planned, Moscow. Kishi, meanwhile, was faced with obstruction of parliamentary proceedings by the opposition parties, and found some factions in the LDP manoeuvring against him.

By failing to have the treaty passed by the House of Representatives by 26 April, Kishi missed the 26 May deadline for the House of Councillors to ratify it by the end of the parliamentary session, necessitating an extension to the session.

---

[39]   For details of the revisions to the Security Treaty and the issues involved, see Chapter 12. On the politics of the crisis, see George Packard III, *Protest in Tokyo: The Security Treaty Revision Crisis of 1960*, Princeton, NJ, Princeton University Press, 1966.

[40]   All-Japan Federation of Student Self-Governing Associations.

[41]   Elements from these groups broke into the Parliament compound on 27 November 1959 and unsuccessfully tried to stop Kishi from leaving Haneda Airport on 16 January 1960 to sign the revised treaty in Washington.

[42]   An American U2 spy plane was shot down over the Soviet Union and the pilot detained.

He then compounded his problems by inviting President Eisenhower to Japan for 19 June, assuming that the treaty would have been ratified by that date. This meant it had to pass the lower house by 19 May.

When 19 May arrived and the treaty still had not passed the lower house, Kishi decided on drastic action. Late in the evening he called police into Parliament to remove Socialist parliamentarians and their male secretaries who were physically preventing the Speaker from calling a vote to extend the session.[43]

Kishi now stood accused of subverting parliamentary procedure, and even democracy itself, which many realized was still fragile. Socialist actions, such as imprisoning the Speaker, were also criticized, but in general less harshly. In the month that followed before the treaty came into force, Eisenhower's press secretary was mobbed in his car by demonstrators and had to be rescued by helicopter (10 June), and on 15 June a massive demonstration outside Parliament led to an invasion of the parliamentary compound and pitched battles with police. There were many injuries and one female student was killed. The next day Kishi cancelled the US President's visit on the ground that he could not guarantee his safety. The revised Security Treaty duly passed the House of Councillors on 19 June, and four days later Kishi announced his resignation. The LDP did not split, though it came close.[44] The demonstrators went home.

The suddenness with which the 1960 crisis was over suggests that basic stability underlay the political turbulence. It is true that there were some disturbing instances of political violence following the crisis.[45] The next few years, however, were relatively calm and uneventful. Ikeda Hayato, the next Prime Minister, also came from the bureaucracy and was a protégé of Yoshida. Government remained in the hands of the conservative, business-oriented LDP.

Ikeda was a great contrast to his predecessor. He was conciliatory to the opposition, projected a low-key image, played down contentious political issues and sought to restore the normal working of Parliament. His trump card was economic growth. The economy was now recording double-digit growth rates, and Ikeda issued a plan for 'income doubling' over a ten-year period. He promoted Japanese participation in international organizations, such as the OECD, which Japan joined in 1964.

---

[43] A proposal to involve the Self-Defence Forces was apparently vetoed by the Defence Agency Minister, Akagi Munenori, who can be considered an unsung hero of Japanese democracy. He may well have prevented a far worse crisis that would have greeted a military presence in Parliament.

[44] One powerful faction leader, Kōno Ichirō, came close to pulling his faction out of the party. Interestingly, it was his son, Kōno Yōhei, who in 1976 led a defection from the LDP over the Lockheed scandal.

[45] In June 1960 the JSP leader, Kawakami Jōtarō, and in July Kishi himself, were injured by stabbing, in both cases by ultra-rightist individuals. In October 1960 the JSP Chairman, Asanuma Inejirō, was assassinated in front of television cameras by a 17-year-old youth influenced by ultra-rightist groups. In February 1961, an ultra-rightist intending to kill the editor of *Chūō Kōron*, a leading intellectual journal, wounded the editor's wife and killed a female servant. Later the same year, an amateurish plot to assassinate the whole Cabinet was discovered in time.

During the 1960s the political opposition tended to fragment, with the previous dominance of the JSP coming under challenge by other groups. In 1959 a right-of-centre group led by Nishio Suehiro (prominent in the coalition governments of the late 1940s) broke away from the JSP and formed the Democratic Socialist Party (DSP, *Minshatō*), in protest at the Socialists' drift to the left.[46] The DSP did not do particularly well at the polls,[47] but its defection upset the ideological balance within the JSP. During the early 1960s the JSP leader Eda Saburō promoted a policy of Structural Reform (*kōzō kaikaku*), which was reformist rather than revolutionary in its implications. His grip on the party organization, however, was fragile, and by 1965 he had been replaced by leaders further to the left.[48]

The JSP was poorly organized and heavily dependent on labour unions affiliated with the *Sōhyō* federation. Unlike the German Social Democrats at about the same period, who were broadening their appeal, the JSP was narrowing its appeal to the ranks of organized labour, principally indeed to unions in the public sector. This left the way open to other groups to encroach on traditional areas of Socialist support. One such was a Buddhist organization called *Sōka Gakkai* which since the war had attracted several million unorganized workers, small shopkeepers and middle-aged housewives in cities. In 1964 it founded the Clean Government Party (CGP, *Kōmeitō*), which attacked corruption and campaigned on behalf of the disadvantaged. The party was highly disciplined and won forty-seven lower house seats in the 1969 elections. The other rising force was the JCP, which was rapidly recovering from its setbacks of the 1950s and attracting significant support, especially in big cities. The JSP, by contrast, failed to attract new interests created by the economic 'miracle', and lost fifty seats in the 1969 elections.

Ill-health forced Ikeda to resign as Prime Minister in November 1964 (he died the next year) and he was succeeded by Satō Eisaku, younger brother of Kishi.[49] Satō was another former bureaucrat and protégé of Yoshida, and was to remain in office until June 1972 – a record tenure in the premiership that still stands. He presided over the later stages of the economic 'miracle' that by the late 1960s had given Japan a larger GNP than those of Britain, France and West Germany, and smaller only than those of the US and the USSR. Japan was becoming a major force internationally, although political initiative lagged behind economic weight.

Satō was a cautious and conservative Prime Minister, though the Vietnam War meant that relations between government and opposition were more polarized than under Ikeda. His most tangible achievements, but also his major

[46] In March 1959 the JSP Secretary-General, Asanuma Inejirō, remarked in Beijing that 'American imperialism is the common enemy of Japan and China'.

[47] The DSP, until it merged with other parties to form the New Frontier Party in 1994, usually polled between 6% and 8% of the vote and gained between 17 and 35 lower house seats.

[48] For a perceptive analysis of 'Structural Reform' and the reasons for its failure, see Stephen Johnson, *Opposition Party Politics in Japan: Strategies under a One-Party Dominant Regime*, London and New York, Routledge, 2000, pp. 24–57.

[49] The difference in surname was occasioned by one having been adopted into a different family.

setbacks, were in foreign policy. In 1965 he concluded a treaty with the Republic of Korea (South Korea). He avoided a repeat in 1970 of the 1960 crisis over the Security Treaty by securing an automatic extension. He secured the return of Okinawa, which had been US-administered since the end of the war, to Japan with effect from May 1972.[50] In 1974, after he had left office, he was awarded the Nobel Peace Prize for his declaration in 1971 that Japan would not manufacture, stockpile or introduce nuclear weapons on its territory.[51]

Japan saw a great deal of student radicalism in the late 1960s and early 1970s, though Satō's Universities Control Bill in August 1969 had a dramatic effect in returning things to normal.

Satō's final year in office was seriously troubled. In August 1971 President Nixon introduced measures in part designed to force Japan to revalue the yen, which had remained at 360 yen to the US dollar since the Occupation. As a consequence the yen rose unevenly against other currencies until the 1990s. It was, however, China policy that caused the Prime Minister to leave office. Nixon did not consult Japan when he announced, in July 1971, his intention to visit the PRC. The two 'Nixon shocks', as they were known, led to much rethinking in Japan. Satō was unwilling (or unable) to change his China policy radically, whereas the media and much articulate opinion was calling on him either to move towards recognizing the PRC or step down as Prime Minister. Another set of issues rapidly emerging in the early 1970s related to the environmental consequences of rapid economic growth. Satō initiated measures for environmental control, but degradation of the environment favoured opposition candidates in the cities at this period.

In July 1972 Satō was replaced by Tanaka Kakuei. The new Prime Minister was a man of limited formal education and no bureaucratic background, who had made his career in business and in the LDP machine. The tide of disillusionment with Satō was probably what robbed his preferred successor, Fukuda Takeo – a man of similar background to his own – of the succession. Tanaka took initiatives in two directions. He moved at once to recognize the PRC, which meant severing diplomatic relations with the Republic of China (ROC) on Taiwan. He also produced a plan for the 'Reconstruction of the Japanese Archipelago', involving dispersal of industry and population away from the big cities. His China initiative quickly succeeded, but the 'Reconstruction' plan created a speculative boom in designated land prices, further fuelling inflationary trends that were already apparent. He also tried, but failed, to reform the lower house electoral system to the advantage of the LDP.

The fourfold oil price increases precipitated by OPEC late in 1973 further stimulated inflation, and brought economic growth to a shuddering halt.

---

[50]   Okinawa and the surrounding Ryūkyū islands saw one of the bloodiest battles of the Asia–Pacific war. With Japan's defeat, they came under American jurisdiction, though Japan was given 'residual sovereignty'. As a key US base for the Vietnam War, holding nuclear weapons, Okinawa became a major source of political conflict in Japan.

[51]   In the 1970s and early 1980s the third of these principles – 'introduction' (*mochikomi*) – aroused controversy when it became clear that nuclear weapons were coming into Japanese ports on US naval vessels.

Tanaka's government limped along through 1974, but revelations about his financial dealings were given wide coverage, and he resigned in November of that year.[52] His successor was Miki Takeo, a veteran faction leader on the left of the LDP. He was chosen through behind-the-scenes consultation among party elders, who were no doubt seeking someone with a 'clean' reputation. A further motive for his appointment may also have been to forestall any move by Miki to take his faction out of the party in a protest against corruption.

Miki relied on a weak power base within the LDP, and indeed for some months in 1975 he relied on opposition party votes in support of those of his bills that were opposed by the LDP right wing. He had a modest success with a watered-down version of the Anti-Monopoly Law, which enabled the Fair Trade Commission (FTC, *Kōsei torihiki iinkai*) to pursue cartels rather more effectively than hitherto.[53] He succeeded in bringing about ratification of the Nuclear Non-Proliferation Treaty, long after its signature in 1970.

In February 1976 a US Senate committee uncovered evidence that several million dollars had been given to politicians in Japan and elsewhere to influence aircraft contracts. This caused a sensation in Japan, and the 'Lockheed scandal' dominated the nation's politics for a long period. Miki broke with tradition and allowed official investigators a free hand to probe the affair as deeply as they wished. Sensationally, Tanaka was arrested in July and made to answer charges about his part in the affair. Though quickly released and still a member of Parliament (he later resigned from the LDP), he had to face protracted court proceedings and eventually received an adverse verdict in 1983. His case was still under appeal in 1986 when he suffered a stroke, which ended his political career. Until that point, however, he remained an LDP faction leader (despite no longer being an LDP member!), and during the 1980s his faction was not only the largest in the party, but the one that in effect determined who should be Prime Minister.

The Lockheed scandal brought about the one serious defection suffered by the LDP between 1955 and 1993: that of six parliamentarians led by Kōno Yōhei, who formed a small party called the New Liberal Club (NLC, *Shin jiyū kurabu*). The NLC remained in existence for ten years, never escaping from minor party status, but probably had a catalytic effect on the LDP. It was incorporated into a coalition government with the LDP in 1983, and most of its members were reabsorbed into their former party in 1986. Kōno was to be LDP President (but never Prime Minister) between 1993 and 1995.

In the lower house general elections of December 1976 (following the NLC defection) the LDP barely maintained its majority of seats. As a result, the party lost control of a number of House of Representatives standing committees, thus

---

[52] Articles in the press outside Japan often repeat the statement that Tanaka was brought down as a result of the Lockheed aircraft scandal (see below). This is wholly incorrect, since the Lockheed scandal first came to light in February 1976, 15 months after his resignation.

[53] Michael Beeman, *Public Policy and Economic Competition in Japan: Change and Continuity in Antimonopoly Policy, 1973–1995*, London and New York, Routledge, 2002.

complicating its legislative task.[54] An era dubbed the Era of Parity (*hakuchū jidai*) had begun and was to last until June 1980. Some commentators were confidently predicting that the opposition parties would soon attain a majority and even replace the LDP in power.

Miki resigned following the elections, and was replaced by Fukuda Takeo (Tanaka's great rival). Loss of committee control meant that Fukuda had to incorporate tax reductions into the 1977 budget. Economic growth, though, had started to resume, and with it the beginning of trade imbalance problems with the US, which were to cause much contestation in the 1980s.

Fukuda was active in promoting economic relations with South-East Asia, and in February 1978 signed a large-scale trade agreement with the PRC. This was followed in August by the Sino-Japanese Treaty of Peace and Friendship. These two treaties were to lead to sustained growth in the economic relationship between Japan and China, which has continued into the twenty-first century. On the other hand, relations between Japan and its Soviet neighbour deteriorated in line with the emergence of the 'second Cold War' from the late 1970s.

The opposition parties appeared to be riding high in this period, but left–right divisions continued to plague their ranks, particularly those of the JSP.[55] The JCP resurgence was also faltering. By the late 1970s there were signs that the swing to the left among the electorate apparent earlier in the decade was over, and that conservative electoral support was stabilizing. From the late 1960s left-of-centre chief executives had been elected to head many urban and metropolitan local authorities, arriving on the back of a concern with the environment, welfare and quality of living, all of which had suffered during the period of rapid economic growth. Though these individuals had many achievements to their credit,[56] they had not always proved competent administrators. With the change in public mood towards the end of the decade, most of them were defeated in elections and replaced with candidates backed by essentially conservative coalitions.

In 1978, for the first time, the LDP President was elected through a primary election of all party members, prior to the main election by LDP parliamentarians and some local representatives. This had the perverse effect of extending factional divisions down to the rank-and-file membership. Central factions competed to recruit new local members, and in November 1978 the combined organizational strength of the Ōhira and Tanaka factions proved too much for the incumbent Prime Minister, Fukuda. In a four-cornered contest Ōhira Masayoshi beat Fukuda and the other two candidates by a wide margin, and Fukuda decided not to contest the run-off election.

---

[54] The allocation of committee memberships to parties is proportional to party representation in the house. This means that in a situation of near parity between government and opposition parties, the LDP would lose control of those committees for which it was required to provide the (non-voting) chairman.

[55] In 1977 a JSP splinter opposed to Marxist influence broke away and formed the Social Democratic League (SDL, *Shaminren*), led by Eda Saburō, who unfortunately died shortly after its formation, so that the leadership passed to his son, Eda Satsuki. The SDL lasted until 1994.

[56] For instance, Governor Minobe of Tokyo, the best-known 'progressive governor', had initiated great improvements in the safety of pedestrians throughout the city.

The fact that Tanaka had beaten Fukuda to the succession in 1972, and then Ōhira, in alliance with Tanaka, had displaced him as Prime Minister in 1978, caused acute inter-factional tension. Ōhira in fact turned out to be an innovative Prime Minister, and several policies taken up in the 1980s by the better-known Nakasone can be traced back to the Ōhira period. Nevertheless, Ōhira's position was constantly under threat. The LDP performed marginally worse in the 1979 lower house general elections than in 1976, though it just retained its parliamentary majority.[57]

Following the 1979 elections Ōhira's tenure was challenged from within his party, and a forty-day crisis ensued, resolved only when the LDP put forward two candidates, Ōhira and Fukuda, in the parliamentary election to determine who should be Prime Minister.[58] Ōhira narrowly won the contest, but his troubles did not end there. On 16 May 1980 the JSP presented to Parliament a no-confidence motion, citing corruption, proposed defence spending increases and rises in public utility charges. Quite unexpectedly, sixty-nine LDP parliamentarians, from the Fukuda, Miki and Nakagawa factions,[59] abstained from voting on the motion. In essence, this revolt was part of a continued attempt by anti-Ōhira factions to bring him down. The government was defeated by 243 votes to 187 and resigned. For the first time a simultaneous double election was called for both houses of Parliament.

Although it seemed as if the LDP was faced with disintegration, the shock of the government's resignation led to a closing of ranks. This mood of unity was further strengthened when on 12 June Ōhira died from a heart condition, perhaps exacerbated by the defeat. A caretaker Prime Minister was chosen, and the LDP went to the people on 22 June carrying black-edged posters of its dead leader. In an extraordinary reversal of its fortunes, the party won a clear victory in both houses and in the lower house secured its safest majority since 1969.[60] The ruling party was once more in charge of all parliamentary committees, and therefore had regained its former power over legislation. The LDP had gone to the people leaderless, but scored a convincing victory on a high turnout. Following the elections Suzuki Zenkō, the new leader of what had been the Ōhira faction, became party President and thus Prime Minister. He was an unexpected choice.

There are important lines of continuity between the Ōhira, Suzuki and subsequent Nakasone cabinets. Priorities in the 1970s had been to attack the environmental crisis and also to improve what had been gravely inadequate welfare provision.[61] These initiatives involved major increases in public expenditure, and

---

[57] A proposal by Ōhira to introduce new indirect taxation may have contributed to this result.

[58] Had the opposition parties chosen to do so, they could have easily determined the choice of Prime Minister by voting for one or other LDP candidate, but instead they each voted for their own party leader.

[59] The Nakagawa faction was a small nationalist-inclined grouping. It appears to be widely believed that the larger and more important Nakasone faction abstained, but this is not correct.

[60] For a fuller analysis of the 1980 crisis, see J. A. A. Stockwin, 'Japan's Political Crisis of 1980', *Australian Outlook*, vol. 35, no. 1 (April 1981), pp. 19–32.

[61] The Tanaka government declared 1973 'Year One of Welfare' (*fukushi gannen*).

although this would not have caused problems had the high growth rates up to 1973 been sustained, the much slower growth following the first oil crisis meant that finances became seriously strained. Ōhira recognized this problem, but it was left to his successors, who enjoyed more stable parliamentary majorities, to put in place measures of financial retrenchment. In March 1981 the government set up the Provisional Commission on Administrative Reform (*Rinji gyōsei chōsakai*, or *Rinchō*). At first it seemed designed to rationalize and curb bureaucratic power, but the *Rinchō* quickly turned into an exercise in budget-cutting. When Nakasone replaced Suzuki as Prime Minister in November 1982 he had the means, and the will, to ensure that its main recommendations for zero-increase budgets were adhered to.

In the early 1980s important changes were taking place in the internal politics of the LDP. In retrospect, the party alternated between periods of acute factional conflict over the leadership and periods in which a single faction could impose its will, or at least act as arbiter of who became leader. If the late 1950s and early 1960s, as well as most of the 1970s, exemplified the former, the Satō period (1964–72), as well as the 1980s and the early 1990s, exemplified the latter. The ultimate arbiter of power in the LDP from around 1980 was the Tanaka (from 1986 Takeshita) faction. Ever since the Lockheed scandal of 1976, Tanaka had been recruiting new members into his faction, which by the early 1980s had become the largest in the party. Members of other factions often envied the resources available to Tanaka faction members. Three factors were important here. One was the disruptive legacy of factional conflict in the 1970s. The second was the sheer size of the Tanaka faction. Even though no faction of the LDP has ever accounted for a majority of its parliamentarians, the Tanaka faction became big enough to make it difficult for its rivals to combine against it. The third reason was Tanaka's political skill and financial resources, which were inherited to a greater or lesser extent by his successors.

The dominance of this group was long-lasting, and may be said to have ended only with the choice of Mori Yoshirō as Prime Minister in 2000, whereby power moved decisively to the faction that had been led by Tanaka's great rival Fukuda in the 1970s (see Chapters 5 and 6). In October 1983 the Tokyo District Court finally handed down its verdict on the Lockheed case. Tanaka was fined 500 million yen and sentenced to four years in prison, though he appealed and the appeal was still proceeding when he suffered a severe stroke in 1986. It seems extraordinary that he could continue to exert crucial political influence within the LDP despite the Lockheed verdict. In part this reflects the Japanese political dynamic of personal loyalty to a paternalistic leader able and willing to reward his followers. It also resulted from the unusually charismatic and inspirational character of Tanaka himself.

With Tanaka's support, Nakasone Yasuhiro succeeded Suzuki as Prime Minister in November 1982. During his five-year tenure of office he favoured a presidential style of government – unusual in Japan – and launched a number of major policy initiatives, not all of them successful. He was widely regarded as a nationalist, who manoeuvred outside the LDP mainstream, but as Prime Minister he applied his considerable charisma to political advantage. His most important policy initiatives concerned privatization, defence, trade relations with the United States, taxation and education.

In seeking to privatize, Nakasone was influenced by the fashion for the small state and market liberalism that had emerged in the US, the UK and elsewhere during the 1980s. Most importantly, he privatized the Japan National Railways (JNR, *Kokutetsu*). His purpose here was partly to tackle a staggering deficit that the JNR had accumulated, and partly to smash the National Railwaymen's Union (NRU, *Kokurō*), replacing confrontational with cooperative unionism. The JNR was divided into six regional (and one freight) companies, the union was split, and many militants lost their jobs or were redeployed.

Nippon Telegraph and Telephone (NTT, *Nippon denshin denwa*) was privatized rather differently, though with similar intent. It was transformed into a single joint stock corporation, and the element of competition remained strictly limited. The NTT union, the Japan Telecommunication Workers Union (JTWU, *Zendentsū*), fared much better than the NRU because under the able leadership of Yamagishi Akira it cooperated with the changes proposed.[62]

On defence, Nakasone sought to push back the limits of what was permitted. True to his nationalist belief system, he spoke of 'settling accounts with the post-war period' (*sengo jidai no sōkessan*), thus signalling his dislike of much Occupation policy. He did not achieve all he desired in defence policy, since the minimal defence orthodoxy remained strong. But his efforts bore some fruit. He broke – though marginally and only for a year or two – the 1 per cent of GNP ceiling for total defence spending. He broke the ban on overseas sales of military equipment, albeit only to the extent of permitting export of military-related technology to the US. He also committed Japan to defending the straits between its main islands, and to protecting its sea-lanes. He promoted 'interoperability' between US and Japanese forces, and allowed Japanese assistance at sea for US naval vessels. He spoke openly of a 'common destiny' of Japan and the US, and the need for coordinated deterrence against the USSR. He sought to raise the Japanese profile on the global stage. On one occasion he paid an official visit to the Yasukuni Shrine in Tokyo, though he backed off subsequently in the face of protests. This was to be a far bigger issue when Koizumi led Japan between 2001 and 2006. Although actual progress in the direction he desired was modest, he set the agenda for later developments of a similar kind.

Japan–US trade relations were contentious throughout the 1980s, with a build-up of criticism across the Pacific at Japanese trade surpluses and a seemingly closed Japanese domestic market. The Plaza Accords of September 1985 meant a major revaluation of the yen, but the resultant rises in the price of Japanese exports merely stimulated greater efficiencies at home and failed to rectify the trade balance. Nakasone also commissioned the Maekawa Report (issued in April 1986) with a view to deregulating the economy and decreasing government control. But most of the report's recommendations failed to be implemented.

Nakasone sought to redress the balance between direct and indirect taxation in favour of the latter, by proposing a form of value added tax. As with Ōhira

---

[62] Mike Mochizuki, 'Public Sector Labor and Privatization', in Gary D. Allinson and Yasunori Sone (eds), *Political Dynamics in Contemporary Japan*, Ithaca, NY, and London, Cornell University Press, 1993, pp. 181–99.

previously and Takeshita in 1988–9, this proved to be an electoral hot potato, and Nakasone withdrew his proposal three months after introducing it in February 1987.

Like other conservative politicians since the Occupation, Nakasone was unhappy with the educational system and practice. He therefore set up the Ad Hoc Council on Education (*Rinkyōshin*) with a brief to look critically at the structures set up by the Occupation under American influence, and also to provide more educational choice. In the event, the Ad Hoc Council was too closely controlled by the Ministry of Education to recommend radically liberal reform, but some of Nakasone's ideas can be detected in later educational reform of the 1990s.[63]

Nakasone faced two lower house general elections as Prime Minister. In the first, held in December 1983 soon after the Tanaka verdict, the LDP fared poorly, but in those of July 1986 (held simultaneously with upper house elections) the ruling party had its best result since 1980.[64] Prior to the 1986 elections most of the NLC – part of a coalition with the LDP since 1983 – rejoined its former party, thus ending ten years of separate existence. Nakasone was at the height of his prestige, and was able to escape from the Tanaka faction's powerful influence over his government. We therefore need to explain the rapid deterioration in LDP fortunes that followed the high point reached in July 1986.

The late 1980s was a time of economic boom, with land prices rising to stratospheric levels, in part because companies were buying up urban land and using it as security for bank borrowing. Economic difficulties between Japan and the US were growing, as the Americans put pressure on Japan to open markets and threatened retaliation against Japanese products entering the US. The period saw a new sort of literature about Japan written by Americans or for the American market, claiming that Japan worked to different rules from the rest of the non-Communist world, and portraying Japan as a threat. The principal 'revisionist' authors, Clyde Prestowitz, Karel van Wolferen, James Fallows and Chalmers Johnson, in fact had divergent views and concerns, but they were united in criticizing what they saw as US complacency with regard to Japan. American official attitudes to Japan were also toughening, and when, under US pressure, Japan lifted import restrictions on beef and citrus fruit, farmers and their organizations became increasingly critical of government policies.

With Tanaka out of politics from 1986 following his stroke, Takeshita Noboru took over the bulk of the Tanaka faction, and replaced Nakasone as Prime Minister in November 1987. Takeshita was not internationally known as Nakasone had become, but he was a skilled grass-roots politician, and in command of the 'king-making' faction within the LDP. He found it difficult, however, to consolidate his power, for several reasons. Lifting of some agricultural

[63]   Leonard Schoppa, *Education Reform in Japan: A Case of Immobilist Politics*, London and New York, Routledge, 1991. For a more positive view of the long-term impact of Nakasone and the Ad Hoc Commission, see Christopher P. Hood, *Japanese Education Reform: Nakasone's Legacy*, London, Routledge, 2001.

[64]   Both were double elections, for both houses at the same time. How far this affected the result in favour of the LDP is controversial.

import restrictions was alienating the farmers. He was the third Prime Minister to attempt introduction of a value-added tax, and though he finally succeeded, with a 3 per cent consumption tax (*shōhizei*) coming into effect in April 1989, it aroused determined opposition from housewives, small businessmen and others. In addition, the government became mired in corruption scandals, the most notorious of which, the Recruit scandal, implicated many politicians across the political spectrum.[65]

The political opposition, meanwhile, was showing signs of resurgence. After years of electoral stagnation and ideological complacency, the JSP, under its Chairman Ishibashi Masashi, revised its 1964, Marxist-influenced, platform, issuing a new platform approved in January 1986. The party was nevertheless defeated in the July double elections of the same year, and Ishibashi took responsibility for the defeat and resigned. In his stead the JSP elected Doi Takako, the first woman in Japanese history to head a political party. Despite lack of experience, she established a rapport with sections of the electorate that did not normally vote Socialist. In 1988–9 she succeeded beyond all expectation in exploiting the boiling discontent over loss of agricultural protection, the introduction of consumption tax, the Recruit and other scandals, and skyrocketing land prices. In an appeal to the female vote, Ms Doi endorsed numbers of women candidates for elections.

In April 1989 Takeshita, by now desperately unpopular, resigned as Prime Minister. His hapless successor, Uno Sōsuke, was soon implicated in a sex scandal. Elections for half the seats in the fixed-term House of Councillors were held in July 1989, and the LDP suffered a major reverse. Since only half the seats were contested, the LDP did not lose its overall majority, but the JSP amazingly polled more votes than the ruling party in the national constituency, elected by proportional representation.[66]

Uno resigned after the elections, and was replaced by Kaifu Toshiki, one of the few Liberal Democrats not implicated in the Recruit scandal. It may not have been apparent at the time, but an era of economic growth and relative political stability was coming to an end. What was to replace it is discussed in Chapter 5.

[65]   The Recruit company, on floating a subsidiary, Recruit Cosmos, distributed unlisted shares in the new company to politicians and others, who would make a killing once the shares were listed at the stock exchange.
[66]   In 26 constituencies that elected one member in each three-yearly election, the LDP held 24 before the elections and only 3 following them. The JSP won 12 and the *Rengō* labour federation a further 11.

Chapter 5 | One Step Forward and One Step Back: Attempting Political Reform in the 1990s

Eric Hobsbawm's creative idea of the 'short' twentieth century, lasting from 1914 (the outbreak of the First World War) to 1989 (the ending of the Cold War) might in a sense be applied also to Japan, even though many aspects of the Japanese political system continued as before.[1] For Japan, 1989 was a momentous year for leadership transition, in a symbolic as well as a real sense. If 1978 was for the Catholic Church the year of the three popes, 1989 was for Japan the year of the two emperors and the three prime ministers. The *Shōwa Tennō* (best known outside Japan as Hirohito) died on 7 January 1989.[2] Even though he had no political power, his death was highly symbolic in a nation most of whose people had known no other *Tennō* in their lives. Having been *Tennō* since 1926, he embodied so much of Japan's modern history that his passing was seen by

---

[1] Eric Hobsbawm, *The Age of Extremes: The Short Twentieth Century*, London, Michael Joseph, 1994.

[2] Customs relating to the naming of Japanese emperors often cause confusion among non-Japanese. Even though the *Shōwa Tennō* bore the name 'Hirohito' and his son, the current *Tennō*, bears the name 'Akihito', these names are seldom used in ordinary discourse in Japan. The normal way of referring to a current *Tennō* is *Tennō heika* (roughly translated as 'His Majesty the Emperor'), though *kinjō heika* ('the current emperor') may also be used. Attached to the reign of each *Tennō* is an 'era name' (*gengo*), and the counting of years according to era name became official in 1978 following a referendum. Thus 1985 was 'Shōwa 60' since the *Shōwa Tennō* came to the throne in 1926 (Shōwa 1) and his reign was given the era name 'Shōwa' (enlightened peace). And 2005 was 'Heisei 17', since the current *Tennō* came to the throne on the death of his father with the era name 'Heisei'. A *Tennō* is only referred to by his era name after his death. Interestingly, the first week of 1989 was 'Shōwa 64' and the rest of the year was 'Heisei 1' (*Heisei gannen*), since the *Shōwa Tennō* died on 7 January. It is said that in choosing a new era name, any name beginning with 'S' had to be avoided, because many computers coded 1985, for instance, as 'S60'.

many as a historic turning point. He was, of course, a highly controversial figure, as much within Japan as abroad,[3] despite official efforts to play down the fact.

In his inauguration speech, the new *Tennō*, aged 55 at the time of his accession, used everyday expressions rather than archaic court language. He addressed his audience as *minasan* (literally 'everybody', but perhaps best translated as 'Ladies and Gentlemen'), and boldly declared that he supported the post-war Constitution, 'the only one he had ever known'.[4]

The three prime ministers who presided in quick succession during 1989 were, as we have seen, Takeshita, Uno and Kaifu. The third of these, Kaifu, would not normally have been seen as a possible leader,[5] but after the Recruit scandal he had the supreme advantage of being clean. He was a member of the small Kōmoto (formerly Miki) faction and had some ministerial experience (notably as Education Minister), but his power base within the LDP was weak. Even so, he could survive so long as he retained the support of the Takeshita (formerly Tanaka) faction.

Kaifu, who included two women in his first Cabinet to counter Ms Doi's appeal to women, faced general elections for the House of Representatives on 18 February 1990. The LDP was returned with a reduced, but still comfortable, majority of 275 out of 512 seats, and the Socialists, though they could not match their spectacular performance in the upper house elections seven months earlier, won 136 seats as against 83 at dissolution.[6] Fifty-six JSP 'new faces' were elected, rejuvenating a party that had been dominated by older entrenched members. Seven of 12 women elected belonged to the JSP.

Beginning in August 1990, the world faced its first international crisis of the post-Cold War world, namely the situation following Iraq's invasion of Kuwait. For Japan, this created particular difficulties, including the peace clause of the Constitution, political fluidity and the recent loss by the LDP of its upper house majority.

The Kaifu government took a number of measures against Iraq, but failed in its attempts to pass legislation permitting the despatch of what was termed a 'peace cooperation corps' to participate in the expeditionary force tasked to remove Saddam Hussein's forces from Iraq. Instead, Japan provided 13 billion US dollars towards the costs of the expedition (a substantial proportion of the total cost), but in several successive commitments, and with implied reluctance.

[3]   Stephen Large, *Emperor Hirohito and Shōwa Japan; A Political Biography*, London and New York, Routledge, 1992.

[4]   The *Tennō* does not express formal opinions on political subjects. Nevertheless, reports of informal conversations suggest a man strongly committed to democratic values and unwilling to be seen to support nationalist positions. For instance, he does not visit the Yasukuni Shrine, and was reported in 2004 as opposing the coercion of school authorities to hoist the national flag and have pupils sing the national anthem: *Asia Times Online*, 6 November 2004.

[5]   In this his situation was similar to that of Suzuki nearly a decade earlier. In both cases exceptional circumstances required a leader from outside the normal pool of party presidential aspirants.

[6]   They won 24.4% of the total vote, as against 17.2% in 1986.

The UN Peace Force Cooperation Bill did not receive sufficient parliamentary support – even for a force that would have engaged in civilian, not military, activity – and on 9 November 1990 the government withdrew it. Once war broke out in January 1991, Japan pledged 9 billion US dollars to add to the 4 billion already given for the expeditionary force. But the bill to approve this funding needed to pass both houses of Parliament, and the LDP now lacked a majority in the House of Councillors. Here the CGP (Kōmeitō) was a major obstacle, since its votes were essential to enable the bill to pass. The government therefore entered into negotiations with that party over how to release this enormous amount of money.[7]

The ways in which the Kaifu government attempted to deal with problems posed for it by the Gulf crisis and war had crucial short-term and medium-term effects on the development of political change in the 1990s.[8]

First, the loss by the LDP of its majority in the House of Councillors meant that any LDP government had to negotiate with opposition parties (mainly the smaller ones) in that house.[9] Without a majority in the upper house, an LDP government lacking a two-thirds majority in the House of Representatives can pass its bills into law (apart from the budget and treaties) only if it can persuade other parties to join it in support of its legislation and thus create a composite majority.

From the time of the Gulf crisis negotiations, however, the CGP (and also the DSP, though with some differences of emphasis) began to come round to the government's position. A key actor in this process was Ozawa Ichirō, LDP Secretary-General during the Kaifu administration, who was to become a key figure in the reformist politics of the 1990s. In the course of his negotiations with the CGP, he became aware that that party was unhappy with the performance of Suzuki Shunichi, Governor of Tokyo Prefecture since 1979, who had been elected for three terms with LDP and CGP support. On Ozawa's initiative, therefore, the LDP transferred its support to another candidate in the elections scheduled for 7 April 1991. The octogenarian Suzuki, however, refused to withdraw, stood as an Independent, and won easily against his LDP-backed rival, and all other candidates. Ozawa took responsibility for this failure by resigning as LDP Secretary-General, but he had secured CGP support for the 9-billion-dollar contribution to driving Iraqi forces out of Kuwait,[10] and forged links with the CGP that would become of great future importance.

---

[7]   Essentially, the government proposed raising taxation, whereas the CGP wanted reductions in official expenditure.

[8]   For a much more extensive account of how the crisis was handled, see the third edition of the present book: J. A. A. Stockwin, *Governing Japan: Divided Politics in a Major Economy*, Oxford and Malden, MA, Blackwell, 3rd edn, 1999, pp. 72–9.

[9]   Between 1989 and 2007 the LDP never regained an overall majority in the House of Councillors.

[10]   Financial contributions alone, however large, did not guarantee gratitude. Later in 1991 the Kuwaiti government publicly thanked the states that had contributed to the military operation that had driven out Saddam Hussein's forces. Japan was pointedly omitted from this list.

Second, the Gulf crisis dealt a serious blow to the popularity of the JSP, which had been riding so high from 1989. The hard line taken by the Socialists against any Japanese participation in, or contribution to, peacekeeping activities proved unpopular with the electorate. Doi Takako saw her popularity plummet, and the candidate the party picked to contest the Tokyo governorship won a mere 7 per cent of the vote.

The effects of the Gulf crisis on Japanese politics show multiple contradictions. The Kaifu government failed in its attempts to provide a physical (as distinct from financial) contribution to the international force. But at the same time it went some way towards nullifying the LDP loss of its House of Councillors majority by bringing the CGP (and DSP) rather provisionally into the camp of its allies. This alliance, however, had sown the seeds of the LDP divisions which led to its downfall in August 1993, when it was to lose office to a multi-party coalition. In retrospect it is evident that LDP dominance had always relied on exclusivity, and when external parties had to be given a say in policy, the structure risked becoming fragile and even collapsing.[11]

The JSP resurgence from 1989 with Doi Takako as leader implied that the system was moving away from single-party dominance, but JSP credibility had been badly damaged by its negative attitudes in the Gulf crisis. Even so, the ending of the Cold War, and the Gulf crisis that followed it so closely, created a situation in which the JSP and the newly reorganized labour union movement,[12] as well as the Buddhist-based CGP, were potential allies in a possible coalition government supplanting the LDP. There is a further irony in respect of the JSP, namely that though it entered government in 1993 and remained part of a government coalition for all but nine weeks of the period August 1993 to October 1996 (even providing the Prime Minister for more than 18 months of that period),[13] yet the ultimate result of its excursion into government was to be its virtual collapse.

In November 1991 Kaifu resigned as Prime Minister. Kaifu had proposed reform of the lower house electoral system away from one based on multi-member constituencies to one mixing single-member constituencies and seats elected by proportional representation. The proposed reform was fairly similar to that eventually put in place in 1994, and, like the latter, was designed to root out corruption, correct malapportionment of votes and move from personality voting to voting on the basis of party and policy. But in 1991 Kaifu's proposals were used as an excuse to get rid of him; he had a weak power base and had always been regarded as merely a stopgap leader by those who had put him there in the first place to divert attention from the Recruit scandal.

The new Prime Minister was Miyazawa Kiichi, leader of the faction that had produced the prime ministers Ikeda, Ōhira and Suzuki, a former Ministry of

---

[11]   One is reminded of the 1850s and 1860s, when the Shogunate accorded an advisory role to certain *han* lords, only to find its own authority eroded by this decision to consult.

[12]   A new union federation, *Rengō*, replaced both *Sōhyō* and *Dōmei* at the end of the 1980s.

[13]   Those nine weeks ran from April to June 1994, the period of the Hata government.

Finance official, one of the few politicians at the time with excellent English fluency and in policy terms a centrist. It is ironic that such a man should have presided over the downfall of the LDP, after nearly thirty-eight years in office, in August 1993.

The Miyazawa government achieved one important thing, namely the passage through Parliament of the Peace Keeping Operations (PKO) bill in July 1992. Even though it was limited in scope, and fell far short of providing for unqualified participation by Japan in UN peacekeeping missions, it marks a crucial turning point in the development of Japanese foreign policies towards greater international engagement (see Chapter 12). Where Kaifu had failed, Miyazawa succeeded because by mid-1992 the CGP and DSP had abandoned their objections to any participation in UN peacekeeping missions, and were prepared to vote for the bill. They had changed course because public opinion, reacting to international criticism of Japanese passivity, had swung round in favour of participation in such missions.[14]

By far the most important party political event to occur in 1992 was the split in the hitherto dominant Takeshita faction of the LDP. A precipitating factor was the disgrace of the faction's leader, Kanemaru Shin. The most important of several financial scandals aired in the press during the year was that involving a road delivery company called Sagawa Kyūbin. In September Kanemaru admitted breaking the Political Contributions Control Law (*seiji shikin kisei hō*) and paid a 200,000-yen fine.[15] Previously the police had raided his house and discovered a huge cache of money and gold bars. The derisory value of the fine evoked a public outcry. Kanemaru resigned all his political offices, including leadership of the Takeshita faction, and resigned his parliamentary seat in October. In November Takeshita himself was called upon to testify before Parliament in relation to a case whereby in 1987 he had allegedly had contacts with a gangster organization (*bōryokudan*). These cases shook the faction to its core, and brought into relief existing strains within it over its future leadership. In December, Hata Tsutomu and Ozawa set up a breakaway group, known as Reform Forum 21. About half the Takeshita faction joined this group and the rest coalesced around a more orthodox leader, Obuchi Keizō.

Two further events occurred during 1992 that were to feed into the flood tide of change that came rushing in during the summer of the following year. The first was the foundation of a completely new party (as distinct from parties formed by splinter groups from existing parties), called the Japan New Party (JNP, *Nihon Shintō*).[16] Its founder was Hosokawa Morihiro, who was to become

---

[14]   A poll in November 1990, when Kaifu's bill was before Parliament, asked: 'Do you support overseas despatch of a basically civilian peace cooperation organization?' 21% of respondents supported and 58% opposed: *Asahi Shinbun*, 6 November 1990. In September 1992, following the passage of the PKO bill and when Japan was sending peacekeeping troops to Cambodia, a further poll asked: 'Do you support the despatch of Self-Defence Forces to the PKO in Cambodia?' 52% supported and 36% opposed. Of those who supported, 32% gave as the main reason 'to fulfil our responsibility to international society'. *Asahi Nenkan*, 1993, p. 205.

[15]   Approximately US$2,000.

[16]   The name has nothing to do with the religion *Shintō*, which is written with quite different characters meaning 'way of the gods'.

one of the most significant politicians of the 1990s. Hosokawa, who some years previously had been an LDP member of the House of Councillors, was currently Governor of Kumamoto Prefecture in Kyūshū. His maternal grandfather was Prince Konoe Fumimaro, Prime Minister shortly before the Asia–Pacific war, and even though Japan no longer had an aristocracy, Hosokawa's aristocratic background gave him a certain cachet. The newly formed JNP won four seats in the House of Councillors elections held in July 1992.

The second development was the emergence of a progressive social democratic movement grouped loosely around Eda Satsuki of the Social Democratic League (SDL, *Shaminren*) and a number of newly elected JSP members. This group became a force on the moderate left favourable to the kinds of reforms that came on to the agenda with the formation of a new government in August 1993.[17]

Changes in the domestic economy and in international politics formed an unsettling, but opportunity-creating, backdrop to reform.

In the late 1980s economic boom conditions led to asset inflation, severe trade frictions with the US, and unwise investment decisions by banks, funds and companies. In 1991 the 'bubble economy' collapsed and the economy entered into a period of prolonged stagnation. This led to calls for painful economic and institutional adjustment. Allegations of corruption among politicians, businessmen and, increasingly, public servants filled the mass media.

The period 1989–91 saw the most far-reaching changes in international politics since the late 1940s. For Asian countries the changes were less profound than for Europe or North America (see Chapter 12), but for Japan the removal of the Soviet threat to its north created a situation with altered parameters. This was important for political change in one crucial respect: the domestic political divide that had closely mirrored themes from the Cold War was coming to an end (though it had not completely ended by 1993), and this permitted the shaping of new forms of political alliance. There was, in particular, now much less inhibition about having moderate labour unions as part of the ruling structure.

The immediate issue that brought about the downfall of the LDP was electoral law reform. The Miyazawa government had proposed a lower house electoral system based entirely on single-member constituencies, with candidates elected by the first-past-the-post system. The JSP and CGP countered with a proposal close to the German system, based largely on proportional representation. Compromise proved impossible, so in June 1993 the government shelved its proposal.

This opened the flood gates. All the non-Communist opposition parties combined to put forward a no-confidence motion in the Miyazawa government, and this was voted on in the lower house on 18 June. Miyazawa's attempts to win over Reform Forum 21 (the Hata–Ozawa group) failed, and thirty-nine LDP members, including thirty-four from this group, voted in favour of the motion, while a further sixteen absented themselves from the voting.[18] The government had no choice but to dissolve Parliament. Over the following few days, not one, but two groups of LDP parliamentarians formed new parties outside the LDP.

[17] See J. A. A. Stockwin, 'From JSP to SDPJ: The New Wave Society and the "New" *Nihon Shakaitō*', *Japan Forum*, vol. 3, no. 2 (October 1991), pp. 287–300.
[18] *Asahi Nenkan*, 1994, p. 108.

On 21 June Takemura Masayoshi, another former prefectural governor, formed a small party called the New Party Harbinger (NPH, *Shintō Sakigake*), which inclined towards the centre-left on a number of policy issues. The second party, called the Japan Renewal Party (JRP, *Shinseitō*) was formed on the 23rd by the Hata–Ozawa group itself, consisting of forty-four former LDP parliamentarians (from both houses). In these confused circumstances a general election for the House of Representatives was held on 18 July 1993, and the LDP, for the first time since it was founded in 1955, found itself well short of a majority.[19]

The Miyazawa government had evidently been complacent, assuming that, even if there were defections, the defectors could be persuaded to enter a coalition government in which the LDP would be the leading player. But all the LDP's best efforts to form a coalition in the days following the election were frustrated by the adroitness with which the other non-Communist parties managed to put together a coalition government of their own.

On 9 August 1993 a new eight-party coalition government was formed (see Table 5.1), excluding the Communists and the LDP, who found themselves strange companions in opposition. The period of uninterrupted LDP rule, nearly thirty-eight years in duration, was at an end. Hosokawa Morihiro was the new Prime Minister, having been elected to the House of Representatives only the previous month along with thirty-four other members of the JNP. A new start seemed possible for the political system, which had become so discredited by the endless stream of corruption allegations over the preceding years.

The JSP became the largest party in the coalition government, but it had lost nearly half its seats in the elections. It had suffered an electoral reverse far worse than that of the LDP, but by the irony of strategic numbers the JSP found itself in government for the first time in nearly forty-five years. Its period in office was not to be a happy one.

Creation of the coalition government required skill and foresight. Its principal creators were Ozawa Ichirō, Hosokawa Morihiro, Yamahana Sadao and Yamagishi Akira. Ozawa may be regarded as the most strategic thinker among them. He had a vision of reform and the political skill to fashion a new government. He was also substantially in control, as seen by the fact that his JRP took the lion's share of Cabinet positions.[20] Hosokawa was essential for the image he was able to project of a new kind of politician leading a new party formed from outside the political establishment. The JSP Chairman, Yamahana, was important in that he was committed to the idea of Socialist participation and was able to deliver on this commitment. The JSP, despite its disastrous election, was the

[19]   The LDP actually increased by one seat the total it held immediately before the election (but following the defections), lending credence to the view that it was the split in its ranks, rather than its desertion by the electorate, that brought about its downfall. Given the strength of local electoral machines, many voters seem to have continued to vote for the same candidates, whether they had remained in the LDP or had joined the JRP or NPH.

[20]   JRP members obtained the posts of Foreign Minister, Finance Minister, Minister of Agriculture, Forestry and Fisheries, Minister of International Trade and Industry, and Defence Agency Director. *Asahi Shinbun*, 22 December 1993.

Table 5.1   Composition of the Hosokawa government, August 1993

Parties	Seats	% of total vote
Government parties[a]		
Japan Socialist Party (JSP, *Nihon Shakaitō*)	70	15.4
Japan Renewal Party (JRP, *Shinseitō*)	55	10.1
Clean Government Party (CGP, *Kōmeitō*)	51	8.1
Japan New Party (JNP, *Nihon shintō*)	35	8.0
Democratic Socialist Party (DSP, *Minshatō*)	15	3.5
New Party Harbinger (NPH, *Shintō sakigake*)	13	2.6
Social Democratic League (SDL, *Shaminren*)	4	0.7
Opposition parties		
Liberal Democratic Party (LDP, *Jiyūminshutō, Jimintō*)	223	36.6
Japan Communist Party (JCP, *Nihon kyōsantō*)	15	7.7
Independents	30	6.9

[a]The eighth participant in the new government was the union-based Minkairen, with representation only in the House of Councillors.

largest party in the coalition, which could not have been formed without it. Yamagishi had created the *Rengō* union federation, whose most vital function was to unite the divided union movement. This in turn created the conditions for reconciling the JSP and the DSP – previously backers of rival union federations – and allowing them to coexist in the same coalition.

Unfortunately, both the coalition and its key leaders also had weaknesses, which were to emerge in the following months.

The Hosokawa government was well received at first, and the Prime Minister recorded an unprecedented level of support, 71 per cent, in early public opinion polls. A radical reform programme was announced, covering revamping the lower house electoral system, bringing in anti-corruption legislation, substantially deregulating industry, commerce and banking, and devolving some central government functions to local authorities. In terms publicized by Ozawa, the key government strategist in its early stages, Japan should be run by politicians responsible to the electorate rather than by unelected bureaucrats, competitive party politics (preferably with two parties alternating in office) should replace single-party dominance, and individual endeavour should be encouraged. More power should be given to local regions and local authorities, and local control by central ministries should be scaled back. The electoral system should be restructured to replace the politics of factions, money and personality voting with competition between parties over matters of policy. In foreign policy, Japan should evolve into a 'normal state' having the right and means to defend itself.[21]

---

[21]   Ichiro Ozawa, *Blueprint for a New Japan*, Tokyo, New York and London, Kodansha International, 1994.

It was not surprising, given its composition, that the government should contain diverse views on issues of reform. The JSP provoked the first crisis when, at its September Congress, its Chairman, Yamahana Sadao, was forced to assume responsibility for the poor showing of the party at the July elections by resigning his party post. He nevertheless retained his Cabinet post as minister without portfolio in charge of electoral system reform. Yamahana, broadly speaking, represented the right wing of the party. His successor, a 70-year-old politician from Kyūshū, Murayama Tomiichi, was identified with the left.

Reforming the electoral system for the House of Representatives was the one great achievement of the coalition, but it was accomplished with great difficulty and cost. Details of the reform will be left to Chapter 8, but here we shall summarize what happened in outline.

To achieve reform, it was necessary to consult the opposition LDP; but LDP views were incompatible with those widely held on the left wing of the JSP. The reform as drafted in August 1993 proposed 250 first-past-the-post single-member constituency seats and 250 seats to be filled by proportional representation. The LDP, and those on the right of the coalition, favoured the largest possible number of single-member seats, while the JSP – especially its left wing – wanted the proportional representation element to be maximized. On proposed anti-corruption legislation, those on the right of the spectrum favoured a relaxed regime, whereas the left wanted rigorous measures against 'money politics'.

In November, the Prime Minister and the newly elected LDP President, Kōno Yōhei, finalized a compromise package, based on 274 single-member seats and 226 proportional representation seats, and this passed the lower house. Two months later, however, the same package was defeated in the House of Councillors, with seventeen JSP members voting against it and three being absent. The LDP voted against, though there were five LDP votes in favour. A few days later Doi Takako, President of the lower house, negotiated a compromise proposal between Hosokawa and Kōno, based on 300 single-member and 200 proportional representation seats (the latter to be elected from eleven regional blocs).[22] The legislation passed a joint session of both houses on 29 January 1994.[23]

Other strains in the coalition appeared as well. It was widely reported that relations between Ozawa and the NPH leader and Chief Cabinet Secretary, Takemura Masayoshi, had deteriorated. In the early weeks of the coalition, the press had been reporting that Hosokawa's JNP and Takemura's NPH were so close in spirit that they might merge. But in February 1994 the Prime Minister, under pressure from the Ministry of Finance, proposed unilaterally to increase the consumption tax from 3 to 7 per cent. When Takemura objected, Hosokawa attempted unsuccessfully to remove him from his post. Hosokawa had been moving towards the Ozawa emphasis on financial reconstruction regardless of the objections of vested interests. In retrospect he saw as his greatest achievement

---

[22]   The original proposals had envisaged a single national proportional representation constituency, as in the House of Councillors.

[23]   Ironically, by helping to defeat the earlier bill in the upper house, the Socialist defectors had ensured that an even less favourable bill – from their perspective – went onto the statute books.

as Prime Minister the ending of the previous total ban on rice imports for direct consumption, as the price of signing up to the Uruguay Round of global trade liberalization. He was happy to curb the power of the agricultural lobby in favour of rational market economics.[24]

Despite these difficulties and strains, it was a great surprise when in April 1994 Hosokawa announced his resignation as Prime Minister, citing obscure corruption allegations from the past.

Though of brief duration and rather chaotic character, the Hosokawa government must be considered one of the most important administrations of recent times. Not only did its formation show that it was possible to force the LDP into opposition, but it set an agenda of reform across a range of policy areas, which no subsequent government could easily ignore. It opened up the possibility of alternative kinds of government, and thus in various ways affected and altered prevailing habits of political behaviour. It succeeded, against the odds, in rewriting the lower house electoral law, and although this did not produce the radical effects its proponents had hoped for, it shook up long-standing forms of political activity and organization. The effects of the new electoral system remain highly controversial, but it is at least arguable that it was a blow in favour of representative and responsible politics.[25]

The Hosokawa government did not live up to its initial promise, and was cut off in mid-course. Government officials, after their initial shock at finding they had to deal with a (partially) different set of politicians from those they were used to dealing with, discovered that the new, mostly inexperienced, ministers were often easier to manipulate than those from the LDP. A programme of reform also gave bureaucrats new things to administer, and since they could choose to a great extent what had to be 'deregulated', they excluded the things that were really important to them. The various parties and personalities in the government bickered extensively, especially in the later stages, but they also set an agenda for reform and embarked upon implementing it with a determination rarely seen in LDP governments.

The next government was led by the JNP leader, Hata Tsutomu. It was supposed to consist of the same parties that formed the Hosokawa administration, but the JSP quickly pulled out and the NPH refused to co-operate. The JSP withdrew because Ozawa had devised a scheme to unify all the parties of the coalition, *except the Socialists*, into a single party to be called Renovation (*Kaishin*). When the scheme became public knowledge, the recently elected JSP Chairman, Murayama, led his party out of the coalition, thus depriving the Hata government of a parliamentary majority.

The government was kept in existence in order to pass the budget, and once the budget was passed, the coalition leaders attempted to tempt back the two parties that had defected, so as to restore the government's majority. This effort was in vain, however, since the two parties were simultaneously talking with the LDP leaders, and on 29 June a new government was announced, combining the

---

[24]   Interview, 27 September 1995.
[25]   The opposite argument has some weight also (see Chapter 8).

LDP, the JSP and the NPH. Although the LDP was by far the largest party in the new coalition, the JSP Chairman, Murayama, became Prime Minister and the NPH leader, Takemura, became Finance Minister.

The arrangement caused astonishment for a number of reasons. First of all, Japan found itself with a Socialist Prime Minister for the first time since the resignation of Katayama Tetsu in 1948, nearly 45 years earlier. Second, the new Prime Minister was from the left wing of his party, and had been little known to the public before becoming JSP Chairman a mere nine months before. Surprising as this was, however, it could easily be explained as part of the price exacted by the Socialists for allowing the Liberal Democrats back into office. Much more surprising was the fact that the LDP and JSP, sworn political enemies for so many years and apparently far apart in their political ideologies, were now prepared to run a government together. Since the LDP–JSP–NPH coalition government was to prove more durable than most had expected, and indeed turned out to be the ruling force in Japan throughout the mid-1990s, we need to dwell a little on the rationale for its formation.

From an LDP point of view, deprivation of office had been an extraordinary shock. Since the 1950s the party had woven itself into the fabric of both legislation and administration so seamlessly that to be in opposition was hard to tolerate. The party's appeal had rested heavily on being able to convince a rather parochial electorate that it was more advantageous to support a party that was at the centre of government, and could therefore deliver material benefits, than to support opposition parties that were only capable of delivering empty rhetoric. To be out of office for a long time, therefore, risked disaster at the polls. Moreover, if the forces that had constituted the Hosokawa and Hata governments had been able to consolidate themselves in office, the LDP might have suffered additional defections as some of its parliamentarians repositioned themselves to 'get with the strength', weakening the party yet further.[26]

The three parties together had sufficient numbers for a comfortable majority in both houses, and since the Cold War had ended the ideological distance between the LDP and JSP was no longer so acute (though important differences of policy and emphasis remained). Moreover, some LDP strategists seem to have believed that participation in a coalition with the LDP would be the kiss of death for the JSP.[27] In this they would be proved uncannily perceptive.

The carrot dangled by LDP negotiators before the eyes of JSP leaders was the offer of the post of Prime Minister.[28] The Socialists also received other more or

---

[26]   The reverse process may be observed following the general elections of October 1996 and in the early months of 1997, when opposition parties were having difficulty stopping their members defecting to a revived LDP, and indeed some of the smaller opposition parties were tempted to move right into the LDP's orbit. See *Asahi Shinbun*, 8 February 1997.

[27]   For instance, the former Prime Minister, Takeshita Noboru, was quoted as saying: 'We have swallowed the Socialists and we have them in our stomach. All that remains is for the gastric juices to digest them.' *Tokyo Insideline*, no. 30, 30 July 1994, p. 1.

[28]   Years later, Ozawa mused that he should have made the same offer to the Socialists: Oka Takashi, private communication.

less significant positions in Cabinet and the LDP organization.[29] In policy terms, the new coalition made more sense than was immediately apparent. During the Hosokawa government the JSP (especially its left-wing factions) had become seriously disillusioned with the reformist instincts of Ozawa, and indeed of Hosokawa himself, given that these politicians gave first priority to deregulation and to reducing the influence of vested interests. The strongest traditional base of support for the JSP had always lain in the labour movement, and particularly in those unions whose membership was in the public sector. The old conservative attitudes of excluding labour involvement in decision-making had become to an extent eroded with the formation of the *Rengō* union federation at the beginning of the decade, so it was less surprising to find the Socialists cooperating with the Liberal Democrats than it would have been a few years earlier.[30]

Murayama, as Prime Minister, had a number of modest legislative successes.[31] But he also changed some of the fundamentals of JSP policy. In August 1994 he announced that the party would no longer regard the Self-Defence Forces as unconstitutional, that it would cease to oppose the Japan–US Mutual Security Treaty, and that it would no longer campaign against the compulsory raising of the rising sun flag and singing of the national anthem, *Kimigayo*, in schools.[32] These new policies were endorsed by majority vote at a JSP Congress in September, after some fierce debate. The fact that the policies were proposed by the leader of the party's left wing no doubt helped their acceptance among those elements in the party most likely to have opposed such tampering with time-honoured policy. Even so, strains within the party were extreme during this period and, as we shall see, it very nearly split apart in January 1995.

After the fall of the minority Hata government in June, most of its constituent parties negotiated to form a single large party in opposition to the Murayama government. The middle months of 1994 witnessed a kaleidoscopic scene of defections from parties (especially the LDP), the formation of small splinter parties, party amalgamations and failed attempts at amalgamation. In December 1994 a major new party was born, the New Frontier Party (NFP, *Shinshintō*).[33] Into it

[29]   In the Murayama Cabinet, the LDP had 13 positions, the JSP five and the NPH two. This more or less reflected the balance of strength between the three parties.
[30]   There were also similarities between the JSP and the NPH in respect of their basic policy attitudes at this time, even though a plan to unite the two parties was later to prove elusive.
[31]   For instance, a bill to assist surviving victims of the atomic bombings of Hiroshima and Nagasaki became law in December 1994, reflecting elements on the JSP agenda.
[32]   The flag and anthem issues were controversial because of the association of both with pre-1945 nationalism and the emperor system, as well as symbolizing attempts by the Ministry of Education, allied with right-wing LDP parliamentarians, to suppress 'progressive' tendencies in education. The *kimi* in *Kimigayo* is commonly understood to refer to the *Tennō*, and the anthem as a whole to constitute an invocation of the *Tennō*.
[33]   An accurate English translation would be 'New Progress Party', but 'New Frontier Party' was chosen in conscious echo of US President Kennedy's New Frontier. For several months before its launch the embryo party was known as the 'New, New Party'. In Japanese this was also *Shinshintō*, since the character for 'new' and the character for 'progress' are both pronounced '*shin*', though they are written differently.

were merged the Democratic Socialist Party (*Minshatō*), which split from the JSP in 1960, the Clean Government Party (*Kōmeitō*), founded in 1964,[34] Hosokawa's Japan New Party (*Nihon shintō*), founded in 1992, Ozawa's Japan Renewal Party (*Shinseitō*), which split from the LDP in 1993, and the Liberal Reform League (*Jiyū kaikaku rengō*), formed late in 1994 by the former Prime Minister Kaifu Toshiki and a handful of defectors from the LDP. Kaifu was elected head of the New Frontier Party by a wide margin. At the time of its foundation it had 178 members in the House of Representatives and 36 members in the House of Councillors. It was thus much the largest opposition party, but somewhat smaller than the LDP.

Meanwhile, on the government side, the Prime Minister was facing a crisis within his own party. The former JSP Chairman, Yamahana, representing right-of-centre opinion in the party, was preparing to lead a major defection in January 1995. But on 17 January, the very day when Yamahana's new party was due to be launched, a major earthquake hit Osaka, Awaji island and, most severely, the city of Kōbe. Enormous damage was caused, and over 6,000 people were killed. The new party launch was put on hold and in effect, collapsed.

The political impact was complex. On the one hand, the threatened split in Murayama's party was averted. On the other hand, the rescue effort in and around Kōbe was slow and badly coordinated, reflecting poorly on central government. The issue became linked with that of political and administrative reform. Many critics argued that political checks and balances, combined with vertically articulated administrative structures having poor horizontal coordination, had produced a system that badly needed restructuring. The Murayama government became the butt of criticism for its handling of the crisis, though the problem lay in long-established administrative structures and practices rather than in the shortcomings of a particular government.[35]

There was a further impact of the earthquake with long-term consequences. In the absence of a prompt and effective official rescue effort, many individuals and voluntary groups went to the stricken area to do what they could. This became the germ of a newly emergent voluntary sector in a society that had long lacked the institutions and habits of mind of civil society independent of government (see Chapter 11).[36]

Some weeks later another disaster occurred, this time man-made, not in a provincial city but in the central government district of Tokyo. On 20 March several individuals planted canisters containing the highly toxic gas sarin in underground railway stations and trains. Over 5,000 victims fell ill and at least ten died. Suspicion quickly fell on a religious sect called *Aum Shinrikyō* ('Supreme Truth Religion'),[37] led by a nearly blind guru who had adopted the name Asahara

---

[34]   Before merging into the NFP, the CGP decided to split its organization, so that its local branches and some of its upper house members would remain independent, while lower house parliamentarians would enter the new party. This decision reflected the complex relationship between the CGP and the *Sōka Gakkai* religion.

[35]   It was rumoured that the Prime Minister did not know about the earthquake until he learned about it from the morning television news.

[36]   See Frank J. Schwartz and Susan J. Pharr (eds), *The State of Civil Society in Japan*, Cambridge and New York, Cambridge University Press, 2003.

[37]   *Aum* is a Tibetan word having mystical significance. The Japanese pronunciation is *ōmu*.

Shōkō. The sect had its headquarters on the lower slopes of Mount Fuji, where, as investigations showed, they had been manufacturing toxic chemicals and engaging in various kinds of criminal activity, including kidnapping and murder.[38]

The affair became a media sensation, especially when it became clear that some of the sect's leading members were highly educated, having science degrees from leading universities. It brought into the arena of debate the relationship between politics and religion (see Chapter 11). Evidence emerged that the sarin gas attack might have been part of a bizarre scheme to mount a *coup d'état*.

The *Aum* affair also served to highlight how fundamental religion had become in the struggle for political power between the parties. In the July 1995 regular elections for the House of Councillors the opposition NFP won nineteen more seats than at the elections three years before. Central to the electoral strategy of the NFP was the impressive electoral organization developed by the former Clean Government Party, part, though not all of which had been absorbed into the new party, as we have seen. The vast majority of those who had voted for the CGP (and now voted for the NFP) were members of the *Sōka Gakkai* sect, Japan's largest 'new religion'. These people were much more likely to vote than the general population. It followed that a low general turnout (44.52 per cent in the 1995 upper house elections) favoured the NFP, for whose candidates the *Sōka Gakkai* directed its members to vote.[39] In October 1995 the LDP sought parliamentary approval for a Religious Corporate Body Law (*shūkyō hōjin hō*). Although precipitated by the *Aum* crisis, it seems that the LDP was seeking to weaken the *Sōka Gakkai*, whose political effectiveness it recognized as a challenge.[40]

An important aim of the Prime Minister and his party in the early months of 1995 was to persuade Parliament to pass a resolution expressing regret and apology for Japan's actions during the war. After much negotiation, the three parties constituting the coalition government agreed to a compromise form of wording in which the Liberal Democrats made concessions to the JSP position. The resolution, passed by Parliament on 9 June, fell well short of what many critics of Japan's war record would have liked, but the resolution had a certain symbolic force. This, however, was weakened by the fact that the NFP members, disagreeing with its wording, absented themselves *en bloc* from the vote. On 15 August (the fiftieth anniversary of the end of the war), the Prime Minister

---

[38] See Ian Reader, *Religious Violence in Contemporary Japan: The Case of Aum Shinrikyō*, Richmond, Surrey, Curzon Press, 2000. The renowned novelist Murakami Haruki carried out a fascinating series of interviews with victims of the Tokyo underground poisoning, published as Haruki Murakami, *Underground: The Tokyo Gas Attack and the Japanese Psyche*, London, Harvill Press, 2000.

[39] It seems that Ozawa's links with the CGP, which went back at least to the Tokyo governorship election campaign of 1991, were forged in the full understanding of the electoral potential that lay in this factor.

[40] The LDP attempted to have Ikeda Daisaku, revered head of the *Sōka Gakkai*, testify to Parliament. This was fiercely resisted by the NFP, and a lesser official was brought in to testify instead. A watered-down compromise bill was eventually passed.

made an official statement including the following words: '[Japan] brought great damage and suffering on the peoples of many nations, and particularly on the nations of Asia, by its colonialism and aggression'.[41]

A related issue which came to the fore at this period was that of former 'comfort women' (*ianfu*), from Korea and other (mainly Asian) nations, who had been forced to serve as prostitutes for the Japanese armed forces during the war. As more and more evidence emerged of how widespread and degrading this practice had been, Japanese governments had resisted demands for an apology and compensation to the women who still survived, maintaining that the issue of compensation had been settled in earlier treaties between Japan and other Asian states. The Murayama government made limited moves to recognize this issue, but it remained controversial and the question of compensation was particularly thorny.

In the later months of 1995 the two largest parties both changed their leaders. In September Kōno Yōhei, who had become LDP President after the collapse of the Miyazawa government in 1993, withdrew from the leadership contest after it became clear that a rival candidate, Hashimoto Ryūtarō, would beat him. Kōno was thus the only LDP President since the party's foundation in 1955 not to become Prime Minister. Hashimoto, widely seen as a more traditional conservative than the centrist Kōno, easily fought off a challenge from the much younger Koizumi Junichirō, a 'Thatcherite' radical whose chance would eventually come five and a half years later. And then in December the NFP held its leadership election, with the election thrown open to any member of the general public willing to pay 1,000 yen for the privilege of participating. As a result, Ozawa polled about twice as many votes as his opponent, the former Prime Minister Hata Tsutomu, and was duly elected.

Early in January 1996, Murayama stepped down as Prime Minister and was replaced by Hashimoto. Now both the government and the principal opposition party were led by their central strategists of the two contending teams, rather than by leaders to some extent peripheral in each case.

Whereas 1995 had seen electoral advances by the NFP, its challenge to the LDP lost momentum in 1996, and there were signs that the coalition of parties and disparate leaders that it contained was beginning to unravel. Politics in the early part of the year were dominated by a government plan to rescue a number of housing loan companies (the *jūsen*), which were in effect bankrupt because of non-performing loans negotiated during the boom period of the 1980s and early 1990s . This in turn threatened the viability of the major banks to which they were indebted. The government wished to use taxpayers' money to rescue them, but this met with fierce criticism. Nevertheless, when the NFP staged a lengthy sit-in in Parliament so as to block the legislation, this caused an adverse reaction. Moreover, the *Sōka Gakkai* gave indications that it might not support NFP candidates at the next lower house elections.

---

[41]   The Japanese text of the June resolution is given in *Asahi Shinbun*, 10 June 1995. The text of Murayama's 15 August speech is given the paper's evening edition of 15 August 1995.

Meanwhile, attempts continued to create a viable third force on the moderate left. These resulted in the formation of the Democratic Party (of Japan) (DPJ, *Minshutō*), in September 1996. The JSP, which had been declining electorally since the early 1990s, split shortly before the DPJ was formed, and its right-of-centre factions joined the new party. In January 1996 the JSP had changed its name to Social Democratic Party (SDP, *Shakai minshutō* or *Shamintō*). Other participants came from the NPH, NFP and elsewhere. This was a period of great fluidity in party affiliation, and there is even a case of a parliamentarian who changed party seven times in the 1990s.[42]

Prominent among the DPJ leaders were the two Hatoyama brothers, Yukio and Kunio, grandsons of Hatoyama Ichirō, Prime Minister 1954–6, and Kan Naoto, a moderate social democrat from Tokyo. Kan (then a member of the NPH) was Minister of Health and Welfare in the first Hashimoto Cabinet early in 1996. In this capacity he had dramatically broken with precedent by apologizing (on his knees) to the families of haemophiliacs made ill by blood transfusions contaminated with HIV during the 1980s. Officials of his ministry stood accused of having knowingly supplied contaminated blood, but ministers did not normally apologize on behalf of their ministries. This act made Kan popular and gave him a high profile, which also rubbed off on to the image of the new party. These two issues – the *jūsen* bankruptcies and the contaminated blood scandal – symbolized the spread of corruption into the bureaucracy, though there is some question how far this was perception and how far reality. Government officials, in any case, now felt they were under redoubled attack from political reformers.

On 20 October 1996 the first general elections to the House of Representatives were held under the new system (see Chapter 8). The LDP gained nearly 30 seats, but still fell short of a majority in its own right; the NFP fell slightly short of its pre-election total; the SDP (formerly JSP), now once again chaired by Doi Takako, suffered its worst ever defeat; and the NPH was almost wiped out. The Japan Communist Party, which had refused to join any political grouping or coalition, came close to doubling its representation. Hashimoto formed a minority administration supported by the much-reduced SDP and NPH contingents. At this period there were many 'floating' members of Parliament, with weak party affiliation, and LDP officials worked hard to tempt them to join (or rejoin) their party. Through a process of gradual accretion, the LDP achieved a majority in the lower house in September 1997, 11 months after the elections. On the other hand the NFP was suffering defections, the most prominent of which was that of the former Prime Minister, Hata, who had clashed with Ozawa. In December 1996 Hata formed a small group engagingly entitled the Sun Party (SP, *Taiyōtō*). Hosokawa followed in June 1997, forming his own group of five members known as 'From Five' (title in English).

Hashimoto used his second period in government to put forward various reform programmes, particularly in the field of financial services, where he sought major liberalization of the Tokyo financial market, so that it could compete on an equal footing with New York and London. This ambitious reform agenda was

---

[42]   Inge Engel-Christensen, 'New Party Success and Failure in Japan: The Experiences of the Liberal Party, 1998–2003', DPhil thesis, University of Oxford, 2006.

to take four years, and was regarded with great seriousness by the corporate world. In addition he proposed to reduce drastically the number of government ministries, and reorganize the government bureaucracy as a whole. The reform of the bureaucracy was finally put in place long after Hashimoto ceased to be Prime Minister, in January 2001. In 1997, however, it seemed evident that Hashimoto was adopting the main points of the agenda of the Hosokawa Cabinet earlier in the decade.

At the end of December 1997 Ozawa announced the dissolution of the NFP, thus ending its three-year existence. The reasons for its demise were complicated, involving personality clashes, differences over policy and the fact that it had plainly lost the initiative to a resurgent LDP under the quite innovative Hashimoto. Also, the elements in the party based on the *Sōka Gakkai*, though organizationally beneficial in elections, had proved difficult to assimilate and maintained a semi-separate existence. No fewer than six mini-parties were formed from the wreck of the NFP, and the first few months of 1998 were spent attempting to form a viable successor party capable of challenging LDP dominance. In April 1998, several of the small parties that had been formed when the NFP collapsed merged with the DPJ to form a party accounting for nearly 100 lower house members. The new party – sometimes referred to as the 'relaunched' DPJ – was headed by the popular Kan Naoto. Absent from the new party were various groups backed by the *Sōka Gakkai*, and a small party formed separately by Ozawa called the Liberal Party (LP, *Jiyūtō*). The first half of 1998 was a period of great party political confusion, though some order was brought back once the 'relaunched DPJ' was consolidated.[43]

Japanese politics from the latter half of 1997 was overshadowed by a series of financial crises affecting several East and South-East Asian nations, and collectively known as the Asian economic crisis. Thailand, Malaysia, Indonesia and South Korea experienced severe economic effects, and in Indonesia a near-revolutionary situation developed in the middle months of 1998, leading to the resignation of President Suharto after thirty-two years in office. Given that the Japanese economy was by far the largest in the region, it was expected that Japan would help its neighbours return to economic health. Japan itself, however, was in severe economic difficulties, from which escape appeared problematic. Indeed, from 1991 the Japanese economy had entered a period of economic stagnation, and although in the first half of the decade there were periods of fitful economic growth, the second half of the 1990s actually saw the economy contract over several quarters.

Several factors contributed to these difficulties. The most important was a huge overhang of debt affecting the financial sector, from the collapse of the 'bubble economy'. Smaller banks had become vulnerable (some went into liquidation) and even the larger banks were in difficulties – a situation requiring major restructuring of the banking system as a whole. Since the system had been geared to economic expansion and worked on the basis of high debt-to-equity ratios, in an economic recession it was most vulnerable. Distortions were also caused by the political power of numerous vested interests – for instance, the

---

[43]   See Chapter 9 for details of the parties formed after the collapse of the NFP.

construction industry and agriculture – which were able to call upon government protection. Macroeconomic management had been generally poor during the 1990s, and consumer confidence was low, with consumers showing their lack of faith in the future by saving, not spending.[44]

With effect from April 1997, Hashimoto, who had been intensively lobbied by the Ministry of Finance, increased the rate of consumption tax from 3 to 5 per cent. The Ministry had been worried for years about a taxation revenue shortfall, and believed that too much of the tax burden was concentrated in direct taxation, particularly income tax. This had been a most sensitive issue with the public since the 1980s, but Hashimoto was prevailed upon to take up the challenge and increase the rate. In so doing, he jeopardized his chances in the general elections for the House of Councillors in July 1998, where the LDP did unexpectedly badly. Needing to win 60 seats out of the 126 contested simply to maintain its pre-election strength, Hashimoto's party retained only 44, losing many seats in the big cities. The main beneficiaries were the Democratic Party led by Kan Naoto, the JCP and Independents, leading to comparisons with the LDP defeat in the upper house elections of 1989. No doubt reflecting the anxiety of voters about worsening economic conditions, voting turnout was over 14 percentage points higher than in 1995.

Hashimoto took responsibility for the electoral defeat and resigned as Prime Minister. Three candidates contested the succession to the LDP presidency: Obuchi Keizō (born 1937), who had taken over the leadership of the Takeshita faction at the time of the Ozawa defection, Kajiyama Seiroku (born 1926), a feisty senior politician who proposed to sort out the banking crisis by forcing some banks into liquidation, and Koizumi Junichirō (born 1942), whose pet project was to privatize postal services, especially the postal savings bank, and thus release enormous sums of money to be tested by the discipline of the market. Tanaka Makiko, daughter of the former Prime Minister Tanaka Kakuei, and later to be Foreign Minister briefly under Koizumi, when asked by a journalist how she would describe the three candidates, replied without hesitation: '*bonjin, gunjin, henjin*' (an ordinary man, a military man, an eccentric man).[45] At this point in the political process it was the *bonjin* (Obuchi) who became Prime Minister; the *gunjin* (Kajiyama) never became leader (and died in 2000), while the *henjin* (Koizumi) was to become one of Japan's most controversial and radical prime ministers between 2001 and 2006 (See Chapter 6). In 1998, however, Koizumi seemed far from his goal. In the LDP elections Obuchi, though he had failed to excite the electorate, won 225 votes, Kajiyama won 102 and Koizumi a mere 84. The result showed how far the preferences of the electors, most of whom were LDP parliamentarians, differed from those of ordinary voters. It also demonstrated that even now, towards the end of the 1990s, factional strength was the key factor in getting elected as leader. Since the beginning of the 1980s (or even earlier) the Tanaka faction line was much the most powerful

---

[44]   The 1990s came to be known, in a telling phrase, as the 'lost decade' – a phrase attributed to the economist Yoshikawa Hiroshi. In the end, the 'lost decade' lasted into the 2000s as well.

[45]   More colloquially, *henjin* translates as 'an odd fish', 'a weirdo'.

within the LDP. Obuchi became LDP President and thus Prime Minister largely because he commanded the largest faction in the party.[46] Nevertheless, when he departed, the supremacy of his faction also evaporated.

The banking crisis, and economic recession, were the most serious problems faced by the new Prime Minister. For Finance Minister, he chose the former Prime Minister Miyazawa Kiichi, already 78 but widely experienced in financial matters. Obuchi declared that his Cabinet would be a 'Cabinet for financial reconstruction'.[47] He announced extensive tax cuts, and major public works programmes, to stimulate the economy. This was the first of a number of such exercises under the Obuchi Cabinet, but they hardly succeeded in their aim of economic stimulation. The best that can be said is that they prevented the recessionary situation becoming even worse.

Faced by a serious economic situation (in which the economy was actually contracting), Obuchi set up a Council for Economic Strategy (*Keizai senryaku kaigi*),[48] precursor of a more powerful body that came to dominate economic policy under Koizumi. Lacking a stable parliamentary majority, he engaged in intensive talks with opposition parties about strategy to rescue the banking sector, burdened with non-performing loans,[49] and this led to legislation with considerable opposition party support.

Having served as Foreign Minister immediately before becoming Prime Minister, Obuchi was able to bring to a conclusion certain agreements he had negotiated in his previous post. One was an international treaty to ban land mines, which Japan ratified at the end of September.[50] Another was the Guidelines Agreement with the United States, designed to strengthen bilateral arrangements under the Mutual Security Treaty (discussed in Chapter 12 below). President Kim Dae Jung of South Korea visited Japan on 7 October, and the visit from an unusually pro-Japanese President inaugurated a relatively friendly phase in the often tense relations between the two countries. Obuchi visited Russia in November for talks with President Yeltsin, and the two leaders agreed on the aim of signing a peace treaty by 2000.

In domestic politics, Obuchi's principal problem was his lack of a stable parliamentary majority, as we have seen, with the House of Councillors posing a perennial problem. In November 1998, therefore, he began negotiations with Ozawa Ichirō, leader of the Liberal Party, with a view to bringing that party into a coalition government. As his price for entering such a government, Ozawa demanded that policies be devised to promote real reforms to the political and administrative system, as well as in the areas of national security and taxation.

---

[46]   Whereas the House of Representatives gave its majority to Obuchi as Prime Minister, the House of Councillors chose Kan Naoto, leader of the DPJ, flush from its victory in the upper house elections. Following the Constitution, article 67, the decision of the lower house prevailed, and Obuchi was confirmed as Prime Minister.
[47]   *Asahi Shinbun*, 31 July 1998.
[48]   *Asahi Shinbun*, 25 August 1998.
[49]   *Asahi Shinbun*, 18 September 1998.
[50]   *Asahi Shinbun*, 1 October 1998.

The coalition between the LDP and the LP was launched in January 1999, and lasted until April 2000. The experiment was given a certain poignancy by the fact that Obuchi and Ozawa – the two rivals for control of the Takeshita faction of the LDP in 1992 – were now apparently reconciled. The number of Cabinet ministers was reduced by two to eighteen, and the Liberal Party received one portfolio, that of the Home Ministry. Forming a two-party coalition slightly improved the government's popularity, but in a public opinion poll at the time of its launch, those who said they did not support it exceeded those who said they did support it by 37 per cent to 32 per cent.[51]

At the outset, the two parties reached agreement on some reforms. They agreed on the basic principle that the powers of the Prime Minister should be strengthened, and that Cabinet ought to be strengthened by introducing deputy ministers (*fukudaijin*) and junior ministers (*seimukan*) to coincide with the reorganization of ministries earlier decided on and scheduled for January 2001. They also made a pact to abolish the long-standing practice whereby senior public servants would sit next to Cabinet ministers in Parliament and, when required, answer questions on the minister's behalf, and they agreed that the total number of public servants should be reduced by 25 per cent over a ten-year period. From Ozawa's perspective, however, early hopes that the arrangement would make it possible to inject into the policy-making process the full set of reform measures that he and his Liberal Party colleagues favoured were soon disappointed. One of the main reasons for this was that in October 1999 the recently re-formed CGP also entered the coalition, which thereby became a three-party grouping in government.[52]

For the Liberal Party, the new coalition spelt a reduction in its strategic importance, since it was no longer the sole force committed to supporting the LDP in parliamentary votes. Moreover, on certain issues the interests of the CGP were diametrically opposed to the prescriptions of Ozawa and the LP. This difference came to the fore when the LP argued for the number of members elected by proportional representation from eleven regional blocs in House of Representatives elections to be reduced from 200 to 150. In Ozawa's thinking, this was in order to tilt the balance further in the direction of a British-style voting system, and bring forward the day when two large competing parties would vie for power with relatively even chances. To achieve this, it was essential to reduce the number of seats apportioned by PR, so as to eliminate, so far as possible, small parties from Parliament. For the CGP, however, this was a life-and-death matter. Those who voted for the CGP (mostly *Sōka Gakkai* members) formed a plurality in hardly any constituencies (even in big city areas, where its strength lay), so that it could realistically expect to win numbers of seats only in those constituencies elected by proportional representation. The CGP therefore fought fiercely against the Liberal Party proposal, and a compromise was eventually reached whereby the number of such seats would be reduced to 180.

[51] *Asahi Shinbun*, 19 January 1999.
[52] With the dissolution of the NFP in December 1997, the former CGP elements began to refashion themselves as a single entity, known as the New Party Peace (NPP, *Shintō heiwa*). In November 1998 it mutated into the New Clean Government Party (NCGP, *Shin kōmeitō*), though it soon came to be referred to by its pre-1994 title of CGP (*Kōmeitō*).

In April 1999 the highly significant election for the governorship of Tokyo prefecture was held, simultaneously with various other local elections. Electing the Tokyo Governor had on some previous occasions heralded future trends. For instance, when Minobe Ryōkichi was first elected in 1967, this signalled the beginning of the 'progressive local authority' phenomenon,[53] which ran right through the 1970s. In 1991 the re-election of Suzuki Shunichi despite the best efforts of Ozawa to displace him heralded a difficult time for the LDP. And on this occasion, in 1999, a maverick nationalist, Ishihara Shintarō, was elected Governor, trouncing all other candidates, including those backed by the LDP and the DPJ. Indeed, the LDP candidate, the celebrated Akashi Yasushi, who had been UN representative during the 1990s in first Cambodia, then Yugoslavia, was relegated to fourth position in the elections.[54] Ishihara, an intelligent populist with a strong following in the capital city, was to influence public opinion in the direction of sometimes extreme nationalist sentiment in the years to come.

One highly significant piece of legislation that passed both houses of Parliament in May was the 'Guidelines' agreement between Japan and the United States, designed to strengthen the Mutual Security Treaty by obliging Japan, among other things, to give various kinds of back-up assistance to US naval forces in case of a naval clash in waters close to Japan. This was part of a longer-term consolidation of security relations between the two countries that had been developing for some time and would continue to progress over the years to come.[55] The bill was supported by the two parties in the coalition government, and also by the CGP, which was to join the coalition later. Some critics began to complain that the size of this three-party compact was giving the Obuchi government much more scope to pass bills than in the past, and that the government was abusing this new-found power by rushing through legislation that previously would have been blocked as reactionary.[56]

Another measure of this kind was a wire-tapping bill, permitting the police to listen in to electronic conversations in defined circumstances, which went through Parliament in June. This was the subject of intense parliamentary debate, but was supported by the same three now dominant parties. Yet another was a bill legitimizing as national symbols the rising sun flag and the *Kimigayo* anthem, both of which (but especially the anthem) had been subject to controversy as reminiscent of wartime militarism. At this stage there was no proposal to make observance of flag and anthem compulsory in schools.[57] This bill passed the House of Representatives by 403 votes to 86. Opposing votes came from the JCP and the SDP. The DPJ gave a free vote to its members, who split evenly, with

[53]   From the late 1960s to the late 1970s many urban local authorities were under the control of elected chief executives connected with left-of-centre parties.

[54]   *Asahi Shinbun*, 12 April 1999.

[55]   See Christopher W. Hughes, *Japan's Re-emergence as a 'Normal' Military Power*, Abingdon and New York, Routledge, 2005 (Adelphi Paper 368–9), esp. Chapter 4.

[56]   See e.g. Yamaguchi Jirō, *Kiki no Nihon seiji* (Japanese Politics in Crisis), Tokyo, Iwanami Shoten, 1999.

[57]   *Asahi Shinbun*, 11 June 1999. It will be recalled that Murayama, as Socialist Prime Minister in 1994, had prevailed on the JSP to lift its objections to the flag and anthem. They nevertheless remained a subject of dispute, especially among teachers.

45 supporting the bill and 46 opposing it.[58] Further examples were a national identity card bill, a bill to establish a Japanese version of the British 'Prime Minister's Questions' as a regular feature of parliamentary procedure, and a bill to enforce ethical standards among public servants.

Most important in terms of later developments was a bill, debated in July and August, to set up committees in both houses of Parliament to examine the 1946 Constitution. Even though the road towards constitutional revision would be extremely lengthy, the bill showed which way the political wind was beginning to blow. The committees were convened in January 2000.

Whereas support for the Obuchi Cabinet was initially low, in September 1999 a regular *Asahi* poll for the first time showed its approval rating at more than 50 per cent.[59] Even though this level later fell back considerably, it seems reasonable to suppose that Obuchi's record of frenetic activity in shepherding reformist legislation through Parliament had struck a chord with a large part of the electorate.

Certainly, within the LDP Obuchi's position was secure. In September he faced biennial LDP presidential elections, in which three candidates stood: Katō Kōichi, Yamasaki Taku and Obuchi. Katō was the current leader of the factional line previously led by the former prime ministers Ikeda (in the early 1960s), Ōhira (in the 1970s), Suzuki (in the early 1980s) and Miyazawa (in the late 1980s and early 1990s). This faction had a relatively liberal record and Katō was commonly regarded as left-of-centre in LDP terms. Yamasaki was a right-of-centre politician who had recently founded his own faction. Interestingly enough, Katō and Yamasaki, together with Koizumi (who had contested two previous LDP presidential elections), were often lumped together as 'new leaders', intent on challenging the older and more venerable establishment. The media routinely dubbed them 'YKK'. Of the three, however, only one, Koizumi, was to fulfil the promise that YKK projected.

The result of the election was never in doubt. The verdict of an electorate consisting of all LDP parliamentarians of both houses, along with a small number of party members and party 'friends', was: Obuchi 350 votes; Katō 113 votes; and Yamasaki 51 votes.[60] The next month Obuchi brought the CGP into coalition with the LDP and LP. In retrospect this period marked the high point of his administration.

Also in September, the Democratic Party held elections for its top position, known, in suitably democratic fashion, as 'Representative' (*daihyō*). How far it is appropriate to speak of 'factions' in the DPJ is a matter of some dispute, and intra-party groupings were nothing like so tightly organized as the factions (*habatsu*) of the LDP. Nevertheless, different leaders and leadership aspirants were heirs to the different political traditions that had merged to form this conglomerate party, which at the time was a very recent creation. The three candidates were the current Representative, Kan Naoto; his main challenger, Hatoyama Yukio; and the former Socialist Yokomichi Takahiro. Kan had successively inhabited two mini-parties of the centre-left, the Social Democratic League and

---

[58]   *Asahi Shinbun*, 22 July 1999.
[59]   *Asahi Shinbun*, 17 September 1999. The percentage of approvals was 51%.
[60]   *Asahi Shinbun*, 21 September 1999.

the New Party Harbinger. He based much of his support on citizens' movements, mainly urban-based. Hatoyama had been a Liberal Democratic parliamentarian until he defected to the NPH in 1993. He was from a famous political family, being grandson of Hatoyama Ichirō, Prime Minister in the mid-1950s, and son of a man who had been Foreign Minister in the 1960s. Yokomichi, who had been Governor of Hokkaidō, had spent long years in the JSP, where his father had been one of the leading critics of the Prime Minister, Kishi Nobusuke, while the latter was taking the revised Japan–US Security Treaty through parliament in 1960.

Yokomichi was eliminated in the first round of a two-stage election, and at the second stage Hatoyama prevailed over the incumbent, Kan, by 182 votes to 130. The DPJ's leadership had been contested by these two men from the party's foundation in 1996. Between September 1996 and September 1997 the position of Representative was shared between them; for the next two years it was occupied by Kan; then Hatoyama was Representative until December 2002, when Kan replaced him once again. But the following year Kan was forced to resign (see Chapter 6), and the long-running 'Hato–Kan show' at last came to an end.

On 1 October a serious incident involving spillage of radioactive material occurred at the Tōkai village (*Tōkai mura*) nuclear power station in Ibaraki Prefecture, north of Tokyo. The local authorities instructed residents within 10 kilometres of the site to remain indoors, and investigation unearthed an extraordinarily slack security regime at the plant. The press carried stories of regulations being ignored and the spillage being cleared away in buckets.[61] This caused an outpouring of angry criticism, and the incident became for a while a symbol of the incompetence that was alleged to have led to Japan's 'lost decade'. It threw a shadow over the last months of the Obuchi government, and was probably a significant factor in the decline of the Prime Minister's popularity.

The three-party coalition government was launched in October, with the CGP brought in to supplement the LDP and LP. Signs of disagreement within the coalition, but particularly between the CGP and LP, soon began to surface. One issue was that already mentioned of reducing the number of lower house seats to be elected by proportional representation. Another was a proposed bill in relation to nursing care, which Ozawa maintained was only part of the real task of reforming the welfare system. He was also concerned with other areas of reform, namely education, national security and the running of Parliament, where he felt that the coalition was not adhering sufficiently closely to the agreements made at the outset of the coalition government.[62] On this occasion the Liberal Party agreed to support the supplementary budget, and thus narrowly averted the likelihood that it would defect from the coalition.[63]

---

[61]   *Asahi Shinbun*, 1 October 1999 and subsequent days.

[62]   Under national security he was especially concerned with, first, ensuring a Japanese obligation to assist the American forces in areas outside any battle zone, and second, the need for 'emergency legislation' (*yūji rippō*), which would impose obligations on citizens in case of a military or natural emergency.

[63]   *Asahi Shinbun*, 25 November 1999. In his press conference on the 24th, Ozawa raised several further issues on which he thought action was needed, including imposing a limit on the number of times provincial governors and mayors could be elected, redenomination of the currency, and giving voting rights to resident foreigners. Ibid.

The first parliamentary session of the new millennium began in January 2000, with the three main parties of opposition – the DPJ, JCP and SDP – boycotting the session, which in defiance of them passed a bill authorizing a reduction in the number of proportional representation seats in the House of Representatives from 200 to 180. This was the final result of the compromise hammered out with great difficulty between the three parties of the coalition government, with the LP pressing for a 50-seat cut and the CGP fighting this tooth and nail. The three opposition parties continued their boycott for a fortnight, so that parliamentary business did not return to normal until 9 February. When it did, the Prime Minister faced representatives of the opposition parties in the innovation of a British-style Question Time.

On 1 April, the tensions that had been building up within the coalition between the Liberal Party and the other two parties came to a head, and the Liberals left the coalition. This was not, however, to the taste of all its parliamentary members. On 3 April, 26 LP members launched the Conservative Party (CP, *Hoshutō*), which remained with the coalition. Meanwhile, on 2 April, Obuchi suffered a stroke and fell into a coma, from which he never recovered. He died on 14 May. The Obuchi Cabinet, which had lasted for one year and eight months, held an emergency meeting at which it resigned *en masse*. Obuchi's successor, chosen in haste and controversially by a small group of LDP 'elder statesmen',[64] was Mori Yoshirō, who declared that news of his appointment was 'like an earthquake and a fire happening all at once'.[65]

Japanese politics during the 1990s are not easy to summarize. The period is most famously dismissed as 'the lost decade', though the phrase was principally devised with economic failures in mind. In politics, the most memorable event was the departure of the LDP from power on 9 August 1993. It is difficult to overestimate the degree of shock felt by the erstwhile ruling party at being deprived of the oxygen of power. The fact that it was back in power a mere nine months later in a strange, though surprisingly durable, coalition with the Socialists, has led to the view that the period of non-LDP coalition governments was an aberration. The Hosokawa and Hata administrations were indeed fragile. But it was also the fault of two crucial bad judgements, the first by Hosokawa (in resigning) and the second by Ozawa (in trying to form a new party without the Socialists) that the LDP was able to claw its way back into power. Much depended on timing. There is ample evidence, in terms of successive defections from the LDP during the period it was out of office, that if it had stayed in opposition for, say, two or three years, the party might well have gone the way of the Democristiana in Italy over the same period.[66] The one concrete achievement of the Hosokawa government was the new lower house election system, even if its effects may not have been as its authors wished.

---

[64]   Accounts differed over whether Obuchi had remained conscious for a while after becoming ill and given his blessing to Mori as his successor.
[65]   *Asahi Shinbun*, 9 April 2000.
[66]   The Democristiana was the Christian Democratic Party that dominated Italian politics from the late 1940s until the early 1990s, when it imploded.

The LDP–JSP–NPH coalitions of the mid-1990s provided a political tone that may perhaps be described as Japanese conservatism with a human face, as Murayama in particular took up a number of humanistic causes that the LDP had never been prepared to touch, such as that of the 'comfort women', and also tackled the vexed issue of war apology. But the willingness of the JSP to ally itself with its old LDP enemies in return for the prime ministership turned into a Faustian bargain, leading in a few years to the near-destruction of the JSP itself. The disappearance of the ancient left-wing pole of Japanese politics unbalanced the system, and even though new parties of opposition emerged (first the New Frontier Party and later the Democratic Party), it was always uncertain how far these parties were really prepared to *oppose*, as distinct from *appease*, the LDP.[67]

The final point to be made about the decade is that economic stagnation and political instability gradually led to a new political agenda, which was destined to lead Japan into altered directions in the new millennium. This was partly about revamping political and economic institutions to make them more efficient, and appropriate for a globalizing world. But it was also about conforming to what were regarded, sensibly or not, as 'American standards' in a world that had become unipolar since the ending of the Cold War. And moreover, it was to lead the country into more right-wing – and less liberal – political territory than had been experienced since the 1950s. Finally, there were already signs that the East Asian region was beginning to change in ways that would profoundly affect Japan. These are themes that we shall pick up in Chapter 6.

[67]   See J. A. A. Stockwin, 'To Oppose or to Appease? Parties out of Power and the Need for Real Politics in Japan', *Japan Forum*, vol. 18, no. 1 (March 2006), pp. 115–32.

Chapter 6 | New Politics for the New Millennium: The Koizumi Effect

The unexpected transition of the post of Prime Minister from the incapacitated Obuchi to the surprised Mori may be seen, with the advantage of hindsight, to signify a paradigm shift in the direction of politics in Japan. This did not become fully evident until Mori himself had departed from the scene a year later in favour of Koizumi. But the change of prime minister in April 2000 marked a major shift in the balance of factional control within the LDP. Since the late 1970s or early 1980s it was the Tanaka faction line that had been the strongest influence over the composition of governments, and especially, over who should be the next Prime Minister. This did not mean that every Prime Minister was from this faction, but it was the Tanaka faction under first Tanaka himself, and then his successors, that was kingmaker (to a greater or lesser degree) for Ōhira, Suzuki, Nakasone, Takeshita, Kaifu, Miyazawa, Hashimoto and Obuchi. Of these only Takeshita, Hashimoto and Obuchi were actually from the Tanaka faction line, but the others owed much to that faction's backing. With the selection of Mori, however, the baton moved to the Fukuda faction line, of which Mori was the current leader in 2000 and to which not only Mori but also his three successors, Koizumi Junichirō, Abe Shinzō and Fukuda Yasuo, belonged.

We need to consider carefully the implications of this shift. Generalizations about LDP factions have to be treated with some analytical delicacy. Even so, and with all the necessary caveats, it seems possible to assert that whereas Tanaka and his followers were relatively pragmatic in policy terms, but greatly concerned with organization, power, finance and the more traditional trappings of factional existence, the Fukuda faction line was more ideological, interested in promoting a certain set of policy ideas that went back to the 1950s. This is perhaps most evident in the case of Abe, Prime Minister from September 2006 to September 2007, whose revered grandfather was Kishi Nobusuke, the Prime Minister who negotiated the Japan–US Mutual Security Treaty in 1960.

Too much should not be made of this distinction. There were those in the Tanaka faction line who were every bit as ideologically right-wing as the mainstream members of the Fukuda factional line, and the rivalry between the two was as much personal and organizational as it was ideological. Moreover, when we come to Koizumi (Prime Minister from April 2001 to September 2006), we have to take into account factors specific to his personality, charisma, abilities and vision. But the distinction is not without validity, and the effects of the factional shift were very marked, particularly once Koizumi took over the reins of power.

Mori Yoshirō, the new Prime Minister, was well known for his interest in rugby. Having been a journalist and then secretary to a parliamentarian, he first entered the House of Representatives in 1969 at the age of 32, and since then had occupied at various times the portfolios of Education, Trade and Industry, and Construction, as well as party positions, including most recently that of LDP Secretary-General. Throughout his parliamentary career he had been identified with right-wing ideological positions, but, unlike some others with similar views, he came over less as an intellectual than as a bluff, rugby-playing, no-nonsense individual with an earthy sense of humour.

The Mori Cabinet, like the Obuchi Cabinet in its final months, consisted of three parties, the LDP, the CGP and now the newly formed Conservative Party that had broken away from Ozawa's Liberal Party in order to stay within government. The Cabinet began with modest but respectable approval ratings.[1] It was not long, however, before Mori began to develop a reputation for unfortunate remarks. In mid-May, speaking at a meeting to celebrate the thirtieth anniversary of the founding of the parliamentarians' congress of the Shinto Political Federation (*Shintō seiji renmei kokkai giin kondankai*), he expressed the opinion that 'Japan is a country of the gods, centred upon the Emperor'.[2] This phrase, with its connotations of wartime emperor-worship, elicited a protest from the *Sōka Gakkai*, which had suffered under the wartime regime and deeply distrusted the legacy of State Shinto. Coming from the backer of one of the parties in the coalition, this was a criticism that needed to be taken seriously. Mori apologized for 'causing misunderstanding', but did not retract the statement. Hatoyama Yukio, Representative of the opposition Democratic Party, urged him to resign.[3] The opposition presented to both houses motions of no-confidence in the Prime Minister, but both were rejected by votes taken on party lines.[4]

On the other hand, Mori's popularity was severely dented by this episode. An *Asahi* poll taken in mid-June showed the Cabinet's approval rating down to 19 per cent, though a *Yomiuri* poll taken in late May found 28 per cent of those polled approving of the Cabinet.[5] Although these levels of approval were to stabilize around 20 per cent for a few months before plunging again at the end of the year, it was clear that he was having problems convincing the electorate that

[1] A *Yomiuri* poll on 18 April gave the Mori Cabinet a 41.9% approval rating, slightly better than its 40.7% for the Obuchi Cabinet in March: *Yomiuri Nenkan*, 2001, p. 270.
[2] *Asahi Shinbun*, 16 May 2000.
[3] *Asahi Shinbun*, 19 and 27 May 2000.
[4] *Asahi Shinbun*, 1 June 2000.
[5] *Asahi Shinbun*, 13 June 2000; *Yomiuri Nenkan*, 2001, p. 270.

he was the right man for the job. In early June publicity was given – by a press now straining every ear for prime ministerial gaffes – to Mori's statement in a political speech delivered in Nara that possible cooperation between the Democratic Party and the Japan Communist Party might make it difficult to defend Japan's 'national polity' (*kokutai*). The term *kokutai* had been used up to 1945 as a rather mystical concept embracing the essence of the emperor system, and was thus highly sensitive, even a taboo term, in contemporary Japan.

General elections for the House of Representatives were held on 25 June 2000. Taken together, the three parties of the coalition government lost seats, while retaining a secure majority. But most of these losses were accounted for by the fact that the newly formed Conservative Party, which having had 26 seats when it broke from the Liberals three months earlier, was reduced to a mere seven in the elections. The Liberal Democrats fell back, but only marginally. The big winner was the DPJ, which increased its seat total from 95 to 127. Even though this was far behind the LDP total of 233, it meant that the core of opposition to the government was reinforced and consolidated.

In late July, the G8 Summit was held in Okinawa. For Japan, this was a prestigious event, and to mark the occasion the government issued 2,000-yen banknotes for the first time. The Summit was an opportunity for top-level meetings, and the Minister of Foreign Affairs, Kōno Yōhei, shortly afterwards met the North Korean Foreign Minister in Bangkok to discuss normalizing relations between Japan and North Korea.[6] This was a time when breakthroughs in relations between Japan and its neighbours seemed a genuine possibility. Vladimir Putin, the new Russian President, visited Japan in September, and in a joint statement the two leaders spoke of their continuing efforts to conclude a long-delayed peace treaty, although by now it was evident that the target date of 2000 set by Yeltsin and Hashimoto in 1997 was unrealistic.[7] The President of South Korea, Kim Dae Jung, also visited Japan in September, discussing with the Japanese side voting rights for Korean residents in Japan, as well as the issue of Japanese economic aid to North Korea and the prospects for normalization of relations between them.[8] In October Mori met the Prime Minister of China, Zhu Rongji, to discuss continuing Japanese aid to China.[9] Finally, in January 2001, Mori visited several countries in Africa, in furtherance of Japan's growing links with that continent.[10]

In October the four opposition parties boycotted parliamentary debate on the government proposal concerning the proportional representation constituency of the House of Councillors (in which the whole country functions as a single constituency). The proposal was designed to enable voters to show preference for an individual candidate, and not just for a party. The LDP had always disliked the proportional representation element in the upper house electoral system, because the party thrived on name recognition. When voters were simply

[6] *Yomiuri Nenkan*, 2001, pp. 164–5.
[7] *Asahi Shinbun*, 6 September 2000.
[8] *Asahi Shinbun*, 24 September 2000.
[9] *Asahi Shinbun*, 14 October 2000.
[10] *Asahi Shinbun*, 10 January 2001.

asked to express a preference among parties, they were less likely to choose the LDP than if they were asked to choose an individual candidate. In the latter case, many chose LDP candidates because of name recognition and strong local links.[11] Despite the opposition boycott, however, the legislation passed the House of Representatives in October.[12]

The following month, what nearly turned into a major defection from the LDP was narrowly averted. On 20 November the four opposition parties presented a motion of no confidence in the Mori government on the floor of the House of Representatives. Such an initiative was a fairly regular occurrence, but what made it dramatic in this case was the support for the motion offered by Katō Kōichi, the moderate leader of a faction that was part of the original Ikeda faction line. He was also a member of the YKK group (Yamasaki, Katō, Koizumi) of so-called 'new leaders', and thus a credible aspirant for the post of Prime Minister. In the face of incipient revolt from within LDP ranks, Mori threatened any Katō faction members who voted with the opposition in favour of the no-confidence motion with expulsion from the party. As a consequence, Katō was unable to persuade enough of his faction members to support the motion, and the revolt collapsed. Most damagingly, the former Prime Minister and previous leader of the same faction, Miyazawa Kiichi, refused to support the revolt. The political career of Katō Kōichi never recovered from this setback. Yamasaki – another YKK member – also voted in favour of the motion, which was defeated by the force of numbers of the three government parties.[13]

In January 2001 the long-gestating reorganization of the government ministries, which had been decided in 1997 under the Hashimoto Cabinet, finally saw the light of day. Previously competing ministries were merged into a smaller number of super-ministries, a Cabinet Office was created in order to strengthen the power of the Prime Minister and Cabinet, and the venerable title of the Ministry of Finance – Ōkurashō ('Treasury Ministry') – was transmuted into the more prosaic Zaimushō ('Financial Affairs Ministry). The details of this reform will be treated in Chapter 7. In the same month a body was created that would become highly influential under Koizumi in economic policy-making: the Council on Economic and Fiscal Policy (Keizai zaisei shimon kaigi).

In February 2001, an event occurred that was to damage Mori's reputation and brought the end of his tenure as Prime Minister closer. Off Oahu in Hawaii an American submarine rose rapidly to the surface and collided with a Japanese fisheries training vessel. Several young Japanese died in the incident. The Prime Minister came under criticism for allegedly continuing to play golf even after having been informed of the incident.[14] There were further ramifications of this issue, and a public opinion poll testing his popularity showed his approval rating

---

[11]   For further details, see J. A. A. Stockwin, Dictionary of the Modern Politics of Japan, London and New York, RoutledgeCurzon, 2003, entry on 'election systems', pp. 49–57, at p. 56.

[12]   Asahi Shinbun, 27 October 2000. The bill also included a reduction by ten seats in the size of the upper house.

[13]   Asahi Shinbun, 22 November 2000.

[14]   Asahi Shinbun, 15 February 2001.

down to single figures (9 per cent).[15] This disillusionment no doubt partly reflected the continued failure of the economy to improve its stagnant performance. For the first time since the war a deflationary trend had become entrenched. It was becoming increasingly clear that Mori could not remain in office much longer.

In early March, a no-confidence motion brought by the four opposition parties was once again defeated by the numerical superiority of the government parties,[16] but Mori let it be understood that he intended to step down once the annual budget had passed through the parliamentary process. He nevertheless remained active in international diplomacy. He paid an official visit to the United States, where he received an apology from President George W. Bush concerning the fishing vessel tragedy off Oahu. In addition, he visited the Siberian city of Irkutsk, where he met President Putin and discussed with him the issue of disputed territory to the north-east of Hokkaidō. At this period intensive efforts were being made by officials of the two sides to bring about a resolution of the issue, but the momentum went out of the process when Mori finally resigned his position in April.[17]

The ending of Mori's year as Prime Minister came at a time when the LDP was preparing for the regular three-yearly House of Councillors elections scheduled for July 2001. Given Mori's lack of popularity, there was a sense of crisis in the ranks of the LDP, and a fear of severe defeat in the coming elections. Party rank and file therefore regarded the choice of their next President (who would inevitably become Prime Minister) as crucial. It may not be too much of an exaggeration to say that the party was looking for a saviour. The procedure followed on this occasion to choose the next LDP President involved a two-stage election. The first stage was a set of primary elections, organized by each of the 47 prefectural branches of the party according to its own procedures, followed by a run-off election among LDP-affiliated parliamentarians.

In the primary elections held on 23 April four candidates stood: Asō Tarō, a thrusting and ambitious right-wing revisionist who was a grandson of the post-war Prime Minister Yoshida Shigeru; Hashimoto Ryūtarō, who had been Prime Minister between 1996 and 1998 and had long been a central figure in the Tanaka faction line; Kamei Shizuka, a party heavyweight who favoured protection of politically strategic interests; and Koizumi Junichirō, often regarded within the LDP as a maverick for his single-minded determination to privatize postal services, but more broadly a believer in free-market capitalism. This was his third bid for the party presidency.

In spectacular fashion, Koizumi swept the primaries. Of the branches in the 47 prefectures, Koizumi won 41, Hashimoto five, Kamei one (his own base of Hiroshima) and Asō none at all. Most of the prefectural branches ran a 'winner-take-all' election,

[15]   *Asahi Shinbun*, 20 February 2001.
[16]   Ibid., 6 March 2001.
[17]   For an interesting perspective on relations between Japan and Russia at this period, see Kazuhiko Togo, *Japan's Foreign Policy 1945–2003: The Quest for a Proactive Policy*, Leiden, Brill, 2005, pp. 228–58, esp. pp. 256–8.

and each branch was entitled to three votes. The results of the primaries, therefore, were as follows: Koizumi 123; Hashimoto 15; Kamei 3; Asō 0.[18] Before the run-off election Kamei withdrew and gave his support to Koizumi. The results of the run-off election were therefore: Koizumi 298; Hashimoto 155; Asō 31.

Popular reaction to this decision was enthusiastic. In a public opinion poll whose results were published on 30 April, the new Prime Minister scored an approval rating of 78 per cent,[19] and a poll a month later was to give him a wholly unprecedented 84 per cent.[20] Given that in the last few weeks in his post Mori's recorded approval rating had been in single figures, this was an extraordinary resurgence. Part of the explanation was no doubt a sense of relief that, after a long period of economic stagnation and unimpressive top leadership, here was a dashing new Prime Minister capable of pulling the country together and giving it a sense of purpose. The new leader's image was clearly important, and Koizumi proved adept at projecting an interesting image in an increasingly image-conscious world. He made good use of the internet, not only to explain his policies but also to polish his image. His wavy hairstyle made him instantly recognizable,[21] and his laconic replies to questions suggested a certain mysterious reserve. Koizumi dolls and other memorabilia became all the rage, and surprising numbers of people would brook no criticism of their new idol.

Another reason for his early popularity was that he had appointed Ms Tanaka Makiko, daughter of Tanaka Kakuei, as his Foreign Minister. She had become one of the country's best-known political personalities, famous for her direct and unelliptical style of discourse in the mass media. In a political culture where deliberate ambiguity was an art form, many ordinary people found her attacking style to be refreshing. As it turned out, she was a problematic minister, and did not survive more than a few months in her post. With her departure early in 2002, Koizumi's popularity fell to more 'normal' levels for an incumbent Prime Minister. But it was to remain throughout his five-and-a-half-year tenure of the office at levels higher than some of his predecessors attained for most of their tenure.

While it is not entirely true that Koizumi ignored factional demands in constructing his first Cabinet, he decisively broke with the principle of Cabinet construction in proportion to factional strength. In particular, he appointed only two members of the Hashimoto (former Tanaka) faction, thus reinforcing the

---

[18] The Osaka prefectural branch used proportional representation, so that Koizumi received two votes and Hashimoto one. In Tottori, no candidate had an overall majority, so that Hashimoto received two votes and Koizumi one. *Asahi Shinbun*, 24 April 2001.

[19] *Asahi Shinbun*, 30 April 2001.

[20] *Asahi Shinbun*, 29 May 2001.

[21] Photographs of Koizumi a very few years before he became Prime Minister show a man with relatively short hair, whereas by 2001 it was long and wavy. By contrast, photographs of Tony Blair in the earlier stages of his political career reveal abundant hair, which became progressively shorter as his career progressed. This suggests that there is no single model for what works in the industry of image creation.

break with its long years of dominance within the LDP.[22] Three members of the Mori (formerly the Fukuda) faction entered Cabinet – four if we include the Prime Minister, who claimed technically to be outside any faction. Three members of the Cabinet were not members of Parliament (the Constitution permitted up to 50 per cent in this category, but in the past few non-parliamentarians had been appointed), and one each came from the two other parties of the coalition, the Clean Government Party and the Conservative Party. An unprecedented five members of the 18-strong Cabinet were women, including Ms Ōgi Chikage, leader of the CP.

What was to be a crucial appointment was that of Takenaka Heizō, an academic economist from Keio University, who remained in successive cabinets almost throughout Koizumi's tenure of office. Appointed as Minister of Economics and Finance, he was to become crucially important in shaping the economic policies of the Koizumi regime. His instincts, like those of the Prime Minister, were to deregulate the economy so far as possible on the model of free-market economics, and to resist the demands of the vested interests that had, in his view, stifled economic progress. He was well aware that such interests were strongly represented within the LDP. In an effort to broaden the debate beyond the narrow confines of these sectional groups, Koizumi and Takenaka began a long-running programme of 'town meetings', visiting provincial areas to explain the nature of the proposed 'Koizumi revolution'.

Partially fulfilling the hopes of the worried LDP branch members who had voted for him in April, Koizumi led his party to a somewhat improved performance at the elections for half the seats in the House of Councillors held on 29 July. The party was still, however, well short of a majority in the upper house, a goal that had eluded it since the electoral disaster of 1989. Whereas the LDP pre-election strength had been 107 seats out of 250, it had now risen to 111 seats out of the reduced total of 247. The Democratic Party also improved its position, from 55 seats to 59. These gains were at the expense of smaller parties, particularly the Socialists and Communists. But the LDP was still not in a position to govern without the other two parties of the coalition because without them it was unable to pass legislation through the House of Councillors.

With the election out of the way, the Prime Minister initiated a line of policy that he was to continue throughout his tenure – one that led to increasing difficulties for his government in foreign affairs, especially in its relations with China and South Korea. On 13 August 2001 he paid the first of many visits in his official capacity to the Yasukuni Shrine in Tokyo. Japan is not the only country defeated in war where commemoration of the dead of that war has become controversial.[23] In the Japanese case, however, the question of prime ministerial visits to the Yasukuni Shrine was difficult largely because in 1978 a decision had been made to 'enshrine' the souls of 14 Class A war criminals (so defined by the Tokyo war crimes trials of the late 1940s) at Yasukuni. No earthly remains were interred there, but people were invited to pray at the shrine for the souls of those who had died in the war, including the controversial 14. Nakasone, as Prime Minister in

---

[22] Despite being the daughter of Tanaka Kakuei, founder of this faction, Tanaka Makiko stayed clear of any factional affiliation.
[23] Another obvious example is that of Germany.

the 1980s, had paid one visit to the shrine in his official capacity, but in the face of widespread criticism had refrained from further visits, Most of his successors had regarded shrine visits as a political hot potato and had not gone.[24]

It is significant that Koizumi went on 13 August, not the fifteenth, which was the anniversary of the 1945 defeat. This was in order to dampen Chinese and Korean sensitivities, and in subsequent years he also chose dates other than 15 August. But shortly before his retirement in September 2006 he finally visited the shrine on the anniversary of the defeat. By this time Chinese and Korean criticism hardly mattered, since he was about to leave office, but in the years he was Prime Minister the Yasukuni Shrine question became a major source of bad feeling between Japan and China, as well as between Japan and South Korea.

There are three possible reasons why Koizumi persisted in these problematic visits. The first was an explanation he himself gave on various occasions, citing a personal experience of having visited a provincial memorial to the war dead, where he was immensely moved to learn of the suffering that young Japanese servicemen had had to endure during the war. There is no need to reject this as at least a partial explanation for his visits.[25] In some circumstances Koizumi was inclined to act intuitively and on the basis of feeling and emotion. A second explanation, by contrast, is more mundane and political. Like many LDP politicians, he was supported by ex-servicemen's organizations, who favoured prime ministerial visits to commemorate those who had fallen during the war. This, however, was a factor affecting successive prime ministers, so that we have to look for further factors that may have affected Koizumi specifically.

The third factor that seems to have been salient in his specific case was a political judgement that Japan ought not simply to bend before criticism from its neighbours. His period as Prime Minister coincided with a period of rapid growth in the Chinese economy, and fears in Japan that the balance of economic and political influence was shifting away from Japan in favour of China were widespread. It was also well recognized in Japanese government circles that verbally attacking Japan was a tactic frequently used by the Chinese government for domestic political purposes, so that it made sense for Japan not simply to lie down in the face of such attacks.[26]

From a different point of view, however, the Chinese and the Koreans could be said to have good reason to remember the horrors perpetrated during the war, so that it was reasonable for them to object to signs of revisionist sentiment in Japan, such as the prime ministerial visits to the Yasukuni Shrine or the tendency by some prominent politicians and others in Japan to deny the facts of the

---

[24]   Interestingly, even Mori, as Prime Minister, had declined to visit the Yasukuni Shrine, despite an ideological outlook compatible with such a visit, and the fact that nine members of his Cabinet went there to pray for the souls of the war dead: *Asahi Shinbun*, 16 August 2000.

[25]   For his explanation that he did not seek to justify the war, but rather to pay his respects and give thanks for those Japanese servicemen who laid down their lives during the war, see *Asahi Shinbun*, 3 June 2005.

[26]   Ambassador Nogami Yoshiji, private conversation, 18 November 2004.

Nanjing massacre by Japanese troops in 1937.[27] Indeed, from the beginning of the new millennium signs of rising nationalism, including positive re-evaluation of Japan's international actions in the 1930s and early 1940s, were coming to trouble observers on the continent of Asia and elsewhere. Needless to say, in addition, the Japanese and Chinese economies were deeply interlocked, to the advantage of both, so that a worsening of relations that might start to unravel that economic relationship was hardly in the national interest of either country.

On 11 September 2001 planes hijacked by Al Qaeda operatives brought down the Twin Towers in New York and severely damaged the Pentagon in Washington DC. Nearly 3,000 people were killed, of many nationalities including Japanese. This event altered the course of world history.

For Japan, it was to mean a strengthening of its ties with the United States. Faced with an American President giving high priority to fighting a 'war on terror', governments of other states were faced with difficult choices in the years to follow about how far to align their countries with American policy. The Japanese government under Koizumi seems to have been troubled by few doubts on this issue, and in the aftermath of 9/11 the Prime Minister gave firm assurances of his willingness to cooperate with President Bush in counter-terrorist activities.[28] An anti-terrorist bill was quickly shepherded through Parliament. On the basis of this, Parliament sanctioned the despatch overseas of contingents from the Self-Defence Forces, whether to aid US forces or to rescue refugees. The bill passed with the support of the opposition Democratic Party, although Yokomichi Takahiro, its Deputy Representative and former member of the JSP, voted against.[29]

From the political perspective that Koizumi represented, the national interest was seen to lie in close coordination with the United States, even though terrorist activities from Middle Eastern groups were a far less serious problem for Japan than for many other countries. For Japan, the United States was, and had been for half a century, the principal guarantor of national security. With the economic, political and strategic balance shifting in favour of China in the East Asian region, it made sense to consolidate a process already under way of integrating Japanese and American military systems in the region. Despite the history of anti-war activism in Japan in earlier years, there was surprisingly little public dissent from this approach.

The coordination, however, went further than promoting interoperable military systems. Koizumi was ideologically committed to globalization, in the sense of cutting through the multifarious obstacles to market capitalism that had existed in Japan's managed economy. The United States saw itself as the principal international promoter of globalization in this sense, even though America's trading practices did not always adhere strictly to its own official precepts on the matter. Thus Koizumi, early in his period in office, began the long and difficult task of unscrambling the huge postal services empire, in order eventually to put

---

[27]   Ishihara Shintarō, the high-profile Governor of Tokyo, was a prominent and influential Nanjing massacre denier.

[28]   *Asahi Shinbun*, 9 October 2001.

[29]   *Asahi Shinbun*, 30 November 2001. For this infringement of party discipline, the DPJ imposed a three-month suspension from party office.

its various parts into the private commercial sector. The postal savings bank, which alongside mail delivery and insurance constituted one of the three sections of the empire, had at its disposal enormous funds from small savers, and these funds were channelled into various governmental purposes. Indeed, the funds were the basis of what was often known as the 'second budget': the Fiscal and Investment Loan Programme (FILP, *Zaitō*). Believing that this 'second budget' distorted market mechanisms and entrenched vested interests, Koizumi was determined to destroy the system on which it was based.

Another target for reform was the group of four public corporations dedicated to road-building (*dōro 4 kōdan*). The four corporations were to be privatized and the public subsidy to them was scheduled for abolition. Here again, as in the case of postal services, entrenched interests fought hard against the privatization. The government also privatized sixteen out of 163 special corporate bodies (*tokushu hōjin*), and abolished or amalgamated 18 others.[30] A public housing finance corporation (*jūtaku kin'yū kōko*) was earmarked for abolition over a five-year period. Koizumi was quoted as saying that 'houses get built even without such a corporation; there's no need to privatize it, we shall just abolish it'.[31]

In a book published in 2002 the Australian scholar Aurelia George Mulgan argued that Koizumi's reform programmes were being frustrated by a combination of forces that one would not expect to be so obstructive in a Westminster-type system of Cabinet government. The bureaucracy, even after its reorganization came into effect in January 2001, retained enough initiative to block or constrain initiatives coming from the Prime Minister and Cabinet. Another source of obstruction was provided by members of Parliament organized into 'tribes' (*zoku*) tightly organized to control specific areas of policy. The 'tribes' often worked in close conjunction with relevant parts of the government bureaucracy. And the third policy bottleneck was to be found in the complex committee system of the LDP, where policy from Prime Minister and Cabinet was vetted and sometimes rejected.[32] We shall examine these arguments in Chapter 7, but it is worth noting here that Koizumi later had some success in overcoming these obstacles.

In the early weeks of 2002 a simmering feud came to a head involving the Minister of Foreign Affairs, Tanaka Makiko, senior officials of the Foreign Ministry and an LDP politician from Hokkaidō called Suzuki Muneo, who was the current Chairman of the House of Representatives Management Committee. The immediate crisis was prompted by the allegation that Suzuki had exerted undue pressure on the ministry regarding participation in an NGO involved with providing aid to Afghanistan. Replies to parliamentary questions given by ministry officials and by the minister herself had differed on material points, causing much criticism within Parliament of how foreign policy issues were being handled. This was, however, only the latest in a series of disagreements between the sharp-tongued Tanaka Makiko and officials of the Foreign Ministry,

[30]   *Asahi Shinbun*, 6 October 2001.
[31]   *Asahi Shinbun*, 15, 25 November 2001.
[32]   Aurelia George Mulgan, *Japan's Failed Revolution: Koizumi and the Politics of Economic Reform*, Canberra, Asia Pacific Press, 2002.

while the activities of Suzuki Muneo were inviting suspicion on various counts, including accusations of interfering in aid projects to the Northern Territories (Southern Kuriles). Despite Tanaka's popularity, Koizumi decided to lance the boil of an increasingly untenable situation and dismissed her from her post. He simultaneously replaced the vice-minister (*jimu jikan* – a public servant, not a politician) who had clashed with her, and around the same time Suzuki resigned his chairmanship of the House of Representatives Management Committee.[33] A few weeks later Suzuki admitted having interfered in aid projects to the Northern Territories, and resigned his membership of the LDP. In June he was arrested on charges of corruption. Koizumi appointed as his new Foreign Minister another woman, Kawaguchi Yoriko: not a member of Parliament but already a minister in charge of the environment portfolio.[34] The new Foreign Minister supervised a revision of the guidelines for the ministry, and more dismissals of officials followed.

Without his popular Foreign Minister, Koizumi's approval rating promptly fell from above 70 per cent to below 50 per cent, and although it later recovered to some extent, it never again matched the high levels of his first nine months.[35] Economic recovery was still nowhere to be seen; indeed, at this period the economy was contracting, while deflation had become endemic. Major companies were refusing any wage rises for their workforces.

In April Koizumi took the opportunity of a spring festival at the Yasukuni Shrine to pay an official visit to it, after which he reiterated a no-war pledge. He said that he would not go to the shrine in August, but this did not prevent a protest from the Chinese authorities, who reacted by postponing a visit by the Japanese Defence Agency Minister.[36] This pattern of playing with dates to try to minimize international reaction (without much success) was repeated in subsequent years.

Economic conditions began to improve slightly during the year, and there was some talk that the economy was at last bottoming out of its recession. This was conducive to somewhat calmer politics than had prevailed in the recent past. But Koizumi was about to take an initiative that was to have profound repercussions for Japanese politics in the months and years to come. For much of the year talks had been going on between Japanese officials and officials of the Democratic People's Republic of Korea (North Korea). At the beginning of September the Chief Cabinet Secretary, Fukuda Yasuo,[37] announced that the Prime Minister would visit Pyongyang, the capital of North Korea, on 17 September for talks with President Kim Jong Il. This was the first time that a Japanese prime minister had visited the reclusive North Korean state, and it

---

[33] *Asahi Shinbun*, 30 January 2002.

[34] His first choice was Ogata Sadako, the highly respected former United Nations Commissioner for Refugees, but she was unable to break existing commitments.

[35] In a poll taken shortly after the dismissal of Tanaka Makiko, 69% of those polled thought her dismissal was wrong: *Asahi Shinbun*, 4 February 2002.

[36] *Asahi Shinbun*, 24 April 2002.

[37] Son of Fukuda Takeo, Prime Minister 1976–8.

seemed possible that a new era might be about to begin in relations between the DPRK and Japan, and perhaps on the Korean peninsula as a whole.

Japanese officials had long experience of dealing with their North Korean counterparts, and although negotiations were always difficult, they had developed a good sense of the mentality of the people they were seeking to do business with. The issues that were normally discussed included Japanese demands for information about their nationals allegedly kidnapped by North Koreans from Japan, North Korean demands for apology and compensation for Japanese colonization of Korea, and security issues such as missiles and weapons of mass destruction. For the Japanese side the real sticking point was the abductions of mostly young Japanese from Japan to North Korea in the late 1970s and early 1980s, apparently to train spies in the Japanese language and customs. Security issues also loomed large. In July and August, a series of meetings were held between officials of the two sides, at which the Japanese side began to sense a readiness among their North Korean counterparts to address some at least of the Japanese concerns. This was around the time that the North Koreans were introducing price reforms, suggesting some loosening of tight economic control, possibly in the direction of a more open regime. Thus it was that a summit meeting was arranged between the Japanese Prime Minister and the North Korean President for 17 September.

Koizumi flew to Pyongyang and back on the same day, emphasizing the proximity of the two capitals. Out of the Koizumi visit came the Pyongyang Declaration, consisting of four articles, summarized here:

1   The two sides resolved to normalize relations and resume talks to that end during October.
2   'Settling accounts with the past' was dealt with by a Japanese apology, provision for economic assistance after diplomatic relations were normalized, mutual waiving of property claims from before 1945, and the promise to discuss the status of Korean residents in Japan.
3   On abductions, the North Korean side agreed to ensure that no similar incidents would occur in the future. (President Kim Jong Il made a forthright apology for what had happened, but this was not part of the declaration.)
4   On security and peace issues, the two sides agreed to promote regional cooperation and confidence-building, to observe international agreements and to resolve security issues including nuclear and missile questions 'by promoting dialogues among countries concerned', as well as bilateral discussions. North Korea agreed to keep its moratorium on missile launching 'in and after 2003'.[38]

Undoubtedly this was the most promising development relating to Korea that had occurred for many years, but sadly it was to prove abortive. The first thing that spoiled the favourable impact of the Koizumi visit was the information given by North Korean officials to the Japanese side that of the 13 Japanese

[38]   *Asahi Shinbun*, 18 September 2002.

nationals that both sides now agreed had been abducted – mostly from Japanese coastal areas – in the late 1970s and early 1980s, eight had died. Since their age at the time of abduction was young (the youngest had been 13),[39] it seemed implausible that so many should have died, except by violent means, if all the eight were indeed dead (as some in Japan came to doubt).

At this news, public opinion in Japan, amply reflected in the media, erupted in anger, and the abduction issue came to overshadow other aspects of the visit and the Pyongyang Declaration. To an extraordinary extent, this issue domi-nated media reporting and discussion in the months and years to come. The anguish of the families concerned was real enough, and the affair undoubtedly touched a deep stratum of feeling in the Japanese population. The idea that young people should have been kidnapped from beaches by agents of a ruthless foreign government and held for years with no possibility of contacting their parents, who knew nothing of their fate, would have outraged public opinion in any country. The story also remained in the public eye long afterwards partly because the five surviving abductees were returned to Japan in October 2002,[40] and their stories became the subject of intense and continuing media interest. Nevertheless, it is difficult to escape the conclusion that the North Korean abduc-tions were used by radical conservative politicians in the Japanese government as part of a broader agenda to justify moves towards a harder line on foreign policy and defence, and indeed to put pressure on the media to support official policies (a case of official pressure on the national broadcasting network, NHK, in relation to the abduction issue is discussed towards the end of this chapter).

Subsequent developments involving North Korea in effect scuppered Koizumi's promising initiative. An American delegation to Pyongyang in October claimed it had found confirmation that the North Koreans had been pursuing a uranium enrichment programme, in violation of agreements made in 1994. The American administration of President George W. Bush was now taking a tough and uncom-promising stand in its dealings with the North Korean regime, thus arguably augmenting the paranoia that infected the Pyongyang regime's view of the out-side world. Far from preventing the development of a nuclear weapons capacity by North Korea, it may even have accelerated it. So far as Japan was concerned, at a meeting on 30 October 2002 between officials of Japan and North Korea in Kuala Lumpur, the North Koreans simply refused to discuss nuclear weapons, and wanted only to talk about normalizing relations.

The position of the Koizumi government was reasonably stable at this period, but in December a change of leadership took place in the main opposition party, the DPJ. Hatoyama Yukio, who had been the Representative of the Party since September 1999, was forced to resign in face of internal criticism for having conducted negotiations – allegedly without authorization – with the Liberal Party and the Social Democratic Party, with a view to merging the three into a

---

[39]   This was Yokota Megumi, abducted in 1977. A film has been made of her tragic story: *Abduction: The Megumi Yokota Story*, distributed by Safari Media LLC (www.safarimedia.net).
[40]   *Asahi Shinbun*, 16 October 2002.

single party.[41] An election was held to replace him, at which the winner was the man whom Hatoyama had earlier supplanted, Kan Naoto. As we shall see, however, this neither produced stable leadership nor ended attempts to bring together the various parties in opposition to the Koizumi government. The DPJ, LP and SDP were able, at least, to coordinate their economic policies in Parliament at the end of 2002.[42]

The year 2003 saw a gradual rise in the temperature of parliamentary debate on the subject of Iraq. Once it had become evident that the US President was determined to remove the Iraqi regime of President Saddam Hussein by force, the question of what policies Japan should adopt became a live issue. Kan Naoto, now once again leader of the principal opposition party, was an effective parliamentary debater, and on various occasions he accused the Prime Minister of blindly following the policies and preferences of the United States without expressing his own independently formed views.

The Japanese government indeed took a hard line against the Iraqi regime at the United Nations, calling for a second resolution by the Security Council sanctioning military action against Saddam Hussein. When attempts to pass such a resolution failed, and the deadline imposed upon the Iraqi President to leave the country had passed without action on his part, American and British forces entered Iraq and quickly overthrew the Saddam Hussein regime. The fact that the UNSC resolution did not materialize, as well as the lack of evidence of weapons of mass destruction discovered by the UN inspectors of the Blix Commission (whose work was halted by the invasion), made the invasion of Iraq from the start a matter of enormous controversy. Koizumi and his team, however, gave the appearance of harbouring few doubts about the validity of the US and British decision.

In July, the long and complex negotiations for amalgamation of opposition parties reached resolution, with the announcement that the Democratic Party, led by Kan Naoto, and the Liberal Party, led by Ozawa Ichirō, were to merge (the Social Democratic Party, however, was not included). This was not so much a merger of equals as the absorption of the LP by the DPJ, whose name, structure and principal policies would live on in the new party. This decision meant a much strengthened opposition party, reinforced by the reformist approaches that had been a feature of Ozawa and the Liberal Party.[43]

The merged party held its first Congress in October, issuing a 'manifesto' (the English word was used), consisting of five promises and two proposals. The promises were:

1   Abolition within four years of all subsidies from the bureaucracy having strings attached.
2   Total disclosure of political financial contributions.
3   Abolition of the public road corporations, and free travel on high-speed roads within three years.

---

[41]   *Asahi Shinbun*, 4 December 2002.
[42]   *Asahi Shinbun*, 29 December 2002.
[43]   *Asahi Shinbun*, 24 July 2003.

4   A reduction of 10 per cent within three years in both the number of parliamentarians and the personnel expenses of public servants.
5   Cancellation of projects for two dams and one land reclamation project (a list of these was appended).

The proposals were:

1   To use the consumption tax to fund the basic pension, and establish a new pension system.
2   To restrict primary school classes to thirty pupils, and re-examine the five-day school week.[44]

In September, Koizumi too had announced a party 'manifesto' – this being the current buzz-word in party political circles. This was in the context of his campaign for re-election as President of his party. Among items relating to economic revival, pensions, health care, nursing care, inter-generational equity, national defence, human security, employment, the environment, technology, science and culture, and administrative decentralization, he emphasized three items that were central to his approach. One was privatization of postal services, to begin in April 2007. The second was privatization of the four public road corporations – a process to start in 2005. And the third was a pledge to reform the LDP.[45] Koizumi launched his manifesto in an upbeat mood, which he could afford to do as the economy was belatedly showing signs of renewed vigour.

It was hardly surprising, therefore that in September 2003 Koizumi was easily re-elected as LDP President, ensuring the continuation of his position as Prime Minister for another two years. The results were as follows: Koizumi Junichirō 399; Kamei Shizuka 139; Fujii Takao 65; Kōmura Masahiko 54.[46] It was perhaps significant that Koizumi received 68 per cent of the votes of local representatives, but only 54 per cent of the votes of LDP parliamentarians, among whom his early promise to 'smash' (bukkowasu) the LDP, and subsequent pursuit of radical reform, made him enemies as well as friends. He appointed as the new Secretary-General of the party Abe Shinzō, a right-wing radical from a leading political family, at the time regarded as young for the job at 49. This was a significant appointment in the light of later events.

On 9 November general elections for the House of Representatives were held, to renew a house that had last faced election in June 2000. The Liberal Democrats fell back slightly, from 247 seats before the elections to 237 after them. Impressively, the DPJ, now incorporating members of the former Liberal Party, progressed from 137 seats to 177 (out of a total of 480). This was the best result for a party of opposition since the 1950s, and continued a trend whereby the DPJ had improved its position in each election since it was first founded in 1996. Frustratingly, however, it was still well short of overtaking the LDP. In the 11 blocs elected by proportional representation it was ahead (DPJ 72; LDP 69), but

[44]   *Asahi Shinbun*, 6 October 2003.
[45]   *Asahi Shinbun*, 9 September 2003.
[46]   *Asahi Shinbun*, 21 September 2003.

in the single-member seats it was well behind (LDP 168; DPJ 105). This pointed to the major advantage the Liberal Democrats, with their superior funding and local power networks, had over the Democrats in the single-member seats, and showed graphically that elections were not simply fought on policy lines.

Two other elements in these election results should be noted. The Conservative Party (by now called the New Conservative Party and still in coalition with the LDP) saw its seat total reduced from nine to four, so the party was disbanded and the remaining elected members joined the LDP, boosting its total by four seats. Second, the parties of the left, already much reduced, were routed. The JCP was reduced from 20 seats to nine, and the SDP from 18 seats to six. Doi Takako, the first woman to head a Japanese political party, resigned to take responsibility for the defeat.[47] All of this had the effect of continuing a process that had been developing progressively over the three elections held so far under the new electoral system (1996, 2000, 2003), whereby minor parties were diminished to the benefit of the larger parties.[48]

After the elections Koizumi reshuffled his Cabinet. One of the most significant appointments was a re-appointment: that of Takenaka Heizō, his unbending market-liberal adviser, to the economics and finance portfolio. Another, significant in terms of the impending decision whether to send a contingent from the Self-Defence Forces to Iraq, was the appointment of Ishiba Shigeru, a strong defence advocate, to be minister in charge of the Defence Agency. At the same time the former LDP President, and later Foreign Minister (but never Prime Minister), Kōno Yōhei, became Speaker of the House of Representatives. Taken together with the recent retirement of a tough senior LDP administrator called Nonaka Hiromu, this meant that the two most prominent supporters of the 1946 Constitution still active in the ruling party had in effect left the scene. The reshuffle thus indicated a further distinct move to the right within government.

This period also saw the development of new ideas in relation to financing of local government. Hitherto, much local government funding had been provided by government ministries from national taxation, for the fulfilment of purposes determined by each ministry. The new idea was to give a substantial proportion of these tax revenues directly to the local authorities, thus endowing them with greater freedom of choice about how the money should be spent. This was known as 'Three Reforms in One' (san'i ittai kaikaku).[49]

Another government initiative was the introduction into Parliament of a bill to provide for a range of contingencies in the case of military emergency. These were defined to include armed attack by a foreign power, but also terrorist

---

[47]   Her successor was a woman called Fukushima Mizuho, a progressive lawyer.

[48]   The one exception was the Clean Government Party, a member of the government coalition, which slightly increased its seat total from 31 to 34. Its capacity to survive was largely the result of its religious support base and tight discipline among adherents. Even so, 25 of its seats were won in the proportional representation constituencies and only nine in single-member constituencies.

[49]   Asahi Shinbun, 20 November 2003. The 'three reforms' were (1) to reduce subsidies to local authorities; (2) to transfer sources of tax to local authorities so that they could have sufficient revenues for free use; (3) to revamp the local grants taxes distributed to local authorities to make up revenue shortfalls. Asahi Shinbun, 13 November 2004.

attacks. Local authorities were to be given wider authority to act in such emergencies. This was an area where constitutional inhibitions had led to governmental reluctance to bring in effective legislation. The issue had been discussed for many years, but now the Koizumi government was determined to create a robust legislative framework to deal with such matters as protecting the lives and property of citizens in the event of a military emergency.[50] The final package of bills became law in February 2004.[51]

The government's determination to maintain close military–strategic links with the United States created a favourable atmosphere for possible cooperation between Japan and the US in the development of missile defence systems. In the thinking of both governments, the imminent or actual possession of nuclear weapons and their means of delivery by North Korea made it prudent to develop systems that could destroy attacking missiles before they reached their targets. The huge cost and problematic viability of such systems did not deter intensive activity to this end.

Perhaps the most crucial item on the government's agenda as 2003 drew to a close was the proposal to send a contingent from the Self-Defence Forces to Iraq. A rude reminder of the dangers inherent in involvement in Iraq was given at the end of November when two Foreign Ministry officials on a national fact-finding mission, travelling on a road north of Baghdad, were shot and killed from a car overtaking their vehicle. The Prime Minister declared that this would not change government policy of sending troops to Iraq, but it shocked public opinion and increased the sensitivity of the issue.[52]

In order to be able to legislate for the despatch of troops, it was crucial for Koizumi to obtain the support of the CGP, which had become conspicuous as the element within his coalition most inclined to be sceptical about military initiatives. This caution seems to have derived in part from the strength of anti-war feeling among members of the *Sōka Gakkai* (especially women members), who were the party's principal source of support. Even so, in December the CGP leaders came to the conclusion that they wanted to stay within the coalition. Although they were plainly unhappy about the proposal to send troops to Iraq, they eventually agreed to 'respect the judgement of the Prime Minister'.[53] The decision to send troops to Iraq was formally announced on 9 December 2003. They would be stationed at Samawa, in the south of the country – a location regarded as relatively safe – and their tasks would be strictly non-military, described as 'humanitarian aid activities for rehabilitation' (*jindōteki fukkō shien katsudō*). These comprised principally projects in the fields of education, health and public works (water supply, road-building, etc.).[54] The contingent was to be severely restricted in respect of the arms its members could carry, and so would need to be protected by the troops of other nations participating in the Iraq

---

[50] *Asahi Shinbun*, 22 November 2003.
[51] *Asahi Shinbun*, 25 February 2004.
[52] *Asahi Shinbun*, 1 December 2003.
[53] *Asahi Shinbun*, 4 December 2003.
[54] For a full text of the Basic Plan for Despatch to Iraq, see *Asahi Shinbun*, 10 December 2003.

operation. The advance guard was sent to Iraq on 19 January 2004, and the contingent built up to full strength (600 troops in all) in the weeks following. Although the despatch of troops was politically controversial, and public opinion was equivocal on the matter, the exercise did not create the kinds of determined opposition that such an event would have evoked one or two decades earlier. When, in April 2004, three young Japanese nationals engaged in voluntary work in Iraq were kidnapped by Iraqi irregulars, who demanded the withdrawal of Japanese troops as a condition of their release, Koizumi immediately rejected the demand. When the three were later released and repatriated, they met with surprisingly little sympathy and a good deal of criticism. A public opinion poll conducted by the *Asahi* immediately following their release showed 73 per cent of those polled agreeing with the Prime Minister's rejection of the kidnappers' demand for Japan to withdraw its troops from Iraq. This contrasted with more or less evenly divided opinion over the rights and wrongs of sending troops at the time this was initially decided.[55] Shortly after the release of the three voluntary workers, two Japanese freelance journalists who had been kidnapped in Iraq were also set free.

Deregulation had been an issue on the political agenda for at least a decade, but for various reasons it had proved difficult to bring about across the board. The imperative, however, of rescuing the economy from its long stagnation was generally thought to require greater freedom for economic actors to show initiative without having to confront suffocating regulatory constraints. The government therefore hit upon the idea of sanctioning ad hoc deregulation in circumstances where it could be shown that lack of rules would not create harm. What was proposed was the device of authorizing 'special zones for structural reform' (*kōzō kaikaku tokku*), and in the summer of 2003 the government set up a bureau to promote such zones, headed by the Prime Minister. 'Zones' did not have only a geographical but in some cases also a functional meaning. Examples included a 'special zone' to promote trade in goods by having customs posts open twenty-four hours a day; relaxation of the law concerning tax on *sake* to permit the production of a home-brewed variety (*doburoku*); a 'special zone' for English-language education; and a 'special zone' to permit a company to borrow agricultural land (normally highly regulated) for the production of olives. By mid-February 2004 no fewer than 236 of these zones had been approved.[56]

In May several leading politicians found themselves in trouble over non-payment of pension contributions. Pensions had become a big economic and therefore political issue because of the rapid ageing of the population and the difficulty of maintaining a viable pension scheme to provide for increasing numbers of elderly people. The current pension system was a complex mixture of public and private provision, which the government was striving to rationalize. But the fundamental long-term problem was that the ratio of those in receipt of a pension to those still in the workforce was rapidly shifting in such a way that it was unlikely to be possible to pay pensions to those still in work at the levels currently prevailing when the time came for them to retire. Japan was both the

[55]   *Asahi Shinbun*, 9, 16, 17 April 2004.
[56]   *Asahi Shinbun*, 15 February 2004.

longest-lived and the most rapidly ageing society in the world, so that the point had almost been reached at which the population would peak and begin to decline. Moreover, the baby-boom generation of the post-war years was now close to retirement,[57] so that the strain on the resources of pension schemes would rapidly increase.

Given the intense interest in the need to reform the pension system, the discovery that prominent politicians had not been paying pension contributions became a major controversy, from which the alleged culprits could not easily hope to emerge unscathed. Up to a certain point in the past, contributions had been voluntary, but later they had been made compulsory. Not to have made contributions when there was no compulsion to do so was not so much of a problem (the Prime Minister himself was in this position), but once payment had become an obligation, then it was difficult to escape the consequences. On 7 May the Chief Cabinet Secretary, Fukuda Yasuo, tendered his resignation.[58] But then, three days later, Kan Naoto, who as Representative of the Democratic Party had been leading vigorous parliamentary criticism of the Koizumi government over a range of issues (including Iraq), had to confess his own delinquency over the question of pension contributions. Kan resigned after only ten months back as his party's leader.[59]

Kan's departure necessitated new elections for the leadership of the DPJ. The obvious candidate was Ozawa, but it turned out that he was also in trouble over non-payment of pension contributions, and so he withdrew his candidacy. This left a younger candidate, 50-year-old Okada Katsuya, who was elected unopposed.[60] Okada had the reputation of being something of a theorist rather than a hands-on politician, and was said not to recognize factional loyalties within his party. He nevertheless proved a more successful leader than many had anticipated from the rather unsmiling and rigid image he projected.

On 22 May 2004 Koizumi paid his second visit to Pyongyang. His main purpose seems to have been to reach understanding on aspects of the abductions issue, which had blown up into a huge controversy in Japan. An association of families of those who had been abducted had been formed, widely known as the 'Families Association' (kazoku kai). The parents of Yokota Megumi (abducted aged 13 in 1977 and said by the Pyongyang authorities to have committed suicide in the early 1990s),[61] took a leadership role in the association, and became among the most familiar faces on Japanese television. They consistently took a hard line against North Korea, and on this occasion Megumi's father, Yokota

[57] In Japanese the baby-boomers are known as the 'lump generation' (dankai sedai).

[58] Asahi Shinbun, 8 May 2004.

[59] Asahi Shinbun, 11 May 2004

[60] Asahi Shinbun, 18, 19 May 2004.

[61] It turned out that Yokota Megumi had married a Korean man, by whom she had a daughter, now a high-school student in Pyongyang. Later press interviews with the daughter, Kim Ki Gyeon, who apparently had not known her late mother was Japanese or that she had been abducted, were to be one of the most sensational episodes in this affair.

Shigeru, publicly expressed his suspicion that the Koizumi government had offered economic aid to North Korea as a *quid pro quo* for the return of the children of the abductees.[62]

Among the five abductees earlier returned to Japan were two couples, who had met and married in North Korea. Between them they had five children, and simultaneously with the Koizumi visit to Pyongyang, these five – aged between 16 and 22 – were allowed to visit Japan. The fifth abductee earlier returned, Ms Soga Hitomi, was married to Charles Jenkins, who had deserted from the US forces in South Korea in the 1960s. This couple had two daughters, whose repatriation posed more complicated problems, which took some more months to sort out. Koizumi met Jenkins in Pyongyang and discussed his situation with him.

Koizumi did not confine himself to the abduction issue on this visit. In his meeting with Kim Jong Il, he expressed his desire to implement the Pyongyang Declaration of September 2002, to turn relations of enmity into relations of friendship, and to turn confrontation into cooperation. He called for a nuclear-free Korean peninsula and a moratorium on missile tests. And he promised food aid and medical aid to the people of North Korea, to be channelled through international organizations.[63]

As a reminder of continuing perils in Iraq, two Japanese freelance journalists were shot and killed near Baghdad at the end of May.[64] The government considered it essential to keep Japanese casualties to an absolute minimum, and even though these men were not part of the SDF contingent in Samawa, this incident risked turning public opinion against Japanese involvement in Iraq.

In early June the Pensions Reform Bill passed all parliamentary stages and became law. The Democratic Party, as well as the SDP and JCP, strongly contested it. When the Chairman of the House of Councillors Welfare and Labour Committee cut off debate on the bill while opposition party members were still within their time allocated for questions, the opposition parties moved a motion for the dismissal of the Chairman. This was, of course, defeated by strength of pro-government numbers. The DPJ and SDP members then absented themselves from the final session on the bill.[65] This was another instance, of which there had been many in the past, of parties out of power boycotting a vote, or a session, as a means of expressing their dismay at the actions of government parties. Votes taken in the absence of opposition party members were often described as 'forced votes', implying that government was exploiting its 'tyranny of the majority'. Behind this was a cultural norm rather at variance with standard decision-making by majority vote, namely that decisions ought to be made consensually, and that if elements of the opposition indicated their strong unhappiness by boycotting a session, the parties in power should maintain consensus by making concessions to them (see Chapter 3).

---

[62]   *Asahi Shinbun*, 23 May 2004.
[63]   Ibid.
[64]   *Asahi Shinbun*, 29 May 2004.
[65]   *Asahi Shinbun*, 6 June 2004.

As we have already seen, in a society with a declining birth rate and a growing proportion of elderly people,[66] pensions were a charged political issue. The government was facing the urgent imperative of rescuing pension schemes from bankruptcy. But the tough stand taken by the DPJ on a pensions bill that would result in reduced benefits did it no harm at all, at a time when upper house elections were imminent. A public opinion poll published on 12 June showed 67 per cent unhappy about the new law on pensions. It also showed that while 20 per cent hoped that the LDP would win more seats in the upper house elections (down from 29 per cent in May), now 28 per cent hoped the DPJ would win more seats (up from 20 per cent in May).

Elections for half the seats in the House of Councillors were held on 11 July. As predicted, the Democrats won more seats than their Liberal Democrat rivals, reversing the results in 2001. Since, however, only half the seats were contested, the LDP retained a plurality of seats in the house as a whole, while being well short of an overall majority. Specifically, of the seats contested, the LDP had 50 seats at dissolution but dropped to 49. The DPJ held 38 seats at dissolution but rose to 50. The CGP gained 1 seat (rising from 10 to 11) and the SDP retained the same number of seats as before (5), but the JCP was routed, losing all but 4 of 15 contested seats. This meant that the totals for the whole house were (previous totals in brackets): LDP 115 (116); DPJ 82 (70); CGP 24 (23); JCP 9 (20); SDP 5 (5); unaffiliated 5 (4): total 242 (245). There were strong indications that the pensions issue had swung numerous votes towards the DPJ.[67] The leadership of Okada Katsuya, who was something of an unknown quantity when he first took over the DPJ leadership a few weeks previously, was consolidated by the result. On the other side of the political divide, Koizumi's key Economics Minister, Takenaka Heizō, won a seat, having previously sat in Cabinet as a non-parliamentary member. The results may be interpreted as a further step in a trend towards a system dominated by two major parties.

A few days before the elections, Charles Jenkins, his wife Soga Hitomi and their two daughters were reunited in Jakarta after more than 18 months of separation. This family presented a delicate diplomatic problem for Japan, the United States and North Korea. Jenkins, as a deserter from the US armed forces, could be subject to extradition if he returned to Japan, where, however, the family was the object of widespread sympathy. The North Korean authorities may have been reluctant to let him go as someone who knew too many North Korean secrets. Eventually a compromise was reached whereby the family would be reunited in Indonesia, then flown back to Japan, where Jenkins would receive urgently needed medical treatment. He would then report to US military authorities in Japan and suffer a period of incarceration. In the event he spent about a month with the US military, no doubt telling them what he knew about North Korea; then he was released, and the family resumed their life together on Sado Island, off the Japan Sea coast.

---

[66] The latest birth rate figures were the lowest yet: 1.29 children on average born per woman: *Asahi Shinbun*, 10 June 2004.

[67] *Asahi Shinbun*, 12 July 2004. The total number of seats had been cut by nine since the 2001 elections.

In September, the Cabinet embarked on a course that was to dominate politics for the next year and more. It took the decision to privatize postal services, meaning that the savings bank, insurance, mail delivery and window network arms of the postal services should be divided into separate private companies, registered on the stock exchange. This initiative was based on Koizumi's long-held belief that having postal services under public ownership had led to massive misuse of funds, inefficiency and the kinds of corruption that were fed by infusions of public money into vested interests and pet projects.[68] He attracted determined criticism from within the LDP on the issue, but at the outset of the parliamentary session that began in January 2005, after lengthy attempts to negotiate with dissenters, he declared that he would not give ground on the issues involved.[69]

Near the end of September, Koizumi reshuffled his Cabinet. He retained six ministers in their existing, mostly heavyweight, posts. Asō Tarō, a right-wing politician with clear prime ministerial ambitions, remained as General Affairs Minister; the Ministry of Finance was left in the hands of Tanigaki Sadakazu, a moderate who had recently inherited the faction previously led by the ill-fated Katō Kōichi; Nakagawa Shōichi, a politician of the extreme right from Hokkaidō, retained the portfolio of Economy, Trade and Industry; a leading woman politician, Koike Yuriko (an Arabist with a degree from Cairo University), remained as Minister for the Environment; and Hosoda Hiroyuki, of the dominant Mori faction, was still Chief Cabinet Secretary. Most importantly, perhaps, the free-market aficionado Takenaka Heizō was kept in place as Minister for Economics and Finance. His responsibility to oversee the privatization of postal services was clearly signalled. Of the changes, perhaps the most important concerned the Foreign Affairs portfolio. Whereas the last two Ministers of Foreign Affairs had been women,[70] the new Minister was Machimura Nobutaka, who had previously held a top position in the LDP.

In October the report was handed to the Prime Minister of the government Commission on Security and Defence Strength (*Anzen hoshō to bōeiryoku ni kansuru kondankai*) that had been set up the previous April. The commission's report reflected the increasingly close links between the US and Japan in military matters, and recommended closer cooperation with the US in combating terror. It also recommended a relaxation of the long-standing embargo on the export of armaments manufactured in Japan.[71] Later in the same month a controversy within Cabinet was reported, relating to the definition of the 'Far East' in the 1960 Mutual Security Treaty between Japan and the United States. Some ministers wished to expand the geographical definition of the term as used in the treaty, so as to permit Japan to project its forces in aid of American military operations over a wider area. In the end an assurance was made that nothing would be done outside the ambit of the treaty.[72]

---

[68]   *Asahi Shinbun*, 11 September 2004.
[69]   *Asahi Shinbun*, 22 January 2005.
[70]   Successively the controversial Tanaka Makiko, and the more measured Kawaguchi Yoriko.
[71]   *Asahi Shinbun*, 5 October 2004.
[72]   *Asahi Shinbun*, 21 October 2004.

Relations with China started to rise on the Japanese political agenda late in 2004. In November an unidentified submarine apparently entered Japanese territorial waters near to Okinawa. Evidence was strong that it was nuclear-powered, and that its nationality was Chinese.[73] Later in the month, two top Chinese leaders, Hu Jintao and Wen Jiabao, successively protested to Koizumi about his repeated visits to the Yasukuni Shrine.[74] These events were to mark a stage in the progressive deterioration in official relations between China and Japan over the rest of the period that Koizumi was to remain Prime Minister. Indeed, less than six months later, in April 2005, serious anti-Japanese riots broke out in various parts of China, and stones were thrown from a huge crowd through the windows of the Japanese Embassy in Beijing. It is unclear how far these riots were spontaneous and how far organized with government assistance, but in the end they threatened to get out of hand and were curbed by official action.[75] These events caused shock in Japan, and a reassessment of relations with China. An attempt was made to put the relationship on a better footing when Koizumi and the Chinese Party Chairman Hu Jintao met in Jakarta in late April.[76] But in May the Chinese Vice-Premier, Ms Wu Li, on an official visit to Japan, citing Yasukuni visits by ministers, cancelled a scheduled meeting with Koizumi, who commented to the press: 'I don't need to meet someone who doesn't want to meet me.'[77] The Yasukuni issue also caused strains between the parties of the coalition, with the CGP calling on the Prime Minister to show restraint in his pilgrimages to the shrine, in the interests of maintaining good relations between Japan and China.[78]

If relations with China were strained, relations with North Korea developed in bizarre directions under the influence of developments surrounding the abductions. A third round of talks began in Pyongyang between officials of the two sides regarding the eight abductees said by the North Koreans to have died and two others of whom they said they had no knowledge. The Japanese side pressed their Korean counterparts to produce concrete evidence of the deaths and how they had happened. The Koreans admitted that previous documentation about the deaths had been forged. Eventually the North Korean authorities provided what they said were samples from the body of Yokota Megumi, whose case had been strongly contested by her parents. DNA testing by a Japanese laboratory was reported to reveal that the samples did not come from her body, but from two other unknown individuals.[79] North Korea later formally claimed that the Japanese test results were falsified.[80] Under the influence of these and earlier developments, most Japanese now regarded the North Korean regime with extreme distaste and some apprehension, making it difficult for Japanese leaders to attempt serious dialogue with it.

[73]   *Asahi Shinbun,* 17 November 2004.
[74]   *Asahi Shinbun,* 23 November and 1 December 2004.
[75]   *Asahi Shinbun,* 10 and 20 April 2005.
[76]   *Asahi Shinbun,* 24 April 2005.
[77]   *Asahi Shinbun,* 24 and 25 May 2005.
[78]   *Asahi Shinbun,* 26 May 2005.
[79]   *Asahi Shinbun,* 16 November and 9 December 2004. Having earlier told the Japanese side that Megumi had died in March 1993, they now changed the month to April 1994.
[80]   *Asahi Shinbun,* 27 January 2005.

In December, the government decided to extend for a further year the Self-Defence Forces mission to Iraq. Scepticism about the project – and even calls for the troops to be withdrawn – was being expressed even within the government parties, so the Prime Minister needed to defend the decision with care. He argued publicly that the force was needed because the security situation in Iraq remained unresolved, because he expected the rather quiet Samawa region to remain outside the areas of conflict, and, perhaps most importantly, because Japan need to pay its dues to the US–Japan alliance, given the unstable international situation in East Asia.[81] Japan's increasing defence readiness was underlined by the New Defence Plan Outline (*shin bōei keikaku taikō*) announced around the same time.[82]

Further evidence soon emerged that relations with neighbouring states were likely to experience persistent problems, this time concerning Japan's relations with South Korea. There was an outstanding territorial dispute between the two countries about some rocky islets to the east of the Korean peninsula, known in Korean as Dokdo (Lonely Island) and in Japanese as Takeshima (Bamboo Island). On older Western maps they were also known as the Liancourt Rocks.[83] Their disposition had been contested since the end of the Second World War: they were in the possession of South Korea but claimed by Japan. The total land area concerned was about the size of two or three football pitches. In March 2005, Shimane Prefecture, on the Japan Sea coast and the nearest part of Japan to Takeshima, held a 'Takeshima Day', to emphasize a continuing Japanese claim.[84] This triggered a hostile reaction from the South Korean government of President Rho Moo Hyun, who was not disinclined to stir up anti-Japanese feeling in order to distract attention from domestic political problems. Relations between Japan and the Republic of Korea went into a difficult period that contrasted with the friendly interlude of the pro-Japanese President Kim Dae Jung in the late 1990s, and the time of euphoria generated by the joint Japanese–Korean sponsorship of the football World Cup in 2002.

An ongoing issue of supreme importance both domestically and in terms of future international repercussions was the government's aim of revising the 1946 Constitution. On 4 April 2005 the LDP committee charged with drafting a revised constitution issued its report.[85] The committee's chairman was the former Prime Minister Mori Yoshirō. Its recommendations will be summarized in Chapter 10, but it is pertinent to mention at this point its proposals on defence. These were that the 'Self Defence Forces' (*Jieitai*) be renamed 'Military Forces for Self Defence' (*Jieigun*),[86] and enabled to contribute to international peace and security; that the Prime Minister have supreme command of the armed

[81]   *Asahi Shinbun*, 10 December 2004.
[82]   *Asahi Shinbun*, 11 December 2004.
[83]   On this and other territorial disputes in the region, see Kimie Hara, *Cold War Frontiers in the Asia–Pacific: Divided Territories in the San Francisco System*, Abingdon and New York, Routledge, 2007.
[84]   *Asahi Shinbun*, 17 March 2005.
[85]   *Asahi Shinbun*, 5 April 2005.
[86]   The more usual translation 'Self-Defence Army' is misleading in that it appears to ignore the navy and air force.

forces; and that the principle of civilian control be embedded in the Constitution. In early August the LDP became the first party since the war to issue a complete draft of a revised constitution.[87]

Both houses of Parliament had appointed committees that had been working on constitutional revision for many months, but, with parties having substantially different ideas about reform, both committees were finding difficulty in producing agreed reports. Nevertheless, the committee of the House of Representatives published its final report at the end of April.[88] Polls taken around this time showed declining levels of resistance to constitutional revision as such, but polarized opinions on whether to revise the peace clause (article 9).[89]

Much the biggest issue in domestic politics in 2005 was postal services privatization. For Koizumi, this was both his flagship policy and also something that cut to the core of a hugely important section of organized support for the LDP, namely the massed forces of postmasters throughout the land. Late in May the National Special Postmasters Association (*Zenkoku tokutei yūbinkyokuchō kai*) held its annual conference, at which it expressed wholehearted opposition to 'unprincipled' privatization of postal services. Instead of inviting representatives from the LDP, as in previous years, the association invited – for the first time since the war – the chairmen of the two postal services labour unions, with which it was normally at loggerheads. The unions, moreover, were close to the DPJ. Those who did attend from the LDP were members firmly opposed to privatization, such as the former Speaker of the Lower House, Watanuki Tamisuke.[90]

A revised bill was approved by the LDP at the end of June on a majority vote, including substantial concessions to the privatization opponents. Nevertheless, on 5 July, the bill only barely passed the House of Representatives with a majority of five votes. Thirty-seven LDP parliamentarians (including Watanuki) voted against, and a further 14 were absent or cast invalid votes.[91] This was a major revolt in a party that normally maintained tight discipline over its members' voting behaviour in Parliament. A vote was then taken in the House of Councillors on 8 August, in which the government bill was defeated by 125 votes to 108. Negative votes were cast by 22 LDP parliamentarians, while a further 8 either absented themselves or cast invalid ballots.[92]

This confronted Koizumi with the greatest challenge of his prime ministership, and in the crisis caused by defeat of the postal services privatization bill, he proved himself to be a brilliant political strategist.

The Prime Minister dissolved the House of Representatives, and under article 54 of the Constitution declared new elections for 11 September – a date not without significance.[93] He refused to allow LDP endorsement of the members

---

[87] *Asahi Shinbun*, 2 and 3 August 2005.
[88] *Asahi Shinbun*, 1 May 2005.
[89] *Asahi Shinbun*, 3 May 2005.
[90] *Asahi Shinbun*, 10 June 2005.
[91] *Asahi Shinbun*, 6 July 2005.
[92] *Asahi Shinbun*, 9 August 2005.
[93] Article 54: 'When the House of Representatives is dissolved, there must be a general election of members of the House of Representatives within forty days from the date of dissolution ...'

who had opposed the bill in the lower house, and proceeded to select candidates to run against them in their constituencies. This would force them either to stand as Independents or to form new parties. After discussions with the head of the CGP, Kanzaki Takenori, he announced that if the elections were won, he would re-introduce the postal services privatization bill into Parliament. Immediately after the bill's defeat, the Democrats brought in a no-confidence motion against the government, but because of the dissolution no vote on it was taken.

There were immediate indications that Koizumi's bold and decisive actions had struck a favourable chord with the electorate, and that his popularity was rising as a result.[94] The alternative candidates selected to contest the constituencies of the rebels quickly came to be described both as 'the assassins' and as 'Koizumi's children'. The new candidates included a young, American-style businessman called Horie Takafumi, founder of the Livedoor Company, who was receiving widespread press coverage for what were in the Japanese context unorthodox business methods. Horie contested the constituency of the formidable leader of the privatization rebels, Kamei Shizuka, who in mid-August, with Watanuki and others, had formed a new mini-party called the People's New Party (PNP, *Kokumin Shintō*), consisting of former LDP parliamentarians refused endorsement.[95]

The elections produced a spectacular victory for Koizumi and the LDP and a devastating setback for the DPJ. The Liberal Democrats, who had occupied 249 seats at dissolution in August (and only 212 after the privatization rebels had been expelled), now won 296 out of a total 480 seats. Their main rivals the Democrats were reduced from 175 at dissolution to 113. The CGP lost 3 seats to win 31. The Communists retained their pre-election total of 9, and the Social Democrats rose from 6 to 7. Of the newly formed parties, the People's New Party of Watanuki and Kamei won a mere 4 seats. Kamei, however, with his formidable local electoral machine, beat off the challenge from Horie and was re-elected. A few weeks later Horie, who had spectacularly cocked a snook at the business establishment, found himself in trouble with the law and committed to gaol. Two seats were won by minor parties and 18 unaffiliated candidates were returned.

Koizumi, who had promised to 'smash' the LDP, had led it to its best election result in years. But he had done so by changing its structure and in part also its ethos, getting rid of those who resisted change and replacing them with his own nominees – 'Koizumi's children' – who became a new and dynamic force within the party. The DPJ, which had been advancing from election to election, was stopped in its tracks. Subsequent analysis of reasons for such a result suggested that while the LDP victory was largely due to Koizumi, the DPJ defeat was most importantly the fault of that party.[96]

---

[94]   For instance, 48% of those polled supported his dissolution of Parliament: *Asahi Shinbun*, 10 August 2005.
[95]   *Asahi Shinbun*, 18 August 2007. At around the same time two other mini-parties were formed: the New Party Japan (*Shintō nihon*), founded by the controversial Governor of Nagano Prefecture, Tanaka Yasuo; and the New Party Earth (*Shintō daichi*), based in Hokkaidō and led by the maverick Suzuki Muneo.
[96]   *Asahi Shinbun*, 14 September 2005.

Okada Katsuya, the DPJ Representative, promptly resigned to take responsibility for his party's defeat. Two candidates contested the succession: the perennial Kan Naoto, trying to make yet another comeback, and a 43-year old parliamentarian from Kyoto called Maehara Seiji, who held the shadow defence portfolio. In a close vote on 17 September, Maehara beat Kan by 96 votes to 94. As leader, he sought to move party policy sharply to the right, causing deep internal divisions.

In October, the six related postal services privatization bills that had been rejected by the House of Councillors in August passed all stages of parliamentary procedure and became law. A timetable was set up for full privatization to begin in October 2007.[97] Most of those LDP upper house members who had voted against the bills in August voted for them this time, no doubt bowing to the inevitable and anxious to secure their positions within the principal ruling party.

In the same month the Prime Minister made his fifth annual pilgrimage to the Yasukuni Shrine. As usual this elicited a critical reaction from the Chinese and South Korean governments, and on this occasion the Chinese side cancelled a planned visit to China by the Japanese Foreign Minister, Machimura, five days before it was due to begin.[98]

An issue that required delicate political handling at this period was that of the imperial succession. The imperial family had not produced a male heir since the 1960s, which left the ultimate prospect that no male successor would eventually be left. The Crown Prince and Princess had a young daughter, but the current succession law did not admit female succession. With prime ministerial backing, therefore, the idea of changing the law to permit a female heir to become *Tennō* was actively discussed, though it met with resistance from traditionalists.[99] This solution was proposed by a committee of experts that reported in November.[100] In February 2006, however, it transpired that the wife of the brother of the Crown Prince was pregnant, and in September 2006 she gave birth to a boy. This last minute reprieve for the traditionalists essentially took the issue off the political agenda once again.

At the end of October 2005, Koizumi reshuffled his Cabinet. This time, two ministers were retained in their previous posts, one of them being Tanigaki Sadakazu, the Minister of Finance. The durable Takenaka Heizō was moved to the General Affairs portfolio, where he remained in charge of postal services privatization. A distinguished woman academic and diplomat, now parliamentarian, Inoguchi Kuniko, was put in charge of a portfolio to combat the low birth rate and to promote equality of men and women. The new Minister of Justice, Sugiura Seiken, brought the death penalty issue to the fore by declaring that on grounds of conscience he would not sign execution warrants, and

[97]   *Asahi Shinbun*, 15 October 2005.
[98]   *Asahi Shinbun*, 19 October 2005.
[99]   *Asahi Shinbun*, 26 October 2005.
[100]   *Asahi Shinbun*, 25 November 2005. A poll showed 71% in favour of allowing a woman *Tennō*: *Asahi Shinbun*, 29 November 2005.

expressing the view that the death penalty was on the way to being abolished.[101] Very promptly, however, he was forced to retract his statement, with the Prime Minister himself endorsing the death penalty.[102] Abe Shinzō, who ten months later was to be Koizumi's successor, became Chief Cabinet Secretary. Perhaps the most surprising appointment was that of the outspoken Asō Tarō as Minister of Foreign Affairs. Asō had been carving out an ideological position as an uncompromising right-winger, not overly concerned if he offended foreign sensibilities.[103]

In December the government extended by a further year the Self-Defence Forces mission to Iraq, while leaving open the option of at least partial withdrawal before the year was up.[104] The force had been effective within its limited brief, and had managed to avoid casualties, but the qualified character of the announcement tended to confirm the view that this was a minimal contribution, made as a necessary down payment to cement Japan's American alliance. The war in Iraq had not gone well (and would get worse), support for it was in decline in Japan as elsewhere, and the government prudently judged that its commitment should not be open-ended. Indeed, in June 2006 the decision was announced that the mission would be rapidly scaled down to the point of complete withdrawal.[105]

In February 2006 information emerged into the open that was to change the top leadership of the Democratic Party. One of the party's parliamentary members had alleged in the lower house budget committee that a senior LDP official had solicited a large sum of money from the Livedoor Company (now under police investigation), to be paid to the official's son. The DPJ, however, was unable to provide evidence to back up the allegation, and had to apologize. The man who had made the allegations was suspended from his parliamentary status by the party for six months, and the DPJ parliamentary committee chairman had to resign.[106] For a while it seemed that the party Representative, Maehara, would survive the crisis, but in the end he too was forced to step down.[107] He had proved a divisive leader, and his resignation gave an opportunity to the party to return to a path more acceptable to the bulk of its members.

This time the choice of a successor fell to Ozawa Ichirō, who beat the only other candidate, the persistent contender Kan Naoto, by 119 votes to 72.[108] Thus began the latest stage in the career of a remarkable reforming politician. He could have been Prime Minister at the start of the 1990s, but rejected this opportunity in favour of promoting reform of the whole system of politics. He was then the principal guiding force behind the Hosokawa and Hata governments of 1993–4, founded the New Frontier Party at the end of 1994 and led it

---

[101]   The last time that a Minister of Justice had refused to sign execution warrants was during the Miyazawa Cabinet of 1991–3.
[102]   *Asahi Shinbun*, 2 October 2005.
[103]   For reporting on the reshuffle, see *Asahi Shinbun*, 1 November 2005.
[104]   *Asahi Shinbun*, 11 November and 9 December 2005.
[105]   *Asahi Shinbun*, 20 June 2006.
[106]   *Asahi Shinbun*, 1 March 2006.
[107]   *Asahi Shinbun*, 1 April 2006.
[108]   *Asahi Shinbun*, 8 April 2006.

for part of its three-year existence, founded and led the Liberal Party after the collapse of the NFP in December 1997, brought the LP into coalition with the Obuchi government for a limited period in 1999–2000, and finally merged the LP into the DPJ in July 2003. During the 1990s he had generally been considered a right-wing reformer, but as the political balance had shifted to the right, particularly under Koizumi, the prevailing perception of Ozawa was of a politician on the centre or even centre-left. For instance, in relation to the Iraq war, he opposed the sending of troops except with the full backing of a UN resolution.[109]

Within the same month a 26-year old female candidate of the DPJ narrowly won a by-election in a constituency of Chiba Prefecture, near Tokyo. Disillusionment with the situation in Iraq, as well as concerns with widening income and wealth discrepancies, seem to have affected the result.[110] The Democrats sensed that they were on the rise again, after seven months of failure and turmoil.

In May final agreement was reached between Japan and the United States on what was termed the 'road map' for reorganizing the disposition of US troops and bases in Japan. The most sensitive issues related to bases in Okinawa, the island prefecture between the Japanese mainland and Taiwan, where the concentration of American bases on limited land space had long been subject of dispute with the local population. But the 'road map', which set out plans up to 2014 and beyond, also envisaged Japan taking over progressively wider defence responsibilities.[111]

On 5 July, North Korea conducted tests of seven missiles that fell into the sea south of the Russian coast in the vicinity of Vladivostok.[112] Even though analysis suggested that some of the missiles had malfunctioned and not completed their planned trajectories, the launches were a reminder that the North Korean regime was intent upon arming itself with credible deterrent capacity against possible attack, most probably, as it feared, from the United States. Repeated attempts to engage the regime in genuine dialogue had failed to prevent such an outcome, just as they were later to prevent its testing of a nuclear weapon. The behaviour of North Korea was of course a crucial factor motivating the consolidation of the military–strategic relationship between Japan and the United States. This included plans for missile defence.

Around the same time there was a further twist in the saga of the abductees. Kim Young Nam, the Korean husband of Yokota Megumi, abducted from Japan aged 13 in 1977, was interviewed in Pyongyang by the Japanese press, and confirmed that she had committed suicide in 1994. This story, which had attracted such intense media interest in Japan, was given added piquancy by the possibility that Kim Young Nam had himself been kidnapped from South Korea (though he claimed he had been picked up by North Koreans while drifting in a boat).[113]

[109]   I am grateful to Oka Takashi for insight into the political career of Ozawa.
[110]   *Asahi Shinbun*, 24 April 2006.
[111]   *Asahi Shinbun*, 2 May 2006.
[112]   *Asahi Shinbun*, 6 July 2006.
[113]   *Asahi Shinbun*, 30 June 2006. There were so many uncertainties in this affair that the press referred to him as 'Megumi's *alleged* husband'.

Koizumi had long insisted that he would not seek to remain as Prime Minister beyond the ending of his term as LDP President in September 2006. As the Koizumi era drew to a close, the President of the Bank of Japan announced that the Bank would raise interest rates above the 'zero-interest' level that had prevailed for several years.[114] This was a good indication of the fact that the economy was now in a period of sustained growth after the long period of low or negative growth and price deflation. In a phrase current in the summer of 2006: 'Japan is back'.

In foreign policy, on the other hand, the insistence of the Prime Minister on making regular visits to the Yasukuni Shrine guaranteed that relations with China and South Korea remained tense. In his final year in post, he finally chose the sixty-first anniversary of Japan's surrender, 15 August 2006, as the date to pay his last official visit. In July, however, material had been released showing that the *Shōwa Tennō* (Hirohito) had refused to visit the shrine on the grounds that fourteen Class A war criminals had been enshrined there in 1978. There was much resistance in Japan to such visits, and by now the Chinese, realizing that Koizumi would soon be replaced, brushed off the final visit without too much fuss.

The three candidates for the LDP presidency, and thus in effect for the premiership, were Abe Shinzō, who from the start of the campaign was far ahead of the other two, Asō Tarō and Tanigaki Sadakazu. Of these, Abe and Asō were well to the right of centre within the LDP, and Tanigaki was more moderate. Abe declared during the campaign that he placed great priority on revising the Constitution and that he hoped to achieve this within five years. A second priority issue for him was revision of the Basic Law on Education, in particular to promote patriotism. Like Nakasone before him, he hoped to make a break with the post-war period. In the election, 402 LDP parliamentarians from both houses cast their votes, as well as 300 local party representatives, members and 'friends', making 702 votes cast in all. Of these Abe won 464 (267 + 197), Asō 136 (69 + 67) and Tanigaki 102 (66 + 36), meaning that Abe had won a sweeping victory.[115]

Abe's new Cabinet contained only one hold-over from the final Koizumi Cabinet, namely Asō as Foreign Minister. It appeared that in composing his Cabinet Abe had acted in a more traditional fashion than his predecessor, rewarding those who had supported him and allowing himself to be influenced by representations from factions on behalf of favoured members. Significantly, neither Tanigaki (whose views on policy differed widely from those of the new Prime Minister) nor anybody from his faction was appointed to Cabinet.

Deliberately, Abe chose China for his first foreign visit. Given the difficulties between Japan and China that had arisen while Koizumi was Prime Minister, the choice was highly significant. Abe arrived in Beijing on 8 October, only two days before the North Koreans announced that they had detonated a nuclear device underground. The visit to Beijing therefore took on the aspect of an earnest discussion of crisis policy towards the Pyongyang regime.[116] Beijing broke with

---

[114]   *Asahi Shinbun*, 15 July 2006.
[115]   *Asahi Shinbun*, 21 September 2006.
[116]   *Asahi Shinbun*, 9 October 2006.

precedent by accepting the imposition of sanctions on North Korea, and indeed subsequently voted for sanctions at the United Nations later in October.[117] The atmosphere of the visit showed that the Chinese leaders were anxious to stem the deterioration in relations with Japan that had been so evident while Koizumi was still in charge, and Abe, for his part, seems to have indicated that he would – at least for a while – desist from visits to the Yasukuni Shrine.

Abe thus began on a high note, and the LDP victory in two by-elections in October 2006 may have been influenced by the success of his China visit. But several issues in the last weeks of 2006 accumulated in such a way as to cast doubt about his judgement; also, his popularity began to ebb, and the idea spread that he lacked the political flair of Koizumi. For one thing, he lacked the services of Takenaka Heizō, who had been an effective economics enforcer, so that the constant pressure on vested interests was somewhat relaxed, and there was a sense that the relationship between politics and economics was drifting back into the bad old habits of special favours and deals. Moreover, whereas Koizumi had insisted on preventing the postal privatization rebels from rejoining the LDP, Abe initiated a process whereby they were eventually let back into the party. Eleven individuals who had been elected outside the LDP in the September 2005 elections were allowed back in December.[118] There were doubts also about his commitment to freedom of speech. Pressure by the new General Affairs Minister, Suga Yoshihide, on NHK (the national broad-casting network) to give special emphasis to the abduction issue in its overseas service reporting on North Korea created much protest in the media about interference with the network's intellectual autonomy.[119] A statement by the Foreign Minister, Asō Tarō, that Japan's acquisition of nuclear weapons should be openly discussed caused widespread dispute. The priority Abe gave to the tasks of revising the Constitution and making more conservative the rather liberal Basic Law on Education (which dated from the Occupation period) polarized articulate opinion.

In December, the revised Basic Law on Education passed all stages in Parliament and became law. Replacing the previous law, which had lasted for 59 years, it shifted the emphasis from 'individual' (*ko*) to 'public' (*kō*, or *ōyake*), though the word for 'public' has a meaning that shades between 'public' and 'official'.[120] In the preamble to the law, the phrase 'valuing the dignity of the individual' was retained, but 'respecting the public spirit' was added. The new law also incorporated the much debated 'patriotism' clause, which reads: '... fostering respect for tradition and culture, and attitudes of love for our nation and local place (*kyōdo*)'.[121]

---

[117]   *Asahi Shinbun*, 16 October 2006.
[118]   *Asahi Shinbun*, 5 December 2006.
[119]   *Asahi Shinbun*, 11 November 2006.
[120]   The *New Nelson Japanese–English Character Dictionary* gives the following meanings for *ōyake*: public, open, official, governmental, formal.
[121]   The term *kyōdo* has a bundle of connotations, implying local community, local loyalty and solidarity, love of home, and so on.

Ever since the Occupation, education had always been an arena of contention. At the broadest level, the dispute had been between two opposing camps. One promoted a liberal, relatively individualistic educational ethos, and deeply feared reversion to the pre-war officially sanctioned ethos embedded in the Imperial Rescript on Education. The other complained of an 'excess of individualism' and insisted that patriotism and respect for public (often glossed to mean 'official') values and duties should be paramount. The new law shifted the balance of the educational ethos decisively from the belief system of the former to the belief system of the latter.

As the end of 2006 approached, the popularity of Abe as Prime Minister was in decline. Whereas public opinion polls after his accession to the post gave him approval ratings of around 60 per cent, by December his ratings had fallen below 50 per cent, and in January a poll gave him 39 per cent.[122] Although by comparison with the support accorded to many of his predecessors this was still a reasonable level of popularity, the rate of decline was worrying his supporters, especially because there was a sharp drop in his popularity among younger city people, the very sorts of people who had flocked to back Koizumi in September 2005. There were signs that comparison with Koizumi was not in Abe's favour. On the one hand, he was upsetting the market liberals by letting the postal privatization rebels back into the LDP and bending to vested interests. On the other hand, he was upsetting social and political liberals by such measures as revising the Basic Law on Education in what was widely seen as an illiberal direction. He was now, moreover, about to fulfil a further long-standing ambition of the ideological right wing. In January 2007 he oversaw the final stages of a bill to raise the status of the Defence Agency (*bōeichō*) to Defence Ministry (*bōeishō*). This was part and parcel of the defence upgrading that had been in process for several years.[123] When it was set up in 1954 (as the Self-Defence Forces were launched), it was given the low-status title of 'agency' and was formally part of the Prime Minister's Department (*Sōrifu*). Just as in the case of education there was a reasonable fear of reversion to pre-war authoritarian models, so in the case of defence the memory of militarism up to 1945 was the background both to the peace clause of the 1946 Constitution and to the low formal status given to the Defence Agency. Now times had changed, right-wing radicals were in charge, and the Defence Agency became a Ministry of Defence.

The first half of 2007 brought some difficult problems for the Abe government. Six-nation talks over the North Korean nuclear programme resulted in an agreement with the Pyongyang regime to dismantle its nuclear facilities. Even though it remained uncertain whether the agreement would stick, it represented a break on the part of Bush administration with aspects of its previous hard line towards the DPRK, agreed with Japan, and the Abe government was left exposed. Apart from this, equivocal statements emanating from the government about the wartime 'comfort women' (*ianfu*) issue raised protests, not only in China and Korea, but also in the US Congress. One of Abe's ministers, Yanagisawa Hakuo,

---

[122]   *Asahi Shinbun*, 23 January 2007.
[123]   *Asahi Shinbun*, 10 January 2007.

found himself in trouble for referring publicly to women as 'machines for making babies'. Another, the often outspoken Defence Minister Kyūma Fumio, was forced to resign in July after protests at his statement that the atomic bombing of Hiroshima and Nagasaki 'could not be helped' (*shō ga nai*).[124] The Minister for Agriculture, Forestry and Fisheries, Matsuoka Toshikatsu, committed suicide after accusations that he had claimed utilities expenses on premises where these were provided free.[125] Perhaps most damagingly of all, it was revealed that the agency in charge of state pension arrangements had inaccurate information in tens of millions of its files. With the House of Councillors elections looming, the Abe government was making desperate attempts to sort out this problem,[126] but its public support had sunk to low levels.

As anticipated, the House of Councillors elections held on 29 July 2007 dealt a severe blow to the Abe government. Of the 121 seats up for renewal, the LDP pre-election total of 64 was reduced to 32, its ally the CGP found its pre-election total reduced from 12 to 9, while by contrast the DPJ increased the number of its seats from 32 to 60. This meant that, with the addition of those seats renewed in 2004, the grand total stood at: LDP 83 (down from 110), CGP 20 (down from 23), DPJ 109 (up from 81). A further 18 seats were attributed to other parties, and there were 12 Independents (see Appendix 6 for full results). A significant feature of the results was that of 29 constituencies that elect a single member at each election, only 6 were retained by the LDP. These were mostly in rural areas, where resentment at the reduction in government support for agriculture during the Koizumi period seems to have been an important factor influencing the vote. This provided an uncanny parallel to what had happened in the 1989 upper house elections, when previous reductions in agricultural subsidy had triggered an anti-government reaction in rural constituencies. This time, the LDP had lost ground both in city areas and in the countryside, though no doubt for different reasons.

Whereas adverse results in upper house elections had triggered the resignation of Prime Ministers Uno in 1989 and Hashimoto in 1998, Abe refused to follow the traditional practice of stepping down in order to take responsibility for an electoral defeat. Technically, the government parties now enjoyed a two-thirds majority in the House of Representatives and could therefore override legislation blocked in the House of Councillors. Even so, to do this was unlikely to be a popular option. This situation would also provide an interesting test of strategy and tactics for the DPJ, which now held the advantage in the upper house. Rather than taking a wholly confrontational approach, the Democrats, under the leadership of Ozawa (once more in the spotlight), proposed a mixture of confrontation over particular issues and constructive proposals on important issues where they could make an impact on public opinion. The DPJ proposed to introduce bills into the upper house concerning pensions, political funding, agricultural

---

[124] *Asahi Shinbun*, 4 July 2007.
[125] For a case study of this politician in the context of agricultural politics see Aurelia George Mulgan, *Power and Pork: A Japanese Political Life*, ANU E Press and Asia Pacific Press, 2006.
[126] See *Asahi Shinbun*, 12 July 2007.

protection and the family. Even though these bills had little chance of success, they would indicate the direction in which the party wished to take Japan.

The aftermath of the July 2007 elections would provide a test of the resilience of both sides of politics. Could the Abe government, weakened by the electoral backlash, nevertheless recover and reinforce the 'normality' of ruling party dominance? Would it modify its nationalist agenda in the face of an electoral preference for bread-and-butter issues? Could the DPJ, strengthened by the elections, capitalize on its victory and move Japanese politics further in the direction of two-party alternation? Or would its own internal divisions reduce its impact on an easily disillusioned electorate? Were further party realignments in the offing, conceivably leading to a new kind of party system?

On 12th September, citing health problems, Abe unexpectedly resigned. Fukuda Yasuo beat Asō Tarō in an election for LDP President, and became Prime Minister.

Chapter 7 | Who Runs Japan?

Various answers have been given to the question that heads this chapter. No doubt that is true also in relation to other major states, such as the United Kingdom, Germany or the United States. But in the case of Japan, a surprising number of observers – certainly up to the 1990s – would have answered: 'Japan is run by the government bureaucracy.' This view probably owes something to a highly influential book of the early 1980s, *MITI and the Japanese Miracle*, by Chalmers Johnson.[1] The book's argument was not, of course, that the bureaucracy exercised total control over policy-making, but rather that it played the central role in a more or less triangular power structure involving ruling party politicians and corporate interests. Johnson focused on one single ministry, the Ministry of International Trade and Industry, which he argued had played the key role in promoting industrial development over the three decades from 1945 – a pattern of bureaucratic control that had been maturing since the 1920s. His description of Japan as a 'developmental state', operating a 'plan-rational' economy that was neither 'market rational' (as in the United States), nor 'plan-ideological' (as in the Soviet Union), was widely quoted and for a while held sway in much discussion of development strategies, especially for the third world.

There was much accurate observation and perceptive analysis in Johnson's exposition, which also conspicuously flew in the face of much American (and European) economic orthodoxy. The term 'industrial policy', meaning government intervention to influence economic outcomes, was generally derided among Western commentators as likely to distort economic rationality in the interests of non-economic goals such as social welfare. Johnson, however, was at pains to emphasize that Japanese government intervention was strictly for economically rational aims. This was the meaning of 'plan-rational'. Indeed, his project was an ambitious one, namely to describe an alternative, and successful, model of political

[1] Chalmers Johnson, *MITI and the Japanese Miracle: The Growth of Industrial Policy, 1925–1975*. Stanford, CA, Stanford University Press, 1982.

economy, that fitted neither the orthodoxy of American free-market capitalism nor the orthodoxy of the planned economies of Communist regimes in Eastern Europe and elsewhere. He believed that much of the formal structure of the Japanese political system was essentially window-dressing, and that it was necessary to penetrate below the surface to understand how the system really worked.

The cut-off date in Johnson's book was 1975, so that essentially he was treating the period of ultra-rapid economic growth that took place from the 1950s to the time of the first oil crisis of 1973–4. Over that period the government had at its disposal a battery of controls that it could deploy in pursuit of its policies of economic development. Policy-making was in the hands of a relatively restricted number of people, so that if it was decided within MITI that investment should be pumped into a particular type of industrial development, that could happen very quickly with the cooperation of relevant firms, as well as of top politicians. Even in relation to the 1960s, however, there were those economists who argued that autonomous activity within the private sector was more of an engine of economic growth than direction or persuasion from the bureaucracy, particularly MITI.[2]

When we come to the 1990s and 2000s, it is plain that the shape of the political economy differs radically from that described by Johnson. It would be difficult to regard frequently botched attempts by government to bring about economic recovery after the bursting of the asset bubble of the late 1980s as in any real sense 'plan-rational', and indeed the fact that the economy was allowed to overheat to such an extent in that period was itself some indication of failure of government control. By the beginning of the new millennium the economy, and especially the banking system, was in need of some radical surgery. From 2001 Koizumi devoted himself single-mindedly to the task of restructuring, but his recipe led policy in the direction of free-market economics, not 'plan rationality'.

We now need to examine the basic structure of politics and government between the 1950s and the 1990s. This will be followed by an analysis of the extent to which the system evolved over the same period. After this, certain key features of formal and informal structures will be examined in greater detail. We shall focus especially on the government bureaucracy, but also on interactions between government, politics and interest groups. This will lead into an examination of changes from the start of the new millennium.

The Basic Structure of Politics and Government, 1950s–1990s

As we saw in Chapter 4, the power relations embodied in the 1946 Constitution were strongly reminiscent of the 'Westminster model'. In contrast to an American-style separation of powers between the executive and the legislature, a kind of fusion between the two is built into the basic constitutional structure. In regular elections to the House of Representatives,[3] the electorate chooses members of

[2]   See e.g. Hugh Patrick and Henry Rosovsky, *Asia's New Giant: How the Japanese Economy Works*, Washington DC, Brookings, 1976.
[3]   The maximum term for the House of Representatives is four years, but only once since the war (between December 1972 and December 1976) has a government gone full term.

Parliament. From these members a government is formed which, to be viable, must have the confidence of the house. In practice this means that it is formed by a majority party (or party coalition) supported by a majority of members, though occasionally minority administrations are allowed to survive for a while.[4] Throughout the whole period from 1955 to 1993 a single party (the LDP) maintained its lower house majority, with the tiny exception of its coalition with the New Liberal Club between 1983 and 1986. In 1993–4 the LDP was out of power for nine months, and since its return to power in June 1994 it has almost always governed as the dominant party in a coalition with much smaller parties. In this dominant party system, the government not only controlled the House of Representatives by virtue of its parliamentary majority, but also exercised ultimate executive power through the Cabinet, since every ministry had a Cabinet minister (*daijin*) at its head. A government that lost its parliamentary majority and was then defeated in a no-confidence vote was constitutionally required either to resign or to dissolve the House of Representatives and hold new elections.

That outline describes the formal situation; the way things worked on the ground was rather different. Through various mechanisms, government ministries have often played a more dominant, and even controlling, role than the model of a Westminster system would lead one to expect. The historical background is important here. Before the war, government officials maintained a tradition of self-identification as a carefully selected, highly educated elite, dedicated to service of the state and, especially, the *Tennō*. The tradition had deep roots going back several centuries. The removal of the armed forces from political significance after the war conversely reinforced the influence of the civilian bureaucracy, while, as we saw in Chapter 4, the Occupation forces treated government officials more gently than politicians and businessmen because they needed their services to implement Occupation reforms.

There is a third concrete reason why the civil service played such a powerful role after the Occupation. Starting with the administrations of Yoshida Shigeru between 1949 and 1954, numbers of civil servants were elected to Parliament as members of the LDP. This became a phenomenon of major significance. In the late 1960s around a quarter of LDP parliamentarians in the House of Representatives were former officials of the government bureaucracy. The proportion was even higher in the House of Councillors, and as many as half of Cabinet members were in this category.[5] This degree of bureaucratic dominance of Cabinet and the LDP was to decline later, but remained significant, even though the influence of the bureaucracy was hardly monolithic, given sharp inter-ministerial rivalries.

A further mechanism for bureaucratic influence is *amakudari*, translated as 'descent from Heaven', whereby civil servants on retirement take positions on the boards of companies or other institutions, usually related to the jurisdiction of their former ministry. This practice, though often criticized in the mass media, has been lightly policed and was regarded as a useful mechanism for cementing ties between government ministries and the industrial and commercial sectors. It

[4] Most notably the Hata government, between April and June 1994.
[5] Haruhiro Fukui, *Party in Power: The Japanese Liberal-Democrats and Policy Making*, Canberra, Australian National University Press, 1970, pp. 224 and 272–3.

gave able bureaucrats rewarding post-retirement careers. Since the 1990s, vever, when bureaucratic dominance of the political economy started to come er attack, *amakudari* has been placed under critical scrutiny (though it has not disappeared).[6] According to government statistics, between August 2004 and August 2005, 1,206 civil servants ranked section chief (*kachō*) or above had 'descended from Heaven'.[7]

It should not be assumed that the practice of 'descent from Heaven' is solely motivated by the desire to spread bureaucratic influence into the private sector. Ministries need to find external employment for considerable numbers of able and active men (and some women) in early middle age, who are intimately informed about the policies of their ministries. Those who do not make it to the very top of a ministry are likely to retire early; hence the need for external employment, preferably at a good salary. The motivations for this practice are fairly complex, but it has certainly contributed to an environment of regulation and close relationships between the private and public sectors, which free-market advocates such as Koizumi and his Economics Minister, Takenaka, attempted to combat, with mixed results.

It would be wrong to regard relations between civil servants and politicians as a one-way street. Since at least the 1970s groups of LDP parliamentarians, known collectively as 'tribes' (*zoku*), have coalesced around specific policy areas, such as education, defence, telecommunications, transport and construction, and operate in conjunction with their similarly interested counterparts in ministries, companies, think tanks and so on. These may be regarded as 'iron triangles', in the sense that they seek to dominate a particular area of policy in a way that cuts across political, bureaucratic and interest-group boundaries. For many years, for instance, the tobacco 'tribe' was able to resist pressure for restrictions on the advertising of tobacco products, despite the meticulously documented perils to health associated with them. It seems that in face of growing public concern, the influence of this particular 'tribe' is now diminishing; however, it still wields significant influence.[8]

During the 1950s and 1960s powerful oligopolies flourished, despite the anti-monopoly law, which was substantially emasculated during the 1950s. The period of rapid economic growth between the late 1950s and early 1970s was accompanied by a great concentration of economic power in the hands of

---

[6] Recent studies suggest that the practice of *amakudari* remains widespread. Civil servants on retirement are supposed by law to wait two years before joining an organization related to their previous area of work. But it is apparently common for a civil servant to retire and immediately join a special corporate body (*tokushu hōjin*) or other external organization (*gaikaku dantai*) of his ministry, from which it is legal to 'descend' onto the board of a private company: *Asahi Shinbun*, 16 February 2006; see also *Asahi Shinbun*, 25 April 2007.

[7] *Asahi Shinbun*, 16 February 2006.

[8] Proposals by the Ministry of Welfare and Labour to publicize numerical targets for reduction in smoking still met resistance from within the LDP on the ground that 'tobacco production contributes to local finances'. According to a 2004 survey, the proportion of men smoking was 43.3%, and of women 12.0%: *Asahi Shinbun*, 24 December 2006.

keiretsu-type firms.[9] These exercised disproportionate influence on government policy, which saw them as the shock troops of economic progress. Other interests, such as those representing agriculture as well as small and medium industries, also exercised political power, but the big firms occupied the most central position. From the 1970s onwards the economy diversified in such a way as to modify such a skewed system of influence, and anti-monopoly policies came to have some influence.[10]

We now turn to specific features of the political system itself. The first is the role of the Prime Minister. In the British case (or 'Westminster model') some though not all prime ministers have exercised sustained dominance over the political process. In Japan, by contrast, prime ministers have typically been cautious figures, constrained by complex political forces, seeking influence through the careful cultivation of consensus, and usually having limited tenure.[11] There have been exceptions. Satō Eisaku, for instance, was. Prime Minister for seven and a half years, and shaped key areas of policy. Koizumi was more dominant than most of his predecessors, enjoyed relatively long tenure (nearly five and a half years) and benefited from institutional strengthening of the prime ministerial office. But in general, prime ministers in Japan may be categorized as ranging from weak to moderately effective. Moreover, Cabinet has not been the central locus of decision-making one would expect from the British model, though there are differences between time periods and across issues. The average tenure of Cabinet ministers has been short, with many ministers replaced after a year or so,[12] and the business of Cabinet meetings, at least until the 1990s, was normally pre-digested by regular weekly meetings of the Conference of Administrative Vice-Ministers (*Jimu jikan kaigi*).[13] Anecdotal evidence suggests that in many Cabinet meetings little of substance was discussed. Under Koizumi, however, the innovation of a Cabinet Office (*Naikakufu*) and the introduction of junior ministers to some extent increased the power of Prime Minister and Cabinet.

One of the most widely discussed aspects of party politics in Japan is factionalism, although most observers concur that it is now less salient than it used to be, as well as changing in form. We are principally concerned here with factions in the LDP, though they also exist in other parties. A faction (*ha*, or *habatsu*) used to centre on a single leader, who was typically a senior or rising politician. These groupings differed from political factions in British political parties, which have been mainly distinguished by policy differences. In Japanese factions, policy positions may be significant, but their principal functions were power-broking,

---

[9]   *Keiretsu* are loose groupings of business firms, some of whose activities are coordinated. They derived from the pre-war *zaibatsu* groups, but lack the strong central control exercised within those groups.

[10]   Michael L. Beeman, *Public Policy and Economic Competition in Japan: Change and Continuity in Antimonopoly Policy, 1973–1995*, London and New York, Routledge, 2002.

[11]   Between Attlee in 1945 and Brown in 2007, Britain enjoyed the services of 12 prime ministers. Over the same period, between Shidehara and Fukuda, Japan had 29!

[12]   Short tenure, both for prime ministers and ministers, results in part from factional politics, which is discussed below.

[13]   The *jimu jikan* are the permanent heads of ministries.

fund-raising and fund distribution. Before each Cabinet reshuffle, every faction leader would bargain with the Prime Minister over the distribution of Cabinet and party posts. One of the reasons for frequent reshuffles was the need to maintain the Prime Minister's position by satisfying factional demands. Factions were also organized for the collection and distribution of political funding, typically but not only for the purpose of fighting elections. During periods of uncontested LDP dominance, the factions could even serve as a binding force, because, not being primarily policy groups, they served to keep power contests at one remove from policy disputes. There were exceptions to this, as we have seen in Chapters 4 and 5, in the form of bitter factional battles that disrupted the party (in the late 1950s, 1974–80 and 1989–93), but in only one instance (1993) did factional disruption create a serious party split, leading to temporary loss of office.[14]

The pre-1994 lower house electoral system was an important causal factor explaining persistent factionalism in the LDP. In that system, each constituency elected several members, with each elector casting a single, non-transferable vote.[15] In the case of the LDP, which was strong enough to endorse more than one candidate in most constituencies, each candidate set up or inherited a personal support association (*kōenkai*) as the main basis of his or her campaign. The *kōenkai* was in no sense a party branch, but was the exclusive preserve of the candidate concerned. In many cases, however, the *kōenkai* (plural) of LDP candidates in a constituency were more important than the local party branch in gathering the vote. The relevance of all this to factionalism was that each candidate (with occasional exceptions) was backed by a central faction of the party. It was rare for two candidates in the same constituency to be supported by the same faction. This meant that contests between rival candidates of the same party in the same constituency were underpinned by central factional organizations. Leading members of each faction would typically pay visits to constituencies in order to support *their* candidates. When the system of multiple-member constituencies was changed in 1994 in favour of a combination of single-member and proportional representation constituencies, the need for factional backing in elections was reduced, and factions gradually weakened, though they did not disappear.

Styles and methods of electioneering were a crucial feature of the political structure and process. In sharp contrast with British practice for much of the twentieth century, personality and local connections were central to voting decisions, and politicians tailored their campaigns to the realities of this facet of electoral behaviour. One reason for this was a severe distortion of the electoral system in favour of rural areas, resulting from a chronic failure adequately to redraw constituency boundaries to take account of movements of population to the cities in the post-war period. Another reason was the multi-member constituency system, outlined above. The impact on the structure and process of politics and government was important. Members of Parliament were snowed under with constituency business, but much less pressured by the electorate on matters of national or international importance. This in turn meant that

---

[14]   The split leading to the formation of the New Liberal Club in 1976 was minor, and the rebels were re-absorbed into the LDP ten years later.
[15]   For a more detailed treatment, see Chapter 8.

parliamentary interventions into policy-making were much concerned with 'pork barrel' issues, and parliamentarians spent much of their time lobbying bureaucrats and others in order to satisfy the demands of their constituents. Thus, parliamentary oversight of broad policy decision-making was weakened, and bureaucratic power was maintained at a high level. Nevertheless, there has been some reduction in bureaucratic power since the mid-1990s, and we shall seek to explain this later in the chapter.

We need to discuss another significant outcome of personality voting, namely the emergence of political 'dynasties'. Since the late 1980s, some 30 per cent of parliamentarians have been the sons, sons-in-law, nephews, widows, daughters, daughters-in-law or nieces of former parliamentarians.[16] Abe Shinzō, the Prime Minister in 2007, is the son of a former LDP faction leader and grandson of Kishi Nobusuke, Prime Minister in the late 1950s. Koizumi Junichirō, his immediate predecessor, is the son of an LDP parliamentarian who died prematurely. The same is true of Ozawa Ichirō, current Representative of the Democratic Party. When Obuchi Keizō (Prime Minister 1998–2000), died in May 2000, his daughter, still in her twenties, was elected to his parliamentary seat. A former Representative of the DPJ, Hatoyama Yukio, as well as his brother, Kunio (now in the LDP), are fourth-generation politicians: their great-grandfather, Kazuo, entered Parliament in 1892; their great-uncle, Hideo, was a parliamentarian in the 1930s; their grandfather, Ichirō, was Prime Minister 1954–6; and their father, Iichirō, was Foreign Minister in 1976–7. Why is this practice so prevalent, especially, but by no means exclusively, in the LDP? The answer appears to lie in the kind of personality politics that has led to the formation of personal support associations. The easiest way of acquiring such a *kōenkai* is to inherit one, and the easiest way to inherit one is by belonging to a political family. Secretaries of politicians also frequently 'inherit' such associations, and this may be considered an aspect of the same practice, since secretaries are part of the 'family' of a politician. Many politicians in Japan are in effect running small businesses. Who inherits the business is often a family matter.[17] (See Chapter 3 for the social traditions that this practice reflects.)

A further aspect of the way things worked was corruption, or, to use a rather more polite Japanese term, 'money politics'. While the definition of corruption was and is controversial, it was generally agreed that the causes of money politics were both structural and legal: structural, in the sense that it was extremely difficult for a parliamentarian to run his or her political machine without seeking and obtaining funds of dubious provenance, and legal, in the sense that the anti-corruption laws were so full of loopholes that it was easy to evade them. In 1994, however, the relevant legislation was substantially tightened. The mass media played a major part in uncovering instances of money politics – so much so that in the late 1980s and early 1990s corruption became perhaps the most

[16] Since the number of women politicians is small, the first three categories are the most common.

[17] The present writer once met the 20-year-old son of a serving politician and asked him whether he intended to go into politics. His reply was that he had little choice in the matter because the family was responsible for the employees of his father's *kōenkai*.

high-profile political issue. It may well have been the principal factor explaining the widespread alienation from politics of the 1990s, signalled by falling turnout rates at elections and alienation from political parties.

One often neglected aspect of political dynamics during the period of single-party dominance was the relative weakness of opposition parties. During the 1970s, in 1989–96, and again in the early 2000s up to the DPJ reverse of September 2005, they appeared to constitute a threat to LDP dominance, but for most periods a government composed of opposition parties seemed a remote possibility. Nevertheless, the opposition parties between them were able to exercise important veto power over potential or actual right-wing attempts to tamper with the Occupation settlement. At least until the 1990s, such a veto was absolute in relation to constitutional revision (though not constitutional re-interpretation) because the LDP lacked the required two-thirds majority in both houses separately, without which a revision procedure could not begin (see Chapter 10). But it also existed to some extent in relation to other matters, as a result of arrangements made between the LDP and opposition parties to further the smooth running of Parliament. Officials of the parliamentary policy committees of the LDP (*kokkai taisaku iinkai*, or *kokutai*) and major opposition parties met regularly to reach compromises on timetabling issues.[18] At times this had the effect of making some opposition parties act like clients of the LDP, rather than opponents of it, but it had the long-term conservation effect of keeping intact the principal features of the Occupation settlement, much against the wishes of right-wing members of the ruling party.

Finally, there is a real sense in which the structure and process of government and politics over the era of single-party dominance were held in place by the Japan–US relationship throughout the Cold War. It is difficult to establish the precise causality linking the ending of the Cold War with structural change in the politics of Japan, but the long-term effects of such a revolution in international politics clearly included long-term evolutionary changes in Japan. We shall return to this question in Chapter 12.

Evolution of the System to the 1990s

We now turn to the question of systemic change. As we have just suggested, change in the mode of Japanese political operation has been evolutionary rather than revolutionary, but some changes have been extremely significant. Moreover, they are not simply the product of new politics in the new millennium, but in many cases have roots in earlier periods.

There is much discussion today of elected politicians acquiring more power as unelected civil servants reluctantly cede elements of their power to them.[19] But in fact there is evidence of this happening from the 1970s, admittedly in stops and

[18]   This came to be known as 'Parliamentary Policy Committee politics' (*kokutai seiji*). *Kokutai* is here written with different characters from the *kokutai* of the pre-war period, meaning 'national polity'. See Chapter 1.

[19]   See e.g. Takashi Inoguchi, *Japanese Politics: An Introduction*, Melbourne, Trans Pacific Press, 2005.

starts. If the period of ultra-rapid economic growth of the 1960s was the high point of bureaucratic power, thereafter it was possible to detect a gradual rise in the relative influence of the LDP, though this was not a simple or easy progress. The LDP policy 'tribes' began to be noticed in the 1970s, and were soon competing with the ministries by acquiring policy expertise in their chosen policy areas. The length of time that the LDP had been in office gave it the edge, since its experienced parliamentary members now had the capacity to 'sew up' policy-making in particular policy spheres. They did so, however, not independently from ministries and interest groups, but rather in cooperation with them. Within groupings of politicians, civil servants and interest group representatives, it was often unclear who was influencing whom. This indeed leads us to reframe our question, which concerned the relative power of politicians and civil servants (and also interest group representatives). A more relevant question may well be: which combinations of politicians, civil servants and interest group people are more powerful and effective than other similarly constituted groupings? Obviously, the answer will differ from issue to issue and from period to period.[20]

Another dimension of change concerns the relative power of the Prime Minister and his ministers, on the one hand, and the committees of the LDP, on the other. Until the Koizumi period, most policy initiatives of the Prime Minister had to be vetted by the complex committee system of the LDP, which was in a position to reject or emasculate such initiatives.[21] The committees were the focus of lobbying activities by interest groups, so that in general they tended to resist policy initiatives that would risk harming the interests of such groups. Party committees were a thorn in the side of Koizumi administration until Koizumi boldly challenged their influence in July–September 2005.[22]

A key mechanism that Koizumi deployed to good effect in pursuit of his reforming agenda was the Council on Economic and Fiscal Policy (*Keizai zaisei shimon kaigi*). Established a few weeks before the start of the Koizumi regime, this council was used by the new Prime Minister as a principal means of realizing his central reforming goal of postal services privatization. Its membership included all the economics ministers, and other key figures such as the President of the Bank of Japan.[23] The council evolved into the government's most powerful

---

[20] See e.g. Stephen Wilks and Maurice Wright (eds), *The Promotion and Regulation of Industry in Japan*, Basingstoke and London, Macmillan, 1991; Gary D. Allinson and Yasunori Sone, *Political Dynamics in Contemporary Japan*, Ithaca and London, Cornell University Press, 1993.

[21] There were exceptions, for instance in the Satō, Tanaka and Nakasone periods, where the Prime Minister apparently bypassed the LDP committee system in promoting foreign and defence policy initiatives. I am grateful to an anonymous reviewer for pointing this out to me.

[22] For emphasis on the blocking role of LDP committees, see Aurelia George Mulgan, *Japan's Failed Revolution: Koizumi and the Politics of Economic Reform*, Canberra, Asia Pacific Press, 2002.

[23] The Prime Minister, Chief Cabinet Secretary, Minister of Finance, Minister of Economy and Finance, Minister of Public Management, Home Affairs, Posts and Telecommunications, Minister of Economy, Trade and Industry, President of the Bank of Japan, Chairman of the LDP Parliamentary Policy Committee, Chairman of the LDP Policy Research Council and Director of the Financial Supervisory Agency. I am grateful to Professor Nonaka Naoto for materials on the Council.

body in economic affairs, in effect bypassing (or overriding) Cabinet and the LDP committees. It was propelled by the intense efforts put into it by the Prime Minister and his Minister for Economic and Fiscal Affairs, Takenaka Heizō. After Koizumi stepped down in September 2006 it was bereft of such commitment from the very top of government, and its impact was somewhat reduced.

Between the 1950s and the 1990s, the corporate sector grew enormously in size and wealth, and with the removal of many bureaucratic controls which had existed in the earlier post-war period attained much greater independence. Big *keiretsu* firms, newly able to raise capital on the international money markets, became far less dependent on raising capital through the banking system, over which the Ministry of Finance and the Bank of Japan exercised substantial control. From the 1990s measures were put in place to deregulate the Japanese financial sector, so that it became far more integrated into international money markets than it had been in earlier decades, and Tokyo itself was established as one of the world's major financial centres. Gradually, economic management had been transformed from that of a rapidly developing economy in which government played a central role, to that of a leading advanced economy with much lighter, but also more sophisticated, regulation.

When we turn to political parties, we see that relationships between parties based on ideological confrontation had largely given way to relationships based on give and take. This mirrors developments in many European countries, where the span of the left–right spectrum appears to have diminished over time. In Japan the most dramatic indication of this was the near-demise of the Japan Socialist Party (now Social Democratic Party) during the latter half of the 1990s. Throughout the post-war decades, the JSP had confronted conservative governments from a semi-Marxist ideological perspective. It was not until 1986 that most of the Marxism was removed from the party platform, and for a few years after that the JSP acquired new electoral support in face of government mismanagement and corruption. As we have seen, however, ideological confrontation masked *kokutai* politics, whereby LDP and JSP officials often sorted things out behind the scenes. With the Socialists almost removed from the scene by the beginning of the new millennium, the Democratic Party is now the principal party of opposition; and though it hardly sings from the same hymn sheet as the LDP, it at least competes in the same *karaoke* bar.

Major changes also took place in relations between government and interest groups, matching the maturation of the economy over the past half-century. Whereas in the period of high economic growth the corporate sector tended to dominate access to government policy-making and could be regarded as a central part of the real structure of government, by the 1990s many other sectors were in a position to exert significant pressure on government, leading to what Inoguchi, as early as 1983, called 'mass-inclusionary pluralism'.[24] Although governments in the early 1980s resisted pressure from interest groups and put in place the principle of 'zero-ceiling' budgeting (with some areas exempted), later governments were less fiscally orthodox. When the economy stagnated in the

---

[24]   Inoguchi Takashi, *Gendai Nihon seiji keizai no kōzu* (The Structure of Japanese Political Economy), Tokyo, Tōyō Keizai Shinpōsha, 1983, pp. 3–29.

1990s, it became increasingly evident that a stagnant economy combined with excessive interest group influence was a recipe for disaster. This was the vicious circle that impelled Koizumi to take a tough line against interest group pressures, and in particular to confront the powerful postal services lobby. The economy, in his opinion, would recover and flourish only once free-market principles were fully entrenched and interest group lobbying kept within bounds.

A further change that has taken place is the greater unpredictability of the electorate and increasing fluidity in voting behaviour. By the mid- to late 1990s public opinion polls regularly revealed that the proportion of those supporting no political party (the 'no-party supporters', or *mutōhasō*), exceeded the proportion declaring support for any specific party. This phenomenon continued into the new millennium. Those declaring to opinion pollsters that they supported the LDP were more numerous than supporters of any other party, but far fewer than the number required to give the LDP a guaranteed majority.[25] Whereas in the earlier post-war decades political loyalties had been rather stable and predictable, by the 2000s the chances of achieving electoral victory by deploying appeals based on image and charisma had markedly increased. The longevity of Koizumi as Prime Minister may in part be attributed to this factor.

Although corruption scandals had been a more or less constant feature of the political scene throughout the period since the war, from the Recruit scandal of the late 1980s they seemed so pervasive, and were attracting so much media attention, that this in turn began to affect political attitudes within government, leading to passage of the anti-corruption laws of 1994, and making the flow of money for political purposes a good deal more problematic. Moreover, corruption, from which civil servants were previously believed to have been relatively removed, was now involving not only politicians and businessmen, but also some in the bureaucracy. During the 1990s, corruption scandals even touched the prestigious Ministry of Finance, and this, together with accusations that it had mismanaged the financial system after the collapse of the economic 'bubble', led to a decline in its influence.[26]

Finally, a factor of great importance is the change over time in the way promotions were handled in the LDP. By the 1980s, the promotion system had become uncomfortably rigid for the interests of younger LDP parliamentary members. Partly in order to stabilize the party, which had been wracked by factional squabbles during the 1970s, a system was devised whereby virtually no ruling-party parliamentarian would have obtained a full Cabinet post until he or she had been elected for a fifth term, but almost all of them would have experienced one Cabinet post by their sixth term. Beyond the sixth term, only high-flyers could be expected to be given successive Cabinet posts, but the factions were able to satisfy their members by obtaining for everybody at least one

[25] For instance, a public opinion poll published in December 2006, according to which support for the Abe Cabinet was 47%, had 36% of respondents supporting the LDP, exactly the same percentage as those supporting no political party. The DPJ received support from 14% of respondents: *Asahi Shinbun*, 12 December 2006.

[26] For an excellent analysis of the Ministry of Finance during the period of financial crisis, see Jennifer Amyx, *Japan's Financial Crisis: Institutional Regidity and Reluctant Change*, Princeton University Press, 2004.

Cabinet post.[27] Since five successive terms in Parliament usually meant about 15 years (assuming the member was not defeated at any election), the system was frustrating to ambitious younger members, and was an important factor in the defections from the LDP which took place during the 1990s. To some extent generational groups came to replace, or rather supplement, factions.[28] In the turbulent politics of the 1990s it proved much harder to maintain such a 'bureaucratic' mode of promotion. By the end of the decade it was fraying badly, and when Koizumi became Prime Minister in 2001 he was able largely to defy factional demands for Cabinet and party posts, appointing individuals to Cabinet rather according to his estimation of merit.

This factor also proved important in another sense. As we have seen, for much of the post-war period former civil servants made up a substantial proportion of LDP parliamentarians, and frequently enjoyed a dream run into Cabinet. They tended to be those who had attained high positions in their ministries, positions that they could not be expected to reach until their fifties. If, when they moved into politics, they had been required to wait around for a further 15 years before being given their first Cabinet positions, many of them would have by then been too old to fulfil their political ambitions. This led to a lowering of the age of transfer from bureaucracy to Parliament. By the 1980s those making such a move were of a younger age group, and their careers would include a longer political component and a shorter bureaucratic component than those of their predecessors. This may be seen in the context of the shifting emphasis from the bureaucratic to the political in the governmental process as a whole.

The Structure of the Government Bureaucracy

A major restructuring of the government bureaucracy was put in place in January 2001, having been in the pipeline for four years. What had been 22 ministries and agencies of central government were reduced to 13. The main purposes of this reform were threefold: first, to rationalize and bring together functions that had been to some extent scattered in various parts of the government machinery; second, to combat inter-ministerial rivalries over jurisdiction; and third, to strengthen the capacity of Prime Minister and Cabinet to exercise executive power.

Before treating this reform in detail, we need to return briefly to the historical origins of the system. It will be evident that up to 2001 there was remarkable continuity in bureaucratic structures.

When a Cabinet was first instituted in 1885 (preceding by four years the Meiji Constitution), its ministers respectively held the portfolios (each corresponding to a ministry) of foreign affairs, home affairs, finance, army, navy, justice, education, agriculture and commerce, and communications. When the new Constitution came into effect in 1947, the following ministries existed: Foreign Affairs, Home

---

[27]   For details, see J. A. A. Stockwin et al., *Dynamic and Immobilist Politics in Japan*, London, Macmillan, 1988, table on p. 41.
[28]   A famous example is the YKK group, consisting of Yamasaki Taku, Katō Kōichi and Koizumi Junichirō, who worked together for much of the late 1990s and early 2000s.

Affairs, Finance, Justice, Education, Welfare, Agriculture and Forestry, Commerce and Industry, Transport, and Communications. By 2000 the Ministries of Foreign Affairs, Finance, Justice, Education and Transport still remained, but in addition there was a Ministry of Labour and a Ministry of Construction. The Ministry of Commerce and Industry had been replaced by the Ministry of International Trade and Industry (MITI). The former Ministry of Communications became the Ministry of Posts and Telecommunications (though the Japanese title did not change from *Yūseishō* – literally, Ministry of Postal Services). The Ministry of Welfare became the Ministry of Health and Welfare (again, no change to the Japanese title: *Kōseishō*). The Ministry of Agriculture and Forestry had 'Fisheries' added to its title, making it the Ministry of Agriculture, Forestry and Fisheries. The former Ministry of Home Affairs was replaced during the Occupation by the Local Autonomy Agency, a branch of the Prime Minister's Office, and lost some of its earlier powers. But in 1960, on Kishi's initiative, it was upgraded to *Ministry* of Local Autonomy (*Jichishō* replacing *Jichichō*), and soon came to use 'Ministry of Home Affairs' as the English translation of *Jichishō*, thereby seeking to make an important point about its status.[29]

After the Occupation it proved difficult to increase the number of ministries to respond to new functions appearing with modernization; to overcome this problem, a number of commissions (*iinkai*) and 'agencies' *(chō)* were set up under the Prime Minister's Office (*Sōrifu*), which had a formal status equivalent to that of a ministry. These included the Fair Trade Commission, the National Public Safety Commission, the Imperial Household Agency, the Management and Coordination Agency, the Hokkaidō Development Agency, the Okinawa Development Agency, the Science and Technology Agency, the National Land Agency, the Defence Agency and the Economic Planning Agency.

The Constitution, in article 66, defines Cabinet membership as consisting of the Prime Minister and the other ministers of state. Article 2 of the Cabinet Law places an upper limit of 20 ministers of state, plus the Prime Minister, within Cabinet. Until the introduction of junior ministers in 2001, all ministers were members of Cabinet, and there was no provision for an inner cabinet. Since, however, a Cabinet restricted to 13 members (the number of ministries plus the Prime Minister's Office) would have been too small for the breadth of government responsibilities, advantage was taken of article 3 of the Cabinet Law, which permits the inclusion of ministers without portfolio. Several of the more important commissions and agencies of the Prime Minister's Office were therefore designated as requiring a minister of state to head them, thus giving them full representation at Cabinet level. The Chief Cabinet Secretary has also been elevated to Cabinet membership status in this way. Formally speaking, the ministers of state concerned remain ministers without portfolio, despite the fact that their departmental responsibilities may be as great as those of some ministers heading actual ministries. This explains why, for instance, the Director-General of the Defence Agency was a minister of state with full entitlement to sit in

[29] Japanese institutions not uncommonly translate their titles into English with deliberate inaccuracy, so as to make a point (often about status) that may be difficult to state openly in Japanese.

Cabinet. It was not until January 2007 that the Defence Agency (*Bōeichō*) was elevated to the status of Ministry of Defence (*Bōeishō*) – this being a pet project of the new Prime Minister, Abe Shinzō . In the 1990s, cabinets generally comprised 21 or 22 members, so that some ministers had to take on more than one portfolio. Numbers have now been slightly reduced, and the first Abe Cabinet consisted of 18 members.

In the reforms to the government structure put in place in January 2001, the following major changes were effected.

With the aim of strengthening the powers and coordinating role of the Prime Minister, a Cabinet Office (*Naikakufu*) was established, into which was merged the Prime Minister's Office (*Sōrifu*), the Okinawa Development Agency (*Okinawa kaihatsuchō*) and the Economic Planning Agency (*Keizai kikakuchō*). The Prime Minister could thus be directly involved in the delicate politics of Okinawa, where the bulk of US military bases were located, and he also had a path into economic areas, independent of the economic ministries. In addition, the Defence Agency and the National Public Safety Commission (*Kokka kōan iinkai*) were brought within the ambit of the Cabinet Office. The Defence Agency remained intact, but would have to wait another six years for upgrading. A super-ministry was formed out of the Management and Coordination Agency, Ministry of Home Affairs and Ministry of Posts and Telecommunications. It was given a cumbersome name in English but a neat one in Japanese: Ministry of Public Management, Home Affairs, Posts and Telecommunications (*Sōmushō*, which may be translated literally as 'Ministry of General Affairs').[30]

The Ministry of Justice (*Hōmushō*) was left unchanged, as was the Ministry of Foreign Affairs (*Gaimushō*). The prestigious Ministry of Finance (*Ōkurashō*) was left intact for the time being, but its august and ancient title was changed to the more mundane *Zaimushō* (no change in its English title). The Ministry of Education (*Monbushō*) was amalgamated with the Science and Technology Agency (*Kagaku gijutsuchō*) to form the Ministry of Education, Culture, Sports and Technology (*Monbu kagakushō*, or colloquially, *Monkashō*). The Ministry of Health and Welfare (*Kōseishō*) merged with the Ministry of Labour (*Rōdōshō*), to form the Ministry of Health, Labour and Welfare (*Kōsei rōdōshō*). (Some of the functions of the former Ministry of Health and Welfare were transferred to the new Ministry of the Environment.) The Ministry of Agriculture, Forestry and Fisheries (*Nōrin suisanshō*) escaped unscathed from the reorganization, with its name and basic functions unchanged.

The Ministry of International Trade and Industry (MITI, *Tsūshō sangyōshō*, *Tsūsanshō*), remained intact, except that some of its functions were moved to the new Ministry of the Environment, but its name was changed to Ministry of Economy, Trade and Industry (METI, *Keizai sangyōshō*, *Keisanshō*). Another super-ministry was formed out of the Ministry of Transport (*Unyūshō*), Ministry of Construction (*Kensetsushō*), Hokkaidō Development Agency (*Hokkaidō-kaihatsuchō*) and the National Land Agency (*Kokudochō*). It was dubbed the Ministry of Land, Infrastructure and Transport (*Kokudo kōtsūshō*). And finally,

---

[30] This may be another example of the English title being used to make a subtle point. Whereas the Japanese title suggests a single united ministry, the title in English conveys the reality of an organization that was little more than the sum of its parts.

the Environment Agency (*Kankyōchō*), which had been formed in 1971 in the midst of an environmental crisis, was upgraded to Ministry of the Environment (*Kankyōshō*), which acquired some functions from MITI and the former Ministry of Health and Welfare.

In its task of coordinating the functions of central government, the Cabinet has the assistance of the Cabinet Secretariat (*Naikaku kanbō*), the Cabinet Legislation Bureau (*Naikaku hōseikyoku*), the National Defence Council (*Kokubō kaigi*) and the National Personnel Authority (*Jinjiin*).

The Cabinet Secretariat is headed by the Chief Cabinet Secretary (*Kanbō-chōkan*), always a most powerful figure within the government, and a close confidant of the Prime Minister, acting as Cabinet spokesman on many issues, and as a channel of communication with both government and opposition parties. The Cabinet Secretariat, established in 1947, prepares matters for Cabinet discussion, conducts policy research and liaises with the different ministries.

The Cabinet Legislation Bureau was abolished on American insistence during the Occupation but was revived in 1952. It investigates and oversees legislative technicalities, including drafting of legislation, throughout the civil service, helps draft bills if required, and sometimes drafts the 'unified opinions' of Cabinet. Its constitutional interpretations have sometimes taken on the character of Holy Writ, which politicians find it difficult to challenge (particularly on matters of constitutional interpretation).

The National Defence Council is more like a Cabinet committee than an advisory bureau of Cabinet. It consists of the Prime Minister, the Foreign Minister, the Finance Minister, the Director-General of the Defence Agency (now Minister of Defence) and the Director-General of the Economic Planning Agency (before 2001). It was originally set up by the Defence Agency Establishment Law (*Bōeichō setchi hō*) of 1954 as a safeguard for civilian control over the Self-Defence Forces, and the Prime Minister is supposed to refer to it important matters of defence policy, including draft defence plans (article 62 of the Law).

The National Personnel Authority was set up during the Occupation to rationalize the recruitment and conditions of civil servants, and bring them under some sort of centralized control, thus reducing bureaucratic sectionalism. It was deliberately given the status of an independent advisory bureau of Cabinet so that it could exercise authority in personnel matters over the civil service as a whole. Its influence was much resented by the established ministries, which were used to controlling their own personnel matters, so that various attempts were made to weaken it once the Occupation was over. Nevertheless, although its influence is far inferior to that of the major ministries, it has survived, and it makes regular recommendations to Cabinet that civil service remuneration should be kept at least comparable with that in the private sector. This is a controversial and live matter.

Of the ministries themselves, those most closely associated with national economic policy-making have carried most weight politically and in terms of status. From the end of the Asia–Pacific War until the 1990s a career in the Ministry of Finance (MOF) was the most prestigious of any in the civil service. During that decade, however, the ministry was widely criticized for its handling of bankrupt housing loan companies and other matters. It has been argued that under the unstable and shifting coalitions of the period, the tried and tested ways in which the MOF settled issues under its jurisdiction through its linkages with the LDP no longer worked properly. The ability of the ministry to solve the serious problems in the financial system was thus greatly reduced, and the MOF lost influence as a result.[31] The reduction in its influence was given substantive effect with the formation of the Financial Services Agency (FSA, *Kinyūchō*) in June 1997, attached to the Prime Minister's Office (later Cabinet Office), and symbolically with the change of name in January 2001 from *Ōkurashō* to *Zaimushō*. Moreover, another body, set up when Mori was Prime Minister, but used by Koizumi as his key instrument of economic policy reform, also eroded the impact of the MOF. This was the Council on Economic and Fiscal Policy (*Keizai zaisei shimon kaigi*).

The importance of the Ministry of Foreign Affairs (MOFA) has gradually increased as Japan's international role has grown, and the posting of officials of other ministries in embassies abroad facilitates communication between the MOFA and other parts of the bureaucracy. Nevertheless, this ministry, like its counterparts in other countries, lacks a domestic constituency, which weakens its impact upon politics at home. As already seen in Chapter 6, during the early period of Koizumi's term in office the MOFA was adversely affected by internal dissent and unfavourable publicity, though this problem was largely resolved. Over a long period, tensions have sometimes surfaced between strongly pro-American officials and others more 'Asianist' in their orientation. The latter have typically accorded most attention to relations with China.

The Ministry of Agriculture, Forestry and Fisheries (MAFF) has had extraordinary success over the years in protecting the interests of farmers, despite the declining significance of the agricultural sector in the economy as a whole. In doing so it has relied on close liaison with the ubiquitous Agricultural Cooperative Association (*Nōkyō*), and the high proportion of (mainly LDP) parliamentarians having an agricultural background, or representing rural constituencies, or both. It is true that when Japan became a member of the World Trade Organization (WTO) in 1994, it was obliged to open its rice markets to imports from abroad, though the liberalizing effect of this was less than had been envisaged. It is also true that the reforms to the electoral system for the House of Representatives that became law in 1994 created a system less favourable to the agricultural sector than had pertained before. Nevertheless, although the rurally biased malapportionment that had been a feature of the previous system was reduced, even in the new system the value of a vote in the most over-represented constituencies was 2.2 times that of a vote in the most under-represented constituencies in House of Representatives elections; in House of Councillors elections the multiple was 4.8. This bias was largely at the expense of the cities and in favour of the countryside.[32]

---

[31]   Harumi Hori, *The Changing Japanese Political System: The Liberal Democratic Party and the Ministry of Finance*, London and New York, Routledge, 2005.

[32]   See the magisterial work of the Australian scholar Aurelia George Mulgan in her following books: *The Politics of Agriculture in Japan*, London and New York, Routledge, 2000; *Japan's Interventionist State: The Role of the MAFF*, Abingdon and New York, RoutledgeCurzon, 2005; *Japan's Agricultural Policy Regime*, Abingdon and New York, Routledge, 2006; *Power and Pork: A Japanese Political Life*, Canberra, ANU E Press and Asia-Pacific Press, 2006.

The Ministry of International Trade and Industry (MITI) – once known in foreign trading circles as 'notorious MITI', for its policies of 'picking winners', favouring Japanese exporters and discouraging inward investment by multifarious regulations – was by the new millennium mainly an advocate of freer trade. This change reflected the extent to which the economy was being deregulated – a trend which Koizumi promoted vigorously during his time as Prime Minister. Renamed the Ministry of Economy, Trade and Industry, its status in the bureaucratic hierarchy had declined relative to other ministries.

The Ministry of Education (MOE), which in January 2001 acquired the Science and Technology Agency, thus adding culture, sports and technology to its title in English (see above), was for many years locked in confrontation with the Japan Teachers' Union (*Nikkyōso*) and had a deeply reactionary reputation among intellectuals and others. Its control of textbook licensing caused controversy, particularly in the 1980s, when it faced allegations from the Chinese and Korean governments that the textbooks it approved whitewashed Japanese actions on the Asian continent during the Asia–Pacific War. During the 1980s the Ministry resisted attempts to reform the education system, but later came to promote certain kinds of educational reform. With the passage through Parliament of the revised Basic Law of Education in December 2006, the liberal and progressive ethos of education enshrined in the original law of 1947 was shifted radically in a conservative direction. It remained to be seen how the ministry, which had become more moderate in recent years, reflecting the growing pluralism and sophistication of the populace, would interpret this reversion to the conservative ideologies that prevailed some decades in the past.

The Ministry of Justice oversees the judicial system, including appointment of judges, and presides over a court system which, particularly at its higher levels, has a reputation for conservatism. The Ministry of Health and Welfare (now Health, Labour and Welfare, MHLW) has dealt with many difficult and contentious issues relating to health insurance, pharmaceutical issues and drug control; welfare provision, including disaster relief, pensions and population issues (challenging in view of incipient population decline and the ageing society); veterans' affairs; and welfare for the handicapped. Its merging with the Ministry of Labour in January 2001 brought relations with labour unions into its ambit. The Ministry of Labour had been part of the MHW until 1947, when labour-related functions were separated out and a separate Labour Ministry formed. The reuniting of the two ministries after a separation of 54 years suggests that labour affairs were of lessening significance in an industrial environment where unionization rates were in steady decline.[33]

Two ministries promoted in status (the first in 2001 and the second in 2007) deserve comment. The Ministry of the Environment replaced the Environment Agency founded in July 1971, at a time when there had been an environmental crisis but also a time when prevailing attitudes about environmental concerns were still somewhat sceptical. The upgrading of 2001 (and the acquisition of some functions previously belonging to other ministries: see above) signalled an

---

[33] According to *Asahi Shinbun*, 29 December 2006, the proportion of the workforce having affiliation to a labour union was 18.2%.

appreciation of greater national and international concern with environmental matters, influenced by evidence of global warming.

The elevation of the Defence Agency to full ministry status in January 2007 was the fulfilment of an ancient dream of LDP conservatives. Even though the rise in status did not automatically entail an increase in powers, it should be seen as part of a normalization of military preparation and activity, whose apogee (should it be reached) would be revision of the peace clause of the 1946 Constitution.

Finally, the two super-ministries created by the 2001 reforms are significant. The Ministry of Public Management, Home Affairs, Posts and Telecommunications collected together a ragbag of functions, with evident difficulties of coordination between them. It employed more people than any other ministry (over 300,000), of whom more than 90 per cent worked in post offices. Under Koizumi two of its principal functions – relations between national and local governments, and postal services – were subjected to a maelstrom of reforming legislation.

The second super-ministry was the Ministry of Land, Infrastructure and Transport. This combined what had been two major ministries – Construction and Transport – as well as the National Land Agency and the Hokkaidō Development Agency. These four elements were brought together so that social capital could be built up with maximum coordinating efficiency. This meant that roads, railways, harbours, rivers and airports could be brought together under its administrative umbrella, together with other major infrastructural projects. Whereas Hokkaidō had previously been treated as a special case, with its own agency (government authority), it was now placed under a large central ministry. Okinawa, however, retained its own separate agency, because of the sensitive issue of American military bases there.

Article 15 of the 1946 Constitution states, in a complete break with the former tradition of subservience to the *Tennō*, that 'the people have the inalienable right to choose their public officials and to dismiss them. All public officials are servants of the whole community and not of any special group.' This did not mean, of course, that all civil service positions were to be the subject of popular election, but that the civil service was to be subject to popular control through Parliament, to which Cabinet was responsible. Moreover, article 73 of the Constitution stated that '[t]he Cabinet ... shall ... [a]dminister the civil service, in accordance with standards established by law'. Government officials were now 'civil servants' (*kōmuin*), with the implication that they served the people.

Nevertheless, the impact of the Occupation upon the bureaucracy was considerably less than it was in other areas. The Americans needed the bureaucracy to help implement their reforms, meaning that reforming the bureaucracy itself had to take second place. After the Occupation was over, the role of the bureaucracy in administering rapid economic growth became paramount. Thus old patterns of behaviour tended to overlay the newly prescribed patterns. The terms 'public' and 'official' were commonly confused. The character *kō* in *kōmuin* (public servant, civil servant) has the standard meaning of 'public'. Thus *kōkai* means 'public disclosure'. But it can also mean 'official', as in *kōyō* (official use). The confusion is illustrated by a trivial but amusing example. At a provincial state university there was a notice at the entrance to a section of the car park. It read in Japanese: *kōyōsha senyō* (reserved for official vehicles). Underneath, in English, it read: 'public use only'. The example comes from the 1990s.[34]

If bureaucratic arrogance has been perceived as a problem, for many years civil servants were seen as less corruptible than politicians. Boss politics, for instance, of the kind typified in the United States by Mayer Daley in Chicago in the 1960s or Huey Long in the pre-war Deep South, was widespread in local authorities for much of the post-war period. There were occasional corruption scandals involving civil servants, but it was not until the 1990s that the alleged purity and impartiality of the bureaucracy were put in question. Public anger at the contaminated blood scandal involving the Ministry of Health and Welfare, as well as at poor management of the banking and financial system in the 1990s, damaged the reputation of the bureaucracy as a whole. This, however, did not mean that the public came to prefer politicians to bureaucrats. The two were seen as interlocking, and there was much evidence also in the 1990s of disillusion with politicians and parties, as well as apathy about politics in general. As we have already seen, once we come to the Koizumi period, the balance of power between politicians and civil servants was moving significantly in favour of the former. Koizumi had at his disposal the enhanced prime ministerial power provided by the renamed and strengthened Cabinet Office, while Cabinet ministers had also acquired the additional support provided by the introduction of junior ministers.[35] He was also adept at mobilizing the forces of government in favour of a specific set of policy reforms, showing fast footwork in outmanoeuvring opponents within the ranks of his own party.

Interest Groups

Interest groups exercise much political influence in Japan, as in other advanced industrial states. During the earlier post-war years organized groups representing big business provided the ruling party with much of its funding, and had privileged access to the top levels of government. Today, the situation reflects greater pluralism. In the business world, for instance, there are groups representing specific industries, particular *keiretsu* groups (such as Mitsui) and geographical areas, as well as small and medium industry. Farmers are represented by the Agricultural Cooperative Association (*Nōkyō*), to which nearly all farmers have belonged. Combining the functions of lobby group, provider of essential services to farmers and industrial combine, it has had remarkable success in blocking or delaying attempts to liberalize Japanese agriculture.

In May 2002 the Federation of Economic Organizations (*Keidanren*) amalgamated with the Japan Federation of Employers' Associations (*Nikkeiren*) to form the Japan Business Federation (*Nippon keidanren*). The first of the two components of the merged body had represented larger firms over matters of

---

[34] I am grateful to Professor Yabuno Yūzō for this example.

[35] The addition of junior ministers (*fukudaijin*) was designed to strengthen political control over ministries by expanding the total number of ministers and thus providing extra manpower.

general economic policy, whereas the second specialized in labour relations.[36] The new body is in various ways embedded in government, and has also acted as a channel of funding into the LDP. It may be considered Japan's most powerful interest group.

There are many professional bodies, representing doctors, dentists, lawyers and other such practitioners, which are treated seriously by government in relation to their professional spheres. One of the best known is the Japan Medical Association (*Nihon ishikai*), which has exercised great influence in relation to health service matters.

Labour unions were highly active in post-war Japan but, as we have seen, union membership has steadily declined as tertiary industry has increased and secondary industry declined. In general they are less confrontational than they often were in their heyday between the 1950s and the 1970s. What are termed 'citizens' movements' (*shimin undō*) have been sporadically active since the late 1960s, as have more localized 'residents' movements' (*jūmin undō*). These have had some impact on environmental and quality of life issues, and have also provided a political base for a small number of progressive politicians, of whom the most prominent is Kan Naoto, one time Representative of the DPJ. As we have seen earlier, non-profit organizations (NPOs) have been much hindered by government regulation designed to inhibit too much spontaneity in social movements, but since the Kobe earthquake of January 1995, they have developed in a more vigorous fashion than before. What is fashionably called 'civil society' remains much weaker in Japan than in much of North America, Europe or Australasia, but it has been attracting increasing interest and involvement. Consumer movements have also been relatively weak in Japan, although there is widespread interest and concern about food safety. Historically, producer interests have been stronger, and more favoured by government, than consumer interests.

Conclusions

In the third edition of this book (1999, p. 112) we briefly caricatured the way Japan was run as follows:

> Politicians persuade the electorate to elect them, form governments and get legislation through Parliament and thus enable bureaucrats to realize their policies; politicians also provide post-retirement political careers for some ex-bureaucrats; bureaucrats provide much of the legislative initiative and drafting expertise needed by politicians, and implement the policies passed through Parliament (as well as measures not requiring parliamentary sanctions); bureaucrats regulate the economy in such a way as to benefit businessmen, and in turn are rewarded by *amakudari* positions after retirement; businessmen find electoral funding for politicians and support them in electoral campaigns, while in turn relying on politicians to create a benign policy environment for their activities.

[36] For a critical account of *Nikkeiren*, see John Crump, *Nikkeiren and Japanese Capitalism*, London and New York, RoutledgeCurzon, 2003.

To what extent has this picture changed since 1999? First of all, some elements of it remain in place. Numbers of civil servants, for instance, retire from government service into lucrative jobs in the private sector, and some still leave government service to enter politics. But the biggest change is that, since the new millennium began, the power available to the Prime Minister and his ministers has markedly increased. Moreover, Koizumi – a controversial but also clear-headed and determined political leader – managed to deploy the enhanced structural power of Prime Minister and Cabinet to assert their primacy in the struggle against entrenched vested interests within and outside government. Paradoxically but unsurprisingly, it was the long period of economic stagnation that discredited the existing system and provided him with the opportunity to deregulate, privatize and decentralize. Even so, he had to face down a rearguard action of considerable ferocity from those wishing to preserve a system based on favours and special benefits. Indeed, some aspects of that system are still in evidence.

In other areas, particularly foreign policy, not all changes that took place were necessarily beneficial (see Chapter 12). Moreover, possible consequences of the new system, including the resurgence of a reactionary nationalistic ideology, with adverse implications for human rights and a balanced polity, have begun to emerge. Most crucially, perhaps, a single party that may be seen as a congeries of special interests remains in power as though by right. Until alternation in office becomes a real, not theoretical, possibility, the reforms emerging in the new millennium will not be complete.

Chapter 8 | Parliament and Parliamentary Elections: The Changing Character of Electioneering

Parliament

Although Japan has had what could strictly be called a parliamentary system of government only since the Occupation, it has had a parliament since 1890, and the traditional nature of the institution has no doubt contributed to its ready acceptance over the past 60 years. The position of Parliament in the political system is a blend of historical influences. The Meiji Constitution was strongly German in inspiration, and German influences can easily be found even among post-war constitutional lawyers. At the same time the constitutional relationships between emperor, Prime Minister, Cabinet, Parliament and the bureaucracy are reminiscent of British arrangements, while the structure and role of parliamentary committee are American-inspired. Japanese social norms, a long period of dominance of Parliament by a single party and the self-confidence of the government bureaucracy have all put their stamp on the functioning of Parliament in practice.

The key position which the Parliament (*Kokkai*) was expected to occupy in the system of politics and government was forcefully presented in article 41 of the 1946 Constitution, where it was given the title of 'highest organ of state power' and 'sole law-making authority of the State'. There are two houses, the House of Representatives (*Shūgiin*), and the House of Councillors (*Sangiin*), respectively also known as the lower house and the upper house.[1] Both houses are elected (whereas the pre-war upper house, the House of Peers, was largely hereditary or appointed) and 'representative of all the people',[2] a phrase that can be interpreted to mean 'elected by universal suffrage'. The term of the lower house is four years, although it can be ended prematurely by dissolution.[3] Its

---

[1] *Nihonkoku kenpō* (The Constitution of Japan) [henceforth, Constitution], article 42.
[2] Constitution, article 43. See also article 44.
[3] Constitution, article 45.

membership rose from 464 at the time of the 1946 general election to 512 in the late 1980s and stood at 511 when the electoral system was reformed in 1994. Under the new electoral system the membership was 500, reduced to 480 in 1999. Upper house members are elected for a fixed term of six years, with half the membership being elected every three years.[4] Its membership remained at 250 during the post-war period, but rose to 252 with the return of Okinawa prefecture to Japanese sovereignty in 1972. For the 2001 elections this was reduced to 247, and for the 2004 elections to 242. Nobody can be a member of both houses simultaneously.[5]

Relations between the two houses are complex, and reflect the fact that the initial (GHQ) draft – the draft produced by General MacArthur's drafting committee in February 1946 – of the Constitution envisaged a unicameral legislature, so that the addition of a second chamber was one of the few really significant changes that the Japanese government of the day was able to effect in the course of its discussions with SCAP on the drafting of a new Constitution. The constitutional position of the House of Councillors is inferior to that of the House of Representatives. Early hopes that the upper house might differentiate itself from the lower house either by speciality of function or by a difference in the quality and background of members have hardly been fulfilled.

On a number of matters the two houses have identical powers.[6] Each independently judges disputes about the qualifications of its members,[7] keeps and publishes records of its proceedings,[8] selects its president (Speaker),[9] establishes its own rules and punishes its own members,[10] receives petitions,[11] and conducts 'investigations in relation to government' (a power that is the basis of the committee system of each house).[12] The members of each house enjoy freedom from arrest (except in cases provided for by law) while Parliament is in session,[13] and freedom from liability outside the house for speeches, debates or votes cast inside the house.[14] There is no difference in the rights of the two houses concerning revision of the Constitution.[15]

---

[4] Constitution, article 46.

[5] Constitution, article 48.

[6] See Kuroda Satoru, *Kokkaihō* (The Parliamentary Law), Hōritsu Gakkai Zenshū (Collective Works of the Legal Academy), no. 5, Yūhikaku, 1968; Asano Ichirō (ed.), *Kokkai jiten: yōgo ni yoru kokkaihō kaisetsu* (Parliamentary Dictionary; Guide to Parliamentary Law through Terminology), Tokyo, Yūhikaku, 3rd edn, 1997.

[7] Constitution, article 55.

[8] Constitution, article 57.

[9] Constitution, article 58.

[10] Constitution, article 58.

[11] Constitution, article 16. This article gives a general right of petition, without actually specifying Parliament as its receiver.

[12] Constitution, article 62.

[13] Constitution, article 50. In April 1997 the House of Councillors stripped one of its members, accused of fraud, of membership of the house, and thus of parliamentary immunity: *Asahi Shinbun*, 4 April 1997 (evening).

[14] Constitution, article 51.

[15] Constitution, article 96. To revise the Constitution a two-thirds majority of *members* (not just those present at the vote) is required, followed by a simple majority in a national referendum.

On the other hand, only the House of Representatives has the power to force a Cabinet resignation by passing a no-confidence resolution (or rejecting a confidence resolution).[16] Also, dissolution of the House of Representatives means that the House of Councillors must be closed as well,[17] whereas the latter operates on the basis of fixed terms and cannot be dissolved prematurely. The House of Councillors possesses one attribute that is peculiar to it, namely that it may be convoked in emergency session in a time of national emergency. The lower house, however, has to agree to measures taken by such a session within ten days after the opening of the parliamentary session, or they become null and void.[18]

The constitutional inferiority of the House of Councillors is manifest in the restricted nature of its power to reject or delay the passage of legislation originating in the House of Representatives. In the case of ordinary bills, where the upper house differs from the lower house (in other words, when it rejects or amends the proposed legislation), the bill nevertheless becomes law if passed a second time by the lower house by a two-thirds majority of the members present.[19] On the other hand, in such a case another road is open to the House of Representatives, namely to call for a joint committee of both houses to resolve the issue.[20] In order to avoid the possibility of indefinite delay by the House of Councillors, a bill on which that house fails to take action within 60 days of its receipt from the lower house (time in recess excepted) may be regarded by the lower house as having been rejected by the upper.[21]

Between 1955 and 1989, these provisions were largely academic, because the LDP controlled both houses and maintained tight party discipline, at least so far as voting in Parliament was concerned. When, however, the LDP was defeated in

[16]   Constitution, article 69. It was established early in the history of the Constitution that Parliament can be dissolved simply by application of article 7, and does not require a vote of no confidence to be passed. In recent years two governments have been forced to dissolve the House of Representatives after failing to win a vote of confidence: the Ōhira government in May 1980 and the Miyazawa government in June 1993. In June 1994 the minority Hata government resigned without facing a no-confidence motion, which it knew it could not win.

[17]   Constitution, article 54. The double elections of June 1980 and of July 1986 were possible only because the House of Councillors had come to the end of its term.

[18]   Constitution, article 54. This has not happened since the Yoshida government convoked emergency sessions of the upper house, in each case immediately after the close of a lower house session, in August 1952 and March 1953. The first lasted one day and the second three days. In both cases the object was to finish off business from the previous session, rather than to deal with a 'national emergency': Kuroda, *Kokkaihō*, pp. 74–5; Asano, *Kokkai jiten*, pp. 47–8.

[19]   Constitution, article 59, para. 2. A majority of two-thirds of members present is a less onerous requirement than the two-thirds of *members* required to amend the Constitution.

[20]   Constitution, article 59, para. 3. If, however, a bill originates in the House of Councillors and strikes trouble in the House of Representatives, the latter is not obliged to agree to a joint committee of both houses, although the former may request this. *Kokkaihō* (Law No. 79 of 30 April 1947, as amended), article 84, para. 2 (henceforth Parliamentary Law). See Kuroda, *Kokkaihō*, p. 175; Asano, *Kokkai jiten*, p. 29.

[21]   Constitution, article 59, para 4.

the House of Councillors elections of July 1989, the Kaifu government was faced with severe problems during the period of the first Gulf crisis, as we saw in Chapter 5. Since in practice it has normally been impossible for any government to muster the two-thirds majority necessary to override an adverse vote in the House of Councillors, the only practicable strategy available was to seek to *create* an upper house majority by doing deals with parties in opposition there. The politics of the 1990s was much affected by this problem, which was a principal factor compelling the LDP to govern in coalition with parties that would help make up its majority in the upper house.

In the case of matters regarded as outstandingly important, namely the budget, treaties and the designation of a new Prime Minister, the supremacy of the House of Representatives is more marked than with ordinary bills. The relationship between the two houses is also much simpler. The annual budget, unlike other bills, must first be submitted to the House of Representatives.[22] In the case of disagreement between the two houses, reference of the budget to a joint committee is mandatory (not voluntary, as is the case with ordinary bills); but if the House of Councillors has taken no action within 30 days, the decision of the House of Representatives is considered the decision of Parliament.[23] Until 1990, the budget had never been referred to a joint committee, although at least once (in 1954) the upper house failed to take action and the budget automatically came into force after 30 days.[24]

Treaties fall under the same provisions as the budget, except that the Constitution does not forbid a treaty being submitted first to the upper house (though this is very unusual).[25] In Chapter 4 we described how Kishi needed to force the revised Mutual Security Treaty through the House of Representatives by 19 May 1960 if the treaty were to be ready in time for President Eisenhower's projected visit, because it required 30 days in the House of Councillors before it would automatically receive parliamentary endorsement.[26]

The rules are similar for the designation of a Prime Minister, except that this takes precedence over any other business, and the decision of the House of Representatives becomes the decision of Parliament if there is no agreement between the two houses or if the House of Councillors fails to make designation within a mere ten days of action by the House of Representatives.[27] In February 1948, the composition of the two houses was sufficiently different for each to produce a different candidate. After a joint committee had failed to agree and

22 Constitution, article 60, para. 1.
23 Constitution, article 60, para. 2.
24 Kuroda, *Kokkaihō*, p. 178; Asano, *Kokkai jiten*, pp. 28–9, 138–41, 219–21.
25 Constitution, article 61.
26 Langdon quotes the coal debate of 1962 as an instance where the opposition was able to use delaying tactics in the House of Councillors to talk out a piece of legislation, which therefore lapsed at the end of the session and had to be revived in the next regular session. This would normally be impossible in the case of the budget – or of a treaty, although even here the rigidity of session timetables can cause difficulties for governments. See Frank Langdon, *Politics in Japan*, Boston and Toronto, Little, Brown and Co., 1967, p. 160.
27 Constitution, article 67.

ten days had elapsed, the candidate of the lower house, Ashida, prevailed over the candidate of the upper house, Yoshida, and became Prime Minister. In July 1989 Kaifu prevailed over Ms Doi Takako in a similar way.

While the House of Councillors can be used against the government to good effect by an opposition enjoying an upper house majority, another powerful weapon at the disposal of the opposition has been the rigidity of the parliamentary timetable. The 1960 crisis is only one of many instances in which the government of the day has been gravely embarrassed by opposition filibustering, premised on the government's lack of control over the timetabling of parliamentary business. This in turn has meant that the Management (Steering) Committee (*un'ei iinkai*) of the House of Representatives has at times become crucially important, and paradoxically relations between the parliamentary policy committee chairmen of government and opposition parties have been a subtle but crucial factor in maintaining working relationships between the various parties within Parliament.[28]

Provision is made for three types of parliamentary session (apart from the emergency session of the House of Councillors mentioned above). The first is the ordinary or regular session (*tsūjō kokkai*), which is held once every year.[29] This session is normally convoked in January (before 1991, in December) and lasts for 150 days.[30] Since the revision of the parliamentary law in 1955, it may be extended once only, although previously an indefinite number of extensions was permitted.[31] The second is the extraordinary session (*rinji kokkai*), which may be called by the Cabinet, or must be held when a quarter or more of the total members of either house makes the demand.[32] The third is the special session (*tokubetsu kokkai*), called in fulfilment of the constitutional provision that after a lower house dissolution, a lower house general election must be held within 40 days, and Parliament must be convoked within 30 days of the date of the election.[33] Both extraordinary and special sessions may now be extended up to twice;[34] and with all types of session, if there is disagreement between the two houses on, say, the length of the extension, the House of Representatives prevails.[35]

The importance of the length of session is considerable because of the principle in the Parliamentary Law that 'any matter not decided during a session shall not be carried over to the following session', except that in certain circumstances parliamentary committees can continue their deliberations into the adjournment,

[28]   Ishikawa Masumi and Hirose Michisada, *Jimintō – chōki shihai no kōzo* (The LDP – the Structure of its Long-term Control), Tokyo, Iwanami Shoten, 1989, pp. 35–60.
[29]   Constitution, article 52.
[30]   Parliamentary Law, articles 2 and 10.
[31]   Parliamentary Law, article 12, para. 2. Before 1955 as many as five extensions of one ordinary session were known.
[32]   Constitution, article 53.
[33]   Constitution, article 54, para. 1; Parliamentary Law, article 1, para. 3.
[34]   Parliamentary Law, article 12, para. 2.
[35]   Parliamentary Law, article 13.

and matters entrusted to them can then be carried on into the next session.[36] For the most part, however, the government is under strong pressure to complete its legislative programme by the end of the session (extensions included), and this task is not made any easier for it by the fact that the order in which legislation is to be discussed is in the hands of the management committee of each house. Particularly for much of the 1970s, when the balance of parliamentary forces between government and opposition was nearly even, and for periods of coalition and even minority government that intervened in the 1990s, the management committee provided another forum in which delaying tactics could be applied.

Indeed, the opposition parties have a variety of means at their disposal to delay the passage of legislation, so that the length of a particular session may assume magnified importance. During the earlier post-war decades, the left-of-centre opposition parties, most notably the JSP, were famous – or notorious – for obstructionist tactics of various kinds, including 'cow-walking tactics' (*gyūho senjutsu*), whereby they walked extremely slowly to record their votes. In some cases they presented a large number of amendments, and in May 1960 they physically prevented the President of the House of Representatives from taking a vote (see Chapter 4). More recently, such tactics have become much less common. When the JSP engaged in 'cow-walking' in 1992, seeking to delay the Peace Keeping Operations bill, it met a hostile public reaction. In 1996, when the New Frontier Party organized a sit-in in the parliamentary corridors to protest against the use of taxpayers' money to rescue bankrupt housing loan companies, its reputation with the electorate seems to have suffered (see Chapter 5 for accounts of these two episodes).

Opposition party obstruction combined with timetabling rigidity remains on occasion a problem for governments. This is particularly true in the case of the annual budget, where delay is likely to have serious consequences. Since 1947 there have been many instances, relating to the budget as well as to ordinary legislation, where the government makes concessions to opposition parties by modifying the relevant bills, simply in order to have them passed by the end of a session. If, however, as has also happened many times, the government assumes an intransigent position, the opposition parties may decide to boycott the remainder of the session (either the plenary session or the session of the relevant parliamentary committee). The government is then faced with a choice between bargaining with the parties in an effort to persuade them to resume their seats, or brazening it out and pushing the legislation through unilaterally. Experience on a number of occasions, particularly in the earlier post-war years, showed that the latter course carried with it the danger of precipitating a serious political crisis, with the government standing accused of having 'broken consensus', or of having exercised the 'tyranny of the majority'. It should be noted perhaps, that the ideal of 'consensus' serves both as a cultural norm and a political excuse: a cultural norm in the sense that 'winner-take-all' majority decision-making does

---

[36] Parliamentary Law, article 68. The concept of 'non-continuity of sessions' is based on the principle that Parliament has existence only when it is in session and that there is no 'continuity of will' from one session to the next. This is one area where Meiji constitutional practice, itself derived from nineteenth-century German models, has influenced current practice. Kuroda, *Kokkaihō*, pp. 65–7; Asano, *Kokkai jiten*, pp. 37–9.

not sit easily with Japanese social practice, and a political excuse in that parties long excluded from power have managed to hold the line on some issues important to them by invoking the principle of consensus and arguing that they should be part of it. In the fluid politics of the 1990s, the option of actually participating in government became a real possibility for many parties, reducing the attractions of the old forms of obstructionism. In the 2000s that possibility receded except for the CGP, which became a long-term participant in government. For the Democratic Party (the only party out of office that now really mattered), it made more sense to behave responsibly in order to create the image of a party ready for government.

As in the British House of Commons, the overwhelming majority of bills are government-sponsored. Private members' bills are not uncommon, but in contrast to Britain, where private members' bills often concern social issues that are not part of the government's agenda, in Japan they more typically concern constituency matters. Some of them, however, originate in a government ministry that has been successful in finding a parliamentarian prepared to pilot a piece of legislation through the house.

The most 'American' feature of the operation of Parliament is its system of standing and special committees. Based on the constitutional right of each house to 'conduct investigations in relations to government',[37] the system replaces the pre-war practice of taking bills through three successive readings on the floor of the house. Bills initiated by individual parliamentarians or by Cabinet, or referred from the other house, are normally sent straight to the appropriate committee. The committee has the power of 'killing' any bill referred to it (with the exception of bills transmitted from the other house), but it is a comparatively simple matter to pull a bill out of a committee. If, within seven days of a decision by the committee not to submit a bill to the plenary session, its release is demanded by 20 or more members of the house, then it must be submitted to the plenary session.[38] In this respect, at least, the power of Japanese parliamentary committees is much less than that of their American counterparts, the committees of Congress.

Parliamentarians are obliged to belong to at least one standing committee. Before the 1955 revision of the Parliamentary Law, parliamentarians were not allowed to belong to more than two standing committees and, if they belonged to two, the second had to be chosen from a restricted list. Since 1955, however, this restriction has not applied, and the President, Deputy President, Prime Minister, ministers and other Cabinet officials are no longer obliged to belong to any committees.[39] Membership of standing committees and special committees is allocated in proportion to party strengths in the house, with the management committee being the arbiter.[40] Chairmen of standing committees are formally elected from the committee membership by a vote of the plenary session,[41] but in

---

[37]   Constitution, article 62.
[38]   Parliamentary Law, article 56, para. 3.
[39]   Parliamentary Law, article 42. If they do not, their parties are given compensatory weighting in the allocation of members on committees.
[40]   Parliamentary Law, article 46.
[41]   Parliamentary Law, article 25.

practice they are selected by the president according to the distribution of party strengths in each committee.[42] Chairmen of special committees, on the other hand, are elected by the committees themselves from among their members, not necessarily according to their relative strengths.[43]

During the 1990s (as also during the 1970s) the control of parliamentary committees was an exceedingly complicated business, with the LDP sometimes having to concede control of even crucial committees to a combination of opposition parties. For instance, in January 1995 the LDP provided the chairman in only eight out of 20 standing committees of the House of Representatives. Chairmen of the key committees of Cabinet, budget, and foreign affairs, for instance, belonged to opposition parties.[44] Twelve years later, in February 2007, the principal ruling party, having won a convincing victory at the general elections of September 2005, was much more firmly in control. This can be seen from Tables 8.1 and 8.2.

It will be seen by comparing Tables 8.1 and 8.2 that LDP control was firmer over committees in the House of Representatives than it was over committees in the House of Councillors. Given the principle of proportionality whereby the committees of each house are supposed to reflect its party composition, the persistent lack of an LDP majority in the upper house clearly caused problems for its independent effectiveness in the committees of that house. Table 8.2 also brings into sharp focus the extent to which the LDP was dependent for its majority on the Clean Government Party, its junior partner in coalition. On its own, the LDP enjoyed equal representation with all other parties in three out of 17 standing committees, and in two out of six special committees, but in no committee did it have an independent majority. The LDP and CGP taken together, though, had a clear majority of members in all upper house committees, both standing and special. This is true even though the CGP had been allocated only two members in most committees, and no more than four in any of them.

The standing committees of both houses showed continuity with those present in the 1990s, but there had been a certain amount of adjustment after the reform of the structure of ministries in January 2001, in order to bring the committees into at least approximate conformity with the new pattern of ministerial functions, suggesting how important the interaction between government ministries and parliamentary committees remained.[45]

Special committees tended to be ad hoc responses to particular areas of policy concern, though some of them were semi-permanent. Thus the committee of the House of Representatives on disaster policy had existed for many years, as had that on electoral system reform (though its name had been adjusted to take in political ethics), as well as the committee on Okinawa and the Northern Territories. But the committee on youth policy was relatively new, as was

---

[42] Kuroda, *Kokkaihō*, p. 100. The principle here is 'winner take all'. There are, however a number of directors (*riji*) appointed in each committee, and the opposition parties obtain some of these positions even when they do not have the numbers to secure committee chairmanships.

[43] Parliamentary Law, article 45.

[44] *Asahi Nenkan*, 1996, pp. 242–3.

[45] *Asahi Shinbun*, 1 February 2001.

Table 8.1   Committees of the House of Representatives, February 2007

Name of committee	No. of members	Party of chair
Standing committees		
Cabinet	30	LDP
General management	40	LDP
Justice	35	LDP
Foreign affairs	30	LDP
Finance	40	LDP
Education and science	40	CGP
Social welfare and labour	45	LDP
Agriculture, forestry and fisheries	40	LDP
Economy and industry	40	CGP
National land and transport	45	LDP
Environment	30	LDP
Security	30	LDP
Basic national policy	30	LDP
Budget	50	LDP
Audit management	40	DPJ
House management	25	LDP
Disciplinary	20	DPJ
Special committees		
Disaster policy		LDP
Political ethics and revision of the electoral law		LDP
Okinawa and Northern Territories		LDP
Youth issues		DPJ
International terrorism, overseas aid, humanitarian aid to Iraq		LDP
The Japanese Constitution		LDP
Abductions by North Korea		LDP

Source: http://www.shugiin.go.jp/index.nsf/html.index_honkai.htm, 17 Feb. 2007.

Table 8.2   Committees of the House of Councillors, February 2007

Name of committee	No. of members (party breakdown)	Party of chair
Standing committees		
Cabinet	20 (LDP 9; DPJ 8; CGP 2; PNP[a] 1)	DPJ
Finance	24 (LDP 12; DPJ 6; CGP 2; JCP 1; SDP 1; PNP 1; Independent 1)	LDP
Justice	20 (LDP 8; DPJ 6; CGP 3; JCP 1; SDP 1; Independent 1)	CGP
Foreign affairs and defence	21 (LDP 10; DPJ 7; CGP 2; JCP 1; SDP 1)	LDP
Finance	24 (LDP 11; DPJ 10; CGP 2; JCP 1)	DPJ

Table 8.2   *(Continued)*

Name of committee	No. of members (party breakdown)	Party of chair
Education and science	20 (LDP 10; DPJ 7; CGP 2; JCP 1)	LDP
Welfare and labour	25 (LDP 12; DPJ 9; CGP 2; JCP 1; SDP 1)	LDP
Agriculture, forestry and fisheries	20 (LDP 10; DPJ 7; CGP 2; JCP 1)	LDP
Economy and industry	21 (LDP 10; DPJ 7; CGP 2; SDP 1; Independent 1)	LDP
National land and transport	25 (LDP 11; DPJ 9; CGP 2; JCP 1; SDP 1; PNP 1)	DPJ
Environment	20 (LDP 8; DPJ 6; CGP 3; JCP 1; PNP 1; Independent 1)	DPJ
Basic national policy	20 (LDP 9; DPJ 7; CGP 2; JCP 1; PNP 1)	DPJ
Budget	45 (LDP 22; DPJ 16; CGP 4; JCP 2; SDP 1)	LDP
Audit	30 (LDP 14; DPJ 11; CGP 3; JCP 1; SDP 1)	LDP
Management inspection	30 (LDP 14; DPJ 9; CGP 4; JCP 1; SDP 1; PNP 1)	CGP
House management	25 (LDP 13; DPJ 9; CGP 3)	LDP
Disciplinary	10 (LDP 5; DPJ 4; CGP 1)	DPJ
Special committees		
Disaster prevention	20 (LDP 10; DPJ 7; CGP 2; JCP 1)	CGP
Okinawa and Northern Territories	20 (LDP 9; DPJ 7; CGP 2; JCP 1; SDP 1)	DPJ
Political ethics and election system	28 (LDP 16; DPJ 7; CGP 3; JCP 1; SDP 1)	LDP
Abductions by North Korea etc.	20 (LDP 10; DPJ 7; CGP 2; JCP 1)	DPJ
Government development aid etc.	30 (LDP 14; DPJ 10; CGP 3; JCP 1; SDP 1; PNP 1)	LDP
The Japanese Constitution	34 (LDP 16; DPJ 12; CGP 4; JCP 1; SDP 1)	LDP

^aPeople's New Party.

Source: http://www.sangiin.go.jp/japanese/frameset/fset_b01_01.htm, 17 Feb. 2007.

(for obvious reasons) that on international terrorism, to which the issues of overseas aid and humanitarian aid to Iraq were attached. The committee on abductions to North Korea was a response to the political concern with this issue since the Koizumi visit to Pyongyang in September 2001. Committees that existed in the mid-1990s on coal policy, consumer issues, road safety, the relocation of Parliament, local decentralization and deregulation had disappeared.

The special committees of the House of Councillors on disaster prevention and on Okinawa and the Northern Territories were also of long standing. Those on political ethics and the electoral system, North Korean abductions, and overseas development aid were recent. Committees from the mid-1990s on science and technology, the environment, local decentralization and deregulation, and small and medium industry policy no longer operated.

But the most high-profile special committees of both houses were those on revision of the Constitution. These committees were part of a larger movement spearheaded by successive governments to rewrite the 1946 Constitution in the light of developments over half a century and the dislike for the peace clause (article 9) long felt by the right wing of the LDP. These issues will be explored in Chapter 10.

Much more parliamentary time is spent in committee than in plenary sessions. Ministers can speak in committees, as in plenary sessions. They also appear at the request of particular committees, to speak on bills for which they are responsible. There used to be a convention whereby a minister would bring a senior official of his ministry with him to committees (or to a plenary session) in order to assist him in answering difficult or technical questions. This practice, however, has now been abolished, placing more pressure on a minister to be on top of his or her brief. Another innovation designed to increase accountability is the introduction of a regular British-style 'Question Time', whereby the Prime Minister appears to answer questions from members of Parliament.

Although not part of the formal process of government, a further important part of the system is the committee system of the Liberal Democratic Party. Arguably more important in practice than the committees of Parliament, the LDP committees over many years arrogated to themselves immense power to decide policy in conjunction with relevant ministries. When we consider where Parliament fits in to the political system as a whole, we need to bear in mind the interactions between the executive (in the form of the Prime Minister and Cabinet), the government bureaucracy and the internal committees of the LDP. During the period when Koizumi was Prime Minister, a battle royal developed (reaching its apogee in 2005) between the political executive on the one hand and a combination of ministerial interests and LDP committees on the other.

Does this, then, mean that Parliament is irrelevant or politically bypassed? Our answer is that it is not. The constitutional description of Parliament and its functions, though idealized in some aspects, is far from a dead letter. Although there are various devices whereby government can go beyond legislation,[46] government cannot do without it, and for this Parliament is necessary. Indeed, it is probably best to regard Parliament as the *arena* in which power is contested and laws are made, rather than as an independent body exercising power. This is, very broadly, also the way parliaments work in parliamentary systems elsewhere. We would argue that many of the distortions of the political system that have been in evidence result from the dominance of a single political party and its creation of a kind of parallel government structure that in part cooperates with and in part contests the formal constitutional structures of politics and

[46] 'Descent from Heaven' (*amakudari*), the extra-legal practice of 'administrative guidance' (*gyōsei shidō*) and extensive delegated legislation are examples of this.

government. In the 1990s, the LDP power structure came close to collapse, but was allowed to survive, partly because the only alternative at that time appeared to be weak and divided coalition governments. Since the new millennium began, however, the party system has stabilized, and the Democratic Party has come to provide at least the possibility of a credible opposition, perhaps capable of replacing the LDP in power.

Parliament, as the arena of politics, is the reflection of the politics that is conducted within its walls. But in so far as legislation is the central outcome of the political process, Parliament is a pivotal element in the system as a whole. With the gradual and painful development of a more balanced party system, the emergence of a strengthened political executive, and a modest shift in the power balance from bureaucrats to politicians, there are signs that Parliament may be coming to play a more valuable part in the development of Japanese democracy.

Parliamentary Elections

The Japanese system of parliamentary elections has experienced radical reform since the mid-1990s, and the results of the change are only now – more than a decade later – becoming reasonably clear.

The House of Representatives and the House of Councillors have different electoral systems, and this has been the case throughout the post-war period. The system for the lower house was established in 1947,[47] and lasted with occasional modifications until 1994, when it was changed to a wholly different system. In all, 18 general elections were conducted under the former system (which was similar to the system used between 1925 and the war). Four elections have now been held under the new system.

The former lower house electoral system was based on a single, non-transferable vote in multi-member constituencies (SNTV in MMCs). In Japanese, though, it is known simplistically as the 'medium constituency system' (*chūsenkyokusei*), to distinguish it from the 'large constituency system' (*daisenkyokusei*), used in 1946 and some pre-war elections, and the 'small constituency system' (*shōsenkyokusei*), meaning first past the post in single-member constituencies. The essence of SNTV in MMCs was as follows: each elector had one vote, and could not express preferences beyond his or her first preference. But each constituency elected several members. Until the 1980s, all constituencies except one elected (in about equal proportions) three, four or five members.[48] The number of seats increased from 466 in 1947 to 511 in 1994, when the system was replaced.[49] At the time of the 1993 elections (the last under the old system), there were 129 constituencies throughout the country, two electing six members, 47 electing five members, 33 electing four members, 39 electing three members and eight electing two members. Since each elector had a single vote, this was not a preferential voting system, as in Australia, nor a two-stage voting system, as in French presidential elections; nor was it a form of proportional

---

[47] The general election of 1946 was held using a different system.
[48] The exception was the island of Amami Ōshima, between Kyūshū and Okinawa.
[49] The number of seats was 512 for the 1986 and 1990 elections.

representation, even though the number of seats mirrored more closely the number of votes than did the British-type system. Small parties were less disadvantaged than under British electoral arrangements. An unusual feature of the system was that the voter had to write the name of the candidate of his or her choice on the ballot paper.

The system that replaced SNTV in MMCs in 1994 was entirely different. The number of members was reduced from 511 to 500. Three hundred constituencies elected one member each, and the remaining 200 seats were elected by the d'Hondt list system of proportional representation (PR) from 11 regional constituencies. The elector was given two votes, one for the local constituency and one for the regional (PR) constituency, so that vote-splitting was permitted. Unlike the previous system, where the elector wrote the name of the preferred candidate on the ballot paper, the elector now ticked two names (one for each constituency), already printed on the ballot paper. Controversially, candidates may stand for both constituencies, and take a seat in the regional constituency even if defeated in the single-member constituency. Later, the 200 regional seats were reduced to 180, so that the total number of seats became 480. The proportion of seats allocated to the two types of constituency remains an area of contestation.

The House of Councillors is elected on a different system, which, apart from one important change in the early 1980s, is recognizably the same set of arrangements that existed when the upper house was established after the war. Its membership remained at 250, but rose to 252 with the return of Okinawa to Japanese sovereignty in May 1972. For the 2001 elections it was reduced to 247, and for the 2004 elections it went down to 242. Of these, 96[50] are elected from a 'national' constituency (the whole nation as one constituency, elected by PR) and 146[51] from multi-member constituencies that are coincident with the prefectures. The term of the House of Councillors is a fixed six years, but elections are staggered, with half the seats (now 48 from the national constituency and 73 from the prefectural constituencies)[52] being contested every three years in July. As in the current lower house electoral system, each voter has two non-transferable votes, in this case one for the 'national' constituency and one for the local prefectural constituency. Candidates, however, may not stand in both constituencies at the same election.

The basis of election to the 'national' constituency was radically changed in August 1982. Since in each (staggered) election 50 seats were contested in this constituency, the pre-1982 method of election may be described as 'first fifty past the post'). The great expense and uncertainty of campaigning as an individual candidate in an electorate with more than 80 million electors led to a reform whereby the d'Hondt list system of PR was used to elect the 50 'national'[53] constituency seats (now reduced to 48). As in the lower house PR constituency

---

[50]   100 until after the 1998 elections.
[51]   150 between 1947 and 1972, then 152 until after the 1998 elections.
[52]   Between 1972 and 1998 the figures were 50 and 76.
[53]   Although we use 'national' to describe both the pre-1982 and post-1982 constituencies, they are differently named in Japanese. That prior to 1982 was *zenkokku* (all-nation constituency), and that since 1982 is *hirei daihyōku* (PR constituency).

seats, candidates have to be grouped in party (or quasi-party) lists. In time for the 2004 elections, however, the upper house electoral law was revised to permit electors to vote for an individual candidate in the PR constituency, as well as for that candidate's party list.

The electoral law that governs elections for both houses of Parliament, as well as for governors and assemblies of prefectures, mayors and assemblies of cities, towns and villages, is the Public Offices Election Law (*kōshoku senkyo hō*).[54] The purpose of the law given in article 1 is 'to establish an electoral system ... based on the spirit of the Japanese Constitution, to ensure that these elections are conducted fairly and properly according to the freely expressed will of the electors, and thus to aim at the healthy growth of democratic politics'. Any citizen having reached the age of 20 may vote after three months' residence in a constituency (there are some exceptions from this limitation), provided that he or she is not an incompetent or serving a prison sentence. The minimum age for candidacy to all the offices covered by the Election Law is 25, except for membership of the House of Councillors, where it is 30.[55] Voting is not compulsory, as it is in Australia and elsewhere.

Several types of problem have arisen with the electoral systems in Japan, relating to perceived or actual deficiencies in the law, to the characteristics of voting behaviour and candidate behaviour, and to broader issues concerning the structure and process of politics as a whole. Electoral system reform has frequently figured on the political agenda of government. Four prime ministers between the 1950s and 1990s (Hatoyama, Tanaka, Kaifu and Miyazawa) proposed radical reform of the system for the House of Representatives, but all of them failed. Even with the temporary collapse of LDP rule in 1993–4 reforming the system was fraught with difficulty, though it was achieved in 1994. Aspects of the current system are also hotly debated, and many politicians have called for a return to something like the former system. Nevertheless, prevailing arrangements now seem destined to remain in place, albeit with occasional adjustments.

The problem with electoral reform proposals, in Japan as elsewhere, is that the nature of the reform proposed differs depending on the kind of political system (especially party political system) that its proponents wish to achieve. In Japan there is the additional problem that electoral systems having a particular kind of effect elsewhere are apt to have a significantly different effect in Japan, given certain indigenous patterns of social interaction. The following discussion will look first at the effects of the old and new electoral systems, second at the personalizing of elections and the related issue of corruption, and third at malapportionment. Our discussion will concentrate on the House of Representatives, but we shall also discuss briefly the House of Councillors.

We shall first take Yamanashi prefecture, to the west of Tokyo, giving the results of successive elections between 1990 and 2005. This example will illustrate the effects of the transition from the old to the new system. Yamanashi prefecture comprised a single constituency under the old system, electing five members.

---

[54] The Public Offices Election Law is Law No. 100 of 15 April 1950, as amended (henceforth 'Election Law').

[55] Election Law, articles 9–11.

Under the new system, it was split into three single-member constituencies, though other seats were available for candidates who stood in the South Kantō PR bloc. Thus the territory of the original constituency was identical with the three constituencies that emerged from the 1994 reform. This makes analysis easier.

In the 1990 election (see Table 8.3) three LDP candidates and two Socialists were returned. This was the last election for Kanemaru, who was at the time one of the party's highest-profile leaders, but was forced out of politics by scandal two years later. This result shows one of the problems for the LDP of the former system. Kanemaru was *too* popular. If the votes for the four LDP candidates had been evenly distributed, Horiuchi would not actually have been elected, but would have come reasonably close. For the Socialists 1990 was a good year, seeing two of their candidates returned in Yamanashi. The Communist had no chance of being elected in this rural area, but the party ran candidates in nearly all constituencies in order to motivate local organizations and boost its national vote.

In 1993, with Kanemaru out of the picture, Horiuchi rocketed to the head of the poll (see Table 8.4), but of the other LDP candidates (two, not three, this time), the veteran Nakao narrowly retained his seat, whereas the equally long-serving Tanabe was defeated. This time only one Socialist, Koshiishi, was standing, and he was comfortably elected. The Japan New Party of Hosokawa (soon to be Prime Minister), founded the previous year, fielded a successful candidate. Finally, a new candidate, Yokouchi, stood as an Independent and was returned. This man clearly aspired to LDP membership but the party, not wishing to run too many candidates and split the vote between them, refused him endorsement. This was a common pattern under the old system. Having been elected, Yokouchi was then endorsed by the LDP.

In 1996, the three single-member constituencies into which Yamanashi had been carved returned three LDP members (see Table 8.5). Moreover, these were exactly the same men who had been elected under the old system in 1993. The other LDP veteran, Tanabe, stood only in the South Kantō bloc and, in being elected, boosted the LDP representation to four. The opposition parties were left with only one successful candidate between them in Yamanashi: Ozawa (not Ozawa Ichirō), now transferred from the defunct JNP to the DPJ, and also

Table 8.3 House of Representatives election 1990: Yamanashi Prefecture constituency

Result	Candidate	No. of times elected	Party	Votes
Elected	Kanemaru	12	LDP	101,756
Elected	Ueda	2	JSP	94,390
Elected	Koshiishi	1	JSP	80,311
Elected	Nakao	8	LDP	77,282
Elected	Tanabe	8	LDP	75,412
Defeated	Horiuchi		LDP	70,606
Defeated	Sakurai		JCP	17,130

Source: *Asahi Nenkan*, 1994, p. 93.

Table 8.4   House of Representatives election 1993: Yamanashi Prefecture constituency

Result	Candidate	No. of times elected	Party	Votes
Elected	Horiuchi	6	LDP	99,709
Elected	Koshiishi	2	JSP	72,561
Elected	Ozawa[a]	1	JNP	71,038
Elected	Yokouchi	1	Independent	69,704
Elected	Nakao	9	LDP	67,388
Defeated	Tanabe		LDP	63,356
Defeated	Akaike		Independent	31,741
Defeated	Sakurai		JCP	19,696

[a]Not Ozawa Ichirō.

Source: Asahi Nenkan, 1994, p. 128.

elected in the South Kantō bloc. So Yamanashi Prefecture in effect continued to return five parliamentarians. The former Socialist, Koshiishi, now in the DPJ, gave Nakao a run for his money in no. 1 constituency, but the New Frontier Party did badly in all three, and in constituencies 2 and 3 the LDP candidates trounced all opponents.

In 2000 (see Table 8.6) the DPJ candidate in constituency no. 1, who in 1996 had been returned from the South Kantō bloc, now headed the poll, displacing the veteran Nakao as member for the constituency. Nakao was also defeated in

Table 8.5   House of Representatives election 1996: Yamanashi single-member constituencies 1–3

Result	Candidate	No. of times elected	Party	Votes
Constituency No. 1				
Elected	Nakao	10	LDP	52,111
Defeated	Koshiishi		DPJ	45,288
Defeated	Gotō		NFP	25,265
Defeated	Kokoe		JCP	10,610
Defeated	Ichikawa		Minor party	753
Constituency No. 2				
Elected	Horiuchi	7	LDP	90,567
Defeated	Sugimoto		NFP	31,825
Defeated	Akiyama		JCP	15,553
Constituency No. 3				
Elected	Yokouchi	2	LDP	87,683
Defeated	Hase		NFP	31,737
Defeated	Matsuzaki		Minor party	7,250

Source: Asahi Nenkan, 1997, p. 190.

Table 8.6   House of Representatives election 2000: Yamanashi single-member constituencies 1–3

Result	Candidate	No. of times elected	Party	Votes
Constituency No. 1				
Elected	Ozawa	3	DPJ	58,781
Defeated	Nakao		LDP	52,964
Defeated	Akaike		Independent	15,803
Defeated	Endō		JCP	12,538
Constituency No. 2				
Elected	Horiuchi	8	LDP	108,336
Defeated	Akiyama		JCP	22,338
Defeated	Ishii		Minor party	13,738
Constituency No. 3				
Elected	Yokouchi	3	LDP	86,300
Defeated	Gotō		DPJ	54,517
Defeated	Sugazawa		JCP	13,875

Source: Yomiuri Nenkan, 2001, p. 133.

the PR bloc, where the LDP elected six candidates, but he came only ninth. His chances in constituency no. 1 were harmed by the appearance of a new Independent (and aspirant LDP member), Akaike. Although the latter did not do particularly well, he probably took enough votes away from Nakao to ensure that Nakao was defeated. This time Gotō (DPJ), who had been an unsuccessful NFP candidate for constituency no. 1 in 1996, but was now standing for the DPJ, was elected as the third of four successful DPJ candidates in the South Kantō bloc. In constituency no. 2 Horiuchi had become so dominant that the only significant party to run a candidate against him was the JCP. In constituency no. 3 Yokouchi also retained his position, defeating Gotō of the DPJ, who was then 'resuscitated' in the PR bloc. In this election, therefore, Yamanashi returned two LDP and two DPJ candidates.

In the 2003 elections (see Table 8.7) Yamanashi constituency no. 1 saw another victory for the DPJ candidate Ozawa, who easily defeated a new LDP man, Yoneda, also badly beaten in the South Kantō PR bloc. Constituency no. 2 produced a walkover for Horiuchi, where only the Communists bothered to challenge him. In constituency no. 3 a new LDP candidate, Hosaka, won comfortably, although Gotō, of the DPJ, was closing on him to some extent. Gotō, however, this time very narrowly failed to be elected for the PR bloc. The view that the Communists attract a protest vote as well as hard-core support is backed up by the result in constituency no. 2, where, being the only opposition party, their candidate attracted over twice the number of votes gained by their colleagues in each of the other two Yamanashi constituencies. In this election representation from the prefecture was reduced to three members.

Table 8.7   House of Representatives election 2003: Yamanashi single-member constituencies 1–3

Result	Candidate	No. of times elected	Party	Votes
Constituency No. 1				
Elected	Ozawa	4	DPJ	71,623
Defeated	Yoneda		LDP	45,282
Defeated	Endō		JCP	13,545
Constituency No. 2				
Elected	Horiuchi	9	LDP	101,727
Defeated	Hanada		JCP	30,225
Constituency No. 3				
Elected	Hosaka	2	LDP	83,107
Defeated	Gotō		DPJ	62,475
Defeated	Fukazawa		JCP	11,555

Source: Yomiuri Nenkan, 2004, p. 179.

The 2005 election (see Table 8.8) was held in the aftermath of Koizumi's expulsion from the LDP of the postal privatization rebels, and his sponsorship of new candidates ('Koizumi's children') to challenge them in their constituencies. The LDP members for the second and third constituencies, Horiuchi and Hosaka, were among the rebels and so were forced to stand as Independents. Both of them held on to their seats, but in very tight contests. Horiuchi, previously carrying all before him, was this time less than a thousand votes away from defeat by one of the 'Koizumi's children'. Gotō, for the DPJ, was less than

Table 8.8   House of Representatives election 2005: Yamanashi single-member constituencies 1–3

Result	Candidate	No. of times elected	Party	Votes
Constituency No. 1				
Elected	Ozawa	5	DPJ	70,281
Defeated	Akaike		LDP	65,426
Defeated	Endō		JCP	12,173
Constituency No. 2				
Elected	Horiuchi	10	Independent	63,758
Defeated	Nagasaki		LDP	62,821
Defeated	Sakaguchi		DPJ	33,827
Defeated	Watanabe		JCP	7,216
Constituency No. 3				
Elected	Hosaka	3	Independent	63,659
Defeated	Gotō		DPJ	61,716
Defeated	Ono		LDP	51,318

Source: Yomiuri Nenkan, 2006, p. 223.

2,000 votes away from defeating Hosaka, coming well ahead of the new LDP candidate. This time Gotō was easily 'resuscitated' in the South Kantō PR bloc. In constituency no. 1, Ozawa of the DPJ retained his seat against a challenge by the LDP man Akaike, who had stood as an Independent in 2000, contributing to the defeat of the veteran Nakao. An extraordinary result of this election was that no fewer than three defeated LDP candidates in Yamanashi – Akaike, Nagasaki and Ono – were 'resuscitated' in the PR bloc.[56] Adding Gotō as well, this meant that parliamentary representation for Yamanashi, down to three members in 2003, now stood at seven!

This suggests that the new electoral system did not represent such a complete break with the old system as many had thought. In the old system a candidate who came second or third (sometimes even fourth or fifth) in the voting tally of a constituency would still be elected. In the new system it was also possible to be elected without coming first. For instance, in 2005 all three candidates in constituency no. 3 of Yamanashi Prefecture were elected to Parliament – Hosaka for the single-member constituency, Gotō and Ono for the South Kantō PR bloc. The extent of 'losing but still winning' was not as great as in the old system, but was considerable none the less.[57]

This brings us on to the issues of personality voting, involving some tricky problems of analysis. Two questions seem paramount: whether it is the institution of the former electoral system, or the character of Japanese society, that is primarily responsible for the prevalence of personality voting; and how far the change to a different electoral system in 1994 may have enhanced the salience of party, rather than the personality of the candidate, in explaining why and how people vote.

To address the first question, we need to visit the concept of the 'hard vote'. In Japanese electoral parlance, the hard vote (kotei hyō), means essentially those votes that are virtually assured for a particular candidate. Such votes are contrasted with floating votes (fudō hyō), which may be cast for different candidates at different elections. In Britain and elsewhere, the concept of 'floating votes' is familiar, as is the contrasting concept of committed votes; but the essential difference from the Japanese situation is that in the British case votes are committed, or not committed, to parties rather than to candidates.

The former electoral system, based on SNTV in MMCs, appears to have been a causal factor in promoting campaigns based on the personal support associations (kōenkai) of individual candidates, given that candidates from the same party would be competing with each other in the same constituency. It seems plausible to argue, therefore, that the electoral system encouraged personality

[56]   A party could list its PR candidates either sequentially (1, 2, 3 ...), or with equal ranking. If the latter, the 'best loser' (sekihairitsu) provision came into play for candidates standing in both types of constituency. That party's candidates who polled the highest percentage of a winning candidate's vote in single-member constituencies (in the same PR bloc) would be elected, depending on the number of quotas that the party won. To make things even more complicated, a party could rank some candidates and treat others as equal.
[57]   Some candidates eschewed single-member constituencies and stood only in their regional PR bloc. Not very many of them, however, were successful.

voting. On the other hand, this did not affect candidates of all parties to the same extent. The smaller parties, most notably the CGP and JCP, were exceptions to the rule in the sense that they were tightly organized and projected an appeal to *party* loyalty. Neither of those parties, nor the former Democratic Socialist Party (DSP), had enough support to run more than one candidate in any constituency.[58] The Japan Socialist Party (JSP) ran multiple candidates in a number of constituencies, but in most of them it fielded only a single candidate. In practice, the JSP was a kind of halfway house in terms of personality voting versus party voting as the basis of its campaigns.

The party that most consistently and successfully based its campaigning on the cultivation of a 'hard vote' was the LDP. It is at least a reasonable hypothesis that a party attracting sufficient electoral support to run multiple candidates in the bulk of constituencies faced a situation where its candidates were competing with each other locally, and so needed to cultivate personal support in order to maximize their support *against each other*. But on the other hand, it is also plausible to argue that culturally conditioned patterns of social interaction led LDP candidates to cultivate a hard vote that would be loyal to themselves rather than to the party.

To some extent, this is a chicken-and-egg question. Nevertheless, it is a question that needs to be raised, because the LDP's way of optimizing its vote given SNTV in MMCs is not the only possible way, even for a large party. It would have been perfectly possible for the party to take firm charge of the campaign in each constituency, which it would have divided into segments, urging or instructing the voters to vote for one of its candidates in one segment and another in another segment. Indeed, this was precisely the strategy adopted by the CGP (*Kōmeitō*) in the former 'first-fifty-past-the-post' national constituency of the House of Councillors, with astonishing success.[59] The fact that the LDP did not do this, but relied on a decentralized strategy of personal candidate-centred campaigns based on candidates' personal support associations, suggests that it was heavily influenced by the patterns of social interaction in rural Japan, where a deep-rooted sense of mutual obligation helps pork-barrel methods secure the ever-reliable 'hard vote'.

In any case, the LDP methods were so successful for so long that the party was normally able to resist demands for radical change. To turn to our second question, once the electoral system had been reformed in such a way as supposedly to make parties rather than candidates the focus of voter attention, candidate-centred campaigns did not disappear overnight. Most candidates maintained their own *kōenkai*, and indeed reconfigured them to cope with the need to attract to their side a much higher percentage of the (admittedly smaller) local electorate than was necessary under the previous system. Nevertheless, part of the reason for the political turmoil of the 1990s was the frustration of younger parliamentarians with what many of them saw as the straitjacket of the existing system.

---

[58] The only exception is that the JCP elected two candidates in Kyoto no. 1 constituency in the 1972 and 1979 elections.

[59] We also, however, need to factor in the tight discipline that the CGP was able to exert over its voters, most of whom were affiliated with the *Sōka Gakkai*. The LDP could not have hoped to exercise remotely the same level of control over its supporters.

Another factor was the long-term effects of Japanese urbanization, making the rural social element in politics seem anachronistic. Although it is difficult to give numerical values to the changes that were taking place, the new millennium appeared to usher in a state of affairs in which parties were becoming more significant as a focus of elections, and in which the prominence of the local-level personal vote, especially in urban areas, was receding. But this needs to be distinguished from 'personality voting' favouring the LDP led by the charismatic Koizumi in 2005, or in 1989 in favour of the JSP led by Doi Takako. In neither of these examples was party a major factor in voting outcomes. At the local level, however, a change of party in power would be required to marginalize the personal vote.

We now turn to the issue of political corruption, or 'money politics', and its policing.

Corruption was a big political issue in the 1990s, not unconnected with personality politics. Regulation of corruption under the former electoral system had been full of loopholes, but under the non-LDP coalition governments of 1993–4 a serious attempt was made to introduce much tighter legislation. The distinction between political parties and other political organizations in respect of the requirement to declare financial donations was abolished. Previously the threshold above which donations had to be declared had been far lower in the case of parties than in the case of other kinds of political organization. This had led to parties being bypassed, and bodies set up by factions, individual parliamentarians or parliamentary candidates becoming the principal channels of political funding.

Previously, almost unlimited funding had flowed into the political world because politicians could evade maximum limits by setting up several separate funding organizations. Under the new law, corporate bodies could contribute funds for political activities, up to a certain limit, to only a single financial control body representing a party, a political funding body or an individual politician.[60] In cases of infringement of this provision, both the contributor and the receiver of funds would be liable to punishment, including suspension of civil rights.[61] The principle of complicity (*renzasei*) was established, so that a candidate could be penalized for illegal fund-raising activities by members of his family or of his secretarial staff, if the candidate had been privy to those activities.[62] If an elected candidate were convicted, this would not only invalidate his election, but would mean that he could not stand for election in the same constituency again for a period of five years after his conviction.[63] This principle was established in order to plug a gaping hole in the Election Law, which had permitted candidates to escape the consequences of wrongdoing by members of their staff or their families, and to regard any fine that they did incur as part of the cost of campaigning, because it did not bar them from further candidacy.

Widespread corruption in Japanese elections clearly stemmed from the extraordinarily high cost of campaigning, as well as of establishing and servicing political organizations. Given the candidate-centred organizations that had

[60] Political Funding Control Law, section 5.
[61] Political Funding Control Law, section 6.
[62] Ibid.
[63] Ibid.

prevailed under the previous electoral system, much of the cost of maintaining an extensive staff and engaging in political activities had to be borne by the candidate him- or herself. Since one of the objectives of the reforms was to shift the emphasis from candidates to parties, some provision needed to be made to put party financing on a firm footing. The Hosokawa government therefore embarked upon the controversial path of public funding of elections, and this was incorporated in the revised legal structure. The amount of money needed to finance public funding of elections was calculated on the basis of 250 yen per head of population per annum, and in 1994 slightly exceeded 30 billion yen. Much debate was devoted to the question of eligibility to grants from the fund, and in particular on the definition of an 'eligible party'. This came to be defined in the following way: (a) a party containing no fewer than five members of Parliament; or (b) a party which, at the most recent lower house or upper house general election, and in either the single-member or PR constituencies, has received at least 2 per cent of the total valid vote.

In order to avoid the proliferation of minor parties excessively reliant on public funding, it was further provided that the amount calculated to be due to a party (paid normally on 1 January) should not amount to more than two-thirds of its total income. In order to be eligible for public funding, a party also had to be registered as a corporate body (*hōjin*).

In both houses there have been serious problems of malapportionment, in the sense that constituency boundaries have not been adequately redrawn to reflect population movements. The 1947 Election Law contained no effective provision for regular and impartial redrawing of electoral boundaries to take account of movements of population. Despite the efforts of the Electoral System Consultative Council (*Senkyo seido shingikai*), it proved extremely difficult to rectify the resultant discrepancies. It was not difficult to discover reasons for this failure, since the firmest base of support for the LDP was in rural parts of Japan. Reforming the electoral system for the House of Representatives in 1994 was an opportunity to rectify gross imbalances in the value of the vote between different constituencies and areas of the country. Given the massive movements of population from rural areas to the cities between the 1940s and the 1990s, the failure to correct for this adequately had led to a huge advantage being given to rural voters over urban voters. For instance, at the lower house general elections held in October 1979, there were 3.87 times more electors per seat on the electoral roll in urban Chiba constituency no. 4 than in the rural Hyōgo constituency no. 5.[64]

It is true that palliative measures were taken from time to time. In the 1960s and 1970s reforms consisted of adding seats in major conurbations. Spurred by the resultant increase in the number of lower house seats, the government in the 1980s eventually reduced the number of rural seats to compensate for the increase in big city seats. By the 1980s, the courts were interesting themselves in the question of malapportionment from the standpoint of equality of rights, and

---

[64] It is incorrect to regard this as a gerrymander, which means a deliberate drawing of constituency boundaries to favour one party or parties over others. Rather, it is a failure to correct discrepancies that have come about naturally. It may not, however, be entirely inaccurate to call it a 'negative gerrymander', in the specific sense that the failure adequately to correct it may be deliberate.

a judicial guideline was established that no set of voters should find the value of their vote worth more than three times the value of the votes of any other set of voters. The courts, nevertheless, refrained from invalidating any election.[65] With the 1994 reforms all boundaries had to be redrawn, and as a result the extent of malapportionment was substantially reduced. Nevertheless, it still exceeded 200 per cent at the extremes in House of Representatives single-member constituencies,[66] giving a major advantage to candidates and parties based in the relatively conservative rural areas. The 200 (later 180) PR seats did not essentially involve any discrepant weighting in favour of particular areas.

In the House of Councillors the situation was much worse. In the absence of any history of radical reform of its electoral system, malapportionment has been allowed to exceed 500 per cent in the prefectural constituencies. A revision of the upper house election law to remove four overrepresented constituencies, and add four to underrepresented areas, was passed in time for the July 2007 upper house elections. This, however, only reduced the discrepancy to the level of about 480 per cent.[67]

Conclusions

In Japan as in many political systems, the nature of the electoral system has been frequently contested, and is thus an intensely 'political' area. As elsewhere, proponents of different kinds of electoral system wished for different kinds of political outcome. Small parties naturally favoured either proportional representation or SNTV in MMCs, both of which gave them reasonable guarantees of survival. Large parties, especially the LDP, were less clear what they really wanted. Single-member constituencies favoured large, centrally organized parties, but under the former system the LDP had become used to the kinds of decentralized personality-based campaigns that paid off in multi-member constituencies without vote transferability. Rather surprisingly, that system had energized LDP candidates, who had to compete with each other and not just with candidates from other parties, thus helping the LDP as a whole to maximize its vote. On the other hand, it certainly contributed to corruption and 'money politics', and also, perhaps even more seriously, to a perception on the part of the electorate that politicians were people who dispensed favour of a monetary or material kind. This perception has been slow to disappear, despite the change of electoral system in the 1990s, but Japan is now a sophisticated and urbanized society, whose attitude to politicians and political parties has been slowly evolving. The politics of favours and kick-backs is far from disappearing, but a competing politics of policy debate between parties genuinely competing for power has been gradually emerging.

---

[65]   See 'Kanao et al. vs. Hiroshima Prefecture Election Commission', judgment translated in Lawrence W. Beer and Hiroshi Itoh, *The Constitutional Case Law of Japan, 1970 through 1990*, Seattle, University of Washington Press, 1996, pp. 394–405.
[66]   A survey conducted by the Ministry of Public Management, Home Affairs, Posts and Telecommunications late in 2005 showed that the value of one vote in the third single-member lower house constituency of Kōchi (which is remote from major centres) was worth 2.203 times the value of one vote in the fourth constituency of Chiba (an urban centre close to Tokyo): *Asahi Shinbun*, 28 December 2005.
[67]   *Asahi Shinbun*, 26 September 2006.

Chapter 9 | The Politics of Party: The Liberal Democrats and their Rivals

The Party System

The formation of the Liberal Democratic Party in 1955 was a political achievement whose significance can hardly be exaggerated. It led to more than three and a half decades of single-party dominance, covering a period in which Japan moved from relative poverty to becoming the second largest economy in the world – a position that it still holds. Japan then entered a period of economic difficulty and political instability, during which time the dominance of the LDP was seriously threatened. Had it remained out of power for a substantially longer period than its nine months' exile from office in 1993–4, it is quite doubtful that it could have survived as a viable organization. Nevertheless, it was gradually able to reassert its dominance, though from this date it needed the assistance of smaller parties in coalition arrangements.

Koizumi promised to 'smash' the LDP from within, but he ended up consolidating its rule by changing the system in which it operated. It remains to be seen how far the changes he made to the LDP itself will survive. His bold action in expelling the postal privatization rebels in August–September 2005 brought him a spectacular victory in the September elections. Much new blood (the so-called 'Koizumi's children') entered the party, giving it a new sense of purpose. His successor, Abe Shinzō, however, readmitted many of the rebels to party membership, throwing some doubt on the party's capacity to maintain its direction and momentum.

In retrospect, we can see that the party system since the 1950s has been more fluid than is often believed. Some observers and participants long assumed that the LDP had a divine right to rule, or at least that an indefinite extension of LDP rule into the future could be taken for granted. It was therefore a shock to the party to find that, having been ousted from power in August 1993, senior civil servants lost no time in pragmatically disconnecting from the LDP and linking up with the newly formed Hosokawa coalition government. Something that is perfectly normal in British-type political systems when there is a change in government had been outside the Japanese experience for longer than most politicians could remember.

The history of party politics since the 1950s shows that there have been fluctuations in the degree of LDP dominance. Various factors have contributed to this. One is the extent to which the party has been able to reinvent itself, both in the sense of responding creatively to the emergence of new issues and also in the sense of cultivating sections of the electorate that were not necessarily supporting the LDP previously. In the early 1960s Ikeda presented the electorate with a new formula – that of economic growth – and defused much of the tension that had blighted politics under his predecessor, Kishi. A decade later Tanaka saw that LDP support was slipping dangerously, and set out on new paths in environmental and welfare policies, as well as mending fences with China. LDP leaders in the early 1980s energetically tackled problems of government overspending. When, in the 1990s, the necessary leadership to solve the banking crisis was slow to appear, the LDP reaped the whirlwind in terms of loss of electoral support.

A second factor is the relationship between strength of control *by* the dominant party and strength of control *within* the dominant party. This of course relates to the ways in which factions interacted with each other inside the LDP. Speaking very broadly, the 1950s were a period of disputed factional control, whereas in the 1960s the faction led by Satō during his long tenure of office was dominant. The 1970s saw a return to bitter factional contestation, to the detriment of the party's fortunes, whereas during the 1980s the Tanaka faction asserted its ability to control the factional system, and the party did well under Nakasone, who had been Tanaka's nominee (though not of the same faction). In the late 1980s the control exercised by the dominant faction slackened, leading to turmoil, weak party leadership, and a serious party split. The 1990s were spent in attempts to recover LDP fortunes, under a succession of leaders. With the election of Koizumi as party leader and thus Prime Minister in 2001, the LDP once again enjoyed strong and determined leadership and prospered as a result. His successor, Abe, proved incapable of maintaining such momentum.

Third, the reverse side of single-party dominance is opposition party weakness. The role of opposition parties in Japanese politics is often neglected by commentators, but these parties have at times played a vital role in articulating dissent and exerting pressure on government. As with the dominant party, so there have been major fluctuations in opposition party fortunes. For instance, they were resurgent during the 1970s, and again from the late 1980s to the mid-1990s. Their greatest weakness was that they were divided into several discrete parties, and found great difficulty in uniting in such a way as to challenge the LDP effectively.[1] The most important development within the opposition camp during the 1990s was the near-demise of the Japan Socialist Party (now Social Democratic Party) and the emergence of the Democratic Party. For many years

---

[1]   Stephen Johnson, *Opposition Party Politics in Japan: Stategies under a One-Party Dominant Regime*, London and New York, Routledge, 2000.

the opposition was unable to decide whether it wished to challenge the LDP as a potential alternative government, or appease it and receive some access to power, but always in a subordinate role. There are some signs in the new millennium that the Democratic Party is determined on a realistic path of challenge, rather than an old-style combination of ideological rhetoric and behind-the-scenes appeasement.

A fourth factor is institutional change. Two reforms took place during the 1990s that exerted a seminal effect on the party system. The first, in 1994, was the reform of the electoral system for the House of Representatives, already discussed in Chapter 8. In so far as this reform moved the focus of electioneering away from the local, personal and factional level and towards the level of the central party organization, it contributed to a centralizing process within major parties. The second reform (more accurately, set of inter-related reforms) was inaugurated in 1998 under the Hashimoto administration and came into force in January 2001. This was the reform of the structure of ministries, together with a consolidation in the power of Prime Minister and Cabinet. Even though the scope of this set of reforms went far beyond political parties, it exerted a significant impact on the way parties – particularly the LDP – conducted their business. A strong leader now had the means at his or her disposal to challenge, or ignore, demands from sectional interests within the party. It did not, of course, follow, that leaders would act in such a way. If they were of a consensual disposition, they might well prefer to find a balance between competing sectional demands. But the great achievement of Koizumi in 2005 was to show that vested interests within the LDP could be faced down and defeated.

A Profile of the Parties following the September 2005 Elections

The results of the most recent lower house elections at the time of writing – those of 11 September 2005 – reflect the spectacular LDP victory following Koizumi's expulsion of the postal privatization rebels and the entry of 'Koizumi's children'. Table 9.1 illustrates the rejuvenation of the LDP parliamentary membership as a result of these events. No fewer than 83 members of the dominant party, or 28 per cent of its total parliamentary representation, consisted of those elected for the first time in these elections. This contrasted with 20.4 per cent in the elections of 1996 and a mere 7.3 per cent in those of 1980.[2] In the case of the much depleted DPJ, those elected for the second time were the largest group, and most of these had been elected for the first time in 2003, when that party did well. When we come to the CGP, partner in coalition to the LDP, the biggest bloc of members were celebrating their fourth or, especially, fifth election, suggesting that it was needing rejuvenation, and might be sinking into complacency. The other parties, as well as Independents, were too few in number for percentages to be significant.

[2] See J. A. A. Stockwin, *Governing Japan: Divided Politics in a Major Economy*, Oxford and Malden, MA, Blackwell, 3rd edn, 1999, Table 9.2 on p. 136.

Table 9.1   Members of the House of Representatives by party, September 2005 general elections

Party	Total no.	Total no. of times elected									
		1	2	3	4	5	6	7	8	9	10–16
LDP	296	83	33	41	40	21	22	15	14	15	12
(%)		(28.0)	(11.1)	(13.8)	(13.5)	(7.1)	(7.4)	(5.1)	(4.7)	(5.1)	(4.0)
DPJ	113	13	36	18	17	10	11	2	0	2	4
(%)		(11.5)	(31.8)	(15.9)	(15.0)	(8.8)	(9.7)	(1.8)	–	(1.8)	(3.5)
CGP	31	2	2	1	7	14	2	1	1	0	1
(%)		(6.4)	(6.4)	(3.2)	(22.6)	(45.2)	(6.4)	(3.2)	(3.2)	–	(3.2)
JCP	9	1	1	2	1	3	1	0	0	0	0
SDP	7	0	4	3	0	0	0	0	0	0	0
Minor	6	1	0	0	1	1	0	1	0	0	2
Ind.	18	2	5	1	1	2	2	0	1	1	3

Source: *Yomiuri Nenkan*, 2006, pp. 220–41; *Yomiuri Nenkan bessatsu* (additional volume), 2006, pp. 6–18.

Table 9.2   Average age of new members at the time of the September 2005 House of Representatives elections

Party	Average age of new members (years)		
	Sept. 2005	1996	1980
LDP	44.8	56.7	56.5
DPJ	42.8	52.4[a]	
CGP	39.0	(NFP: 52.4)[b]	50.2
JCP	52.0	59.9	53.3
SDP		57.9	57.2
Minor	30.0		
Independent	39.0	48.6	

[a] The DPJ did not exist in 1980.
[b] The CGP was a component of the New Frontier Party in 1996.

Source: as for Table 9.1. Figures for 1980 are from Tables 13–17 in the 2nd edn of this book (1982); figures for 1996 are from Table 9.2 in the 3rd edn of this book (1999), p. 136.

When we turn to the age structure of new members (see Table 9.2), we find that in all parties except the JCP (where numbers are too small for significant comparison) members are entering Parliament at an earlier age than one or two decades earlier. This phenomenon is particularly striking in the case of the LDP, which also had much the largest number of new members in 2005.

The 2005 elections also saw an unusually large influx of women into the House of Representatives. Whereas the proportion of women in Parliament remained small by comparison with parliaments of other major states, it received a significant boost in this poll. Moreover, the most striking feature of the figures in Table 9.3 is the increase in female representation within the LDP. From September 2005, 61.5 per cent of LDP women parliamentarians were new members, and 59.1 per cent

Table 9.3 Number of women in Parliament, by party, following the September 2005 House of Representatives elections

Party	No. elected	Times elected				
		1	2	3	4	5
LDP	26	16	2	4	3	1
DPJ	8	1	6	1	0	0
CGP	4	0	2	0	2	0
JCP	2	0	1	0	0	1
SDP	2	0	0	2	0	0
Minor	0	0	0	0	0	0
Independent	2	0	0	0	0	2
Total	44[a]	17	11	7	5	4

[a] 9.2% of total (480 seats).

Source: as for Table 9.1.

of women in Parliament were members of the LDP. Until the 1980s the number of female parliamentarians largely fluctuated with the fortunes of the Japan Communist Party, which was the only party to run women in winnable seats. During the late 1980s and early 1990s the 'Madonna boom' of the Socialist leader Doi Takako brought substantial numbers of women in under the auspices of the JSP, and in the late 1990s the much weakened SDP (as it was now called) actually had a majority of women parliamentarians. From the late 1990s some women were elected under the DPJ label. But it was unprecedented for women to enter Parliament as Liberal Democrats in substantial numbers, and indeed this is one of the less noticed aspects of change inaugurated by the 2005 elections.

In certain respects, however, change over time seems to have been minimal. Japanese parliamentarians remain overwhelmingly local in origin. One of the great problems of transition from the old electoral system to the new one in the 1996 elections was to find seats in their own areas for sitting members. Since the new constituencies were much smaller than the old ones, it was often possible to accommodate members from the same party who had previously 'shared' a multi-member constituency as strong candidates for single-member constituencies which fell wholly or partly within the boundaries of the old districts. Where this was not possible a member could be placed in a high position on the party list for the local regional bloc. Instances, however, of a defeated member for a constituency in one part of the country moving to a different region and standing for election there remain unusual.[3] From Table 9.4 it appears that there has been only slight change in the situation where a member is typically elected from the constituency – or at least the region – in which he or she was born.

[3] This contrasts with the situation in the United Kingdom, where it is common for a candidate with origins and a previous career in one part of the country to stand for election in a quite distant region. Even so, local loyalties are not entirely irrelevant, and in the UK there have been instances of revolt by local party branches against attempts by the central party HQ to 'impose' a candidate on them (particularly if that candidate is seen as part of the 'London set').

Table 9.4 Local and non-local birthplace of parliamentarians elected in the October 1996 and September 2005 House of Representatives elections (%)

	LDP	NFP	DPJ	CGP	JCP	SDP	Independent
Local[a]							
1996	87.9	80.7	86.5	–	50.0	66.7	80.0
2005	82.4	–	80.5	67.7	55.0	85.7	66.7
Non-local							
1996	12.1	19.3	13.5	–	50.0	33.3	20.0
2005	17.6	–	19.5	32.3	45.0	14.3	33.3

[a]The PR blocs have been used to determine whether 'local' or 'non-local'. In rural areas, however, it is extremely common for a member to have been born within the *prefecture* in which his or her constituency (if single-member) is located. Some members designated 'non-local' by our definition, were nevertheless born close to their present constituency but just over the border in another PR bloc. To this extent, the table may slightly exaggerate the incidence of 'non-local' candidates.

Sources: Asahi Nenkan bessatsu, 1997, pp. 84–97; Yomiuri Nenkan bessatsu, 2006, pp. 6–18.

Table 9.5 Proportion of those non-local to their constituencies, who were born in Tokyo, September 2005 House of Representatives elections

	Born in Tokyo (%)	Not born in Tokyo (%)
LDP	51.9	48.1
DPJ	31.8	68.1
CGP	20.0	80.0

Source: Yomiuri Nenkan bessatsu, 2006, pp. 6–18.

It is interesting to note that of those categorized as 'non-local', a substantial proportion, most significantly in the case of the LDP, were born in Tokyo (see Table 9.5). Without more detailed analysis, it is uncertain why this should be, but it suggests that metropolitan individuals may be able to pursue a political career in the provinces despite their lack of local origins, because of the political weight and prestige exercised by the national capital.[4]

A salient characteristic of Japanese parliamentarians for many years has been a high level of educational attainment. Whereas in earlier decades the LDP led the way and other parties seemed to lag in the level of education achieved by their members, today a high educational level is almost universal, irrespective of party affiliation. Of the 480 members elected in the September 2005 elections, only 14 had failed to experience university education. Respectable

---

[4] It may also be true that some individuals born and raised in Tokyo may capitalize on more or less remote family ties in the provinces.

Table 9.6 Educational background of parliamentarians, by party, after September 2005 House of Representatives elections

	LDP	DPJ	CGP	JCP	SDP	Minor	Independent
Highest level of education							
Prewar school	1						
Senior high school	6	3			2		2
University[a]	289	110	31	9	5	6	16
Of those attending university, the following had attended graduate school:							
	42	19	9	2	1		1
Those attending university were at the following Japanese universities:							
Tokyo	74	28	5	2	1	2	3
Keiō	40	11	3	2	1	2	3
Waseda	40	15	1		2		2
Chūō	20	5			1		2
Nihon	17	3					1
Meiji	10	2	1				
Hōsei	7	1					
Kansai[b]	6			1			
Sophia (Jōchi)	5	4					1
Rikkyō	5						
Gakushūin	4		1			1	
Kyōto[b]		3	5	2	1		
Hitotsubashi	3	4	1				
Ritsumeikan[b]	1	3		1			
Tōhoku[b]	1	3	1				
Sōka			7				
Other universities	51	24	8	5	1	1	4
The following attended foreign universities, mostly graduate schools:							
United States							
Harvard	9						
Columbia	3	1					
Pennsylvania	2	1					
Georgetown	2						
Johns Hopkins		3					
Princeton	1	1					
Washington	1	1					
Cornell			1				
Other	6	2					
United Kingdom							
Cambridge	1		1				
Oxford			1				
Manchester	1						
France							
ENA	1						
EEC	1						

(Continued)

Table 9.6   (*Continued*)

	LDP	DPJ	CGP	JCP	SDP	Minor	Independent
Canada							
Carleton	1						
China							
Heilongjiang			1				
Egypt							
Cairo			1				

[a]Numbers are slightly inflated by some parliamentarians reporting attendance at more than one university. The very small number who reported dropping out of university or high school without graduating are here counted as though they had completed that level of education.

[b]These universities are *not* located in the Tokyo region.

Source: Yomiuri Nenkan, 2006, pp. 6–18.

numbers had also attended graduate school. By now, those raised in the pre-war educational system had virtually disappeared. Table 9.6 gives broad figures for educational attainment broken down by party.

Several points are worth making in relation to Table 9.6. The role of Tokyo University in educating future politicians (just as other members of the elite) remained buoyant. In 1980, 30 per cent of LDP parliamentarians were Tokyo University graduates; this figure had fallen to 21.2 per cent in 1996, but had now risen again to 25.1 per cent. It was a comparable 24.8 per cent in the case of the DPJ, and 16.1 per cent for the CGP. No less than 67.9 per cent of LDP members (67.9 per cent in 1996), and 59.3 per cent of DPJ members, had attended Tokyo, Keiō, Waseda, Chūō, Nihon, Meiji or Kyōto universities, which are among the best-known tertiary institutions in the country. A specific observation should be made about the CGP. This party was originally based on strata of the society having a relatively low level of education, and this used to be reflected in its parliamentary representatives. At the time of the 1980 general elections, a mere 39.4 per cent of CGP members of Parliament had been to university.[5] At the 2005 elections, every one of its representatives in the House of Representatives had attended university. Of these, seven had attended Sōka University, which is closely linked with the *Sōka Gakkai*, the religious backer of the CGP.

Finally, since 1996 there had been a remarkable increase in the number of parliamentarians that had attended foreign universities, mostly graduate schools and most commonly in the United States. Whereas in 1996 the number was a mere seven, in 2005 it had risen to 43 (LDP 29; DPJ 12; CGP 2). At 8.9 per cent

[5] See J. A. A. Stockwin, *Japan: Divided Politics in a Growth Economy*, London, Weidenfeld, 2nd edn, 1982, tables on pages 120 and 187–92.

of total members of Parliament, this was approaching, but still well behind, the level of other East Asian parliaments, such as that of South Korea. It suggested that Parliament, like other bodies, had become significantly more international in its outlook over the past decade.

When we turn from the educational to the professional background of members, we encounter problems of information, definition and interpretation. Much less information is available on the previous career backgrounds of those who have been members for a long time than on more recent members, while in many cases it is difficult to disentangle occupations pursued in parallel with a parliamentary career from those which preceded it. Many members list multiple careers, meaning that the number of occupations much exceeds the number of parliamentarians. Nevertheless, our tentative findings are presented in Table 9.7.

Table 9.7   Career backgrounds of parliamentarians elected in the September 2005 House of Representatives elections

Career	LDP	DPJ	CGP	JCP	SDP	Minor	Independent
Local politician	90	30			4	4	4
Secretary to MP	44	12					4
National government official	34	9	3			1	1
Local government official	2	0					
Company manager/ employee	10	5	1				
Banking manager/ employee	5	2					
Journalist/mass media	14	6	8[a]	1	1		
Education professional	14	4	2	1	1		
Medical, dental, veterinary	6	2	1		1		
Lawyer	11	8	6		1		
Accountant/economist	5	2	1			1	
Party organization	2	0					
Labour union official	0	3					
Researcher	3	1					
Speaker, Deputy Speaker	1	1					
Minister's secretarial staff	5	2					1
Upper house member	7	2		1	1	1	
Other[b]	8	7			1	1	

[a]Several of these worked in the print media of the *Sōka Gakkai/Kōmeitō*.
[b]These include: postal branch head, women's association counsellor, veterans' association executive, economist, youth association executive, professional wrestler, NPO executive, community fund executive, business association executive, Christian priest, actor.
Source: As for Table 9.6.

From this it can be seen that patterns of a decade earlier had, if anything, been reinforced by 2005. As in 1996, the most common career background for a parliamentarian, especially of the LDP, was local politics. Whereas in 1996 the proportion of LDP members of Parliament with this background was 25.8 per cent, following the 2005 elections it had risen to 30.4 per cent. The second most common previous LDP career was that of secretary to a parliamentarian. In 1996 22.8 per cent from the LDP had progressed from this career, whereas in 2005 the proportion had fallen to 14.9 per cent. A significant number (12, or 4.1 per cent) had experienced positions in both these categories. However, while these were also the most frequent past careers for DPJ parliamentarians, for CGP members they did not figure at all. Former national government officials were entering LDP politics in declining numbers. From around a quarter in 1970 the percentage had fallen to 15 per cent in 1996 and was now reduced to 11.5 per cent. This may be an underestimate, given the paucity of information about older politicians, but even so, many older ex-bureaucrats had been so long in politics that they were now professional politicians rather than former bureaucrats. Others had worked in private commercial companies and in banks, though the numbers were quite small. Journalism and the mass media provided quite significant numbers, especially in the CGP, where this was the largest category. Some came from education, the legal and medical professions, and accountancy, but in no case were the numbers large. Labour union officials no longer entered Parliament as they did in the heyday of the Socialist and Democratic Socialist parties. Indeed, their incidence was now almost negligible. Small numbers of lower house parliamentarians had previously been elected to the upper house.

The Japanese party system had gone through turmoil and change during the 1990s, but certain features of it remained much the same. The most important change was the near-demise of the old Socialist Party, and the rise of a principal party of opposition, the Democratic Party. Even though the latter had inherited some former Socialist politicians, they were of declining importance within it, and the DPJ on some (though not all) issues could be regarded as a second conservative party. The smaller parties had either been coopted into semi-permanent coalition with the LDP (CGP), or had declined into insignificance (JCP and SDP). Apart from the Democrats, the many parties that had emerged in the 1990s had soon died, like butterflies, after a brief life in the sunlight. The Liberal Democrats, meanwhile, had once again shown their remarkable ability to adapt to new circumstances in the interests of survival. Koizumi, who had boasted he would smash the party, had made it stronger than ever. Whether his successors would build on his legacy remained to be seen.

We now turn to the individual parties, examining first the LDP and the DPJ before briefly discussing important parties of the past half-century.

Liberal Democratic Party (LDP, *Jiyūminshutō, Jimintō*)

The LDP is in a unique position in that it has normally been entrenched at the very centre of the ruling structure of the state. It went through difficult times in the 1990s, but after briefly experiencing oxygen starvation in the form of opposition status for a few months in 1993–4, it rose to the surface again with redoubled determination to consolidate its ruling position. This, however, it could do only by forging coalition arrangements with smaller parties. After trying out several coalition partners, it eventually fixed on the CGP, a stable minor party that found access to power congenial.

This was not the first time that the LDP had been placed in a position where it needed to change in order to survive. During the 1970s it sensed it was under threat from an electorate unhappy with the ecological effects of rapid economic growth and demanding much more than was on offer in social welfare. Tanaka Kakuei, in his rather brief term as Prime Minister, made a timely contribution to the survival of his party, which had become uncomfortably dependent on electoral malapportionment in favour of the conservative country areas. By the 1980s LDP governments were able to embark on policies of financial retrenchment, secure in the knowledge that the party's base of support was both firm and widely spread in many different segments of society.

While sensitivity to the policy preferences of strategic sections of the electorate was essential for continuing majorities, the methods of campaigning were also an important part of the picture. Turnover of LDP parliamentarians from election to election was comparatively low. Perhaps the most important reason for this was the crucial role played in a candidate's campaign by a network of supporters, or *jiban* ('constituency', or 'base of support').[6] A particular manifestation of *jiban*, which emerged after the Second World War, is the personal support association (*kōenkai*).[7] In one form or another these associations have been adopted by almost all political parties, but the *kōenkai* of LDP candidates have become the central feature of the party's grass-roots campaigning.

The central point to understand about these groups is that they are organized by and for the *candidate*, not the party. This is in part a function of the former electoral system, which in turn explains why this institution became more developed in the LDP than in other parties. In most constituencies, apart from some in the largest cities, the LDP could credibly expect to elect more than one candidate. While it was the function of the party to determine how many candidates a given constituency could take without risking *tomodaore* ('all being defeated together'), it became the function essentially of each individual candidate to organize his (or, rarely, her) individual campaign. The electoral system worked in such a way as to give one LDP candidate almost no stake in the success of another LDP candidate standing for the same constituency. Rather, that person was a rival claimant on more or less the same pool of conservative-inclined votes. In order to ensure that LDP votes were cast in favour of LDP candidate X and not LDP candidate Y, candidate X maintained an association of family connections, school and university friends, business associates, representatives of local interest groups and local notabilities, as well as people falling into none of those categories, charging them with the task of drumming up support for his

---

[6]   For an early description of *jiban* in electoral campaigns, see Nobutaka Ike, *Japanese Politics: An Introductory Survey*, New York, Knopf, 1957.

[7]   The classic account of the working of a *kōenkai* remains that of Gerald Curtis, in his *Election Campaigning Japanese Style*, New York and London, Columbia University Press, 1971.

campaign. Many of the *kōenkai's* activities were essentially social rather than overtly political (though political discussions of course occurred), and the candidate would typically organize (at his expense) trips for its members to Tokyo, or to a hot spring resort.

Several consequences flowed from the function of these associations under the former electoral system. First, the creation, maintenance and servicing of a *kōenkai* (whose members might be in the hundreds) was expensive, and was one of the principal reasons for the seemingly inexhaustible need for electoral funds, leading in turn to so many corruption scandals as candidates took desperate and dubiously legal methods to raise the necessary funding. Second, the *kōenkai* system was hardly compatible with strong local party branches. Even though the party became adept at keeping the number of candidates formally endorsed to a safe minimum,[8] the influence of entrenched candidates within party branches was overwhelming, and hardly conducive to the fostering of new candidates outside the ambit of those already in place.

A third aspect of the *kōenkai* system was that the effort and expense of maintaining an existing concern was a great deal less than those entailed in setting one up from scratch. This was especially true in those constituencies – the majority – where several personal support associations of long standing already existed. Indeed, the easiest way to enter Parliament under the LDP label was to *inherit* a *kōenkai*. The figures on 'inheritance' of seats are truly astonishing. Of all LDP parliamentarians elected in the lower house general elections of October 1996, 37.2 per cent had inherited a *kōenkai* previously controlled by a parent (28.9 per cent), grandparent (2.5 per cent), other relative (2.9 per cent) or spouse (0.4 per cent).[9] A variant of the same phenomenon occurs where a person who has served as the secretary of a deceased or retired parliamentarian takes over his *kōenkai*.[10]

Fourth, under the old electoral system, personal support associations were closely bound up with factions (*habatsu*). It was rare (though not unknown) for LDP members belonging to the same faction to sit for the same constituency. An important part of the reason why an LDP candidate needed to join a *habatsu* was to obtain the funding needed to service his *kōenkai*. This meant setting up and maintaining a complex pattern of linkages connecting faction leaders with various parts of central government and major interest groups, members of Parliament (and candidates), *kōenkai*, and all the local organizations having connections with *kōenkai*.

A final implication of these associations under the former electoral system was that the focus of LDP parliamentarians was highly parochial. So much time and effort were needed to keep the association in working order and its members satisfied that the average member had rather little time to focus on matters of national concern.

---

[8] At each election, however, a small number of 'Independents', who had applied for but been refused LDP endorsement, nevertheless contested the seat and had sufficient local support, typically through their *kōenkai*, to be elected. In most cases they were then readily admitted into the party and officially became LDP members of Parliament.

[9] *Asahi senkyo taikan*, Tokyo, Asahi Shinbunsha, 1997, p. 121.

[10] See Table 9.7 for figures of such secretaries entering Parliament in 2005.

What, then, of the impact upon personal support associations of the reform of the lower house electoral system that took place in 1994? Any expectation that these changes would spell the demise of the *kōenkai* has been negated. It was perhaps rash to imagine that such a deeply entrenched element of election campaigning would disappear as a result of a shift from multi-member to single-member constituencies. The habit of fostering and cashing in on personal relationships as means of being elected to Parliament dies hard in Japanese society, and of course it is not entirely absent from electioneering in other major states, including the UK. There are, though, further reasons for their persistence. One is that the new electoral system partially retains an aspect of the old one in the sense that failure to be elected in a single-member constituency is not the end of the road. A candidate in that position still has the possibility of being elected to a PR seat in his regional bloc; but in order to achieve that he or she must either be high on the party list, or, if the party does not list candidates in order of preference, achieve a high score in the single-member constituency. The implications of this are that such candidates may be competing with other candidates from the same party in the PR regional bloc, much as they used to in the multi-member configuration of the old electoral system.

On the other hand, some real change has taken place in the sense that the local party in a single-member constituency can concentrate its efforts on backing a single candidate. This has fostered a coming together of the local party organization and the personal support association of the local candidate. The party, as a consequence, is very gradually acquiring greater influence over local candidates and their organizations.

Factions (*habatsu*) are another phenomenon long embedded in party politics that has persisted, while being affected by the change in the electoral system for the House of Representatives. Comparison of LDP political factions with factions in European, North American or Australasian political parties is problematic, given some special features in the Japanese case. In particular, individual factions, far from being ephemeral, can often look back on a long history of political activity. Second, though policy issues are not wholly absent from their concerns, power-broking and fund-raising have generally been more important for them. Third, they have tended to exhibit patterns of leadership reflecting norms entrenched in the fabric of society.

Before we address the question of change relating to the reformed electoral system, we shall explore the character of LDP factionalism under the old electoral system. Factions in the LDP were always more powerfully articulated bodies than factions in other parties, no doubt because far more power is available in a ruling party than in a party of opposition. In addition, as we have seen, the multi-member constituency system pitted LDP candidates against each other at local level, which was much less the case in other parties. The high cost of politics (especially campaigning), coupled with intense competition for prestigious positions in government and the party, had led to a situation where factions were the central fund-raisers and power-brokers within the LDP. Factions became so powerful from the late 1950s that prime ministers were motivated to reshuffle their cabinets at least once a year simply in order to provide enough posts to the competing factions to satisfy their ambitions. The result was to weaken the effectiveness of Cabinet and to strengthen the individual ministries, since Cabinet ministers did not have enough time to master their portfolios before being replaced. Ironically, in trying to ensure their own survival by satisfying the factions through frequent Cabinet reshuffles, prime ministers in the long run tended to weaken their own ability to control the policy agenda because ministries were easily able to control Cabinet ministers rather than the other way round.[11]

By the 1980s this procedure was so formalized that it had led to seniority promotions of LDP parliamentarians along lines very similar to those within government ministries. Each faction leader would maintain a seniority list of members which it would present to the Prime Minister preceding a Cabinet reshuffle, and the latter would adjust the claims as best he could so as to maintain an equitable balance between the competing claims. Although there were variations in the way the system worked between different periods, broadly speaking it operated in such a way that 'accelerated promotion' was extremely hard to achieve, even for the exceptionally hard-working and ambitious. This at times created severe tensions between 'generations' of ruling party parliamentarians, and frustration felt by younger members was in turn one of the factors that contributed to the split in the party that occurred in 1993.

Various methods have been used to choose the LDP President – a post that normally carries with it the position of Prime Minister. These have included selection by a cabal of party elders, votes by LDP parliamentarians of both houses plus a limited number of local branch representatives, and use of primary elections among party members and 'friends' at local level. Whatever method has been used, selection has involved factions and factional manoeuvring. Given constant competition between factions, this has contributed to the relatively frequent turnover of prime ministers, as of other Cabinet ministers.

Abundant evidence since the rewriting of the electoral law in 1994 suggests that LDP factions exercise less influence than they did, although they have not disappeared, and most LDP parliamentarians still belong to one faction or another. Both revision of the electoral law in 1994, and the strengthening of prime ministerial authority put in train by the Hashimoto Cabinet in 1998, bequeathed to Koizumi a stronger hand in relation to LDP factions than his predecessors had enjoyed. In constructing his first Cabinet after becoming Prime Minister in April 2001, he pointedly ignored factional claims on Cabinet and party office, and in particular claims from the Hashimoto faction, then the largest in the party.

Factions in the LDP today are more fluid and less tightly structured than they used to be. Whereas in the past the faction leader was dominant to the extent that fund-raising was mainly channelled through that individual, now many members of factions have their own access to funds and are thus less dependent on their faction leader. In short, factions are no longer the 'LDP divisions', as they used to be called, but rather groupings of parliamentarians that show solidarity with each other for limited, but still significant, purposes.

---

[11]   Cabinets under single-party dominance were reshuffled at least once a year, but there was a tendency for ministers in key portfolios to stay in post longer. For data on this, see J. A. A. Stockwin et al., *Dynamic and Immobilist Politics in Japan*, London, Macmillan, 1988, pp. 42–6.

Another informal type of grouping that was noted within the LDP from the 1980s is the so-called policy 'tribes' (*zoku*) that concern themselves with particular areas of policy.[12] Examples of 'tribal' interests include telecommunications, education, construction, transport and defence, though they are also to be found in respect of narrower policy areas, such as the tobacco industry. 'Tribes' were originally conceived as a response to a perceived lack of political influence over many areas of policy where bureaucratic interests prevailed, often (as, for instance, in agriculture), in close conjunction with the sectional interests concerned. Typically, *zoku* parliamentarians do not confront bureaucratic and sectional interests so much as work in conjunction with them. They have been likened to 'iron triangles', on the American model, which aim to sew up a particular area of policy by asserting a political–bureaucratic–sectional control over policy-making initiatives in that area. Generalization about them, however, should only be attempted with caution.

So far, we have said little about the formal structure of the LDP, not surprisingly perhaps, given the great practical importance of informal structures, such as *kōenkai*, *habatsu* and *zoku*. The party, however, has long had a complex structure of committees, which have often exerted great influence on policy. In the past, these have been able to overrule or modify initiatives coming from Prime Minister and Cabinet. Filling the three top party positions (apart from himself) has usually been a delicate balancing act for an LDP president. Apart from his own position as President (*sōsai*), these posts are the Secretary-General (*kanjichō*), Executive Council Chairman (*sōmukaichō*) and Policy Research Council Chairman (*seimu chōsakaichō*). In most periods the occupants of these four party posts, together with the Chief Cabinet Secretary (*kanbō chōkan*) – a Cabinet position – have constituted the effective 'directorate' of a given government. Occupants of those five positions were given constant media exposure, and worked together to hammer out the broad lines of policy that should motivate the government as a whole. As we have seen, however, the 'directorate' has often been frustrated and obstructed by the organized representatives of a range of vested interests. The greater powers now available to a Prime Minister to some extent help to overcome this problem, but it needed a Prime Minister with the tenacity and strategic abilities of Koizumi to make best use of those powers.

The LDP has been in power for more than half a century, with one short break, and latterly with coalition partners. Such long tenure imparts the idea that it is a party of power, and creates the reality that it is a party of patronage. Despite the tightening of electoral campaigning rules from the 1990s, the sense that a ruling-party parliamentarian is a dispenser of patronage dies hard. This is at least part of the explanation for the predominance of personality voting, which the change in the lower house electoral system has reduced only to a limited extent. Table 9.8 illustrates vividly how differently voters behave when voting for an individual candidate in a single-member constituency and when voting for an impersonal party list in a larger-scale PR constituency. The LDP, as party in

---

[12] The classic account of *zoku* is Inoguchi Takashi and Iwai Tomoaki, *Zoku giin no kenkyū* (A Study of Tribal Parliamentarians), Tokyo, Nihon Keizai Hyōronsha, 1987.

Table 9.8   LDP performance by region in the 2000, 2003 and 2005 House of Representatives elections (% of total vote)

		2000	(1)–(2)	2003	(1)–(2)	2005	(1)–(2)
Hokkaidō	(1)[a]	42.5	16.9	43.0	12.0	44.4	15.3
	(2)[b]	25.6		31.0		29.1	
Tōhoku	(1)	46.3	14.3	42.3	4.7	47.9	11.4
	(2)	32.0		37.6		36.5	
N. Kantō	(1)	43.5	12.9	49.5	11.9	53.0	16.5
	(2)	30.6		37.6		36.5	
S. Kantō	(1)	40.2	15.5	45.0	10.4	51.6	9.2
	(2)	24.7		34.6		42.4	
Tokyo	(1)	31.1	11.6	40.4	7.9	49.9	9.7
	(2)	19.5		32.5		40.2	
Hokuriku-Shinetsu	(1)	49.5	14.5	46.4	7.5	47.1	8.8
	(2)	35.0		38.9		38.3	
Tōkai	(1)	36.3	7.7	40.1	5.5	46.7	8.1
	(2)	28.6		34.6		38.6	
Kinki	(1)	28.4	4.7	34.8	4.1	41.4	4.6
	(2)	23.7		30.7		36.8	
Chūgoku	(1)	56.6	21.0	54.4	17.0	49.4	12.7
	(2)	35.6		37.4		36.7	
Shikoku	(1)	53.3	17.3	56.2	18.0	53.2	14.9
	(2)	36.0		38.2		38.3	
Kyūshū	(1)	47.1	15.7	47.4	10.9	46.2	9.1
	(2)	31.4		36.5		37.1	
Overall	(1)	41.0	12.7	43.8	8.8	47.8	9.6
	(2)	28.3		35.0		38.2	

[a](1) = Single-member constituencies.
[b](2) = PR blocs.

Sources: Yomiuri Nenkan, 2001, pp. 145–6; 2004, pp. 194–5; 2006, pp. 236–7.

power, performs much better in the first type of constituency than in the latter. This effect can be seen across all regions of the country, from the north to the south.

Several points stand out when we examine this table. The first is that it shows clearly how far the LDP was able to progress electorally while Koizumi was Prime Minister. Second, the improvement in LDP fortunes took place disproportionately in metropolitan areas where the party had been trailing: namely, Tokyo, Kinki (essentially the Osaka–Kyoto Kobe conurbation), Tōkai (including the Nagoya conurbation), and both North and South Kantō regional blocs (heavily urbanized areas surrounding Tokyo). In Hokkaidō and Tōhoku, in the north, the LDP made only marginal improvements. In Hokuriku-Shinetsu, a less urbanized region on the Japan Sea coast north of Tokyo, LDP support was high but static. In the south-western regions of Chūgoku, Shikoku and Kyūshū, which are more traditional regions without metropolitan cities, support for the LDP remained high but was not markedly increasing. Indeed, in Chūgoku, at the western end of the main island of Honshū, support was the highest in the whole of Japan, but falling.

The third point takes us back to our discussion in the previous paragraph: namely, that there is a wide discrepancy in the numbers of votes for the LDP cast by voters (who have two votes) when voting for a candidate in a single-member constituency and when voting for a party list in a PR constituency. In all cases the LDP received more votes in single-member than in PR constituencies. But the pattern of these discrepancies is intriguing. The difference is not great in the highly urban Kinki (Osaka) and Tōkai (Nagoya) regions, moderate in Tokyo and its immediate surrounds, and high in the remoter and more rural areas at both ends of Japan. This finding is broadly consistent with our observation that personality voting is more prevalent in country regions than in urban and metropolitan areas. When, as under the new electoral system, the voter is given two votes, one for a person and one for a party list, non-metropolitan voters exhibit a tendency to vote for the person but not for the party list. The person (candidate) will have cultivated a network of support in the local constituency, and in this many voters are involved, directly or indirectly. But a party list is a far more impersonal thing, which is less likely to attract that same voter's ballot.

Our final point, however, is that the size of the discrepancy has been reducing somewhat, though patchily, and rather more in country areas than in metropolitan and urban areas. This might suggest that the incidence of personality voting is declining, but the trend is not clear enough to assert this with confidence.

Democratic Party (of Japan) (DPJ, *Minshutō*)

The Democratic Party was founded in September 1996, about a month before general elections. Its birth was precipitated by the split in the SDP (formerly JSP) between its left and right wings, with the right wing being the central element in the DPJ at its inception. It was in a sense refounded nearly two years later, after the collapse of the New Frontier Party at the end of 1997. This brought new members into the DPJ, many of whom originated on the conservative side of politics, though they had passed through the way-station of the NFP. The disparate party and ideological origins of its membership created a problem of identity for the fledgling party, and it experienced many difficulties in hammering out a coherent policy platform.

Establishing effective leadership also presented difficulties. For some years, the top position alternated between Hatoyama Yukio, whose background was on the right, and Kan Naoto, who came from the moderate left, and was associated with citizens' movements (*shimin undō*). For a while, indeed, the two of them set up a duumvirate and attempted to lead as joint 'Representatives' (*daihyō*) of the party, but this did not work well. In 2003 Okada Katsuya became the new leader, and led the party through some encouraging electoral results. On his watch, in September–October 2003, the DPJ merged with Ozawa's Liberal Party, strengthening its parliamentary representation. He was forced to resign, however, to take responsibility for the debacle of the September 2005 lower

Table 9.9　DPJ performance by region in the 2000, 2003 and 2005 House of Representatives elections (% of total vote)

		2000	(1)–(2)	2003	(1)–(2)	2005	(1)–(2)
Hokkaidō	(1)[a]	39.8	8.6	42.9	2.1	44.9	11.1
	(2)[b]	31.2		40.8		33.8	
Tōhoku	(1)	22.4	1.2	35.1	–2.3	38.7	5.1
	(2)	21.2		37.4		33.6	
N. Kantō	(1)	27.4	2.7	37.7	–0.2	36.4	5.0
	(2)	24.7		37.9		31.4	
S. Kantō	(1)	31.7	4.0	39.9	–0.1	35.8	6.3
	(2)	27.7		40.0		29.5	
Tokyo	(1)	33.6	4.6	42.2	2.3	36.4	6.8
	(2)	29.0		39.9		29.6	
Hokuriku Shinetsu	(1)	25.9	0.6	33.3	–3.6	36.4	3.9
	(2)	25.3		36.9		32.5	
Tōkai	(1)	37.1	6.5	45.6	4.8	41.2	6.4
	(2)	30.6		40.8		34.8	
Kinki	(1)	23.1	–0.2	37.3	0.2	36.4	7.4
	(2)	23.3		37.1		29.0	
Chūgoku	(1)	19.6	–2.1	30.0	–3.8	32.4	3.8
	(2)	21.7		33.8		28.6	
Shikoku	(1)	16.5	–4.2	31.0	–0.7	33.3	0.1
	(2)	20.7		31.7		33.2	
Kyūshū	(1)	22.6	2.3	23.7	–7.7	30.4	1.0
	(2)	20.3		31.4		29.4	
Overall	(1)	27.6	1.4	36.7	–0.7	36.4	5.4
	(2)	25.2		37.4		31.0	

[a](1) = Single-member constituencies.
[b](2) = PR blocs.
Sources: As for Table 9.8.

house elections, when the DPJ seat total fell from 177 to 113. He was briefly succeeded by Maehara Seiji, who attempted to shift party policy sharply to the right, but was brought down by a scandal. In April 2006 Ozawa Ichirō took over the leadership, applying his reformist vision to the formation of policy.

Even though the DPJ is the principal party of opposition to a government dominated by the conservative LDP, it is difficult to regard it as other than a second conservative party. The old Socialist element within it is much reduced, and it has been argued that on economic policy its positions may even be to the right of the LDP.[13] In foreign and defence policy, on the other hand, and to some small extent in relation to revising the Constitution, it takes a generally critical stance on government policy.

[13]　Leonard J. Schoppa, 'Neoliberal Policy Preferences of the "New Left": Home-Grown or an Anglo-American Import?', in Rikki Kersten and David Williams (eds), *The Left in the Shaping of Japanese Democracy*, Abingdon and New York, Routledge, 2006, pp. 117–39.

There have been times when the DPJ has appeared divided and fragile, and its severe defeat in the 2005 elections marked the end of a run of electoral successes. Nevertheless, it shows signs of having learned from its recent history of the need to be better melded into a coherent entity[14]. Its victory in the July 2007 upper house elections marked a spectacular comeback.

Finally, when we compare election results for the DPJ in single-member and PR bloc constituencies over the past three lower house elections with those for the LDP, we find that the discrepancy between numbers voting DPJ in the two types of seat is far less marked than in the case of the LDP. Indeed, in the 2003 elections the difference was negative overall, as more people voted for the Democrats in PR blocs than in single-member constituencies. Any explanation would be speculative, but it is arguable that with the DPJ out of power electors would have little expectation of benefits from DPJ candidates, by contrast with LDP candidates. Voters favourably disposed to the Democrats would therefore be at least as attracted by the party as by the personality of a particular candidate. On the other hand, the 2005 results approximate more closely to those of the LDP in that the discrepancy was in all cases positive. This may reflect a negative image of the DPJ as a party, following its criticism of Koizumi's postal privatization bills. However this may be, the figures suggest that the appeal of the DPJ is more to party than to personality, whereas traditional styles of personal, 'pork-barrel' politics remain embedded in the appeal and *modus operandi* of the LDP.

Clean Government Party (CGP, *Kōmeitō*)

Since 1998 the CGP has been governing in coalition with its dominant partner, the LDP. It has thus become the longest-serving government party, except for the LDP, since the Second World War. With 31 seats, as against 296 for the LDP, since the September 2005 elections, it cannot expect many Cabinet positions, but it has provided one minister in successive Cabinets. As junior partner in a coalition government, it can exert only limited influence on government policy, but its trump card is that it is needed by the LDP to make up its majority in the upper house, which has the constitutional right to block bills either first considered by it or passed to it from the lower house. It is believed to have had an impact in some areas of social welfare policy, and also acts as a brake on right-wing elements in the LDP desirous of revising the peace clause of the 1946 Constitution and developing a more forward defence policy. Whether, though, it possesses either the capacity or the will to hold the line firmly against such policy initiatives is subject to serious doubt.

The CGP is the only significant party to be formed by a religious group since the end of the war. Its parent body, the *Sōka Gakkai*, a lay movement of the Nichiren Buddhist sect, experienced sensational growth between the late 1940s and the early 1970s, recruiting several million members. It was widely distrusted for its militant proselytizing. The CGP was formed in 1964, and soon gained

---

[14]   For a comprehensive treatment of the DPJ's origins and later development, see Sarah Hyde, *From Old Socialists to New Democrats: The Transformation of the Japanese Left*, Abingdon and New York, Routledge, 2008.

remarkable electoral successes. In those days it appealed to the less educated, less well-off and less well-organized sections of mainly big-city populations, but from the 1970s it began to cultivate a more middle-class image, placing a strong emphasis on education. Despite early fears that it might be fascist or extreme nationalist, the CGP turned out to be for the most part moderately conservative in its policies, and until the political realignments of the 1990s it generally occupied a centrist position between the LDP and the parties of the left.

The CGP is famous for its effective organizational skills, and the hold that it apparently exerts over those who vote for it. When it merged with the New Frontier Party in December 1994, it provided that party with many lessons on organization. It never, however, entirely abandoned its own independent structure, and when the NFP collapsed three years later it re-emerged in more or less its old form after a few months. Having been one of the parties of the Hosokawa and Hata coalition governments in 1993–4, it had acquired a taste for power, and was then frustrated by the opposition status of the NFP. It was therefore rather to be expected that it would enter a coalition with the LDP late in 1998, and remain there, strategically placed, for most of a decade and perhaps more.

Japan Socialist Party (Nihon shakaitō); Social Democratic Party (Shakai minshutō, Shamintō) from January 1996

In 2007 the SDP was a small party, with a mere seven members of the House of Representatives. But for many years it had been the largest and most significant party of opposition to LDP rule. Its tumultuous history from the late 1940s to the late 1960s, motivated by a mixture of Marxist and pacifist ideas, has been told elsewhere.[15] The Socialists were central to the movement in defence of the 'peace clause' in the Constitution, and in opposition to rearmament and security relations with the United States. But by the 1970s the party had lost much of its dynamism, and it was not until the late 1980s, under the leadership of Doi Takako – the first woman to head a Japanese political party – that it once more captured the popular imagination. This, however, was a brief flowering. The 1990s saw a rapid loss of support, and despite being a key player in the coalition governments of 1993–4, and supplying the Prime Minister (Murayama) in 1994–6, the party was reduced to a rump by the end of the decade, though some of its former adherents played a significant role in the newly formed Democratic Party from 1996. Despite its collapse in the 1990s, its challenging and at times constructive role in the politics of post-war Japan ought not to be forgotten.

Japan Communist Party (Nihon kyōsantō)

The JCP is Japan's oldest political party. Founded in 1922, it led an illegal and clandestine existence until 1945, when it was legalized by the American Occupation. It gained significant support during the Occupation period, when it

---

[15] J. A. A. Stockwin, *The Japanese Socialist Party and Neutralism*, Melbourne, Melbourne University Press, 1968.

tried to gain control of sections of the labour union movement; then sank into electoral insignificance during the 1950s, but from the late 1960s until the late 1970s experienced a resurgence. This was based upon careful attention to the grass roots and moderation of hard-line ideology, but its electoral successes were not carried into the more conservative 1980s. It was resurgent once again in the economic stagnation and political instability of the late 1990s, but this upturn did not last either, and in the 2005 lower house elections it won only nine seats. The JCP has never entered a coalition arrangement with other parties. It holds to a policy of running candidates even in unwinnable seats throughout the country, often splitting the opposition vote by doing so.

People's New Party (PNP, *Kokumin shintō*)

This was a party founded by postal privatization rebels, including Watanuki Tamisuke and Kamei Shizuka, in August–September 2005. Only four of its members were elected to the lower house in the subsequent general elections.

Defunct parties

Democratic Socialist Party (DSP, *Minshatō*)

The DSP was formed in 1960 by the labour leader Nishio Suehiro, in protest against Marxist influence within the JSP during the dispute over revising the Japan–US Security Treaty. Despite its initial ambition to model itself on the British Labour Party, it never developed into a major party. Its support in the *Dōmei* labour union federation was a relatively narrow base, concentrated especially in the Nagoya and Kansai areas. By the 1970s, the party had developed rather hawkish views on defence, putting it in sharp confrontation with the JSP. But when the labour movement was unified in the new *Rengō* federation at the end of the 1980s, the two parties drew closer together, and cooperated in the Hosokawa coalition government from 1993. The formation, however, of the Murayama coalition government in June 1994, combining Liberal Democrats and Socialists, led to renewed estrangement. In December 1994 the DSP entered the New Frontier Party, and several years later most of its members ended up in the Democratic Party.

New Liberal Club (NLC, *Shin jiyū kurabu*)

In 1976 a splinter group, led by Kōno Yōhei, broke from the LDP in protest at corruption, and formed the New Liberal Club. It obtained a handful of parliamentary seats and went into coalition with the ruling LDP following the lower house elections of 1983; then most of its members returned to LDP membership in 1986.

Social Democratic League (SDL, *Shaminren*)

This mini-party was formed in 1977 by dissident members of the JSP, who sought a less ideological form of democratic socialism. It remained in existence until

1994, when its members dispersed. Its leader, Eda Satsuki, and another prominent member, Kan Naoto, both played a significant role in the Democratic Party from 1996.

Japan New Party (JNP, *Nihon shintō*)

The JNP was founded in 1992 by Hosokawa Morihiro, and was largely composed of political outsiders. A few of its members were graduates of the Matsushita School of Politics and Management (*Matsushita seikei juku*), a private college endowed by the founder of Panasonic in order to train new political leaders. It was prominent in the Hosokawa government, but rapidly faded once that administration fell. Most of its parliamentary members moved to the NFP and, later, to the DPJ.

Japan Renewal Party (JRP, *Shinseitō*)

This was the party formed by Hata Tsutomu and Ozawa Ichirō in June 1993 following the split in the Takeshita faction of the LDP. The defection of this group was the most important factor leading to the ruling party's defeat in the July elections. No doubt a principal motive for the formation of the JRP was Ozawa's desire to shake up the political system and form the nucleus of a credible alternative to continuing government by the LDP. The JRP took the largest number of posts in the Hosokawa Cabinet formed in August 1993, and Ozawa's influence was dominant within that Cabinet. The party went into opposition with the formation of the Murayama government and was absorbed into the New Frontier Party in December 1994.

New Party Harbinger (NPH, *Shintō sakigake*)

The NPH was formed by Takemura Masayoshi two days before the formation of the JRP in June 1993, and as part of the splintering of the LDP that was occurring at that time. Its views were more 'progressive' than those of the JRP and initially it appeared likely to merge with the Japan New Party. Tensions between Takemura and Hosokawa that appeared over tax policy in February 1994 made this impossible, and the NPH subsequently found common ground with the JSP, joining it as the third and smallest member of the Murayama coalition government in June 1994. Unusually for the times, the party retained its integrity as a single party into the later 1990s (though suffering defections), but was wound up some time after suffering a crushing defeat at the 1996 lower house elections.

New Frontier Party (NFP, *Shinshintō*)

This party was formed in December 1994 from no fewer than nine parties and groupings – the JRP, CGP, JNP and DSP, as well as various splinter groups that had recently defected from the LDP.[16] Its specific purpose was to challenge the LDP for power, and the long-term aim, as expressed by Ozawa and others, was to create the conditions for an alternating two-party system. In pursuit of this

---

[16] *Asahi Nenkan*, 1995, p. 260.

aim, the party instituted a shadow cabinet system, or 'tomorrow's cabinet', as it was known. Another innovation was that in electing the party leaders any member of the public could vote on payment of a small fee. This ensured that Ozawa was elected leader by a large margin in December 1995 (its first leader was the former Prime Minister Kaifu Toshiki). The party started well, but lost momentum, partly because of disputes among its leaders, and performed less well than expected in the 1996 elections. Defections followed, including that of former Prime Minister Hata Tsutomu. Even though it collapsed in December 1997, the NFP was in some ways a cleverly devised party structure, in that it combined the extraordinary organizational and financial capacity of the *Sōka Gakkai* and the former (and future) CGP with groups originating in the LDP mainstream and elsewhere.

Liberal Party (LP, *Jiyūtō*)

After the New Frontier Party collapsed at the end of 1997, Ozawa Ichirō formed the Liberal Party from his close followers in January 1998. This was one of six fragments into which the NFP split at that time. It was a small party, which began with 43 lower house and 11 upper house members. Its platform reflected Ozawa's ideas of a free market economy, Japan as a 'normal state', and internationalism. Between January 1999 and April 2000 the Liberals were in government in coalition with the LDP under Obuchi, and (for part of the period) with the CGP. Ozawa found this a frustrating arrangement. When he pulled the party out of the coalition it split in two, with nearly half the members opting to remain in government. In September–October 2003 the Liberal Party merged with the Democratic Party.

Conservative Party (CP, *Hoshutō*)

When the Liberal Party split in April 2000, nearly half its members opted to remain in government and formed the Conservative Party. General elections followed in June, when this party's lower house representation was reduced from 18 to 7. For a while it was led by a woman, Ōgi Chikage. The CP later changed its name to 'New Conservative Party', but electoral success eluded it, and its remaining parliamentary members were eventually absorbed back into the LDP.

Conclusions

It can be seen from the preceding brief outline of parties now defunct that the party situation in the second half of the 2000s is far simpler than it was during the turbulent 1990s. Japan now has something close to (though not quite) a two-party system, for the first time since the late 1950s. But neither in the 1950s nor in the 2000s was the principle of alternation of power achieved. Indeed, the situation towards the end of the 1950s was referred to as a 'one-and-a-half-party system', with one dominant party and a much weaker party of opposition. Whether the party system is still that of one-and-a-half parties, or whether it might mutate into a genuine two-party system with a real possibility of changes of party in power, remains to be seen.

Chapter 10 | Some Problems of the Constitution

The Japanese Constitution of 1946 is one of the oldest constitutions in the world,[1] and it has never been revised in any particular. Nevertheless, it remains highly controversial, and the recent Prime Minister, Abe Shinzō, declared on many occasions his determination to revise it.[2] Constitutional revision has returned to the active political agenda after many years in which conservative politicians paid lip-service to the need for revision, but did little to further that end. Issues embodied in the Constitution have haunted Japanese politics since the document was first written.

Debate over the Constitution was at its height in the 1950s and early 1960s. The Hatoyama and Kishi governments aimed at constitutional revision, and the Commission on the Constitution (*Kenpō chōsakai*), set up in 1957, was charged with making proposals for such revision.[3] But when it reported in 1964, the political mood had changed, economic goals had taken precedence over constitutional issues, and its proposals, which in any case were not unanimous, were quietly forgotten.

The politics and political history of the Constitution abound with paradox. The Liberal Democrats have been staunch supporters of the security relationship with the United States, but lukewarm about their 'American-imposed' Constitution. The left, on the other hand, was often anti-American, but strongly supportive of a Constitution whose American inspiration was clear. Its origins in the American Occupation of Japan (and its emergence under the direction of its notably conservative Supreme Commander, General MacArthur), are reflected in its inclusion of many New Deal concepts and also the 'peace clause' (article 9),

---

[1] Lawrence W. Beer and Hiroshi Itoh, *The Constitutional Case Law of Japan, 1970 through 1980*. Seattle and London, University of Washington Press, 1996, p. 4.
[2] See e.g. Abe Shinzō, *Utsukushii kuni e* (Towards a Beautiful Country), Tokyo, Bunshun Shinsho, 2006, pp. 121–3.
[3] In his book Abe writes eulogistically about his grandfather, Kishi Nobusuke, Prime Minister 1957–60: Abe Shinzō, *Utsukushii kuni e*, pp. 15 ff.

which on the face of it banned armed forces in perpetuity. But as soon as 1953, not long after the Occupation was over, an American Vice-President (Richard Nixon) was calling on Japan to scrap the peace clause. Even though politicians could not agree on whether to celebrate or ignore 'Constitution Day' (3 May), the Constitution remains unrevised. Finally, although the Constitution is of enormous significance in having shifted the political institutions and practices of Japan away from domination by the emperor-institution and the armed forces towards democratic norms and values, it has also been the focus of much controversy, a large proportion of which relates to one single article, the 'peace clause', or article 9.

Origins

The origins of the Constitution are crucial to an understanding of the subsequent controversies that have swirled around it. The allegation that General MacArthur 'imposed' the Constitution on Japan, while creating the fiction that it was an indigenous Japanese product, has been the most emotive and powerful charge levelled against it by its opponents.[4] The work of the Commission on the Constitution in the 1950s and early 1960s records the results of exhaustive investigation into this question.[5] The Potsdam Declaration of July 1945 gave positive sanction for a major reform of the Meiji Constitution. It was hardly surprising, therefore, that the Americans, left in near-complete charge of the Occupation of Japan by the conflicts between erstwhile allies, should have placed constitutional revision high on their agenda. Clearly, it was also desirable that constitutional reform should emerge from the Japanese political process itself, and should benefit from adequate popular discussion.[6]

[4]   The conservative *Yomiuri* newspaper called the preamble to the Constitution 'a translation of what was written by a US Navy commander': *Yomiuri Shinbun*, 25 March 1997. By contrast, Beer and Itoh argue that the Occupation officials and members of the House of Representatives were not so far apart in their views. Moreover, in their view, what matters is the enduring support for the Constitution that has been shown by the electorate. Beer and Itoh, *The Constitutional Case Law of Japan*, p. 13. Support, however, has weakened to some extent over the decade since their book was published.

[5]   For a classic account see Robert E. Ward, 'The Commission on the Constitution and Prospects for Constitutional Change in Japan', *Journal of Asian Studies*, vol. 24, no. 3 (May 1965), pp. 401–29. For a survey of the published documents of the Commission, which run to some 40,000 pages of text, see John M. Maki, 'The Documents of Japan's Commission on the Constitution', *Journal of Asian Studies*, vol. 24, no. 3 (May 1965), pp. 475–89.

[6]   This was also a theme of the 'United States Initial Post-Surrender Policy for Japan', issued as a presidential directive to General MacArthur on 6 September 1945. The issue was also complicated by an ambiguity in the Potsdam Declaration between coercive and voluntarist principles. See Robert E. Ward, 'The Origins of the Present Japanese Constitution', *American Political Science Review*, vol. 50, no. 4 (December 1956), pp. 980–1010, at p. 983.

In accordance with the latter principle, the Shidehara government was invited to submit proposals for reform late in 1945. A committee was set up under a Cabinet minister, Dr Matsumoto Jōji, and had worked out the draft of a revised constitution by the beginning of February 1946.[7] This, however, conceded few changes to the text of the Meiji Constitution, and was rejected by SCAP as too conservative.

On 7 January 1946 General MacArthur had received a document called SWNCC-228 from the State–War–Navy Coordinating Committee in Washington. This document urged that the Japanese should be encouraged to reform the Constitution along democratic lines, but warned the Supreme Commander against a coercive approach, on the unimpeachable grounds that pressure from the occupying power would seriously prejudice the ultimate acceptability of any resulting constitution.[8]

At the beginning of February, the pace of events suddenly quickened. On 3 February the Supreme Commander summoned his Government Section and gave its members instructions to prepare, with the utmost despatch, a draft constitution to be used as a 'guide' to their work for constitutional revision. Among the items that MacArthur specifically ordered to be included in the draft were a clause to the effect that the *Tennō* should be 'at the head of state', but that his duties and powers should be 'exercised in accordance with the Constitution and responsible to the basic will of the people as provided therein', and another specifying that the right to wage war and to maintain the means of waging it should be abolished.[9] The Government Section, under Major-General Courtney Whitney, but with Colonel Charles Kades effectively in charge, worked under great pressure from 4 February and completed its draft (now known as the 'GHQ draft') in no more than six days. It was presented on 13 February to Cabinet, which accepted it 'in basic principle' on 22 February.[10]

We need, however, to return to the midwinter of 1945–6, and examine why it was that MacArthur moved with such speed in early February 1946. It seems that the urgency was rooted in the imminent inauguration of the Far Eastern

[7] The former Prime Minister, Prince Konoe, also busied himself with proposals for constitutional reform, but his efforts were repudiated by MacArthur.

[8] Theodore McNelly, 'The Japanese Constitution, Child of the Cold War', *Political Science Quarterly*, vol. 74, no. 2 (June 1959), pp. 176–95.

[9] Supreme Commander for the Allied Powers, *Political Reorientation of Japan, September 1945 to September 1948*, 2 vols, Westport, CT, Greenwood Press, 1970 (repr. of original, published by US Government Printing Office, 1949), vol. 1, p. 102.

[10] Ward acidly comments: 'This awesome display of speed and "efficiency" without a doubt represents the world's record time for the devising and acceptance of a constitution for a major modern state': Ward, 'Origins', p. 995. Yoshida, in his memoirs, after pointing to the impending general elections as a probable reason for haste, concludes: 'The fact remains, however, that there was a good deal of the American spirit of enterprise in the undertaking of such a fundamental piece of reform as the revision of the Constitution within two months of Japan's defeat; as for wishing to see that reform realised in so short a period as half a year or a year, one can only put it down to that impulsiveness common to military people of all countries': Shigeru Yoshida, *The Yoshida Memoirs: The Story of Japan in Crisis*, trans. Kenichi Yoshida, London, Heinemann, 1961, p. 136.

Commission in Washington, decided upon at the Big Three summit conference in Moscow in December 1945. The Far Eastern Commission, on which representatives of 11 nations were to sit, could have its decisions vetoed by any one of the US, the UK, the USSR and China, which on the face of it gave the Americans a fairly free hand if they were prepared to use the veto. From MacArthur's point of view, however, the crucial difficulty lay in the following provision: 'Any directives dealing with fundamental changes in the Japanese constitutional structure or in the regime of control, or dealing with a change in the Japanese Government as a whole, will be issued only following consultation *and following the attainment of agreement* in the Far Eastern Commission.'[11]

As late as 30 January 1946, General MacArthur met the Far Eastern Advisory Commission (precursor of the Far Eastern Commission) and told them that, because of the Moscow Agreement, he no longer had authority to take action on constitutional reform, which he hoped would be carried out on Japanese initiative.[12]

What exactly happened when the GHQ draft was presented to a shocked and disbelieving Cabinet on 13 February has never been completely cleared up. What is certain is that substantial pressure was brought to bear upon the Cabinet by the officials of Government Section, including Whitney himself. The precise nature of that pressure, however, has been a subject of some dispute, and upon it hangs in part the controversy about whether the Constitution was 'imposed' or 'written in cooperation'. According to one account that gained wide currency, Whitney told members of the Cabinet that if the Japanese government did not present a revised constitution similar to the GHQ draft, the *person* of the *Tennō* could not be guaranteed.[13]

This account was the basis of the later charge by Dr Matsumoto, whose constitution-drafting efforts have already been mentioned, that the Americans threatened to indict the *Tennō* as a war criminal if Cabinet did not accept the GHQ draft as the basis for a new constitution. If the statement was actually made, however, a more likely interpretation would appear to be that it was meant as a warning, to the effect that without drastic action to forestall the Far Eastern Commission, SCAP would find it difficult to stave off demands from the Soviet Union and other countries for the emperor to be tried in person.[14] It has, moreover, been doubted whether Whitney ever spoke in such terms. Whitney mentions this comment nowhere in his own published account of the meeting,[15]

---

[11] Quoted in SCAP, *Political Reorientation of Japan*, vol. 2, p. 421.
[12] McNelly, 'The Japanese Constitution', p. 184.
[13] This account is that of Satō Tatsuo, who was a leading official of the Cabinet Bureau of Legislation, and closely involved with the constitutional drafting process, for part of the time as assistant to Matsumoto. See also Koseki Shōichi, *The Birth of Japan's Postwar Constitution*, ed. and trans. Ray E. Moore, Boulder, CO, Westview, 1997. Koseki's book is an excellent account of the origins of the Constitution.
[14] McNelly, 'The Japanese Constitution', p. 187.
[15] Whitney, on the other hand, has an account in which he boasts of telling the Cabinet members that he and his aides had been 'enjoying your atomic sunshine': Major-General Courtney Whitney, *MacArthur, his Rendezvous with History*, New York, Knopf, 1956, pp. 250–2.

and Professor Takayanagi Kenzō, later Chairman of the Commission on the Constitution, casts doubt on the reliability of the original account.[16]

Even if Takayanagi's doubts can be sustained, however, it is not quite so easy to agree wholly with his thesis, courageously and persistently argued during the hearings of the Commission on the Constitution, that the Constitution was a 'collaborative effort' between the Americans and the Japanese. A recent study, by Moore and Robinson, details a number of instances where Charles Kades, Chairman of the Government Section drafting committee, and others put pressure on the Cabinet and also Parliament to accept certain concepts or refrain from bringing back elements from the pre-war political order. A case in point was the question of 'national polity' (*kokutai*), central to the philosophy of the Meiji Constitution and the order built upon it. When Kanamori Tokujirō (a constitutional scholar who became a minister in the first Yoshida Cabinet) challenged Kades in July 1946 with an assertion of the continuing relevance of the 'national polity' idea, Kades forced him to retract. Nevertheless, Moore and Robinson judge that, despite a degree of American coercion on some aspects of constitutional drafting, in broad terms the new Constitution may be regarded as the product of a partnership rather than simply the result of American imposition.[17]

Whitney by his own account threatened to place the draft before the people over the heads of Cabinet if ministers refused to accept it.[18] As Ward commented in 1956: 'Given the traditional distrust of Japanese officials for popular sovereignty in any form, rendered particularly acute by the country's desperate and tumultuous economic and social circumstances and the unprecedented scale of left-wing political activities, it is difficult to conceive of any more ominous development from the standpoint of Japanese officialdom than a constitution formulated in the "marketplace".'[19]

After the meeting on 13 February, the Cabinet made one more attempt to persuade SCAP to accept the Matsumoto draft as a basis for negotiation, but this was flatly rejected.[20] Finally, the Cabinet capitulated and hammered out a draft constitution, following the GHQ draft closely. This was delivered to SCAP on 4 March. There followed an extraordinary session, some 30 hours long, in which Cabinet and the Government Section arrived at a mutually acceptable draft. Here also the Americans kept up a relentless pressure upon the Japanese government. Whitney gave an ultimatum that he would 'wait until morning' for a final draft to be produced, and then proceeded to reverse most of the changes that the

---

[16] Kenzo Takayanagi, 'Some Reminiscences of Japan's Commission on the Constitution', in Dan F. Henderson (ed.), *The Constitution of Japan: Its First Twenty Years, 1947–67*, Seattle and London, University of Washington Press, 1969, pp. 71–88, at pp. 77–8. See esp. fn. 13.

[17] Ray A. Moore and Donald L. Robinson, *Partners for Democracy: Crafting the New Japanese State under MacArthur*. Oxford and New York, Oxford University Press, 2002.

[18] SCAP, *Political Reorientation of Japan*, vol. 1, p. 105.

[19] Ward, 'Origins', p. 996.

[20] Ward, 'Origins', p. 999.

Japanese had attempted to introduce into the GHQ draft. The only significant concession made at this point by the Americans was the substitution of a bicameral for a unicameral assembly.[21] The document was published on 6 March and subsequently went through an intensive process of debate in Parliament. The House of Representatives passed it on 24 August by 421 votes to 8 (6 of the dissenters being Communists); it was agreed to by the House of Peers on 6 October and by the Privy Council on 29 October.

During this process, some changes were made in the text, but for the most part they were not of great importance, and in any case they were all cleared with SCAP. Beer and Itoh emphasize the importance of the fact that it was a largely new body of parliamentarians, rather than the Cabinet left over from the war, that debated and approved the constitutional draft in the House of Representatives.[22] The overwhelmingly affirmative vote certainly reflected the mood of the times and the enthusiasm with which democratic reforms were being embraced by many Japanese. It was also true that by this time many of the more conservative parliamentarians had been removed by the purge edict. Also, some who may have had qualms about the new Constitution possibly calculated that no real alternative course of action was possible in conditions of Occupation control other than to accept it.

There is force in the argument that the post-war Constitution was imposed on a reluctant Japanese political establishment, even though, following Beer and Itoh, it is also arguable that that establishment was discredited and about to be replaced, in part if not in its entirety. SCAP undoubtedly twisted the arm of the Cabinet by writing a constitutional draft based on popular sovereignty and threatening to take it to the people if the Cabinet should fail to sponsor it as its own creation. An official view was then maintained that the new Constitution was a Japanese product, and the press was forbidden to make critical comment.[23] Whether and to what extent the course of action taken by SCAP was justified by pressing political circumstances – in particular the opportunities that the establishment of the Far Eastern Commission appeared to create for Soviet interference – is a matter for argument. In so far as this bears on the legitimacy of the Constitution, there is a strong argument that its subsequent history is a more important factor than its origins. As Beer and Itoh put it: 'The intent of the SCAP framers seems to matter little now. Japanese interpretations and judgements will determine whether or not constitutional change is advisable.'[24] Or, in the words of Moore and Robinson, 'Democracies are often instituted by undemocratic means.'[25]

[21]   Ward, 'Origins', p. 1002.
[22]   Beer and Itoh, *The Constitutional Case Law of Japan*, p. 13.
[23]   Kazuo Kawai, *Japan's American Interlude*, Chicago, Chicago University Press, 1960, p. 52. See also John Dower, *Embracing Defeat: Japan in the Aftermath of World War II*, London and New York, Allen Lane/Penguin Press, 1999, pp. 346–404.
[24]   Beer and Itoh, *The Constitutional Case Law of Japan*, p. 13.
[25]   Moore and Robinson, *Partners for Democracy*, p. 336. This does not mean that the use of undemocratic means will guarantee democratic rule, as events in Iraq have shown.

Disputed Aspects

One way in which the survival of the Constitution was facilitated was by making it very difficult to revise. Article 96 sets as the requirements for constitutional amendment 'a concurring vote of two-thirds or more of all the members of each House', followed by a simple majority 'at a special referendum, or at such election as the Diet shall specify'. This has been frustrating to revisionists.[26] Until at least the 1990s, no government could ever fulfil the requirement for a two-thirds majority of parliamentary members, and public opinion polls indicated that the chances of attaining a simple majority in a referendum of the people were slim. Following the first Gulf War, however, when Japan suffered international criticism for its failure to send, not just money, but troops, most polls showed a majority in favour of constitutional revision. On the other hand, this is sharply qualified by the nature of the revision proposed. Moreover, the near-disappearance of the JSP (SDP) since 1996 has taken away the one party that unequivocally defended the Constitution, with its slogan: 'The Constitution defends you, and we defend the Constitution.' The Democratic Party, its principal successor, is much more equivocal about defending the Constitution.

A second argument used by revisionists is that the Constitution was too hastily written, that this is reflected in some of its wording, and that some aspects of it are ill-suited to Japanese social and political traditions. To this it may be replied that Japan in 1946 was ripe for radical political change, so that a dramatic new approach was needed. In any case, successive governments have not found it difficult to interpret its provisions flexibly. Flexibility, however, is not limitless. A piece of elastic may be stretched to a certain point, but beyond that there is the risk it will snap.

The Peace Clause (Article 9)

For many, the peace clause is the Constitution's very essence, often leading to the neglect of other important parts of it. The term 'Peace Constitution' conferred on the whole document attests to the dramatic impact and controversial nature of this particular clause.

Both the origins and the subsequent history of this clause are interesting and important. It is apparent that it did not originate in instructions received by MacArthur from Washington. The document SWNCC-228, for instance, merely required that 'the civil be supreme over the military branch of the government'.[27] It was natural to assume, therefore, that the author and originator of the clause was MacArthur himself. The idea of having Japan renounce war and the means of waging it through a clause in the body of its Constitution may perhaps have appealed to the visionary element in MacArthur's temperament,[28] and may also have been designed to forestall interference from the Far Eastern Commission,

---

[26] The LDP draft revision proposal of October 2005 reduced the parliamentary hurdle to a simple majority in each house: *Asahi Shinbun*, 29 October 2005.

[27] D. C. S. Sissons, 'The Pacifist Clause of the Japanese Constitution: Legal and Political Problems of Rearmament', *International Affairs*, vol. 37, no. 1 (January 1961), pp. 45–59, at p. 45.

[28] At one point the Cabinet attempted to have the clause relegated to the preamble, but this was not acceptable to SCAP.

mentioned above. He regarded retention of the *Tennō* as vital to the success of the Constitution. As a stratagem, therefore, it made sense to create a Constitution so radical that it not only replaced imperial with popular sovereignty, but even removed from Japan the right to wage war, *and yet retained the* Tennō. The context was a situation in which the USSR and other powers wished to put the *Tennō* on trial as a war criminal. If this version of events and motivations is correct, the revisionists could argue with force that the obnoxious peace clause was very specifically 'imposed'.

Unfortunately for the credibility of this version, MacArthur in his testimony to a US Senate Committee in May 1951 claimed that not he, but Shidehara, who was Prime Minister in early 1946, was the originator of the peace clause.[29] According to MacArthur, Shidehara had come to see him on 24 January 1946, and had proposed that a new Constitution should incorporate a renunciation of war. This was substantially corroborated in Shidehara's biography,[30] and was used by Takayanagi in his argument against the 'imposed Constitution' thesis.[31] Shidehara allegedly said nothing of this at the time to his Cabinet colleagues, and since no third person was present at the meeting (and both parties to it are dead), it is impossible to be sure exactly what happened. Not all of Shidehara's colleagues were prepared to accept this version of events.[32]

The wording of the peace clause went through a number of changes between its enunciation by MacArthur in his instructions to the Government Section on 3 February 1946 and the final version. All the versions contained two paragraphs, the first renouncing the right to war, and the second stating that armed forces would not be maintained.

General MacArthur's initial version read as follows:

War as a sovereign right of the nation is abolished. Japan renounces it as an instrumentality for settling its disputes and even for preserving its own security. It relies upon the higher ideals which are now stirring the world for its defence and protection.

---

[29] *Military Situation in the Far East* (Hearings before the Committee on Armed Service and the Committee on Foreign Relations, United States Senate, Eighty-second Congress, First Session ... Part 1), Washington, US Senate, 1951, p. 223. The relevant section is quoted in Sissons, 'The Pacifist Clause of the Japanese Constitution', p. 45.

[30] Shidehara Kijurō, *Gaikō gojūnen* (Fifty Years in Diplomacy), Tokyo, Yomiuri Shinbunsha, 1951, pp. 211–13. Shidehara in effect claims responsibility for the peace clause, without specifically mentioning a meeting with MacArthur. He relates an encounter with a young man on a tram, who was emotionally haranguing his fellow passengers on the despair and destruction that the war had brought upon Japan. Shidehara contrasts this with the enthusiastic support which the people gave the government in the Russo-Japanese War, and says this brought home to him how utterly people's attitudes to war had changed. He therefore decided, as Prime Minister, but unbeknown to others, that war and armaments should be banned in perpetuity. So far as he was concerned, the Constitution was not imposed by the Americans against the will of the Japanese.

[31] Takayanagi, 'Some Reminiscences', pp. 86–8.

[32] Sissons, 'The Pacifist Clause of the Japanese Constitution', p. 46. For instance, Yoshida, who was a Cabinet minister at the time, and later succeeded Shidehara as Prime Minister, thought it more likely that MacArthur suggested the peace clause to Shidehara, who may then have 'replied with enthusiasm'. *The Yoshida Memoirs*, vol. 1, p. 102.

No Japanese Army, Navy or Air Force will ever be authorised and no rights of belligerency will ever be conferred upon any Japanese force.[33]

In the GHQ draft worked out by the Government Section and presented to the Japanese Cabinet on 13 February 1946 the sentence about 'higher ideals' was dropped, as, more significantly, was the phrase 'even for preserving its own security'. There was a further change in the text of the agreed draft published on 6 March, the first paragraph of which read: 'War, as a sovereign right of the nation, and the threat or use of force, is forever renounced as a means of settling disputes with other nations.' This version, in which war, instead of being simply abolished as a sovereign right of the nation, is renounced *as a means of settling disputes with other nations*, could conceivably be regarded as permitting defence against invasion, or participation in international sanctions.[34]

The most important change to the wording of the article was introduced on the initiative of Ashida Hitoshi (later to be Prime Minister, in 1947–8) during the course of debates in Parliament. An additional phrase was attached to the beginning of each of the two paragraphs of the article, ostensibly to reinforce and clarify its pacifist purpose. The final version, therefore, read as follows:

> Aspiring sincerely to an international peace based on justice and order, the Japanese people forever renounce war as a sovereign right of the nation and the threat or use of force as a means of settling international disputes.
>
> In order to accomplish the aim of the preceding paragraph, land, sea and air forces, as well as other war potential, will never be maintained. The right of belligerency of the state will not be recognized.

The real significance of the additional phrases (as Ashida admitted later) was one of qualification rather than reinforcement. Now that the 'aim' of the first paragraph was 'an international peace based on justice and order', the ban on land, sea and air forces in the second paragraph could be regarded as qualified in so far as it was now designed to accomplish the 'aim' of the first. Presumably, in an imperfectly peaceful world, other aims, such as defence preparedness against aggression, might be regarded as legitimate. The logic of this interpretation may well be regarded as flawed, since the 'aim' of the first paragraph might better be seen as the renunciation of war by Japan. Nevertheless, this was the interpretation that took hold, in right-wing circles at least.

There is evidence that this interpretation was understood at the time by SCAP, who did not disapprove.[35] If this is the case, it goes some way to supporting the conclusion that article 9 was initially intended as a stratagem, to forestall criticism and interference from the Far Eastern Commission, and that later on, even before the onset of the Cold War had started to change American foreign policy priorities, SCAP was content to see the original purport of the article emasculated. It is ironic indeed that despite this article 9 should have become a potent weapon in the hands both of left-wing opponents of American foreign policy

---

[33]   Quoted in SCAP, *Political Reorientation of Japan.*, vol. 1, p. 102.
[34]   Sissons, 'The Pacifist Clause of the Japanese Constitution', p. 47.
[35]   Ibid., p. 48.

within Japan and of conservative politicians such as Yoshida, who could use it to combat American pressure for heavy Japanese defence spending, exerted during the period of economic recovery in the 1950s.

The existence of article 9 did not prevent the emergence of the euphemistically named Ground, Maritime and Air Self-Defence Forces (*Rikujō, kaijō, kōkū jieitai*), formed under their present names in 1954. Their existence, size, cost, location, equipment and permitted roles were to attract recurrent controversy. Although a Cabinet minister was in charge of defence matters, the Defence Agency (*Bōeichō*) was not elevated to the status of Defence Ministry (*Bōeishō*) until January 2007.

Up to the 1990s public opinion was firmly in favour of retaining the peace clause. When pollsters asked whether the Constitution should be revised in order formally to permit the existence of armed forces, the response was negative.[36] Many polls showed that the peace clause concerned respondents much more than any other constitutional issue.[37] These same polls, however, coming after criticism of Japan over its role in the first Gulf crisis, showed that respondents wishing to revise the Constitution (already an increasing proportion)[38] were worried especially that article 9 inhibited Japan from making an international contribution.[39]

A decade later the threat from terrorism, following the September 2001 attacks in the United States, the problems with North Korea and the emergence of China as a major power, were plainly affecting Japanese public opinion about the Constitution. The context was further changed by the government having placed constitutional revision on its active agenda. A poll by the *Yomiuri* (revisionist in editorial policy) on 8 April 2005 gave 61 per cent of respondents in favour of constitutional revision, with 44 per cent in favour of revising the peace clause, 28 per cent of the opinion that the existing article could be flexibly interpreted and did not need revision, and a further 18 per cent taking a strict constructionist view of the article.[40] Polls conducted by the relatively pro-constitution *Asahi* consistently recorded lower levels of revisionism, but by the 2000s revisionists were in a clear majority even in *Asahi* polls. The question 'Should the Constitution be revised?' elicited support from 46 per cent of those polled in 1997, 47 per cent in 2001, 53 per cent in 2004, 56 per cent in 2005 and 55 per cent in 2006.[41] So far as the peace clause was concerned, 36 per cent in 2005,

---

[36]   In favour, 13%; against 81% (*Asahi Shinbun*, 1 January 1991); in favour, 5.1% of those expressing a revisionist view (*Yomiuri Shinbun*, 31 March 1994).

[37]   For instance, 51%, ahead of 28% for environmental issues (*Yomiuri Shinbun*, 2 May 1991). For rather similar poll results in the 1990s, see *Mainichi Shinbun*, 27 April 1993; *Yomiuri Shinbun*, 31 March 1994; *Yomiuri Shinbun*, 6 April 1995; *Yomiuri Shinbun*, 5 April 1996. This last poll gave a lead of 9% for the peace clause over the environment.

[38]   Pro-revision 33.3%, anti-revision 51.1% (*Yomiuri Shinbun*, 2 May 1991); pro-revision 46.7%, anti-revision 36.4% (*Yomiuri Shinbun*, 5 April 1996).

[39]   For instance, 53.7% of those favouring revision (*Yomiuri Shinbun*, 5 April 1996).

[40]   *Yomiuri Nenkan*, 2006, p. 348. In the same poll 47% thought that issues relating to the peace clause were the most important constitutional issue, as against 27% citing issues relating to the imperial family, 26% citing privacy issues and 24% the environment.

[41]   *Asahi Shinbun*, 3 May 2006. Opponents of revision amounted to 39% (1997), 36% (2001), 35% (2004), 33% (2005), and 32% (2006).

and 43 per cent in 2006, thought that it should be revised, whereas 51 per cent in 2005 and 42 per cent in 2006 thought it should remain intact.[42]

Increased interest in constitutional revision since the 1990s elicited a number of proposals for revision from various political perspectives. These are usefully translated and discussed in *Japan's Contested Constitution* by Hook and McCormack.[43] The best-known of these is a complete revised draft Constitution published by the *Yomiuri Shinbun* in 1994. This relatively conservative newspaper tackled the issue of article 9 by replacing its second paragraph with a new article specifically authorizing a self-defence organization, while placing it securely under the authority of the Prime Minister and banning conscription. A new article was also proposed authorizing international cooperation activities, including participation in peacekeeping missions. But perhaps the most surprising amendment was a sentence in the first paragraph of the article banning weapons of mass destruction, glossed as chemical, biological and nuclear weapons. The existing Constitution does not contain such a ban.[44]

The following year (1995) the more progressive *Asahi Shinbun* produced a document which, though not a draft Constitution as such, presented six broad proposals. These included retaining the peace clause intact, enacting an international cooperation law, creating a peace support corps, scaling down the Self-Defence Forces to confine their mission to the defence of Japan, replacing Cold War security arrangements by emphasis on peace in Asia as a whole, and taking the initiative to reform the UN into a healthier world body.[45]

Around the same period the intellectual journal *Sekai* (World) sponsored a proposal for minimal Japanese defence capacity coupled with international efforts towards world peace. The authors of the report did not draft a revised constitutional text, but outlined how pacifist ideals might be developed through constitutional means.[46]

A proposal from a more conservative standpoint was made by Ozawa Ichirō, as leader of the Liberal Party, in 1999. His solution to the peace clause issue was to maintain the two paragraphs of article 9 intact, but to add a third paragraph that would read: 'The regulation in paragraph 2 does not prevent the maintenance of military power for the purpose of exercising Japan's right of self-defence against military attack by a third country.' Central to Ozawa's view of the world was a belief in the United Nations, which he described as 'the only global organization for peace'. He therefore proposed a new article, to follow article 9, in the following terms: 'In order to maintain, and restore, international peace and

---

[42]   Ibid. The 2006 poll gave respondents the choice of revising the first paragraph of the article, revising the second paragraph, or revising the whole article. The 43% in favour of revision represents the total of responses to these three options, which were, respectively 9%, 16% and 18%.

[43]   Glenn D. Hook and Gavan McCormack, *Japan's Contested Constitution: Documents and Analysis*. London and New York, Routledge, 2001.

[44]   Ibid., pp. 55–91.

[45]   Ibid., pp. 129–60.

[46]   Ibid., pp. 92–128.

safety from threats to, the collapse of, or aggressive actions against, peace, the Japanese people shall contribute positively to world peace, through various means including taking the lead in participating in international peacekeeping activities, and supplying troops.'[47]

In October 2005 the Liberal Democratic Party published its own proposal for a revised Constitution. It seems likely that this will be the basis for whatever revision it may eventually present to Parliament and the people for approval. The draft retained intact the first paragraph of article 9, but scrapped the second paragraph and in its place substituted three paragraphs, making four in all:

Article 9 (1). Aspiring sincerely to an international peace based on justice and order, the Japanese people forever renounce war as a sovereign right of the nation, and the threat or use of force as means of settling international disputes [unchanged].

(2) In order to guarantee the peace and independence of our nation, as well as the security of our nation and our people, we shall maintain Military Forces for Self Defence (*Jiei gun*), under the supreme command of the Prime Minister.

(3) Military Forces for Self Defence, in carrying out activities in pursuance of its duties under the preceding articles, shall submit to the approval of the Diet and other authorities.

(4) Apart from activities in fulfilment of its duties established in the first paragraph, and according to the provisions of the law, the Military Forces for Self Defence may act to cooperate internationally so as to maintain the peace and security of international society, as well as maintaining public order in emergency situations, and in order to defend the people's livelihood and freedom.[48]

Given the proclivities of the LDP under the Koizumi administration, perhaps the most surprising aspect of this proposal was that the party proposed to retain intact the first paragraph of the peace clause. Takemi Keizō, a member of the House of Councillors' special committee on the Constitution, spoke on the matter in the following words: 'If we were to change paragraph 1, Japan's pacifist beliefs might be shaken, so it is better to leave it as it is.'[49] The limitations, however, that article 9 imposed on military operations overseas lay essentially in the second paragraph, as nearly all revisionists were well aware. With 'the right of belligerency of the state' not recognized in the Constitution, justifying despatch of troops overseas was like stretching a piece of elastic to breaking point; in other words, revision by interpretation had obvious limits. The controversial change in designation proposed from 'Self-Defence Forces' (*Jieitai*) to Military Forces for Self-Defence (*Jiei gun*) looked radical but did not impose new legal obligations, whereas paragraphs 2, 3 and 4 set out the legal framework, basic tasks and obligations of the Forces, with the duty of contributing to international peacekeeping clearly indicated.

[47]   Ibid., pp. 161–76.
[48]   Full text in *Asahi Shinbun*, 29 October 2005.
[49]   Ibid.

Judicial Review

The 1946 Constitution for the first time gave to the Supreme Court the power of constitutional review. Article 81 reads: 'The Supreme Court is the court of last resort with power to determine the constitutionality of any law, order, regulation or official act.'

Under the Meiji Constitution of 1889, the courts had no power whatever of reviewing governmental acts. Constitutional issues were politically, not legally, determined. The introduction of judicial review in the post-war Constitution had a strong American flavour, and was obviously derived in large measure from the famous case of Marbury v. Madison. In the Suzuki case of 1952, which related to the constitutionality of the National Police Reserve (predecessor of the Self-Defence Forces),[50] it was determined that the Supreme Court should not act as a constitutional court to determine matters of constitutionality in the abstract, but should act 'only where a concrete legal dispute exists between specific parties'. Otherwise the Supreme Court would be in danger of assuming 'the appearance of an organ superior to all other powers in the land, thereby running counter to the basic principle of democratic government: that the three powers are independent, equal, and immune from each other's interference'.[51] In practice, the Supreme Court has been reluctant to exercise its power of judicial review, in contrast to the situation in the United States. The *Yomiuri* proposals envisaged the establishment of a separate constitutional court, rather on the German model, to examine acts of the executive and legislature involving issues of constitutionality. Such a court could take up issues referred to it by one-third or more of the members of either house of Parliament, by request from another court, or in relation to appeals against Supreme Court decisions.[52]

The LDP draft published in 2005 did not propose a constitutional court, but provided for a military court, of lower status than the Supreme Court, in order to try cases relating to military matters.[53] This of course was premised on revisions to the peace clause that would legitimize the Self-Defence Forces as Military Forces for Self-Defence. The historical background was a series of judgments by the Supreme Court that had basically opted out of pronouncing on the constitutionality of either the Self-Defence Forces or American military bases on Japanese soil.

The most famous of these cases was the Sunakawa decision of 1959, which was the first to involve the peace clause directly. In 1957 seven demonstrators were charged with breaking into the US Air Force base at Tachikawa, in the western suburbs of Tokyo, following a protest against the extension of a runway onto agricultural land. The penalty they faced, under a law derived

---

[50]   A translation of the judgment is given in John M. Maki, with translations by Ikeda Masaaki, David C. S. Sissons, and Kurt Steiner, *Court and Constitution in Japan: Selected Supreme Court Decisions, 1948–60*, Seattle, University of Washington Press, 1964, pp. 362–5.

[51]   Maki, *Court and Constitution*, p. 48.

[52]   Hook and McCormack, *Japan's Contested Constitution*, pp. 78–9.

[53]   This was placed as an extra paragraph in Constitution, article 76. Text in *Asahi Shinbun*, 29 October 2005.

from the Administrative Agreement accompanying the Japan–US Security Treaty of 1951, was heavier than it would have been had they been found guilty of trespass onto civilian property. The Tokyo District Court acquitted the defendants, on the specifically constitutional grounds that the Security Treaty, and thus the Special Criminal Law based on the Administrative Agreement, was illegal under article 9 of the Constitution. The Tokyo Public Prosecutor's Office immediately appealed to the Supreme Court, which quashed the lower court decision.[54]

A wide variety of opinions was expressed by the 15 judges, but the formal judgment used the doctrine of the 'political question'. The judgment pointed out that the Security Treaty was of a 'highly political nature' in the context of the present case, and possessed 'an extremely important relation to the basis of the existence of our country as a sovereign nation'. Arguing, therefore, that it was Cabinet, Parliament and ultimately the 'sovereign people' that should decide on matters such as this, the court concluded that 'the legal decision as to unconstitutionality ... falls outside the right of judicial review by the courts, unless there is clearly obvious unconstitutionality or invalidity'.[55]

Four successive cases in the 1970s and 1980s – the first, second and third Naganuma Nike Missile Site cases (1973, 1976 and 1982) and the Hyakuri Air Base case (1989) – permitted further testing through the courts of the constitutionality of military bases.[56] In 1973 the Sapporo District Court in Hokkaidō held that the construction of an anti-aircraft missile base for the Self-Defence Forces violated the Constitution, and was therefore not in the interests of public welfare as prescribed by the Forestry Law. This was the first time that the SDF had been found to be unconstitutional by a district court. But later both the Sapporo High Court, in 1976, and the Supreme Court, in 1982, managed to avoid the issue of constitutionality in passing judgment on the Naganuma Nike Missile Site case. The 1989 Hyakuri Air Base case concerned the sale of a parcel of land to the Defence Agency. The sale was challenged on constitutional grounds, but the Tokyo High Court in1981 and the Supreme Court in 1989 found technical grounds on which to avoid the issues of constitutionality.

In a further case, in 1990, a group of citizens of Okinawa failed in a bid to overturn on constitutional grounds expropriation of property for American military bases, since the Naha District Court held such seizure to be in accordance with the Constitution.[57] As we shall see in Chapter 12, the issue of American bases on Okinawa was to become a matter of sharp political dispute and tension from 1995 onwards. The issues are tangled, but it would be difficult to argue that the courts were an effective instrument in upholding either the letter or the spirit of the Constitution on issues related to military bases in Okinawa.

---

[54]   For a translation of the judgment, supplementary opinions and opinions of the various Supreme Court judges in the Sunakawa case, see Maki, *Court and Constitution*, pp. 298–361.
[55]   Maki, *Court and Constitution*, pp. 305–6.
[56]   For details of these cases, see Beer and Itoh, *The Constitutional Case Law of Japan*, pp. 30–2 and 83–141.
[57]   Beer and Itoh, *The Constitutional Case Law of Japan*, p. 32.

Rights and Duties of the People

Chapter 3 of the Constitution contains a long list of rights and duties, and in 1946 this part of the document was remarkably progressive by international standards. The rights guaranteed are both more extensive and less qualified by concomitant duties than in the corresponding section of the Meiji Constitution. Of the 31 articles in chapter 3, only four are qualified by consideration of the 'public welfare'. Articles 12 and 13 provide general qualifications, and read as follows:

> Article 12: The freedoms and rights guaranteed to the people by this Constitution shall be maintained by the constant endeavour of the people, who shall refrain from any abuse of these freedoms and rights and shall always be responsible for utilizing them for the public welfare.
>
> Article 13: All of the people shall be respected as individuals. Their right to life, liberty and the pursuit of happiness shall, to the extent that it does not interfere with the public welfare, be the supreme consideration in legislation and in other governmental affairs.

Whereas the 'public welfare' in articles 12 and 13 presumably refers to the whole of chapter 3, in articles 22 and 29 it qualifies specific freedoms, namely that of choosing one's place of residence and occupation (article 22), and the right, as defined by law, to own property (article 29).

The LDP draft published in October 2005 contained some important amendments to articles 12 and 13, in both cases strengthening the qualifications to the freedoms expressed in the articles. In article 12, the phrase 'responsible for utilizing them for the public welfare'[58] was changed to 'responsible for utilizing these rights in the awareness that freedoms and rights are accompanied by responsibilities and duties, and always enjoying freedoms without interfering with the public good and public order'.[59] In article 13, the phrase 'to the extent that it does not interfere with the public welfare'[60] was altered to 'to the extent that it does not interfere with the public good and public order'.

These linguistic subtleties are extremely important. As suggested in Chapter 3, the words *kōkyō* and *ōyake* are to an extent ambiguous between 'public' and 'official',[61] whereas in English there is a clear distinction between those two concepts. Now, *kōkyō* is used both in the existing articles 12 and 13, and in the proposed revisions of them. But there is a subtle difference between 'public welfare' (*kōkyō no fukushi*) and 'the public good' (*kōeki*), especially when 'the public good' is combined with 'public order' (*ōyake no chitsujo*). 'Public welfare' suggests the welfare of the people, whereas 'the public good' and 'public

---

[58]   *Kōkyō no fukushi no tame ni riyō suru sekinin o ou.*

[59]   *Jiyū oyobi kenri ni wa sekinin oyobi gimu ga tomonau koto o jikaku shitsutsu, tsune ni kōeki oyobi ōyake no chitsujo ni hanshinai yō ni jiyū o kyōju shi, kenri o kōshi suru sekimu o ou.* In this and subsequent articles of the LDP draft, translations are by the present writer.

[60]   *Kōkyō no fukushi ni hanshinai kagiri.*

[61]   The *kō* of *kōkyō* is written with the same character as *ōyake*.

order' suggest a situation desired by the State, or by officialdom. Those who drafted the proposed revisions would perhaps contest this interpretation, but experience indicates that this is the sense in which the revised wording is likely to be regarded by servants of the state.

In the early years of the Constitution the courts had to deal with cases involving regulations of local authorities governing demonstrations, with some authorities seeking to control demonstrations through a licensing system and others merely requiring prior notification.

Beer and Itoh drew up a sixfold classification of more recent cases: (1) equality of rights under the law; (2) freedom of economic activities; (3) rights related to quality of life; (4) rights of political participation; (5) procedural rights of the person; (6) rights and freedoms of the spirit.[62]

Cases in the first category include an obscure but significant dispute over a ruling upholding more severe punishment for killing one's father than for other kinds of unlawful killing. This pitted the Confucian respect for lineal ascendants against the principle of equality before the law. The Supreme Court in 1973 overturned its own ruling of 1950 upholding more severe penalties for patricide.[63]

In the second category, that of economic freedoms, many cases have reflected a clash between property rights and the right to engage in private enterprise against *raison d'état* or, more commonly, the sectional interests of a particular department of the government bureaucracy. The Supreme Court has sometimes found it difficult to adjudicate between these two principles, both conservative but in different ways.[64]

Cases under category 3, related to quality of life, touch on several politically sensitive issues, including the rights of employees in the public sector, such as teachers and local civil servants, to engage in union or other protest activity. The Supreme Court has tended to take a restrictive view of such rights.

The fourth category touches issues at the core of democratic practice. Electoral malapportionment had been allowed to reach a serious level by the 1980s, despite palliative measures to redress severe imbalances in the value of a vote in different parts of Japan. As late as 1983 the Supreme Court ruled acceptable a discrepancy of 526 per cent (5.26 times!) in the value of votes in a House of Councillors election. Later, the Court ruled that in the House of Representatives elections, malapportionment should not exceed 300 per cent, but even so, when the lower house electoral system was revised in 1994, the discrepancy between best and worst remained more than 300 per cent.[65]

Category 5, concerning procedural rights, touches on a range of issues, some of which have political implications, such as the role of confessions in criminal investigations by police, other aspects of police investigations, problems of delay in judicial proceedings, and court procedures in the trial of political dissidents.[66]

62   Beer and Itoh, *The Constitutional Case Law of Japan*, pp. 29–30.
63   Ibid., pp. 32–3 and 143–81.
64   Ibid., pp. 34–6 and 183–221.
65   Ibid., pp. 38–41 and 355–421.
66   Ibid., pp. 41–4 and 423–48.

The final category, that of rights and freedoms of the spirit, covers a rich vein of judicial interpretation on a wide range of issues, many with political overtones. Their diversity is summarized by Beer and Itoh in the following words:

> government seizure of allegedly obscene publications, visa denial in relation to political speech, press disclosure of untruths classified as state secrets, the newsman's privilege to refuse to identify confidential sources, published response to a newspaper advertisement attacking a political party, press defamation of public figures, the legality of vote canvassing, discriminatory restraints on courtroom note taking, separation of the *Shintō* religion from the state, and the downplay of unpleasant wartime history in high school textbooks certified by the Ministry of Education, Science and Culture.[67]

Cases concerning the separation of religion and the state deserve elaboration. Article 20 of the 1946 Constitution was designed to guarantee freedom of religious belief and avoid the kind of state manipulation of *Shintō* that had occurred up to 1945. But when the municipal authorities of the city of Tsū in Mie Prefecture participated in a *Shintō* ground-breaking ceremony, they no doubt assumed they were engaging in a customary social activity and were surprised to fall foul of the constitutional prescription that 'the State and its organs shall refrain from ... religious activity'.[68] The case brought against them reached the Supreme Court, which found in a majority verdict that the ceremony in question, though connected with religion, was in essence social and secular, and 'will not have the effect of promoting or encouraging *Shintō* or of oppressing or interfering with other religions'.[69]

In 1988 the Supreme Court pronounced on a case in which the Christian widow of a deceased member of the Self-Defence Forces had challenged the constitutionality of a decision to 'enshrine' the soul of her late husband, without her permission, in a *Shintō* shrine. Her case failed in the Supreme Court on complex grounds.

These cases illustrate the difficulty of maintaining the letter of article 20, where religion and society at the local level are intertwined; but they also show that the legacy of State *Shintō* up to 1945 continues to reverberate in the political and judicial arenas.

Apart from the amendments to the general articles 12 and 13 made in its 2005 draft revision of the Constitution, the LDP proposed a number of specific revisions to the later articles of chapter 3.

Article 14 bans discrimination on grounds of race, creed, sex, social status or family origin. To this the revised draft added disability.

A second clause was added to article 19, which guarantees freedom of thought and conscience, in order to meet current concerns about privacy in the electronic age: 'No person [shall face a situation in which] information about himself is unjustly obtained, stored or used. Secrecy of communication shall not be violated.'

---

[67]   Ibid., p. 44.
[68]   Constitution, article 20, paragraph 3.
[69]   Beer and Itoh, Beer and Itoh, *The Constitutional Case Law of Japan*, pp. 478–91, at p. 483.

A substantive revision was proposed to the contentious third paragraph of article 20, concerning freedom of religion. The existing clause reads: 'The State and its organs shall refrain from religious education or any other religious activity.' This had led to court cases such as that in the city of Tsū, described above. It was therefore proposed that it should be amended and expanded to read: 'The State and its organs shall refrain from religious education and other religious activities *exceeding the sphere of social etiquette and customary activities*,[70] as well as activities having religious significance that amount to aid, encouragement, promotion, pressure or interference in respect of a particular religion.'

In the 1946 Constitution, the second paragraph of article 21 reads: 'No censorship shall be maintained, nor shall the secrecy of any means of communication be violated.' This first clause here was retained, but a change in the second was proposed: 'The State has the responsibility to explain to the people concerning national administration.' The altered formulation gives the government greater discretion in matters of surveillance and disclosure.

The LDP draft proposed the addition of two extra paragraphs to article 25 (which guarantees minimum standards of wholesome and cultured living), so as to take into account environmental concerns and the rights of crime victims: first, 'The State shall strive to conserve the environment, so that the people will be able to receive the benefits of a satisfactory environment,' and second, 'Victims of crime have the right to receive treatment consistent with their dignity.'

An expansion was proposed for the second paragraph of article 29, on property rights. The existing paragraph reads: 'Property rights shall be defined by law, in accordance with the public welfare.' To take into account intellectual property rights, the following amendment was proposed: 'The content of property rights shall be determined by law, in order to be in conformity with the public good and public order. In these circumstances, attention shall be paid, concerning intellectual property rights, to improving the intellectual creativity of the nation and bringing about an energetic society.'

Other, more minor, amendments in the LDP draft are not considered individually here; but it can be seen from the extracts given above that the amendments sought to combine some 'traditional' LDP themes (redressing the balance between rights and duties, softening the ban on state involvement in religious ceremonies, etc.) with the introduction of new themes touching on contemporary concerns (rights of the disabled, environmental rights, rights of crime victims, intellectual property rights, etc.).

Parliament (National Diet)

Proposed changes to chapter 4 of the Constitution, on Parliament, were rather few; but among them was an amendment to paragraph 1 of article 54, to clarify the primacy of the Prime Minister's role in dissolving Parliament: 'The Prime

---

[70] Emphasis added. The Japanese is: *shakaiteki girei mata wa shūzokuteki kōi no hani o koeru ...*

Minister decides on dissolution of the House of Representatives under article 69 or under other circumstances.' The draft proposed that an extra section should be added to the final article, 64, of chapter 4, in order to formalize the status of political parties:

> Reflecting the fact that political parties are an indispensable element in parliamentary democracy, the State shall work for the just protection of their activities and for their healthy development.
> 2. No limit shall be placed on the freedom of political activities by parties.
> 3. In addition to that provided in paragraph 2, articles concerning parties shall be established in law.

Prime Minister and Cabinet

The draft proposed a subtle change in the powers of the Prime Minister. Whereas the existing Constitution, in article 72, states that the Prime Minister 'exercises control and supervision over various administrative branches', the LDP draft added the element of coordination: 'The Prime Minister exercises control and supervision over various administrative branches,[71] and conducts general coordination of them.' In the list of functions of Cabinet under article 73, the existing Constitution specifies that Cabinet should 'prepare the budget, and present it to the Diet'. To the budget, the LDP draft added 'bills' – a curious omission in the Constitution as written.

The sixth Cabinet function listed in the Constitution specifies that Cabinet orders 'cannot include penal provisions'. The draft proposed to amend this to 'cannot impose duties or restrict rights'.

In general, the revisions proposed to chapters 4 and 5, which concern the central structure of politics and government, were surprisingly modest.

The *Tennō*

Article 1 of the Constitution reads: 'The Emperor shall be the symbol of the State and of the unity of the people, deriving his position from the will of the people with whom resides sovereign power.'

What seems most surprising about the LDP draft in relation to the *Tennō* is that it left this once contentious article intact. Nor was any explication of the *Tennō*'s status proposed in relation to his duty of '[r]eceiving foreign ambassadors and ministers' (article 7). For many years conservatives had found the status of 'symbol' objectionable, and in particular found it difficult to accept that the *Tennō* was not designated 'head of state'.

Some minor changes were proposed elsewhere in chapter 1, but they amounted to little more than a tidying exercise. The draft did not follow the more radical proposal contained in the 1994 *Yomiuri* draft, that this chapter should become chapter 2, with a new chapter 1 asserting the principle of popular sovereignty.[72]

---

[71]   *Gyōsei kakubu o shiki kantoku suru.*
[72]   Hook and McCormack, *Japan's Contested Constitution*, pp. 56–8.

Preamble

The preamble, however, was another story. The LDP draft proposed a major revision of the existing preamble, presumably on the grounds that it was too strongly American-influenced, and hinted at its origins as an 'imposed' document. The existing preamble reads:

> We, the Japanese people, acting through our duly elected representatives in the National Diet, determined that we shall secure for ourselves and our posterity the fruits of peaceful cooperation with all nations and the blessings of liberty throughout this land, and resolved that never again shall we be visited with the horrors of war through the action of government, do proclaim that sovereign power resides with the people and do firmly establish this Constitution. Government is a sacred trust of the people, the authority for which is derived from the people, the powers of which are exercised by the representatives of the people, and the benefits of which are enjoyed by the people. This is a universal principle of mankind upon which this Constitution is founded. We reject and revoke all constitutions, laws, ordinances, and rescripts in conflict herewith.
>
> We, the Japanese people, desire peace for all time and are deeply conscious of the high ideals controlling human relationship, and we have determined to preserve our security and existence, trusting in the justice and faith of the peace-loving peoples of the world. We desire to occupy an honoured place in an international society striving for the preservation of peace, and the banishment of tyranny and slavery, oppression and intolerance for all time from the earth. We recognize that all people of the world have the right to live in peace, free from fear and want.
>
> We believe that no nation is responsible to itself alone, but that laws of political morality are universal; and that obedience to such laws is incumbent upon all nations who would sustain their own sovereignty and justify their sovereign relationship with other nations.
>
> We, the Japanese people, pledge our national honour to accomplish these high ideals and purposes with all our resources.

The revised preamble in the LDP draft of 2005 was shorter than the original, and less high-flown. It dwelt on internationalist ideals, while adding the theme of patriotism, and sought to reflect the world of the early twenty-first century, rather than that of the mid-twentieth:

> The Japanese people, based on their own will and determination, as a sovereign people establish this new Constitution.
>
> We maintain the symbolic emperor system. We continue popular sovereignty and democracy, liberalism and respect for fundamental human rights, pacifism and internationalism, as unchanging values.
>
> The Japanese people, in the spirit of affection for the country and society to which we belong, hold in common the duty ourselves to defend them, we aim to develop a free, fair and active society, as well as the fulfilment of national welfare, and we value the promotion of education, the creation of culture and the development of local autonomy.
>
> The Japanese people, demanding sincerely an international peace based on justice and order,[73] shall cooperate with other countries for its realization.

---

[73] This phrase is virtually repeated from the beginning of article 9.

Recognizing the plurality of values in international society, we shall make constant efforts to extirpate tyranny and human rights infringements.

The Japanese people, believing in symbiosis with nature, shall bend our efforts to defend, not only the environment of our own country but also the irreplaceable global environment.

Conclusions

Constitutional debate in Japan over more than half a century has principally concerned the peace clause, article 9. But, as we have seen, there are a number of other constitutional issues that are also important. Over the years differences have emerged between the older generation of revisionists, who in certain respects were nostalgic for the Meiji Constitution of 1889, and modern revisionists, who wish to modernize the Constitution by introducing such elements as environmental conservation and privacy guarantees. The former wished to strengthen central executive powers at the expense of the legislature and popular rights, and to make the Constitution more nationalistic and less internationalist. They were concerned with the status of the *Tennō* and of course particularly unhappy about what they regarded (rightly or wrongly) as the imposition of the Constitution upon a defeated nation by the occupying authorities after the war.

Revisionists today have inherited some of these concerns, including a recognition that Japanese social reality is not identical with that of the United States, but they are also more inclined to support modernizing initiatives, which may be positively democratic in character.

Running through the whole debate there remains a fundamental divide. On the one side are those who wish for Japanese defence policy to be that of a 'normal state', so that Japan could constitutionally project military force overseas if required by the dictates of national defence or the need to contribute to international peace and security. On the other side are those who fear a change in the constitutional status quo on defence, conscious that for 60 years under the existing Constitution their country has been at peace, that forward defence brings with it its own perils and that it may not always be wise to trust the intentions of their own government. The balance since the 1990s has swung in the direction of the former, but revisionists are well aware of the latent strength of pacifist sentiment that might scupper chances of constitutional revision.

There is also, for revisionists, the difficult issue of surmounting the obstacles placed in the way of revision by article 96. The LDP draft proposes to lower the requirement of a two-thirds majority of all members of each house of Parliament (followed by a simple majority in a popular referendum), so that it would be sufficient for each house to show a 50 + 1 per cent majority.

Given, however, that revision can be successful only if the *existing* requirements of article 96 are fulfilled, revisionists face the problem that it would be risky to propose too radical a set of revisions. Indeed, this may well explain the generally cautious tone of the 2005 LDP draft. The mid-1990s draft put forward by the *Yomiuri* was decidedly more adventurous, interesting and inherently democratic. There have even been suggestions that the government should propose constitutional revision focusing on one single item: revision of article 96. Then, when the revision hurdles had been lowered, the government would come back with its full revision programme, which would have a much better chance of succeeding. Whether the electorate would fall for such a stratagem, however, and provide the required simple majority in a referendum, seems doubtful.

The 1946 Constitution was based on two main pillars: democracy and pacifism. On both these counts it may be regarded as having served Japan extraordinarily well, whatever its origins. Constitutions do not solve everything, and Japan is neither ideally democratic nor immune to possible future temptations to conflict. There have been problems of accountability in Japanese politics, as well as nodules of irresponsible politico-economic power sometimes given the label of 'crony capitalism'. The changes in the structure of the system since 2001 are in the main positive. There is certainly a case to be made for a new Constitution that would reflect the new reality of an economically and politically mature system. But unfortunately the legacy of the past makes the Constitution not so much difficult to revise (though it is), as difficult to revise in a responsible and enlightened manner. The question is not only *whether* revision of the Constitution should go ahead, but if so *what* revisions should be attempted, in order to write a Constitution appropriate for Japan in the twenty-first century.

Chapter 11 | Issues of Domestic Political Concern

In Japan, as in most other democracies, the average elector is more concerned with economic policies impinging on his or her daily life than with the broad constitutional, environmental or civil liberty issues that tend to interest intellectuals. Similarly, domestic issues in general are more likely to concern electors than foreign policy issues, though the balance changes in time of war or serious international conflict short of war. In the case of Japan, the traumatic events that culminated in defeat on 15 August 1945, and the history that followed, meant that war-related issues of all kinds were prominent in the minds of electors for a considerable period. The end of the war, however, also marked a complete break with the pattern of regular warfare (nearly a war a decade) that all Japanese had known since the late nineteenth century. The six decades from 1945 have been a time of peace, peace has become the norm from the perspective of most electors, and this has fostered a certain parochialism.

Even so, the Japanese electorate is, on average, well educated and capable of reacting to political choices in sophisticated ways. Japanese people have access to a huge range of information sources that touch on political, social and economic issues, some of them superficial and sensational, others of high quality. It is true that since the 1990s interest in politics appears to have declined, but where issues that really interest people arise close to an election, the number of people casting a vote tends to increase.

Japanese electors, much like their counterparts elsewhere, are most concerned with politics where it affects their own interests. But interests are channelled in ways conditioned by predominant social structures and norms, habits of political interaction and patterns of power distribution, as well as what we may call 'historical memory'. This is why, despite much similarity between the ways in which Japanese electors react and the ways in which their counterparts elsewhere react, the former do exhibit some special features which need to be explored.

In the rest of this chapter, we shall group issues under five broad headings: economic, social, environmental, judicial and political, with sub-headings attached to each. Some issues could be placed under more than one heading, in which case our choice of category is to some extent arbitrary. On some issues, our focus will be on the parameters of debate, but on others, we shall concentrate rather on the structure underlying a particular situation. Our selection of issues is by no means comprehensive, but is aimed at giving, so far as possible, an accurate and balanced picture.

Economic issues

Economic system

The Japanese economy over the early post-war decades may be described as a development economy, in much the same way that Chalmers Johnson categorized the Japan as a 'developmental State'.[1] That is to say, the government, together with leaders of major companies, cooperated in a common enterprise of promoting rapid economic growth, with the aim of transforming the economy in as short a time as possible into one that would be at the top rank in international terms. It was not a 'command economy' in the Marxist–Leninist sense, nor was it 'dirigiste' in the way of some European economies of the same period, but government nevertheless exercised a great deal of control over the way the economy moved forward, acting, however, in what Johnson termed a 'market-conforming' manner.[2] Johnson's analysis remains controversial, and flew in the face of much standard economic orthodoxy based on American-style free market capitalism, while also challenging social democratic ideas of the time.

The particular area of controversy that is involved here concerns the extent to which government could actually control, the direction that industry was inclined to take. Putting it crudely, the contrary argument is that the economy would have grown rapidly from the 1950s even in circumstances of a 'nightwatchman state'. Certainly it is true that cheap labour, cheap energy and other factors of production were readily available in the 1950s and 1960s, and Japan benefited from a relatively liberal international trading regime, without being required to open up its own markets to international competition. But it can be argued in defence of Johnson's position that the government reinforced the determination of industrialists to invest in new industries, that much capital for investment was raised through the banking system (over which the government exercised important control), and that the government refrained from diverting a substantial proportion of resources into social welfare.

On the other hand, the circumstances underlying the developmental state of the post-war years did not long outlive the early 1970s. The first and second oil crises, American pressure on Japan to liberalize its economy, revaluation of the yen, greater competition in international markets and various bottlenecks at home required a new politico-economic structure. The economy grew impressively for

[1]   Chalmers Johnson, *MITI and the Japanese Miracle: The Growth of Industrial Policy, 1925–1975*, Stanford, CA, Stanford University Press, 1982.
[2]   Johnson, *MITI*, pp. 317–19.

much of the 1980s, but stagnated through much of the 1990s, following the collapse of what came to be termed the 'bubble economy'. The difficulties of the banking system, saddled with huge quantities of non-performing loans, inhibited investment and made recovery problematic. By the late 1990s the economy had sunk into a deflationary pattern from which it was hard to escape. Unemployment rose to unprecedented levels, even though they seemed low by European standards. Neither supply-side reforms nor Keynesian remedies did much to overcome these problems.

The new millennium saw some economic improvement, though much of the recovery was export-led. The Koizumi government, as we have seen, expended a great deal of energy in its attempts to liberalize the economy and eliminate nodules of vested interest. Japan, in any case, was now a mature economy, so that the rates of economic growth experienced in the post-war years were unlikely to be repeated. It also remained the second largest economy in the world, with a high average standard of living. But the health of the economy remained the most important issue that governments needed to address.

Work and employment

Employment practices have changed to some extent since the 1980s, but it is important not to exaggerate the reach and magnitude of these changes. The most salient characteristic of employment since the war has been that the proportion of employees hired with the expectation that they would remain with the same firm for the rest of their working lives has been much higher than in other comparable economies.[3] This is known as the permanent employment system (*shūshin koyō seido*). Especially in the larger companies, the distinction between regular and non-regular employees is important. Regular employees are hired for an indefinite period, whereas non-regular employees have a termination date, though it may be renewed. Regular employees have more generous fringe benefits than non-regular employees, of whom many are women. For a major company, its non-regular workforce acts as a kind of buffer, giving the firm the flexibility to dismiss labour should economic circumstances worsen.[4]

Several implications of this system are important. First, regular employees on contracts giving indefinite tenure receive annual salary increments until late in their careers, when the increments tail off. This is known as the seniority system (*nenkō joretsu seido*). Second, recruitment to labour unions has mainly been of regular employees in large firms. Union membership among non-regular employees, and employees in general in smaller firms, has been much lower. Moreover, most unions have been 'enterprise unions', that is, unions based on a particular company, or enterprise. Third, the distinction between

---

[3]   For comparative statistics, see Marcus Rebick, *The Japanese Employment System: Adapting to a New Environment*, Oxford and New York, Oxford University Press, 2005, table on p. 14.

[4]   Rebick, *The Japanese Employment System*, pp. 16–33. Rebick points out that the courts tend to give protection to non-regular employees comparable with that due to regular employees (p. 17).

white- and blue-collar workers was less distinct than in much of Europe, for instance. Fourth, a longstanding institution is the 'spring struggle' (*shuntō*), which was established in 1955 and serves to coordinate the wage-bargaining activities of myriad enterprise unions. Finally, there is a debate about whether the celebrated 'loyalty to the firm' of regular employees derives from elements of Japanese culture, or whether material incentives to remain with the same firm may not be a more important explanatory factor.[5] However this may be, commitment to the company by regular employees appears to be particularly high in the Japanese case.

Changes have taken place in response to altered economic circumstances since the 1980s, but the system of employment has been adjusted rather than transformed. The principal adjustments are that there is a slight decrease in employment tenure among men (but an increase among women), firms are using more non-regular workers in the interests of flexibility and cutting labour costs, and performance-related pay is to some extent modifying the seniority system. Employment opportunities for women have been improving, including at senior level.[6] Union membership is in steady decline, and currently stands at around 18 per cent of the workforce. Moreover, the acrimonious labour struggles of earlier years are now much rarer.

Distribution of life-chances

Japan since the rapid economic growth period of the 1960s has been a society in which differences of income and wealth have been comparatively narrow. This led to the widely expressed opinion that, to all intents and purposes, Japan was a 'middle-class society'. Overwhelming percentages of respondents to public opinion polls asking what social class they thought they belonged to replied 'middle class'. It was rather difficult to establish how far this was a reflection of objective reality and how far a matter of perceptions. But it is reasonable to suppose that the declining popularity of Marxist and semi-Marxist political appeals from the 1960s onwards was related to the fact that relatively few people stood out as either extremely rich or extremely poor.

Some observers refused to take the concept of a society in which nearly everybody was middle class as a reflection of that society's true nature. In 1983 the Marxist scholar Rob Steven published *Classes in Contemporary Japan*, arguing that there was a crucial class difference between a labour aristocracy on the one hand – composed of regular workers in large firms, enjoying generous fringe benefits and lifetime guarantees of employment – and on the other hand more marginal employees. The latter included part-time and casual workers in large firms, as well as most of the workforce of small-scale firms. These were often locked into dependent and exclusive subcontracting relationships with one or other of the major companies.[7] Leaving aside the Marxist framework of analysis, some of the points Steven made were cogent, in that the life-chances of

---

[5] Ibid., pp. 17–18.
[6] Ibid., pp. 171–4.
[7] Rob Steven, *Classes in Contemporary Japan*, Cambridge and New York, Cambridge University Press, 1983.

the two 'classes' of employee were indeed significantly different. Also, women were disproportionately represented among casual and part-time workers, though many of them were secondary, rather than primary, breadwinners.

Despite Steven's analysis, however, it was clear that in financial terms the gap between the two 'classes' was not as great as income and wealth differentials in many comparable societies. And with fairly steady, rapid and widely diffused increases in personal income, the psychological impact of these differences was also for the most part tolerable.

Economic stagnation during the 1990s and early 2000s, however, has once more opened up debate about inequalities in Japanese society, with the belief becoming widespread that since the late 1980s discrepancies in life-chances have been widening. As early as 1993, the sociologist Ishida Hiroshi argued that class was the strongest determinant of income inequality and home ownership in Japan. He concluded that 'Class appears as a critical variable in explaining inequality in Japanese society, probably more so than educational credentials or occupational status.'[8] More recently, Rebick has shown that whereas social mobility was rising in the post-war years, especially because of the great movement of population out of agriculture and into urban occupations, it has more recently declined. He suggests that the most important reason for this may be the increase in numbers of children entering private education. Since it requires ample family resources to afford this, it is the children of fathers who are managers who tend to become managers, whereas those whose fathers cannot afford private schools (as well as supplementary cram schools or *juku*) earn less money in their less prestigious careers.[9]

Much recent media coverage has been given to 'freeters' (those moving from casual job to casual job, often with periods of unemployment), and NEETs (those 'not in employment, education or training'). The government has shown concern about the fact that these categories of people are not embedded in the employment system, and has explored various kinds of training scheme.[10] An attempt by the Ministry of Health, Labour and Welfare to regularize the employment of freeters by giving them the status of full employees (*sei shain*) in companies was withdrawn in response to complaints by employers that they would be unreliable.[11] In a society where being outside regular institutions (notably employment) is widely regarded as problematic, the presence of a relatively large number of freeters, NEETs etc. has become a matter of general concern.

Social

Issues of social structure and the family

As we saw in Chapter 3, the Japanese family was officially regarded in the pre-war period as the central building bloc of the social structure. It was hierarchical

---

[8]   Hiroshi Ishida, *Social Mobility in Contemporary Japan*, London, Macmillan, and Stanford, CA, Stanford University Press1993, p. 260.

[9]   Rebick, *The Japanese Employment System*, pp. 108–11.

[10]   *Asahi Shinbun*, 3 November 2006.

[11]   *Asahi Shinbun*, 25 November 2006.

and paternalistic. Marriages were largely by arrangement between two families, though the prospective couple usually had some say in the choice of match. By extension the *Tennō* was portrayed as the 'father' of the Japanese family.

Since the war, families have evolved away from the pre-war model, though some traces of it remain. Worried commentary on the changing state of Japanese families fills the mass media. For instance, absent fathers, spending long hours at work and long hours commuting to and from work, have been seen as a problem weakening the family. Various forms of juvenile delinquency have been obsessively discussed, even though delinquency rates are relatively low by European and North American standards. But the biggest change to have taken place since the war is the declining birth rate. Whereas before the war the average number of births per woman was around five, a report published in December 2006 confirmed that the average was 1.26, equivalent to the lowest figures in European countries.[12]

The problem of a declining birth rate is generally viewed in conjunction with the phenomenon of an ageing population. Since the 1970s, the expectation of life at birth for both males and females has been the highest in the world. In 2006 it was reported as 78.53 for men and 85.49 for women.[13] This is expected to create severe imbalances between age groups within two decades from 2006, the year when the population has apparently peaked at just over 127 million. The need to support the family in order to boost the birth rate forms the key element in a government plan announced in January 2007, which expressed doubts about the efficacy of financial aid to families with small children, though some was being offered. Officials were inclined to link problems of overwork by breadwinners, the prevalence of freeters and the falling birth rate, as the following statement by an official of the Ministry of Health, Labour and Welfare demonstrates: 'The short time spent with families [by fathers] because of long working hours does not bode well for the future of people's lives, while the increase in numbers of young, non-regular, employees who want to have a family but have no family, risks further accelerating the declining trend of births.'[14]

Immigration

One obvious solution to the twin problems of a declining birth rate and an ageing society would be immigration. This, however, is a solution that successive governments have been reluctant to pursue, largely on grounds of social cohesion. During the economic boom of the late 1980s numbers of foreign workers, mainly from other parts of Asia, and also Iran, entered Japan to work on building sites and in other sectors. Some of them were illegal entrants, including visa overstayers, and reports circulated (some no doubt exaggerated) that immigrants were involved in criminal activity. On the other side of the picture, some lacked access to social security and lived in poor housing conditions. In the 1990s the government was prepared to allow immigration from Brazil and other parts of

---

[12]   *Asahi Shinbun*, 21 December 2006.
[13]   *Asahi Shinbun*, 26 July 2006.
[14]   *Asahi Shinbun*, 4 January 2007.

Latin America, mainly of people who had Japanese ancestry. The reason for this preference was that such people would more easily fit into Japanese society, but since most of them were the children or grandchildren of Japanese emigrants, their attitudes were more Latin American than Japanese.

In any case, the numbers of immigrants that would be required to stabilize the Japanese population at its current level would be in the hundreds of thousands, and a practicable level of immigration could make only a marginal contribution to solving the problem. On the other hand, the requirement for recruits into the caring professions (nursing, for example), to look after increasing numbers of elderly people, may be difficult to fulfil from within Japan, so that this is a type of immigration that may well increase.

Social welfare

Japan enjoys a sophisticated system of health insurance, in which large-scale public funding (national insurance, *kokumin hoken*) is combined with widespread private provision, including company schemes for employees. A system of health-care provision based on large public hospitals, smaller private hospitals and individual doctors' surgeries is complex and impossible to describe in a short space. Central policy-making involves the Ministry of Health, Labour and Welfare, interested politicians (including a small number of parliamentarians with a medical background), pressure groups such as the Japan Medical Association (*Nihon ishikai*) and the Ministry of Finance.

Decision-making on social welfare issues involves much bureaucratic politics, with different bureaucratic entities pursuing different if overlapping agendas, and compromises having to be struck at every turn. A major study by John Creighton Campbell on welfare policies towards the elderly gives many examples of muddle and confusion along the way, but identifies a largely consistent policy line, namely that 'much of the burden of the aging process will be borne by the Government'.[15] The political will existed in the early 1980s for an alternative policy, namely a 'Japanese-style welfare society', in which families rather than the state would look after their elderly relatives, but for various reasons the change was never implemented.[16]

A related area is that of pensions policy, where Japan faces a similar problem to that of other advanced states, though in a more acute form because its population is ageing more rapidly than theirs. The problem is one of inter-generational inequality, in that later generations of those active in the workforce risk being burdened with heavier costs of providing for pensions (of lower value) than the present generation. Possible solutions include raising the age from which pensions are payable, increasing premiums and reducing entitlement. A further issue debated between the government and the DPJ concerned what proportion of pension funds should come from taxation and what proportion from insurance. The DPJ wanted to have pensions funded entirely out of taxation, but without raising

---

[15]   John Creighton Campbell, *How Policies Change: The Japanese Government and the Aging Society*, Princeton, NJ, Princeton University Press, 1992, p. 392.
[16]   Ibid.

the level of consumption tax above the existing 5 per cent; the improbability of covering the full cost by this means made it difficult for the party to maintain unity on the issue. The government parties sought to save money by bringing civil service pensions into line with private sector pensions. A report by the National Personnel Authority, however, showed that public sector pensions were actually lower than those in the private sector.[17]

Education

Ever since the American-inspired reforms to education during the Occupation period, the education system has been fertile ground for political controversy. The role, rights, assessment and remuneration of teachers, government control of textbook content, equality versus variety of educational provision, as well as whether it should be compulsory for schools to fly the national flag and have their students sing the national anthem, are all issues with a long history.[18] An issue that is currently much discussed is school violence, including bullying.[19] During the first three decades after 1945 it would have been difficult to find an area in which Japanese were more thoroughly polarized than that of education. The Occupation authorities had sought to reform the content, democratize the structure and expand the scope of the pre-war education system. In place of nationalistic history textbooks, officially sanctioned *Tennō*-worship and government-designed courses on official ethics, the content of instruction was liberalized and modernized. Decision-making was placed in the hands of local 'boards of education' administering schools whose structure was essentially uniform. To make education available to all, the number of state schools and universities was greatly increased.

During the 1950s education was subjected to the reactionary policies of the 'Reverse Course'. The Ministry of Education resumed control from local boards, and refused to negotiate or communicate with the left-wing Japan Teachers Union (*Nikkyōso*). On the initiative of Nakasone as Prime Minister in the mid-1980s, serious attempts were made to reform the system to make it less uniform and to provide more parental choice. Nakasone wanted to encourage creativity and experimentation, but he also disliked the educational legacy of the Occupation. He faced immense difficulties in getting the educational establishment to change its practices,[20] but some reforms along the lines he had proposed were implemented in the 1990s.[21] To some extent reform has been the inevitable consequence of the partial privatization of educational provision, at secondary,

[17]   *Asahi Shinbun*, 9 December 2006.
[18]   A well-made film about teacher protests against coercion of schools in relation to the national flag and anthem is *Kimigayo fukiritsu* (Not Standing for the National Anthem). See http://www.vpress.jp.
[19]   During November 2006 the media reported a number of instances of school bullying leading to suicide of pupils.
[20]   Leonard Schoppa, *Education Reform in Japan: A Case of Immobilist Politics*, London and New York, Routledge, 1991.
[21]   Christopher P. Hood, *Japanese Education Reform: Nakasone's Legacy*, London and New York, Routledge, 2001.

and still more at tertiary, levels.[22] State universities, including the prestigious Tokyo University, in 2004 relinquished Ministry of Education control and took on the status of corporate bodies (*hōjin*).

The question of state control over the contents of school textbooks, most contentiously history textbooks, continued to cause concern in Japan, and serious friction with neighbouring countries, most notably China and South Korea. Right-wing politicians disliked textbooks that focused on Japanese atrocities during the war, such embarrassing issues as the coercive use by the military of 'comfort women' as prostitutes for servicemen, or the human experiments conducted by the notorious biological warfare 'Unit 731' of the Imperial Japanese Army on Chinese and other victims in the early 1940s in Manchukuo. Prominent politicians, including the high-profile Governor of Tokyo Prefecture, Ishihara Shintarō, denied the veracity of standard accounts of the Nanjing massacre by Japanese troops in 1937. One result of textbook control was that many teachers refrained from teaching about the Asia–Pacific War at all, so that many children remained largely ignorant about it throughout their schooldays. In August 2001 the Education Committee of Tokyo Prefecture approved a textbook written by a right-wing group called the Society to Create New History Textbooks (*Atarashii rekishi kyōkasho o tsukuru kai* – often abbreviated to *Tsukuru kai*). Subsequently, however, very few schools indeed actually adopted it.[23]

In December 2006, the Revised Basic Education Law (*Kaisei kyōiku kihon hō*) passed its last parliamentary stage and became law. As discussed in Chapter 6, the new law shifts the balance from the primacy of the individual towards public responsibility, and includes a much debated 'patriotism clause'.

Even though much mass-media space is given to the more dysfunctional aspects of education, schools since the Occupation have delivered high levels of literacy and numeracy to the vast majority of the school-age population. For the most part Japan has avoided the problems seen elsewhere when a barely literate and hardly numerate subclass of the population is allowed to develop, with serious social consequences. In the case of universities, on the other hand, there is a wide gap between the most favoured institutions, some public, some private, and the less favoured ones, almost all private. The less prestigious universities face a critical shortage of students, given that the population of the student age group has sharply fallen. University mergers and closures are in prospect, while many institutions try to make ends meet by attracting overseas students, many of them from China.[24]

Religion

'Separation of church and state' was a basic principle of the Allied Occupation after the war. What this meant in practice was that State *Shintō* should no longer

---

[22]   Some 30% of senior high school pupils (aged 15–18) study at private establishments, and many also attend private cramming schools (*juku*). The bulk of universities have long been in the private sector.

[23]   *Asahi Shinbun*, 8 and 16 August 2001.

[24]   Roger Goodman, 'The Concept of *kokusaika* and Japanese Educational Reform', *Globalisation, Societies and Education*, vol. 5, no. 1, March 2007, pp. 71–87.

have a political role and that the *Tennō* should not be regarded as a god. Religion in Japan, however, represents a very different set of variables from religion in countries whose principal tradition is Christian. The main traditions are Buddhist and *Shintō*, but these are closely intertwined with each other. To be married according to *Shintō* rites, then buried according to Buddhist rites, is not seen as anomalous. Japanese religious thinking is polytheistic rather than monotheistic, and, with some exceptions, adherents of different sects or traditions are tolerant of each other. The concept of war in defence of a particular faith (separately from a clan or nation) is perplexing to most Japanese.[25] Broadly speaking, religious observance is much more widespread than actual belief. Many Japanese will explain that their countrymen are secular, whereas religious observance is clearly widespread. In terms of belief systems, however, Japan is indeed predominantly secular. As we saw in Chapter 10, the separation of religion from the state embodied in article 20 of the 1946 Constitution sometimes caused problems where local authorities wished to participate in ceremonies originally having a religious content.

There have been a number of political issues relating to religion in post-war Japan. After the war many 'new religions' arose, not surprisingly in view of the discrediting of State *Shintō* and the social turmoil that followed the war. The biggest and best-known of these is the *Sōka Gakkai*, the only religious organization to found a significant political party, the Clean Government Party, or *Kōmeitō*, which is now in government. Other religious groups, however, seek to have an impact on politics. For instance, in the 1980s the Religion and Politics Research Association (*Shūkyō seiji kenkyūkai*) represented a number of religious groups, and sought to influence mainly LDP parliamentarians in favour of conservative positions on social issues.

Since the 1980s a number of new sects have appeared, being given the collective title of 'new new religions' (*shin shinshūkyō*). The most extreme of these was the *Aum Shinrikyō*, some of whose members released the poisonous sarin gas on the Tokyo subway system in 1995. This event led to a widespread reaction against religion in general, but particularly to aspects of the charitable status of religious groups embodied in post-war legislation. The police felt that they had been inhibited in their investigations of the *Aum Shinrikyō* by the privileges granted to religious groups under the existing law. In October 1995 Parliament passed a more rigorous Religious Corporate Body Law (*Shūkyō hōjin hō*), against the wishes of other religious groups, in particular the *Sōka Gakkai*.

Women

As we saw in Chapter 9, the number of female members of Parliament has been rising significantly from very low levels in the post-war years, and the 2005 lower house elections saw a remarkable increase in the number of women elected under the LDP label. Koizumi's first Cabinet, formed in April 2001, included no fewer than five women members out of a total of 18 – a record number.

---

[25]   When the present writer has tried to explain the 'troubles' in Northern Ireland to Japanese people, he has met puzzled reactions.

Significantly, two of these were from outside Parliament.[26] Later Cabinets, it is true, had fewer female members than this, but it would now be difficult for a Prime Minister to include no women in his Cabinet, as was the practice, with rare exceptions, until the late 1980s.

The gradual progress of women to some prominence in the profession of politics reflects the significant advances of highly educated women in a range of careers. Even though the bulk of women in the workforce are in positions of relatively low status and pay, increasing numbers of women rise to responsible managerial positions. The reluctance of men to serve under women managers has to a considerable degree dissipated. Given the high-level educational attainments of large numbers of women, they constitute an intellectual and technical resource of enormous value. The high incidence of late marriage, of reluctance to marry at all and of what has been termed the 'birth strike' suggests that large numbers of women now set themselves ambitious career goals. Thus it is surprising that more progress has not already been made.

Cultural values inhibiting career progress by women are no doubt changing, but still appear in unexpected forms. In February 2000, the recently elected woman Governor of Ōsaka Prefecture, Ōta Fusae, wished to present in person the Governor's Prize at the local *sumō* wrestling championships, but was refused permission by the Japan Sumō Association (*Nihon sumō kyōkai*), on the ground that tradition forbade women to enter the *sumō* ring. It appears, however, that public opinion was on her side. The *Asahi* ran a telephone poll shortly afterwards, in which 47 per cent of those polled supported the Governor and 37 per cent supported the Japan Sumō Association. Curiously enough, more men (48 per cent) than women (45 per cent) were on the side of Ms Ōta. In the case of men, responses were about even across the various age groups, whereas women divided sharply, with 50–60 per cent of those under 50 supporting the Governor, but only 32 per cent of women in their sixties and 19 per cent of women in their seventies giving her their backing.[27]

In March 2005 three parties in opposition (DPJ, JCP, SDP) put forward a bill in the House of Councillors to permit married couples to maintain different surnames. This was the eleventh time that such a bill had been proposed since December 1999, though, in the face of cautious and conservative attitudes from the ranks of the LDP, it had only been debated twice.[28] In existing law, a couple on marriage may register their surname either as that of the husband or as that of the wife. In the overwhelming majority of cases it is the husband's family name that is chosen. What the law does not permit, however, is the registration of separate surnames for wife and husband. Impetus for the proposed change came largely from upwardly mobile career women. The bill also proposed a

[26]   *Asahi Shinbun*, 27 April 2001.
[27]   *Asahi Shinbun*, 24 February 2000. The ban on women entering the *sumō* ring has religious overtones, with the ring being considered sacred by traditionalists. This may perhaps explain the negative views of older women, who tend to be the most religious stratum of the population.
[28]   *Asahi Shinbun*, 31 March 2005.

shortening of the period in which remarriage after divorce was forbidden, and the granting of equal inheritance rights for illegitimate and legitimate children.[29] Divorce rates, though rising, have been far lower than in Europe, while the proportion of children born out of wedlock has been static for many years at around 1 per cent. It seems likely that the highly conservative legal framework is part of the explanation for this.

Environmental

Pollution cases

Policies towards the environment have been debated since at least the late 1960s, and have occasioned a number of important government initiatives over the years. After the war Japan was slow to recognize the importance of the environment, which was largely ignored in a headlong rush for economic growth. A number of appalling tragedies resulted, of which the best known was the appearance of 'Minamata disease', a type of mercury poisoning affecting the nervous system, from the 1950s. A company producing nitrogenous fertilizer, at the fishing port of Minamata in Kyūshū, was over a long period discharging mercury effluent into the bay, where it entered the food chain and disastrously affected many hundreds of people.[30] Other cases concerned cadmium poisoning, asthma among schoolchildren and residents close to an oil refinery, and photochemical smog in big cities caused by chemicals in the atmosphere reacting to summer heat.

The urban environment in particular had become so polluted by the late 1960s that the LDP came to perceive it as an issue that could cost it office. The consequent changes in policy are an interesting example of governmental responsiveness to the pressure of an electorate that held the ruling party's fate in its hands. During the 1970s environmental regulations were tightened up, particularly in relation to control of air and water pollution. The air in big cities became noticeably more bearable as polluting factories were forced out, and car exhausts emitted smaller quantities of toxic fumes. The government succeeded in what was perhaps its principal purpose, namely to reduce the political impact of the environment as an issue.

Nevertheless, important problems remained. Although a tightening of regulations made it unlikely that disasters on the scale of Minamata would recur, individual victims of such tragedies still found the task of gaining compensation through the cumbersome court system a time-consuming and exhausting business. Highly polluting factories forced to relocate outside big cities often moved offshore, typically to parts of South-East Asia having less stringent environmental regulations, giving rise to accusations that Japan was exporting its pollution.

[29]   Ibid.
[30]   A moving account of the Minamata tragedy is W. Eugene Smith and Aileen M. Smith, *Minamata*, London, Chatto & Windus, 1975.

Visual pollution

Within Japan itself, even though much has been done to improve the quality of air and water, and to ensure the safety of consumer products, problems of 'visual pollution' persist. Whether it is in the cities or in the countryside, functional but unaesthetic concrete buildings provide an unappealing background to what is often spectacular natural scenery.[31] Similarly, many rivers are encased in concrete, many are dammed,[32] and concrete has invaded long stretches of coastline. These are not life-threatening or health-impairing issues, nor is Japan alone in blighting its landscape, but train journeys in many parts of Japan can be a depressing experience to anyone brought up to expect zoning regulations, preservation of green belts and prevention of ribbon development. Gavan McCormack has used the term 'Construction State' to describe these phenomena.[33] André Sorensen, in a recent book, comments:

> Rapid and unplanned urban growth ... contributed greatly to environmental degradation in Japan. The spread of factories and housing was responsible for a highly visible loss of environmental amenities, as beaches and coastal areas disappeared beneath landfills for industrial complexes, hills and forests were razed and paddies filled in for new housing. [This was exacerbated by] the weak land use planning system, as much development proceeded haphazardly, ... and the issue of urban sprawl ... became widely discussed as a critical problem facing Japanese cities in the 1960s.[34]

The planning system did, however, improve somewhat under pressure from environmental groups in the 1970s and later. Japanese cities, especially in central areas, are more attractive than they used to be, but the legacy of poor or non-existent planning still blights huge areas of rural and semi-rural Japan.

Nuclear power stations

An environmental issue that has attracted particular attention is that of nuclear power stations. It is not surprising that the production of electricity from nuclear power should have been seen as an attractive option for a country as resource-poor as Japan. The government conducted a concerted campaign of persuasion in the late 1970s and 1980s to convince people that nuclear power was an attractive and safe option, producing much less pollution than conventional power stations. A number of well-publicized problems at nuclear power stations over the

---

[31]   It has to be admitted that the earthquake danger makes construction in brick or stone unacceptable. Concrete has replaced wood as the principal building material, reducing the fire hazard from earthquakes and other causes.
[32]   On the cost of dam construction, see *Asahi Shinbun*, 13 February 2004.
[33]   Gavan McCormack, *The Emptiness of Japanese Affluence*, New York, M. E. Sharpe, 1996, pp. 25–77.
[34]   André Sorensen, *The Making of Urban Japan: Cities and Planning from Edo to the Twenty-first Century*, London and New York, Routledge, 2002.

years have, however, from time to time cast doubt on the competence of management in the industry, with particular concern being expressed about cover-ups.[35]

The natural environment

By the 1980s Japan had gained an unenviable reputation overseas for predatory action in relation to the natural environment, particularly concerning whaling, the stripping of tropical timber from Borneo and elsewhere, the importation of ivory and a range of other concerns.[36]

Whaling is an issue that has attracted widespread international publicity. The questions it raises are complicated, but most international observers are puzzled by the strength and persistence of Japanese government commitment on whaling. A moratorium on commercial whaling was imposed in 1982, leading to the virtual demise of the (never large) Japanese whaling industry. Japanese people have also shown little interest in having whale meat back on the menu, and Japan receives widespread international criticism for its pro-whaling stand, which includes killing a certain number of whales for 'scientific purposes'. Nevertheless, the government persists in fighting the issue through the International Whaling Commission, which it has sought to bend to its point of view by recruiting new members sympathetic to its position. While cultural factors are put forward in support of whaling, the explanation for government policy appears to lie elsewhere. The right to catch whales is defended on the grounds of precedent. It is crucial for Japan not to have further restrictions placed on its fishing activities, so that intransigence on whaling is meant as a signal of its determination to defend the principle of using sea creatures as a resource. Bureaucratic politics also seems to be involved, since the Cetacean Research Section of the Ministry of Agriculture, Forestry and Fisheries has been allowed for the most part to control policy in this area.[37]

Judicial

Courts

Japan enjoys a judicial system with a long history and depth of experience. It is often said that Japanese society is non-litigious, and indeed cultural factors may go part of the way towards explaining this, in so far as it is true. But a further factor is that the judicial system has worked to inhibit litigation because of

---

[35]   For instance, an explosion at the nuclear power plant at Tōkai mura, north of Tokyo, led to a decision by government in April 1997 to dissolve Dōnen, the organization responsible for running it.

[36]   On these issues, see Miranda A. Schreurs, 'Domestic Institutions and International Environmental Agendas in Japan and Germany', in Miranda A. Schreurs and Elizabeth Economy (eds), *The Internationalization of Environmental Protection*, Cambridge and New York, Cambridge University Press, 1997, pp. 134–61; Isao Miyaoka, *Legitimacy in International Society: Japan's Reaction to Global Wildlife Preservation*, Basingstoke and New York, Palgrave Macmillan, 2004.

[37]   I am grateful to Roger Smith for insights into the whaling issue. See also Amy L. Catalinac and Gerald Chan, 'Japan, the West, and the Whaling Issue: Understanding the Japanese Side', *Japan Forum*, vol. 17, no. 1 (March 2005), pp. 133–63.

cumbersome court procedures and the length of time it takes for many cases to be brought to a conclusion. Government inhibition of 'excessive' litigation by restricting the number of judges appointed may have contributed to delays in the handling of court cases. Obviously there are pros and cons of a litigious society. A society that is highly litigious is unlikely to be harmonious, as individuals or organizations readily – and sometimes frivolously – pursue disputes against their neighbours through the courts. On the other hand, a society where serious obstacles are placed in the way of legal redress risks giving an unfair advantage to the strong over the weak. As the difficulties experienced by the victims of pollution disasters have shown, the search for redress by the politically and socially weak against the strong and unscrupulous can be a hard and lengthy road. The Japanese ideal of harmony is admirable in many ways, but comes at a cost.

Court cases are investigated by prosecutors, and few criminal cases come to court in which the conclusions of the prosecutors are negated by the court itself. This approach has thrown the spotlight on police handling of suspects. A particular area of contention is the reliance placed on confessions, with evidence suggesting that a great deal of pressure is placed on suspects to confess. This issue is explored cogently in the film directed by Suo Masayuki, *I just didn't do it*, released early in 2007.[38]

Crime

With good reason, Japan is often praised as a nation where the level of crime – particularly violent crime – is low by international standards. One reason cited is the extremely tight gun laws, which make personal ownership of most types of gun virtually impossible, though some guns are in the hands of criminal gangs (see below). Another is efficient control of drugs and prevention of their entering the country. The ways in which the police handle crime may also be significant. Their approach has been based essentially on community policing, with the local police box (*kōban*) being the centre of police relations with the community. The police generally have more detailed knowledge about the comings and goings of people in their area than would be acceptable in most of Europe or North America, but there has been wide support for a high level of intrusiveness in the interests of crime prevention and control.[39] So far as habitual criminals are concerned, the police are used to being tough, and prison regimes are, by most accounts, harsh.

Gangsters

Organized criminal gangs are referred to as *yakuza* or *bōryokudan*. *Yakuza* is a word derived from gambling,[40] while *bōryokudan* literally means 'violent group'. The relations between the police and such gangs remain controversial, and stories may be heard of semi-cooperative relations between the two. The police may indeed prefer to have criminals in an organized environment where surveillance

---

[38]   Suo Masayuki, director, *Sore demo boku wa yatte inai* (I just didn't do it), 2007.
[39]   Schoolteachers are also involved in community policing by keeping their charges out of pleasure arcades and the like.
[40]   *Yakuza* is stressed on the first syllable, not the second.

is easier than in the case of random crime by individuals, though accusations of police corruption in this sphere sometimes surface. In any case, the law relating to criminal gangs has been progressively tightened, forcing some groups to reorganize themselves into semi-legal businesses.[41] The role of *sōkaiya*[42] (criminals who extract payment from companies against a promise not to disrupt shareholders' meetings, or alternatively are employed by companies to keep shareholders' meetings in order) became highly controversial in the late 1990s, with some company directors facing disgrace for having paid off *sōkaiya* – a practice previously regarded as inevitable, if not acceptable. So far as political crime is concerned, it is to be noted that the police, possibly bending to political pressure, have been far tougher on ideologically motivated violence conducted by the far left than on similar activities by the far right.

The death penalty

In Japan, unlike Europe where absence of capital punishment is a requirement for membership of the European Union, the death penalty remains on the statute book, making Japan the only advanced country apart from the United States where this continues to be the case. A small number of convicted murderers are executed every year, with minimum information given by the authorities and limited, though apparently increasing, media interest. Public opinion polls indicate a majority in favour of the death penalty for heinous crimes, and there are some indications that a rise in violent crime has reinforced opinion in favour of it. In the two or three years up to 2004 the death penalty had been imposed in increasing numbers by lower courts, though many of these cases were held up on appeal to the Supreme Court.[43] On the other hand, there has also been increasing pressure for the death penalty to be abolished. A Minister of Justice in the early 1990s refused on religious grounds to approve executions. The Minister of Justice appointed to the new Cabinet in November 2005 indicated that he was in favour of abolishing the death penalty and would refuse to sign death warrants. Within hours, however, he was forced to retract his statement, saying that he had made it 'in his private capacity'.[44]

Political

Political issues relating to the conduct of politics, the nature of the political system, the distribution of power, the Constitution, how election systems work, the problem of corruption, relations between central government and local authorities, and the impact upon politics of culture, history and external influences,

---

[41] Peter B. E. Hill, *The Japanese Mafia: Yakuza, Law and the State*. Oxford and New York, Oxford University Press, 2003.
[42] Again, the stress is on the first syllable.
[43] *Asahi Shinbun*, 28 March 2004. The newspaper lists 47 appeals against the death penalty currently before the Supreme Court.
[44] *Asahi Shinbun*, 1 and 2 November 2005.

have been discussed elsewhere in this book. In this final section of the present chapter, we shall examine questions relating to rights and freedoms, civil society, nationality and minorities, and historical memory.

Rights and freedoms

In Chapter 10 we discussed chapter 3 of the Constitution, concerning rights and freedoms. Included among these rights are equality under the law (article 14), freedom from involuntary servitude (article 18), freedom of thought and conscience (article 19), freedom of religion (article 20), freedom of assembly and association (including speech, press and other forms) (article 21) and academic freedom (article 23). A number of cases have arisen in the recent past concerning rights and freedoms under one or more of these articles.

Hansen's disease

Until 1996 sufferers from Hansen's disease (leprosy) had been separated from society in special sanatoria (*rai ryōyōjo*), despite the fact that with medicines by then available there was no good medical reason why they should not have been allowed to live in the general community. The story goes back to the Leprosy Prevention Law (*Rai yobō hō*) of 1931, and to the Eugenics Protection Law (*Yūsei hogo hō*) of 1948, which prescribed sterilization for sufferers of Hansen's disease. A revised Leprosy Prevention Law was enacted in 1953, prescribing separation of sufferers from society. An association of sufferers was set up in the 1950s and continued to put pressure on the authorities (particularly the Ministry of Health and Welfare) to bring about a change in the law. This was not effected until 1996, when the Leprosy Prevention Law was abolished and the Eugenics Protection Law was replaced by the Maternal Protection Law (*Botai hogo hō*).

In 1998 a group of sufferers brought a case before the Kumamoto District Court in Kyūshū, demanding compensation for years of de facto incarceration, and this was followed by cases in Tokyo and Okayama courts. In 2001 the Kumamoto District Court gave a judgment in favour of the plaintiffs, arguing that at least from 1960 there was no good medical reason to separate sufferers from society. The judgment also criticized the Ministry of Health and Welfare[45] for its failure to remedy matters before the Leprosy Prevention Law was abolished in 1996 – a failure it judged to be 'irrational and clearly unconstitutional'. Members of Parliament were similarly judged responsible. The court therefore awarded compensation against the state to the plaintiffs of 1,823.8 million yen.

The state prepared to appeal against the judgment, but 'wishing for a quick resolution in view of the age of the sufferers', and also no doubt fearing an adverse public reaction, Koizumi, newly elected Prime Minister, announced on 23 May 2001 that the state would not appeal.

Nearly four years later, in March 2005, a commission set up to investigate the issues involved – the Hansen's Disease Investigation Council (*Hansenbyō kenshō kaigi*) – reported to the Minister of Health, Labour and Welfare. The report

---

[45]   Its name before the reorganization of January 2001.

confirmed much of the substance of the Kumamoto judgment, but its most damning finding was that the former Ministry of Health and Welfare had used the separation provisions of the Leprosy Prevention Law in its negotiations with the Ministry of Finance to obtain budgetary allocations for the sanatoria concerned, so as to smoothe the ministry's relations with those sanatoria.[46]

Freedom of expression and communication

Japan enjoys press and media freedoms as extensive as those in other comparable countries. The newspaper world is dominated by four major national newspapers, *Yomiuri*, *Asahi*, *Mainichi* and *Nihon Keizai*, all with circulations counted in millions. There is also a range of local newspapers, serving different regions. Differences exist between the big four: for instance, the *Yomiuri* is usually regarded as somewhat to the right politically of the *Asahi* and *Mainichi*, while the *Nihon Keizai* concentrates on economic matters and is a rough equivalent of the *Financial Times* of London, or the *Wall Street Journal* of New York. Problems found elsewhere of excessive concentration of the media in too few hands are not particularly severe in Japan, though there are links between newspapers and television companies. Apart from the commercial TV stations, there is a national broadcasting channel, NHK (Japan Broadcasting Corporation, *Nippon hōsō kyōkai*), which is funded by the state. Its mission is similar to that of the British Broadcasting Corporation (BBC), namely to broadcast a high-quality output, freed from advertising constraints, and to broadcast news objectively.

NHK has been criticized for blandness, but for the most part it fulfils its mission respectably.[47] Like public broadcasters elsewhere, however, it may sometimes be subject to political pressure. On 12 January 2005, the *Asahi* published an article reporting that certain LDP members had exerted pressure on NHK in respect of a broadcast it was producing. The programme concerned a 'people's court' set up by citizens' groups, which just four years earlier had sought to determine who was responsible for the 'comfort women' system that coerced women into prostitution for the armed forces during the Asia–Pacific War. Sixty-four former 'comfort women' appeared as witnesses. A group of right-wing LDP politicians concerned with history education complained that the broadcast of the 'people's court' (of which they had been shown a preview) was biased in favour of the message it was presenting. Prominent among these parliamentarians was Nakagawa Shōichi, at the time Minister for Economics, Trade and Industry, and Abe Shinzō, then Deputy Secretary-General of the LDP, and later Prime Minister.[48] Whether or not this was connected to the complaints received,

---

[46] *Asahi Shinbun*, 12, 19, 24 May 2001, 2 March 2005. This last reference gives an extensive chronology of events concerning Hansen's disease going back to 1907.

[47] For an intriguing account of news broadcasting on NHK, see Ellis S. Krauss, *Broadcasting Politics in Japan: NHK and Television News*, Ithaca, NY and London, Cornell University Press, 2000.

[48] Nakagawa was Representative, and Abe a former Executive Director, of the 'Society of Young Parliamentarians concerned with the Future of Japan and History Education' (*Nihon no zento to rekishi kyōiku wo kangaeru wakate giin no kai*). The group was critical of school textbooks that discussed the 'comfort women' and related issues.

NHK was in the process of negotiating its budget with the government. Pressure, of course, is a loaded word, but for whatever motives, NHK substantially modified the film before broadcasting it on 30 January.[49]

We discussed in Chapter 6 attempts by the Abe government in November 2006 to put pressure on NHK to emphasize in its overseas broadcasting the issue of abductions of Japanese citizens to North Korea.

Civil society

It has often been observed that civil society in Japan is relatively weak by comparison with its counterparts in Europe, North America and Australasia. On the other hand, the Great Hanshin–Awaji earthquake, centred on the city of Kōbe, in January 1995, to which official bodies reacted in a slow and confused manner, brought into being a number of effective voluntary organizations working on the rescue effort. This gave a boost to the development of non-profit organizations (NPOs) generally. At the time of writing, rather more than a decade after the earthquake, there is undoubtedly more civil society than there was before. On the other hand, by most international comparisons it remains on the weak side. There is an inclination to believe that cultural factors are behind this, and culture should not be entirely dismissed as an explanatory variable. But a comprehensive account of civil society in Japan, edited by Schwartz and Pharr and published in 2003, demonstrates that institutional factors have been of overwhelming importance. At least up to 1998, when an NPO bill was passed, government regulations were heavily weighted against NPOs, unless they were local, service-providing groups without a significant ideological agenda. By contrast, nationwide (or international) groups with sophisticated policy platforms found it hard to gain official accreditation, and were denied tax, postal and other benefits common in other countries. Pekkanen gives the example of an anti-smoking NPO in Tokyo, whose sole full-time employee saved his group money by flying to Seoul to mail material to its mailing list back in Japan.[50]

Governmental attitudes towards civil society reflect a bureaucratic determination to stay in control, so far as possible, of activity that impinges on policy choice. Helen Hardacre, in the same volume, examines the tightening of the regulatory framework affecting religious bodies following the release of sarin gas on the Tokyo underground in March 1995. She shows how this affair enabled the authorities to reassert some of the regulatory control over religious bodies that had been relinquished in the late 1940s.[51] To the extent that civil society has advanced since the mid-1990s, we may detect a certain weakening of bureaucratic will, or power, or both.

[49]   *Asahi Shinbun*, 12 January and 25 July 2005.
[50]   Robert Pekkanen, 'Molding Japanese Civil Society: State-Structured Incentives and the Patterning of Civil Society', in Frank J. Schwartz and Susan J. Pharr (eds), *The State of Civil Society in Japan*, Cambridge and New York, Cambridge University Press, 2003, pp. 116–34.
[51]   Helen Hardacre, 'After Aum: Religion and Civil Society in Japan', in Schwartz and Pharr, *The State of Civil Society in Japan*, pp. 135–53.

Nationality and minorities

The area of nationality involves a range of important issues. Japanese citizenship, in law, is transmitted in principle through patriality, not through place of birth. This has acted as a mechanism whereby the vast bulk of Japanese citizens are of ethnic Japanese origin, and has in turn perpetuated the concept of Japanese as a homogeneous ethnic group all sharing the same citizenship. Much the largest group of ethnically non-Japanese residents, many of whom lack Japanese citizenship, are Koreans. These now include many third-generation residents of Japan, with little or no knowledge of the Korean language. At its height, the number of Koreans in Japan was some 800,000, and most of them were excluded from public service positions (including teaching) because they were not Japanese citizens. The feeling of exclusion from mainstream Japanese society set up numerous frictions between ethnic Koreans and Japanese, and this tension was further exacerbated by the fact that the Koreans in Japan were divided in their loyalties between North and South Korea. A symbolic issue for many Koreans and others was the fingerprinting requirement for the issue of visas. This requirement was relaxed (but not entirely abolished) in the early 1990s.

Another group that has suffered some discrimination is the Okinawans, who tended to be regarded as inferior by mainland Japanese before the war, suffered horrendous losses during the battle for Okinawa in 1945, and were directly administered by the United States between 1945 and 1972. The rape of an Okinawan schoolgirl by three US Marines in September 1995 brought the issue of Okinawa back into the headlines, and though the matters in dispute largely related to US military bases, an underlying theme was the Okinawans' resentment at being treated in certain senses as second-class citizens.[52] A much smaller group is the Ainu in the northern island of Hokkaidō. Most of these intermarried with ethnic Japanese, from whom, nevertheless, they are physically distinguishable. Ainu identity was a live issue from at least the 1980s, with an official tendency to treat Ainu culture in the manner of a theme park being a source of some resentment.

The largest minority group, however, was not an ethnic minority at all, but rather a separate caste (at least in its origins), namely the 'village people subject to discrimination': *hi-sabetsu burakumin*, generally known as *burakumin*. Descendants of various outcast groups from the Tokugawa period, their numbers were estimated at somewhere between a million and a half and three million people. Their greatest concentration lies in western Japan, from Kansai to Kyūshū. Subject to widespread discrimination in the job market and marriage, they were politically well organized and forceful in defence of their own interests. Tension, however, remained high between those who wished to pass as mainstream Japanese and those who were assertive of their own identity.[53]

All the groups briefly mentioned above are long-standing minorities within Japanese society. We have already referred above to immigrants from other Asian

[52]   See Glenn D. Hook and Richard Siddle (eds), *Japan and Okinawa: Structure and Subjectivity*, London and New York, Routledge, 2003.
[53]   See Ian Neary, *The Buraku Issue and Modern Japan*, London and New York, Routledge, 2008.

countries and from Latin America. Though exploitation occurred, some local authorities were making efforts to cater to the needs of this new, if limited, influx of immigrants.

The legacy of history

Even though the sixtieth anniversary of the end of the Asia–Pacific War was passed on 15 August 2005, the legacy of the 1930s and first half of the 1940s continues to haunt Japan. By a strange quirk of history, the first half-century after the defeat was completed under a Socialist Prime Minister, Murayama Tomiichi, in August 1995. Murayama, as we saw in Chapter 6, invested a great deal of effort in persuading Parliament to pass a resolution apologizing for Japanese actions during the war. Even though the resolution was more qualified and less widely supported in Parliament than the Prime Minister would have wished, Parliament went on record as deploring what had happened in the years up to 1945. Prime Ministers Hosokawa and Murayama had made personal statements of regret for the war that went substantially beyond what any of their predecessors had said, though by the exacting standards of some critics even they stopped short of a full apology.

The situation a decade later was rather different. The political balance had shifted to the right, and indeed for a year from September 2006 the Prime Minister was a man of deeply revisionist views, so far as Japanese actions during the war were concerned. In fact, among conservative politicians and their backers there was no consensus about apologizing for the war, and the issue was profoundly divisive politically. A succession of government ministers over the years had made public statements seeking to justify some, at least, of what Japan had done during the war, often citing the impetus created by Japanese military campaigns in Asia towards ridding Asia of European colonial rule. In many such cases such ministers had paid the price of making this kind of statement by being forced to resign their ministerial posts. Even so, it is remarkable that such incidents occurred with some regularity. The issue of official visits by the Prime Minister and various ministers to the Yasukuni Shrine in Tokyo, where the souls of 14 Class A war criminals are 'enshrined', goes back to the Nakasone administration in the 1980s, but was greatly exacerbated as an international bone of contention with Koizumi's regular visits while he was Prime Minister.

Concluding Remarks

In the third edition of this book (1999) we held that Japanese politics was in transition between a decision-making process based on long-standing power relationships and established practices and a much more fluid and dynamic system, in which both the nature of the issues at stake and the best ways of handling them would move on to uncharted ground. We also expected to see the gradual development of a more open and accountable system.

To a certain extent, these guesses about the future have been fulfilled. The greatest achievement of Koizumi's long tenure of office was his ability to challenge vested interests and run policy along lines that paid much more attention to the national interest, and in particular to promote economic recovery through more transparent procedures and rigorous oversight. Some useful measures were also taken to strengthen and give more autonomy to local authorities, which had been both financially stretched and subject to excessive bureaucratic interference from central government.

On the other hand, since the 1990s there has been a clear trend towards illiberal policies in certain areas, and there is much to support the argument that central government power is subject to insufficient restraint, whether from opposition parties, Parliament, the judiciary, the media or the voluntary sector. Right-wing politicians and movements (including some on the extreme right) had made significant political gains and were now focusing on their long-standing goal of revising the Peace Constitution. The need for a rebalancing of the political system was apparent.

Chapter 12 | Issues of Foreign Policy and Defence

After the Cold War

Japanese foreign policy in the mid- to late 1990s was seeking to come to terms with the great structural changes in the international system that had followed the collapse of the Soviet Union and the ending of the Cold War at the beginning of the same decade. There was little sense, however, that policy had changed fundamentally. Indeed, we commented in the third edition of this book that much of what could be said about Japanese foreign policy in the early 1980s might still be said about it in the late 1990s.[1]

At the time, it appeared that there were two principal reasons for the slowness of the Japanese response. One was the economic stagnation that preoccupied governments, coupled with a confused transition in the political system, which we have discussed in previous chapters. The political will for fundamental change in foreign policy was lacking, with the economy in bad shape and political leaders coming and going frequently, having limited impact on policy. The second reason was that whereas the ending of the Cold War in Europe had brought about the kind of systemic change that occurs once or twice a century, in Japan's own region of East and South-East Asia the impact of the Soviet collapse had been considerably less.

Let us now focus on this second factor, which has been given less emphasis than it deserves. In Europe, as the iron curtain that had divided the continent since the 1940s was pulled down, most of the former Soviet satellite states of Eastern Europe, as well as several former republics of the Soviet Union, were absorbed (or themselves sought to be absorbed) into the European sphere, with the European Union and NATO gaining new members in what had been

---

[1] J. A. A. Stockwin, *Governing Japan: Divided Politics in a Major Economy*, Oxford and Malden, MA, Blackwell, 3rd edn, 1999, p. 202.

the ambit of Soviet power. Soviet imperialism was also rolled back in the Caucasus and central Asia, though when Putin became President of Russia in 2000, attempts began to reassert Russian influence in those areas.

Momentous changes also took place in the foreign policies of the United States, which for half a century had focused single-mindedly on its strategic competition with the Soviet Union. For complex reasons that we do not need to address here, the disappearance of the Soviet enemy was followed by a focus on the Islamic world of the Middle East, and in particular, from the new millennium, on the 'war on terror'.

In Japan's region, on the other hand, much less had changed, and what may be described as the 'Cold War residue' had not been swept away. Even though China was undergoing profound economic and social change, politically it remained under the control of the Chinese Communist Party (CCP), which showed little sign of giving up its power in the interests of loosening control over local governments, or introducing elections in any real sense. Whereas a divided Germany had been reunited, the two halves of Korea remained divided, with a high state of tension on the peninsula. Taiwan showed little sign of wishing to reunite with the mainland, though China periodically hinted that it was prepared to use military force to impel it to do so.

Between Japan and Russia, the effective disappearance of a military threat to Japan from the north did not bring the long-running territorial dispute over the Southern Kurile (Chishima) islands any closer to a solution. There were also minor territorial disputes between Japan and South Korea over the Takeshima (Dokdo) rocks, and between Japan and China over Senkaku (Diaoyutai), which continued to simmer on as they had continued to do for years.[2] The Japan–United States Mutual Security Treaty, a product of the early stages of the Cold War, remained in force. The 'war on terror', a new element in international relations that became a major preoccupation for the United States and European countries, had much less impact in Japan, which did not see itself as having a great deal to fear from the terrorist activities of Islamic extremists.

The impact of change was thus significantly less for Japan than it was for either Europe or the United States, or indeed for Russia. This no doubt contributed to an inertial element in Japanese foreign-policy-making in the 1990s and at the beginning of the new millennium. This did not mean, however, that things would remain the same indefinitely, and from the perspective of 2007, it is evident that Japan faces new challenges on a number of fronts.

Options

Before we turn to recent developments, however, it is worth considering the options for foreign policy direction that might have been open to Japan after the collapse of the USSR and the ending of the Cold War. We put forward a number of

[2] For detailed analysis of these and other territorial disputes left over from the Asia–Pacific War, see Kimie Hara, *Cold War Frontiers in the Asia–Pacific: Divided Territories in the San Francisco System*, London and New York, Routledge, 2007.

possible options in the belief that what has actually happened was not inevitable. Political leaders face choices, and until a choice has been made, other choices have not been eliminated.

The first option would have been a transition to a radically pacifist foreign policy, in the spirit, and according to something close to the letter, of article 9 of the 1946 Constitution. This, however, can be ruled out as a practical possibility for several reasons, despite its popularity on the left of the political spectrum in the earlier post-war years. By the 1990s it was simply outside the area of serious consideration, given the composition of government, the balance of public opinion, the influence of the United States, the argument for 'international responsibility', a desire among policy-makers for international influence and the existence of some credible threats to national security.

The second option would have been more or less a continuation of the status quo, with the Mutual Security Treaty retained and the Self-Defence Forces kept at constant strength, but no substantive increase in Japanese defence responsibilities under the Security Treaty. Obviously, in its pure form this option would have been untenable, since it is always necessary to adjust policy to changing circumstances; but Japanese governments could plausibly have resisted American demands for greater participation, while calculating that the Americans would wish to retain the Security Treaty because through it they retained a military presence in the most strategically placed string of islands in East Asia, namely Japan. With such a policy line there was a risk of American abandonment, but a rational case could have been made out that it was a risk worth taking.

A third, and much more radical, option would have been some kind of 'Gaullist' solution, whereby Japan would opt out of most or all of its security linkages with the United States and would boost its own defence potential to the point where it could handle threats to national security and, if desired, contribute to international security, giving priority to Japanese national interests rather than those of the United States. This was a solution that had been aired during the 1960s, when General de Gaulle was still in power in France, but was decisively rejected by the Japanese governments of that period. The context, however, was that of the Cold War, including the nuclear balance between the American and Soviet superpowers. What was emerging after the end of the Cold War was a pluralistic world, although from some perspectives it was also unipolar, with the United States as the single remaining superpower. It was therefore not entirely implausible that Japan might have branched out on its own, to turn its economic power into self-determined political and strategic power, independent of, though not necessarily hostile to, the United States.

An interesting point to make about this scenario is that while it could be expected to appeal to nationalists on the right of the political spectrum, it has a logic that might also appeal to elements on the left. Those who – for often cogent reasons – rail against the increasingly close alignment of Japanese security policies with those of the United States[3] are by implication lending weight to arguments for a Japanese defence strategy that would become much more independent

---

[3]   See e.g. Gavan McCormack, *Client State: Japan in the American Embrace*, London and New York, Verso, 2007.

of the United States. It is of course not inevitable that such a policy would lead in a Gaullist direction, but it is difficult to envisage Japan finding strategic protectors elsewhere, so that Gaullist-type strategies seem a plausible alternative to the alliance with the US.

Following on from this, we should perhaps mention a fourth option that has occasionally been suggested, namely a military alliance between Japan and China. American commentators occasionally express apprehension about this possibility, and it acquires a little intellectual weight from the economic links that have developed between the two countries. Very few in Japan, however, put it forward as a serious option, and the prospect of Japan becoming a tributary state, playing its part in promoting the international ambitions of a new Chinese empire, appear remote.

The fifth option is the one that has proved to be the mainstream option from the late 1990s (and accelerating after Koizumi's accession to power in 2001), namely an increasingly close alignment with US security systems and strategic doctrines. We shall examine the nature and implications of these changes later in this chapter, but here we need to stress that this is a potential and actual set of developments with profound implications for the future of Japan. It also marks a major break with the policies of the past half-century. It seems a strange paradox that the most nationalistic administrations for many years have become wedded to the one foreign and security policy option that seems most likely to restrict the development of policies based on a Japanese perception of national interest.

The International Environment

Even if Japanese foreign policy thinking was slow to react to changes in the international environment following the ending of the Cold War, there were a number of trends, as well as specific events, that contributed to a slow process of change.

The most important regional development, which may be dated from before the Cold War ended, but whose implications have become crystal clear in the new millennium, is the economic rise of China. The famous phrase of Chairman Deng Xiaoping that 'it doesn't matter whether a cat is black or white, so long as it catches mice' has been applied with remarkable effect in China to economic development. It has led to the spectacle of a major state, run exclusively by its Communist Party, promoting largely unregulated capitalist enterprise, with the aim of maximizing national wealth in as short a time-frame as possible. Even though, in GDP terms, the Japanese economy remains more than twice as large as that of its Chinese neighbour, and although there are major economic, political and social problems to be tackled in China, the long-term implications of what is happening in China have profound implications for the world, for the region and for Japan. Beijing's defence spending has already risen to levels that are creating international concern.

A second set of developments with profound importance for Japan has occurred on the Korean peninsula. The collapse of its Soviet protector in 1991 was a catastrophe for North Korea, with grave implications for its economic viability. Many commentators in the early 1990s predicted the imminent collapse of the Pyongyang regime, but despite the famine that stalked the country in the mid-1990s, and the death of its supreme leader, Kim Il-Sung, in 1994, the regime survived, using repressive police state methods. By the mid-2000s the rulers of this impoverished state were testing long-range missiles, having already lobbed a *taepodong* missile into the Pacific the other side of Japan in the late 1990s. They also tested a nuclear device, though a belated international agreement in February 2007 provided for the suspension of the North Korean nuclear weapons programme. Earlier South Korean governments had manifested extreme hostility to North Korea, but from the late 1990s more conciliatory policies took hold, perhaps reflecting the extent to which the economic balance between the two halves of the peninsula had shifted in favour of the South. On the other hand, the US under President George W. Bush between 2001 and 2006 took a rigidly hostile line towards North Korea, forcing the regime into a corner, and quite possibly contributing to its determination to develop a nuclear deterrent as a guarantee of regime survival.

A third significant development was the first Gulf War of 1990–1, which placed Japan in the difficult situation of contributing funds to the expedition to liberate Kuwait, but being unable to supply troops because of constitutional inhibitions. Policy was modified in 1992, after the war had ended, when the Japanese Parliament passed the Peace Keeping Operations bill, permitting the despatch of Self-Defence Forces contingents to UN peacekeeping operations, under certain conditions. The first Gulf War and its aftermath led to a trend in public opinion broadly in favour of a more participatory approach to cooperation in international peacekeeping missions. Thus there was relatively little public opposition to the Koizumi decision to send troops to Iraq (for non-military tasks) in 2004.

A fourth development was the 'Guidelines Agreement' drawn up by the Clinton and Hashimoto administrations in June 1997, to put more substance into cooperation under the Mutual Security Treaty. Under this agreement Japan was obligated, in ways that had not previously applied, to assist US forces engaged in military operations. This turned out to be an early stage in a longer-term process of integration of US and Japanese security systems, involving 'interoperability' and coordination at various levels. Under the Koizumi and Abe administrations, this cooperation was taken to even higher levels.[4] The movement promoted under their leadership to revise the 1946 Constitution should be seen in the context of much closer military ties between Japan and the United States.

The United States in the new millennium has become heavily involved with the question of international terrorism, the situation in Afghanistan, the Iraq War, the Israeli–Palestinian problem and the Iranian nuclear programme. Thus the fifth development is that US foreign policies are now so heavily focused on the Middle East that policies towards other parts of the world are inevitably

[4]   Christopher W. Hughes, *Japan's Re-emergence as a 'Normal' Military Power*, Abingdon and New York, Routledge for International Institute for Strategic Studies, 2005 (Adelphi Paper 368–9).

influenced by this orientation. It seems difficult to believe, however, that the US preoccupations are the principal focus of Japan, at the deepest level, however much Japanese officials may protest Japanese concern.

Sixth, Japanese governments themselves from the 1990s were contending for permanent membership of the United Nations Security Council. This created various repercussions in the international environment. When relations between China and Japan deteriorated while Koizumi was Prime Minister, the Chinese side made it clear that it would not support, and might even seek to block, the Japanese bid. Other states, most notably Germany, India, Brazil and South Africa, also gave indications that they would like to become permanent members. In any case, the Security Council could expand its permanent membership only as part of a radical reorganization of its whole structure. And since the international will for this appeared to be largely absent, the Japanese bid remained stranded in mid-air.[5]

Reflecting on these six crucial aspects of the international environment that had emerged since the late 1990s, it seemed clear that Japan was seeking to pioneer a new international strategy, but that its flexibility in doing so was limited by the choice made several years before to integrate its security and other policies with those of the United States.

We now turn to a more detailed examination of the background of Japanese policies towards the United States, China, the two Koreas, the Soviet Union/Russia, and elsewhere.

The Background of Japan–US Relations

By far the most salient factor in Japan's foreign policy since the Occupation has been its relationship with the United States. As the Japanese economy grew and the war receded into the background, the nature of that relationship changed from a tutelary one in the 1950s, through many painful adjustments and antagonisms, to one based on complex, though largely cooperative, interactions between two major powers.

The American decision from the latter part of the Occupation to treat Japan as a major Cold War ally had profound repercussions on the relationship between the two states. Through the Security Pact of 1951, revised in 1960 as the Mutual Security Treaty, Japan received guarantees of protection in case of attack at fairly low cost in terms of its own defence expenditure. The continued occupation of Okinawa not only provided the United States with its most important strategic base in the Western Pacific, but gave the Americans a hostage to Japanese good intentions, which they did not give up until May 1972. Japan also benefited from considerable quantities of American aid (including military aid), profited greatly from the 'Korea boom' in special procurement orders for the UN forces fighting in Korea, also did well economically out of the Vietnam War, and developed a massive trade with the United States.

---

[5] Reinhard Drifte, *Japan's Quest for a Permanent Security Council Seat: A Matter of Pride or Justice?*, Basingstoke and London, Macmillan, 2000.

One crucial aspect of the Japan–US relationship after the Occupation was that it entailed a radical restructuring of foreign relations away from the pattern that had developed from the Meiji period. Up to 1945, Japan had been largely an Asian power, with an extensive overseas empire that included Korea and Taiwan, and with ever-growing interests in China. In the 1930s Manchuria became a Japanese puppet state, and from 1937 Japan began to occupy large areas of China proper. For many years it was in close and largely hostile contact with Russian (later Soviet) interests in North-East Asia. Finally, for a brief period beginning in 1941, Japan held in its possession a huge colonial empire in East and South-East Asia and the Western Pacific.

With defeat, Occupation and the onset of the Cold War, all this suddenly changed. Japan was now a weak and defeated nation, coopted as a not very significant American ally in the fight against 'international communism'. It is true that Japan became a host for US bases and troops in a strategically impor-tant region. For many years its interaction with its principal neighbours on the continent of Asia was minimal. Diplomatic relations with the USSR were not established until 1956, and even then the two states could not agree on a peace treaty or on the disposition of the variously named 'Northern Territories' or 'Southern Kuriles'. Formal relations with South Korea were not entered into until 1965; with North Korea they are still to be established; and with China, despite enormous pressure from within Japan itself, they were not established until 1972, which meant that formal relations with Taiwan had to be cut. Relations with South-East Asian countries at this period were conducted largely on the economic level, with little political content.

Japan–US relations were briefly shaken by the Security Treaty revision crisis in 1960, but it was not until the early 1970s that a new and more problematic phase in their relationship was inaugurated. In July 1971 President Nixon took a dramatic new initiative, without prior consultation with Tokyo, in announcing his coming visit to Beijing. The following month he announced the floating of the dollar against gold and a 10 per cent surcharge on imports entering the United States, with the primary and successful aim of forcing a revaluation of the yen. Japanese diplomatic recognition of China and the return of Okinawa to Japan from American administration took place the following year, but all these events were dwarfed by the impact of the first 'oil shock' of 1973–4.

The oil shock brought to an end the 15-year period of ultra-rapid economic growth, and forced Japan to restructure its economy and reconsider many of its priorities. From about this period also, America began to take a much more hard-headed view of the Japanese economy, regarding it as potentially threaten-ing to US interests. Such threat perceptions attained their height in the late 1980s, at a time when the Japanese trade surplus had ballooned out and when a specu-lative boom in Japan was prompting many Japanese firms to make daring and in some cases provocative investments in the United States. This in turn led to severe trade frictions between the two countries, a series of top-level negotia-tions – most having little effect – aimed at keeping the relationship afloat, and the emergence of widely read 'revisionist' literature designed to show that the Japanese system was different and threatening.

Over this whole period, however, the cement holding the Japan–US alliance structure together was the common threat perception engendered by the Cold

War. It is hardly surprising, therefore, that the ending of the Cold War should have given rise to fears that, with the threat suddenly removed, the structure might fall apart. The fact that it remained intact has multiple causes, but two stand out. The first is that the Americans had negotiated an advantageous deal in Japan, by which they were able to use an extensive complex of strategically located military bases (notably in Okinawa), at minimum expense, since Japan paid much of the base costs. The second, not fully emerging until the new millennium, was that right-wing conservative politicians saw in closer integration into the US strategic operations in East Asia their best opportunity to push back constitutional restraints on executive power, most particularly in relation to the projection of armed force.

The keystone of Japan–US relations since the 1950s has been the Mutual Security Treaty, and it is to a more detailed analysis of this that we now turn. As we have noted earlier, Yoshida's policy of resisting American demands for a massive Japanese military commitment had considerable success, although under the 1951 Security Treaty and the Mutual Security Assistance (MSA) Agreement of 1954 Japan found its freedom of action in the sphere of defence and foreign policy quite severely restricted by the American presence. Negotiations for revision of the Security Treaty between 1958 and 1960 were motivated on the Japanese side largely by the search for greater equality within the framework of continuing security guarantees. Although his achievement was obscured at the time by the domestic political discord that the whole issue aroused, Kishi obtained, through tough bargaining with the Americans, a number of quite significant concessions that in effect placed Japan in a more equal and favourable position than it had enjoyed under the old treaty.

The first concession, having some symbolic significance, was that the Americans agreed to renegotiate the treaty at all. Thus the stigma that attached to the old treaty, of having been entered into by Japan when it was technically an occupied power and thus not a free agent, was removed. Two specific restrictions on Japanese freedom of action (however academic they may seem in retrospect) were also allowed to lapse. One was the 'internal disturbance clause' in article I of the 1951 treaty. This had provided that American forces stationed 'in and about Japan' might 'be utilized to contribute to the maintenance of international peace and security in the Far East and to the security of Japan against armed attack from without, including assistance given at the express request of the Japanese Government to put down large-scale riots and disturbances in Japan, caused through instigation or intervention by an outside power or powers'. The other was the provision of article II that Japan would not grant, 'without the prior consent of the United States of America, any bases or any rights, powers or authority whatsoever, in or relating to bases or the right of garrison or of maneuver [sic], or transit of ground, air or naval forces to any third power'.

On the positive side, the most important achievement from Japan's point of view was the inclusion of article IV of the new treaty, the 'prior consultation' clause. This read as follows: 'The parties will consult together from time to time regarding the implementation of this Treaty, and, at the request of either Party, whenever the security of Japan or international peace and security in the Far East is threatened.' What this article was supposed to mean in practice was spelled out in the important exchange of notes between Kishi and Secretary of State Herter on 19 January 1960 (the date on which the revised Treaty was signed):

> Major changes in the deployment into Japan of United States armed forces, major changes in their equipment, and the use of facilities and areas in Japan as bases for military combat operations to be undertaken from Japan other than those conducted under Article V of the said Treaty, shall be the subjects of prior consultation with the Government of Japan.

The exact interpretation of this understanding, as well as its propriety, were subjects of recurring dispute between government and opposition parties. One of the main reasons the Socialists put forward in 1960 for opposing the revised treaty was that the 'prior consultation' clause did not provide the Japanese government with a veto over potentially dangerous military activities by the American forces stationed in and around Japan.

The prior consultation clause was at issue in a recurring controversy during the 1970s and 1980s concerning the 'introduction' of nuclear weapons into Japanese ports on US naval vessels. Since the late 1960s, official policy was to ban the 'manufacture, stockpiling and introduction' of nuclear weapons. But it was unclear what was meant by 'introduction' (*mochikomi*). Japanese governments maintained that 'introduction' was subject to the prior consultation clause. The US (unlike Japan) interpreted it as excluding the berthing at Japanese ports of US naval vessels carrying nuclear weapons. US policy was not to comment when asked about possible nuclear weapons on its ships in port, so the Japanese government could argue it was complying with the prior consultation clause, as well as adhering to the three non-nuclear principles. This stretched credibility, however, and caused periodic embarrassment.

In article III of the 1960 treaty, Japan also assumed greater obligations to contribute to a mutual defence effort, though the qualification 'subject to their constitutional provisions' was a ritual obeisance by the US to the peace clause of the Japanese Constitution. There was a similar provision in article V, which sanctioned joint action by the two states in the event of 'an armed attack against either party in the territories under the administration of Japan'.

The 1960 treaty contained three separate references (in the preamble, and in articles IV and VI) to the 'peace and security of the Far East'. This raised questions of geographical definition; there were indications in 1960 that South Korea and Taiwan were included as part of the 'Far East' (and later the Satō government officially designated them 'important' for Japanese security), but in more recent interpretations there was no question of Japanese forces being sent overseas in joint operations with the United States to defend the 'peace and security of the Far East'. The PKO law of 1992 appeared to breach this understanding to a minor degree, but it was not until the new millennium that new interpretations began to emerge.

It need not be supposed that the Japanese government was acting here out of a scrupulous regard for the Constitution as such. But a combination of domestic political pressures, suspicion of Japanese intentions on the part of neighbouring states and a preference not to be too closely identified with American policies in

Asia all contributed to an official interpretation of the Security Treaty which virtually confined the Japanese contribution to a role in the defence of Japanese territory, while providing facilities for American operations elsewhere. Prominent Americans would occasionally complain that Japan was 'taking a ride on the Security Treaty', but in practice the arrangements suited the US authorities well enough. Occasional murmurings emanating from the American military that the real purpose of the Security Treaty was to forestall irresponsible activity by Japan were of course never repeated in any official statement.

Despite the delayed response from Japan to changes in the external security situation following the ending of the Cold War, by the late 1990s the situation was clearly altering. The revised defence cooperation guidelines between Japan and the United States, which came into force in 1999, were reinforced by a Surrounding Areas Emergency Measures bill, passed by Parliament in May 1999. These and other legislative measures ensured that Japan would offer a range of services to the US forces in the case of a military emergency. These included logistical support, as well as supply, communications, transport, evacuation, search and rescue, etc.[6]

In December 2004 a replacement for the 1995 National Defence Programme Outline was published, indicating new defence thinking in relation to peacekeeping, but also concerning possible new types of threat. In addition, it relaxed previous restrictions on export of military technology to the US, and mentioned for the first time states that might pose a future military threat (China and North Korea).[7] This was a further indication of the progressive integration of Japanese defence systems with those of the US forces based in Japan, which had been taking place over the previous several years. Moreover, there were indications that this integration concerned not only threats that might occur in the vicinity of Japan, but also global threats of terrorist attacks such as those on New York and Washington in September 2001. Indeed, 9/11 had given impetus to the development of security thinking in Japan.

The most difficult issue in administering the Security Treaty has always been the question of Okinawa. The return of the islands to Japanese sovereignty in 1972 left American bases there intact, though with nuclear weapons removed. On the other hand, it has been revealed that a secret protocol was signed, permitting such weapons to be brought back in case of a war emergency.[8]

In September 1995, three American Marines raped an Okinawan schoolgirl. This provoked outrage throughout local and national politics, prompting a tenacious campaign by the popular prefectural Governor to have US bases reduced in size and scope, and eventually removed altogether. The fact that a number of base land leases were due for renewal by the summer of 1997 prompted a refusal by the Governor to sanction renewal. Hashimoto, as Prime Minister,

---

[6] For details, see Hughes, *Japan's Re-emergence*, pp. 98–105; Glenn D. Hook, Julie Gilson, Christopher W. Hughes and Hugo Dobson, *Japan's International Relations: Politics, Economics and Security*, London and New York, Routledge, 2nd edn, 2005, pp. 160–1.

[7] Hook et al., *Japan's International Relations*, pp. 166–7.

[8] *Asahi Shinbun*, 5 October 1997.

after consulting President Clinton, decided to override the veto of the Governor, who was later defeated in an election. Okinawan opinion is divided on the American presence, because some sections of the local population gain benefit from the US bases, but there is also an active and persistent movement against the various nuisances that the bases cause. This is hardly surprising given that about 75 per cent of US military facilities in Japan are located in Okinawa, which accounts for 0.6 per cent of the Japanese land area.[9] Around 20 per cent of the main island of the prefecture is accounted for by US bases. Plans to relocate the Futenma air base from an urban part of Okinawa to a location just off the coast of the same island have proved particularly controversial.[10]

The Background of Japan–China Relations

The China issue fundamentally divided political opinion in Japan from the end of the Occupation to Japan's diplomatic recognition of Beijing in 1972, and even to some extent until the Peace and Friendship Treaty of 1978. How to deal with China was central to the debate between supporters of the American alliance and advocates of some form of non-aligned or more independent foreign policy. Japan had signed a separate peace treaty with the 'Republic of China' on Taiwan in 1952, after which Japan had diplomatic relations with the regime in Taipei, but not with the Beijing regime.[11] During the 1960s supporters of Taiwan generally prevailed within the ruling elite, but some trade with the People's Republic was conducted. Japan's official line at this period was that 'politics were separated from economics' (*seikei bunri*), in other words, that unofficial trade was acceptable provided that nothing were done to imply political recognition of Beijing. The Chinese responded by treating trade as a political instrument. In 1970 Zhou Enlai (Chou En-lai) enunciated a set of principles that made it difficult for firms with interests in South Korea or Taiwan to conduct trade with the PRC.

In July 1971 President Nixon announced that he would visit Beijing. This took the rug from under Satō Eisaku, whose prime ministership was fatally undermined by it. His successor, Tanaka Kakuei, moved quickly and effectively to recognize Beijing (and withdraw recognition from Taipei). In the 1972 agreement to restore relations, Japan apologized for the damage it had caused in China up to 1945, and the Chinese agreed to waive reparations. Japan 'fully understood and respected' the Chinese position concerning Taiwan, and in effect renounced any claim to Taiwan. There was no reference to the 1952 treaty between Tokyo and Taipei, nor did Tokyo and Beijing conclude a peace treaty, although there was a reference to 'the termination of the state of war'. Japan was not required to sever de facto relations with Taiwan, nor was any reference made to the Japan–US Mutual Security Treaty or the contentious 1969 Nixon–Satō communiqué. These were quite lenient conditions for Japan.

---

[9]   Hook et al., *Japan's International Relations*, pp. 168–71.
[10]   Ibid.
[11]   Neither Beijing nor Taipei would retain diplomatic relations with a state that recognized the other.

It was to be six years before the problems inherent in the new relationship were satisfactorily ironed out. In particular, the Chinese insisted on an 'anti-hegemony' (meaning anti-Soviet) clause before they would sign a peace and friendship treaty. This point was eventually finessed, and in 1978 two treaties, one being a trade agreement, and the other a treaty of peace and friendship, were successfully concluded.

These treaties more or less coincided with the start of the new economic policies of Deng Xiaoping. Throughout the 1980s and beyond there was a major growth in relations of trade, aid and investment between Japan and China, though the process was not without its problems. After the massacre of protesting students on Tiananmen Square in Beijing in 1989, Japan, like other states, suspended aid, but was the first major state to resume normal economic relations. Subsequently, with the rapid growth of the Chinese economy, Japan–China trade grew rapidly, as did foreign direct investment as Japanese firms relocated to China to take advantage of cheap skilled labour. Japan also granted large amounts of aid to China. In 2002 imports to Japan from China surpassed in value imports from the United States, making China Japan's largest import supplier.[12]

Frictions between the two countries developed on a number of issues, most notably relations with Taiwan, Japanese protection of certain products against imports from China, the phasing down of Japanese overseas development aid to China, various maritime boundary disputes, relations with North Korea, the content of Japanese history textbooks and (under Koizumi) visits by the Prime Minister to the Yasukuni Shrine. The image of each country in the public opinion of the other has deteriorated, so that it is difficult to be entirely confident about the future health of the relationship.[13] On the other hand, the economies of the two countries are now closely interlinked, so that a radical breakdown seems unlikely. On becoming Prime Minister, Abe Shinzō moved quickly to improve relations by visiting Beijing shortly after his inauguration.

Background of Relations between Japan and the Two Koreas

Japan's relations with Korea also have a difficult and stormy history. The legacy of harsh colonial rule over Korea by Japan between 1910 and 1945 created long-standing resentments on the part of the Koreans, while Japanese have tended at times to look down on Koreans. During the Korean War, Japan was a staging post for American forces engaged in the UN operation against North Korea. The outspoken Rhee Syngman of South Korea was so anti-Japanese that no progress was possible towards normalization of relations between the two countries until after his overthrow in 1960. Park Chung-Hee, his successor after a brief interregnum, was prepared to deal with Japan, and diplomatic relations

[12] Hook et al., *Japan's International Relations*, p. 200.
[13] Ibid., pp. 196–202. See also Reinhard Drifte, *Japan's Security Relations with China since 1989: From Balancing to Bandwaggoning?* London and New York, RoutledgeCurzon, 2003.

were – with difficulty – established between the two states in 1965. The rapid growth of the South Korean economy from the 1960s provided plenty of opportunities for Japanese businesses, but relations at most levels remained cool. When the then opposition leader, Kim Dae-jung, was kidnapped from Japan by agents of the South Korean regime, relations between the two governments reached a low point. In the 1980s, however, Nakasone endeavoured to mend fences, with some success. From the latter part of that decade the Republic of Korea gradually transformed itself into a democracy, and by the 1990s it had become an advanced economy, with a relatively high standard of living. These two developments eased relations with Japan. When Kim Dae-jung, who was favourably disposed towards Japan, became President, a period of friendship followed, but things became more difficult under his successor, Rho Moo-hyun, whose conciliatory policies towards the North were at odds with the more hard-line policies of Koizumi and, especially, Abe.

Japan has never entered into diplomatic relations with North Korea, although Koizumi's visit to Pyongyang in September 2002 appeared briefly to open a window into possibly improved relations. As we saw in Chapter 6, however, first the issue of abductees, and then the nuclear issue, derailed this positive approach, so that when in 2006 North Korea tested first missiles, then a nuclear device, relations with Japan were already in poor shape. The six-party agreement signed in February 2007, by which North Korea agreed to freeze its nuclear programme, may relax tension for a while, but the prospects for peaceful change leading to a different kind of regime in the North do not seem bright.

For Japan, therefore, the Korean peninsula remains a pressing concern of its foreign policy, as it has been for more than half a century.

Background to Relations between Japan and the Soviet Union/Russia

Japan and its northern neighbour have rarely enjoyed cordial relations in their modern history.[14] From 1956, when diplomatic relations were entered into but no peace treaty was signed because of the northern islands dispute,[15] until the collapse of the Soviet Union at the end of 1991, the two states regarded each other

---

[14] It is sometimes imagined that Russia is all located to the north and west of Japan, but a glance at the map shows that Russian territory actually stretches for as much as two time zones further *east* than Japan. Part of Russia is Japan's 'Far East'.

[15] Japan claims the two southernmost islands of the Kurile chain (in Japanese, Chishima: 'a thousand islands'), which stretches from the tip of the Kamchatka peninsula in northeastern Russia to near the Nemuro peninsula in eastern Hokkaidō. These islands are called Iturup and Kunashir in Russian, Etorofu and Kunashiri in Japanese. Japan also claims the island of Shikotan and the Habomai archipelago, which are close to the coast of Hokkaidō, of which they formed an administrative part up to 1945. Soviet – and later Russian – leaders have expressed a willingness to return Shikotan and Habomai on concluding a peace treaty, but these only account for some 7% of the total disputed land area, and Japan holds out for Iturup (Etorofu) and Kunashir(i) as well. See Kimie Hara, *Japanese–Soviet/Russian Relations since 1945*, London and New York, Routledge, 1998.

coolly. Memories of the way in which, on 8 August 1945, Stalin unilaterally broke the neutrality pact that Japan and the Soviet Union had signed in April 1941, and of the retention of Japanese prisoners in camps in Siberia for up to a decade after the end of the war, did not entirely disappear, and the two countries seemed to have little in common politically. Relations between Japan and the new Russia have been better, with Japan no longer fearing a military threat from the north, but the territorial dispute seems no closer to a solution. Economic relations have been concentrated in the area of energy supplies, where Russia is an increasingly significant supplier of oil and natural gas.

The Japanese Ministry of Foreign Affairs has over a long period taken a hard line in pursuit of the claim for return of the Northern Territories, maintaining that restraint should be exercised in economic relations until the claim is settled to Japan's satisfaction. The reasons for this position have varied. At the height of the Cold War the ministry was concerned above all to keep intact Japan's security protection by the United States, and determined to prevent any economic links with the Soviet Union that might displease the Americans. With the collapse of the Soviet regime, the concern was more with the territorial claim itself, since economic collapse might have tempted the Russian leaders to trade territory for economic support. This calculation, however, proved illusory, since neither Gorbachev, who visited Japan early in 1991, nor Yeltsin, who met with Hashimoto at Krasnoyarsk in 1997, promising a peace treaty with Japan by 2000, was able to deliver sufficient concessions on the territorial issue to satisfy Japan. During the period when Mori was Prime Minister (April 2000 to April 2001), renewed efforts were made to broker a settlement, but the decision-making process on the Japanese side was muddied by the controversies over the Hokkaidō politician Suzuki Muneo, and when Koizumi replaced Mori he showed less interest in resolving the Northern Territories question than his predecessor had done.[16]

It seems that, for a resolution of the territorial problem in the future to be achieved, two primary conditions would need to be satisfied: first, a more flexible position on the part of Japan over the question of sovereignty, and second, overwhelming economic imperatives that might lead the Russian authorities to make concessions. Neither condition seems likely to be fulfilled in the near future, so that this half-century-long dispute about a group of bleak and sparsely inhabited islands seems likely to continue poisoning relations between two major world powers for some years to come.

Background to Japan's Relations with the Rest of the World

In our discussion above, we have dealt in some detail with Japan's relations with the United States – always the dominant power – and its immediate neighbours, China, the two Koreas and Russia. Japan, however, is an economic power with global reach, whose political and strategic influence should not be underestimated. We therefore need to touch – albeit briefly, as space is limited – on other parts of the world.

---

[16] See Kazuhiko Togo, *Japan's Foreign Policy, 1945–2003: The Quest for a Proactive Policy*, Leiden and Boston, Brill, 2005, pp. 228–59.

South-East Asia

Japan has had extensive relations with the various states of South-East Asia, beginning with trading agreements (in lieu of reparations) in the 1950s, and developing into major trading and investment relationships in the years that followed. Although not a member of the Association of South-East Asian Nations (ASEAN), Japan participates in various regional organizations, most notably ASEAN + 3 (China, Japan and South Korea), the ASEAN Regional Forum (ARF), established in 1994 to discuss security matters, and the Asia–Pacific Economic Cooperation Forum (APEC), which concentrates on economic matters and seeks to promote freer trade. Japan has a prominent role in the Asian Development Bank (ADB), and has made significant contributions to UN peacekeeping missions in Cambodia, in the 1990s, and East Timor, in 2002–4. There have been Japanese initiatives in relation to areas of contention such as Burma (Myanmar) and the Indonesian province of Aceh. Because of its close links with the United States, Japan was not happy about the East Asian Economic Caucus (EAEC) proposed by the then Malaysian Prime Minister, Mahathir Mohamad, in the 1990s, on the grounds that the concept excluded the United States, as well as Australia and New Zealand.

From the 1990s signs could be detected of a desire on the part of Japan to move towards a more regional emphasis in foreign policy, with more involvement in the affairs of the East and South-East Asian region, in their economic, political, strategic and security dimensions. But, as Japanese official attitudes to the EAEC proposals demonstrated, too decisive a shift towards a regional orientation in foreign policy would tend to clash with the dominant relationship with the United States. This dilemma has become sharper as Koizumi and Abe have moved to reinforce the Japan–US security relationship.

Australasia

Japanese relations with Australia developed with great rapidity from the late 1950s, when a huge and lucrative minerals trade was opened up in Australia, with Japan as the principal export market. This led over several years to a surprisingly close relationship, in which the former bitter enemies of the Asia–Pacific War were transformed into partners in a range of mutual endeavours. The economic nexus was different in the case of New Zealand, but after some delay New Zealand also developed close economic links with Japan. The foundation of APEC in the early 1980s was in effect a joint Australian–Japanese initiative, and the two countries have continued to cooperate on economic and other issues. Both Australia and New Zealand became popular tourist destinations for Japanese people, and the Japanese language is widely taught in the schools of both countries.

South Asia

Relationships between Japan and South Asian states have been far less intense than those with the states (and economies) of East and South-East Asia.[17] From

---

[17]   Useful, if now dated, background is given in Purnendra C. Jain (ed.), *Distant Asian Neighbours: Japan and South Asia*, New Delhi, Sterling Publishers, 1996.

a Japanese perspective, the most controversial issue has been that of India and Pakistan successively becoming nuclear powers, a development that brought official protests from Japan. But most of the interactions between Japan and South Asia have been about economics, and the more open economic policies being pursued by recent Indian governments, leading to rapid economic growth, are producing an increased Japanese interest in the region in general, and India in particular. Indian economic growth does not excite the kind of apprehension in Japan caused by the rapid economic development of China.

Middle East

Japanese policy towards the Middle East has predominantly been affected by two considerations: US policies and the need for oil. When the first oil crisis halted Japanese economic growth in 1973–4, Japan promptly substituted broadly pro-Arab for pro-Israel policies in order to secure continued sources of oil. It is probably true to say that up to that time Japan was dependent on the US for much of its Middle Eastern expertise, and tended to follow the US line. But economic imperatives forced a change of policy.

The Iranian Revolution at the end of the 1970s also caused dilemmas for Japan, given its investment commitments in that country, and there were some unsuccessful Japanese attempts to negotiate a settlement in the Iran–Iraq war of the 1980s. The decision of President George W. Bush to invade Iraq in 2003 led to the despatch of a contingent from the Self Defence Forces to engage in limited non-military duties, as we have seen. Even though it seems difficult to regard this as much more than a token gesture towards solidarity with American policies, recent Japanese governments have been prepared to accept, verbally at least, most American priorities in their Middle Eastern policies.

Europe

Europe, as we have noted above, has undergone the most profound transformation of any region since the ending of the Cold War. The process of change can be traced back to the early post-war years, and in particular to the formation of a European entity that eventually became the European Union. With the EU now encompassing most of the former Eastern and East Central Europe, Japan has been increasing its interaction with the various parts of the Union at various levels. In the earlier years of European integration, Japan was more comfortable dealing with the individual states, but as the Union has grown in effectiveness, Japanese interaction with Brussels has grown.

Culturally, politically and economically, Japan has much in common with Europe, and the quite serious trade frictions of earlier years have largely given way to cooperative relationships across a surprising range of areas. Japan recognizes that the EU accounts for almost 457 million people (July 2006) and that Europe has evolved into a major international force, even though it is not (unlike the United States) a single sovereign nation-state. For Japan, however, difficulties arise where European instincts clash with those of the United States. For instance, Europe was far from united in supporting the American-led invasion of Iraq in 2003, whereas the Japanese government aligned itself decisively with the US position. Japan, unlike the individual European states, does not belong to a regional bloc with the degree of depth and influence of the European Union. To some extent, this has given Japan a sense of its own isolation, engendering among some of its citizens chauvinistic and narrow-minded attitudes. But its interactions with Europe have given Japan some idea of how regionalism might work in East and South-East Asia, even though the structures would inevitably be very different.[18]

Africa

Africa, a vast continent with enormous variety and many problems, has seemed for Japan a faraway place. Nevertheless, although it is the *problems* of Africa that generally hit the headlines in the world media, in a quiet way Japan has developed significant interactions with a number of African countries, and is assisting in various development programmes. During the apartheid era Japan had extensive economic dealings with South Africa, and this inhibited relations elsewhere. But since the emergence of a multi-racial regime in 1994, Japan has been able to portray its policies in a more favourable light.[19] In its need for sources of raw materials, China has recently been extending its relations with various African countries, and in the process coming under international criticism for allowing its economic needs to affect its political judgement (for instance, in relation to Darfur). Much of Japan's involvement with African countries is similarly based on commercial motivations, but Japan is also concerned with development projects across the continent.

An Assessment of Japanese Foreign Policy

The transition from an international system based on Cold War attitudes to a post-Cold War world presented serious challenges to Japanese foreign-policy-makers. As we have seen, for a while there was much inertia and little real change. But with the new millennium, new approaches have emerged.

Foreign policy is a multi-layered phenomenon, and in the case of Japan various pressures bearing down on policy-makers have tended to create unclear and complex solutions. Let us consider several kinds of such pressure, and see where they lead.

One kind of pressure is that of national interest and the perception of threats to national security. For Japan, the perceived threat from the Soviet Union was for many years a central element underlying the willingness of policy-makers to accept security guarantees from the United States. It was often reported up to the late 1980s that Soviet military aircraft made several hundred flights through Japanese air space every year. Assistance from a powerful ally in combating that

[18]   For a detailed account of Japanese relations with Europe, see Hook et al., *Japan's International Relations*, pp. 285–347.
[19]   See Kweku Ampiah, *The Dynamics of Japan's Relations with Africa: South Africa, Tanzania, and Nigeria*, London and New York, Routledge, 1997.

threat was consistent with Japan's search for a powerful protector from the beginning of the twentieth century, starting with the Anglo-Japanese Alliance (1902–23), which underpinned Japanese regional policies during the period of its existence.

Another kind of pressure came from public opinion after the 1945 defeat. The Peace Constitution met a genuinely favourable response from the electorate, and pacifist sentiment clearly acted as a constraint on policy for many years. A third source of pressure came from consensus-based decision-making, which tended to make bold and decisive approaches difficult to push through. Foreign policy, in other words, could be regarded as a product of an immobilist political system. A succession of decisions became non-decisions as a result of failure to agree on a bold solution. And finally, pressure emanated from the relative success of policy initiatives based on 'soft power', which arguably maximized national advantage at minimal cost. Despite, or perhaps because of, apparently unassertive policies in its myriad interactions with the international system, Japan was rather successful in promoting its national interests.[20] Broadly speaking, this combination of pressures worked in favour of rather minimalist, or low-key, foreign policy initiatives up to the 1990s.

As we suggested earlier in this chapter, following the ending of the Cold War Japan was presented with genuine alternative paths for its foreign policy. In 1995 the then LDP President, Kōno Yōhei, argued that with the ending of the Cold War Japan was no longer so constrained by loyalty to the Western cause as before, and could work towards the establishment of international regimes that reflected its own interest.[21] This option was tried out to some extent in the 1990s, but largely abandoned in the new millennium in favour of a policy approach that increased Japanese integration into American military systems, policy aims and ways of thinking.

The wisdom or otherwise of the new approach has yet to be fully tested. It may be argued that Japan is in a part of the world that presents problems of instability and potential danger, linked with the problems on the Korean peninsula and a resurgent and possibly militarily ambitious China. Moreover, the problem of terrorism is a global one, against which common action needs to be taken. Koizumi seems to have taken a position close to that of Tony Blair: that in order to secure American protection, it is necessary to give full support to the United States.

On the other hand, there are two principal reasons why the new approach may be regarded critically. One is that the priorities of the United States are not in all ways identical with those of Japan, just as they differ from those of Europe. The US is a continental power, deeply concerned with its own national interests, projecting massive military strength and often acting on the principle that the role of global policeman belongs to it by right. It is also unconstrained by a rival superpower, as it was during the Cold War. Japan, by contrast, is a maritime

---

[20] For the concept of 'soft power' applied to Japan, see Reinhard Drifte, *Japan's Foreign Policy in the 1990s: From Economic Superpower to What Power?*, Basingstoke and London, Macmillan; New York, St Martin's Press, 1996, pp. 87–143.

[21] Drifte, *Japan's Foreign Policy in the 1990s*, p. 87.

power on the edge of Asia, lacking raw materials and depending heavily on global trade for its survival. Its experiment in trying to control its regional environment by military force ended in disaster, and since then it has taken what is essentially the role of a trading state. The essence of this is that economics should be separated from politics: *seikei bunri*. Trading partners should not be alienated by heavy-handed political pressure, and still less by military action. Such an approach may be attacked for lack of principle (for instance, in relation to apartheid South Africa, or China after Tiananmen), or from another perspective it may seem spineless, but it is in fact founded in a hard-headed understanding of national interest and a principled belief that economic intercourse between states is infinitely more desirable (and profitable) than military intercourse.

The second ground for criticizing the new approach is that it represents the doctrines of a particular group of political leaders whose views represent, in certain respects, a throwback to a kind of 1950s nostalgia for a 'purer past'. It seems deeply ironic that the abandonment of a 'trading state' approach should entail closer integration into the world-view of a superpower whose priorities, at the deepest level, are so much at odds with those of Japan.

Chapter 13 | Conclusions: The Analytical Challenge of Japanese Politics

The most fundamental analytical challenge of Japanese politics lies in the fact that Japan is the first, and arguably the most important, nation-state outside the Western, Judaeo-Christian tradition to adopt democratic forms of government. Rather more, therefore, than between states sharing that tradition, it should be possible – in principle at least – to test how far factors of cultural difference affect the working in practice of democratic forms of government.

Japan is also a mature post-industrial state with a consciousness of its own history and national identity going back for many centuries. That history included a long period of near-isolation from the outside world, from the early seventeenth to the mid-nineteenth centuries, when Japan missed out on most of the dramatic modernizing changes that occurred in Europe and elsewhere. During that period, however, Japan pursued its own idiosyncratic path of development. Despite extreme official conservatism in political and social spheres, this included remarkable progress in education and in administrative and commercial skills.

The experience of operating political and governmental institutions under a formal written constitution goes back to 1889, and even though that constitution was not intended to be democratic – though it included limited democratic elements – politics and political conflict occurred in an at least partially structured framework. In 1946 the 1889 Constitution was replaced by the still current Constitution, which was intended to structure politics and government along democratic lines.

The evolution of Japanese politics under the 1946 Constitution reflects many contingent factors, including the massive psychological and structural impact of defeat in war and foreign occupation. Subsequently, after full independence was regained in April 1952, comparative political scientists were offered a feast of elections, parliamentary debates and legislative activity, Cabinet reshuffles, changes of Prime Minister, activities of government ministries and of interest groups, protest movements and demonstrations, judicial challenges to official policy, and so on, operating in a more or less structured fashion. On the face of it, therefore, direct comparison with the politics of other states should be a question of comparing like with like.

Unfortunately, it turned out not to be as simple as that. Institutions and the relations between them tended to operate in ways that seemed puzzling to overseas observers. For instance, the tendency to pre-script debate rather than to have a free-for-all verbal contest suggested that many decisions were taken behind the scenes and then ratified in a formal debating session. The principle that politicians decide and civil servants implement seemed to be turned on its head in the Japanese case, with government ministries exercising semi-independent power in many instances. Formal bodies such as Parliament or Cabinet, even figures such as the Prime Minister, appeared to have less power than informal bodies such as factions within parties, or the non-elected heads of ministries. Informal relationships at all levels – often extremely hard to penetrate – provided a diffuse but potent element that it was necessary to understand in order to grasp what was really happening. Now, in other comparable political systems, one could also find situations in which real decisions were taken behind the scenes, and in which civil servants were more powerful than their political masters, or where obscure personal relationships across formal boundaries determined the way things went. But in Japan these elements seemed more pervasive, and even to give a different character to the whole system of politics (including foreign policy): Japan, it seemed worked 'to different rules from the rest of us'.

This kind of perception of Japanese politics led to a number of attempts to discover some kind of basic key to understanding it. One approach, which originated with Japanese writers in the 1970s (though its roots went back much further), posited the idea that Japanese civilization and culture are somehow 'unique'. Much of its argumentation was specious, and although a few overseas writers accepted its arguments uncritically, others attacked it with vigour.[1] Despite its dreadful faults, this genre of literature at least alerted us to the dangers of a too facile comparison between Japanese institutions and practices and those found elsewhere. Even though it is notoriously difficult to define culture, the idea that culture is irrelevant to the understanding of politics is a dangerous heresy.

Approaches to the study of Japanese politics and government since the Second World War have passed through a succession of phases.[2] In the decade and a half from 1945 a democracy paradigm predominated, focusing on the Occupation's democratic experiment and seeking the causes of authoritarian rule in the 1930s and early 1940s. In the 1960s, however, a very different paradigm took over, prompted by the already obvious successes of the economy, so that many observers came to concentrate their analysis on development and modernization. This

---

[1] For instance Peter Dale, *The Myth of Japanese Uniqueness*, London, Routledge, 1986 and later editions; Ross Mouer and Yoshio Sugimoto, *Images of Japanese Society*, London and New York, KPI, 1986.

[2] Our discussion here will concentrate largely on the debate outside Japan. Discussion of Japanese politics within Japan has had somewhat different, though overlapping, concerns.

included the notion of 'political development', which meant essentially the formation of complex and sophisticated political structures. The modernization paradigm, in turn, was overtaken by New Left criticism from the end of the 1960s. New Left writers directed their fire at the costs of development in terms of human suffering and exploitation, and although much of what they wrote about was pre-war history, they also uncovered exploitative relationships existing within contemporary industry, between large firms and the small firms to which work was subcontracted, and between privileged, permanently employed workers and those casually employed on much lower take-home pay.

This in turn gave way to a 'Japan as Number One' paradigm late in the 1970s. Ezra Vogel developed arguments having much in common with the modernization paradigm, but in addition he maintained that Japan had created a model from which positive lessons could be learnt by Western countries, including the United States. In a sense, his book was as much about the US and its current troubles as about Japan, though ironically, it sold many more copies in Japan than in America.[3]

During the 1980s a different kind of challenge emerged to established approaches to the study of Japan. This was the revisionist paradigm, whose exponents feared what they regarded as predatory trading policies by Japan.[4] The influence of this paradigm on American thinking was most profound during the latter half of the 1980s, when Japan was in the middle of its 'bubble economy' phase, and US–Japan trade frictions were at their height. Revisionists, most prominently Chalmers Johnson, maintained in essence that what drove the Japanese economy was not market economics but bureaucratic control, that the system as it had developed got ahead by exploiting other economies through a closed domestic market, rigged tendering for contracts and predatory export drives, corruption being endemic, not peripheral, and democratic politics being essentially window-dressing.[5]

The 1990s witnessed furious controversy between some exponents of the revisionist paradigm and those favouring a contrasting paradigm newly applied to Japan, that of rational choice theory. So far as Japanese politics is concerned, the most widely noted product of the rational choice paradigm is that of Ramseyer and Rosenbluth.[6] Inspired by the principle that politicians will act in such a way as to maximize their interests within the rules of the political game that exist,

---

[3]   Ezra Vogel, *Japan as Number One; Lessons for America*, Cambridge, MA, Harvard University Press, 1979; Tokyo, Tuttle, 1980.

[4]   Those most commonly associated with the revisionist paradigm were Chalmers Johnson, Clyde Prestowitz, James Fallows and Karel van Wolferen, though other names could be added. Close analysis of their writings would show that their views diverged on various points.

[5]   A variant of this was the view of van Wolferen, which may be caricatured as saying that the system had 'no pilot and no brakes', but that this rudderless and leaderless ship was nevertheless a menace on the high seas. See Karel van Wolferen, *The Enigma of Japanese Power*, London, Macmillan, 1989.

[6]   J. Mark Ramseyer and Frances McCall Rosenbluth, *Japan's Political Marketplace*, Cambridge, MA and London, Harvard University Press, 1993.

these writers arrived at the counter-intuitive conclusion that Japanese politicians essentially controlled bureaucrats, seen by the authors as politicians' agents, rather than the other way round. The book, which was polemically written, attracted fierce attack from revisionists, especially Johnson.[7]

Rather than entering into the detail of a rather sterile controversy between revisionists and rational choice proponents, I shall single out one particular aspect that seems of significance. Ramseyer and Rosenbluth make a particular point of excluding from serious consideration cultural factors, which other writers have brought into play to explain aspects of Japanese politics.[8] Their argument essentially boils down to the view that rational individuals make calculations of advantage within structures of given rules. Others, from very different basic perspectives, have castigated excessive resort to cultural stereotypes to 'explain' Japan. But if by 'culture' we mean those aspects of current practice that are influenced by relatively long-standing patterns of social interaction and by expectations about the behaviour of others conditioned by the norms and values of the society in which individuals operate, then to exclude 'culture' is to risk missing absolutely vital clues about the ways in which politics functions in practice.

As we have sought to demonstrate in this book, important structural changes have been taking place since the 1990s, and particularly since the beginning of the third millennium, in both the economic and the political spheres. In the former arena, the stagnation of the 1990s led to structural readjustment on the part of many companies and banks, as well as a regulatory regime rather more open to foreign investment than previously. Companies reformed their employment practices, though without abandoning the fundamental principle of regular, or semi-permanent, employment contracts for key sections of their workforce. Foreign companies operating in Japan provided a model of different employment practices, which affected domestic practices to some extent.

In politics, the administrative reforms introduced in January 2001, including the creation of super-ministries, and of a Cabinet Office designed – together with the introduction of junior ministers – to strengthen the power of the Prime Minister, were crucial in enabling Koizumi to exercise the kind of prime ministerial power that had eluded most of his predecessors. What in retrospect looks like the culminating point of this increased power was Koizumi's expulsion of the postal services privatization rebels from the LDP in August–September 2005. The ability of a Prime Minister to expel from his party a large group of rebels defying party (that is, prime ministerial) policy, and then convincingly win a general election, marks a crucial turning point in the way Japanese politics is conducted (even though there was evidence of backsliding on this by the Abe administration). It seems plausible to argue that since the turn of the century Japan has turned the corner economically, and at the same time strengthened the capacity of its political system.

Nevertheless, there are reasons to be less than fully sanguine about the future of Japanese politics, and to signal a number of problems that remain far from

---

[7]   Chalmers Johnson and E. B. Keehn, 'A Disaster in the Making: Rational Choice and Asian Studies', *The National Interest*, Summer 1994, pp. 14–22.

[8]   Ramseyer and Rosenbluth, *Japan's Political Marketplace*, pp. 2–3.

resolution. Indeed, in some respects, the very changes that have taken place may have exacerbated some of these problems. We now return to the six crises that we outlined towards the end of Chapter 1.

The first is a crisis of *political power and democratic accountability*. As we have argued at various points in this book, politics in Japan has been based on a single dominant party. This in itself is not necessarily undemocratic, because it may issue from the free choice by the electorate of the same party in successive elections. Nevertheless, it poses problems for accountability in so far as longevity in power may well breed a mentality among the rulers that they rule by right. Some wise words were spoken on this subject by the British political scientist Bernard Crick:

> Politics is a process of discussion ... For discussion to be genuine and fruitful when something is maintained, the opposite or some contrary case must be considered, or – better – maintained by someone who believes it. The hall-mark of free government everywhere ... is whether public criticism is allowed in a manner conceivably effective – in other words, whether opposition is tolerated. Politics needs men who will act freely, but men cannot act freely without politics. Politics is a way of ruling divided societies without undue violence – and most societies are divided, though some think that that is the very trouble. We can do much worse than honour 'mere politics' so we must examine very carefully the claims of those who would do better.[9]

Here Crick is not specifically advocating alternation in power, or occasional changes of government. That, however, is an implication of what he writes, since a classic symptom of single-party dominance is a tendency towards intolerance of opposition. In Japan, opposition is tolerated, but parties out of power find it so difficult to attain power that they have tended historically to appease government authorities rather than actively to oppose them.[10] The identity of 'government authorities' also remains an issue, since, despite the reforms that have been undertaken, the influence of unelected officials over political decision-making remains strong. Moreover, recent governments have shown worrying signs of riding roughshod over opposition, including from the media.

Our second crisis is one of *political participation and non-involvement in politics*. The political confusion of the 1990s led to a marked decline in voting turnout, which has subsequently fluctuated around historically low levels. The 1990s also saw a big increase in the numbers of those who declared no party preference (the so-called *mutōhasō*, or 'non-party strata'). Certain individual leaders do receive enthusiastic support, but some of this plainly relates to 'image' factors mediated through television. It seems a reasonable assumption that the absence of expectation that any combination of opposition parties might accede to power also dampens interest in elections, though participation rates were high in the 1980s when the LDP appeared firmly entrenched in power. As we have seen earlier, civil society has been relatively weak, though

---

9   Bernard Crick, *In Defence of Politics*, London, Penguin, 1964, p. 33.
10   See J. A. A. Stockwin, 'To Oppose or Appease? Parties out of Power and the Need for Real Politics in Japan', *Japan Forum*, vol. 18, no. 1, March 2006, pp. 115–32.

this is partly for regulatory reasons, and voluntary organizations did receive a boost following the Kōbe earthquake of 1995. It may be that this is part of a loosening-up process occurring within Japanese society, and that it may result in greater social pluralism, with a significant impact on politics. That is a question for the future.

The third crisis is a crisis of *the Constitution and political fundamentals*. The apparent determination of the Abe government to press ahead with constitutional revision raised the temperature of politics and was not guaranteed to succeed. Even though public opinion has shifted to a position where in most polls a majority of respondents declare in favour of some kind of revision, there remains a bedrock of support for leaving the document as it is, with the peace clause intact. On the other hand, the peace clause is increasingly at variance with the reality of the policies pursued by the Koizumi and Abe governments of integration of the Self-Defence Forces with those of the United States, and with US demands for Japanese force projection overseas. In late March 2007 a bill was passed through Parliament authorizing a mechanism for a popular referendum on constitutional reform, should both houses approve a revised draft with majorities of two-thirds or more of their membership. Constitutional revision is the most important political issue facing the electorate in the near to medium future. It is highly controversial, and its outcome and consequences are difficult to predict.

The fourth crisis is one of *liberal versus illiberal ideas*. This opposition embraces a set of issues that are at a critical point at the time of writing, in mid-2007. Nakano Kōichi writes of 'the apparently incongruent but extraordinarily common association of economic liberalism with political illiberalism'.[11] Koizumi pursued economic liberalism with zeal, and, being Prime Minister for five and a half years, was able to roll back to a significant extent the vested interests that had for long impeded it. But under Koizumi and his more overtly nationalist successor, Abe Shinzō, a concerted erosion of the liberal reforms that were introduced after the war is also evident. Examples of this include pressure on NHK (the public broadcasting authority) to follow government guidelines in certain areas of reporting, a revised education law introducing for the first time since the war an emphasis on patriotism, and certain elements in the LDP constitutional reform draft of 2005. As mentioned in Chapter 10, this includes a proposal for a specifically military court, and also replacement of the second paragraph of article 21 (proscribing censorship and any violation of communication secrecy) by a clause reading: 'The State has the responsibility to explain to the people concerning national administration.' Moreover, one of the most significant developments of the past decade has been the progressive integration of the Japanese Self-Defence Forces into the structures and procedures of the US forces operating in East Asia. An illiberal and nationalistic set of actual and proposed changes is thus, somewhat bizarrely, linked with increasing intertwining of Japanese and American military systems and policies.[12]

---

[11]   Nakano Kōichi, 'Nationalist Basis of Globalization: A View from Japan', unpublished paper, January 2007.
[12]   For a trenchant attack on this aspect of recent developments, see Gavan McCormack, *Client State: Japan in the American Embrace*, London and New York, Verso, 2007.

The fifth crisis is one of *ageing society and diverging life-chances*. Japan, like many parts of Europe, faces demographic decline and an ageing society. The birth rate is now close to the lowest levels to be found in Europe, while for over 30 years Japan has enjoyed the highest life expectancy at birth of any nation on earth. Population has now peaked at just over 127 million, and although it is arguable that Japan is overpopulated in terms of demand for limited resources and space for habitation, what is now projected as a fairly rapid population decline poses a number of problems. Already, this is causing problems for tertiary educational institutions, which now have excess capacity for a declining number of students. More seriously, the shift in the population profile towards the upper end of the scale imposes increasing burdens on the economically active part of the population, who will have to support huge numbers of elderly people. Japan being a high-technology society, the means of coping with such imbalances will probably be available, but the viability of pension schemes, and inequality between generations, are becoming increasingly contentious issues. The option of mass immigration goes against the grain of official instincts, but in areas such as the caring professions there are signs that this reluctance will soon, perforce, be modified.

The sixth and final crisis is one of *national status and role*. We have written at some length in Chapter 12 and elsewhere of the difficult relationships that Japan has recently had with China, the two Koreas, Russia and other states and groupings. Recent governments have chosen to align policy and military systems closely with those of the United States. This approach is backed by the traditional argument that Japan should be aligned with the world's most powerful international power. But the wisdom of such a path – at least in the rather extreme forms manifested over the past decade or so – may also be questioned with reference to the dangers of too close an alignment with a power that, quite naturally, gives priority to its own national interests, besides being often insensitive to the reality of societies in the Middle East and elsewhere. At this time of writing there is little indication of any change in these policies on the part of the present or any potential Japanese government. Nevertheless, a modus vivendi with China should be at the forefront of Japanese official thinking, given that China is rapidly developing into a great power, and, from the perspective of its own national interest, needs predictable relations with the world's second largest economy, Japan.

Interwoven into these specific considerations is the question of the international status of Japan. Those with experience of teaching the Japanese language and Japanese studies have discovered that many of their students are attracted to Japan because it is 'cool'. The attraction of sophisticated cartoon stories, animation films, fashion, exciting architecture, martial arts and so on exerts a powerful attraction not only in the rest of Asia, but also throughout the world. This is the sign of a society arrived at a high level of sophistication, in contrast to one that attracts attention by the rapidity of its industrial and commercial growth, as was the case in the decades up to the 1980s. Of course, being sophisticated does not absolve Japan from the realities of international power politics, or from the need to prepare against possible security threats. But it does suggest that national status may be enhanced by policies of international cooperation and cultural projection.

The phenomenon of 'Japan-passing', which in the 1990s overtook the 1980s sport of 'Japan-bashing', was perhaps the inevitable consequence of the fact that the 'Japan brand', characterized by industrial organization and rapid economic growth, had faltered, and no longer seemed to present significant lessons to the outside world. The process of Japan-passing speeded up when a new kind of exciting 'China brand' made its appearance. In the first decade of the third millennium an innovative Japan brand has been in the process of formation, emanating, however, spontaneously from the society rather than from the edicts of politicians and officials. If politicians could be persuaded to understand and develop the comparative advantages that Japan now has, as a sophisticated post-industrial society in a globalizing world, the future for the country could be bright indeed. Unfortunately, however, those currently in power appear to be more interested in fighting battles from half a century earlier, and in the process risk turning Japan into a society where human beings suffer oppression in the interests of dubious aesthetic doctrines,[13] masking a readiness to stifle criticism and creativity.

After the LDP defeat in the upper house elections of July 2007, Abe defied precedent and determined to soldier on as Prime Minister. Nevertheless, his power was clearly weakened by the defeat, and it seems reasonable to assume that the prospects for constitutional reform in the foreseeable future have receded. The election results were excellent for the DPJ and for its leadership, but that party was going to have to retain its momentum and present itself as an attractive and credible alternative government, if it was to have any chance of winning the next lower house elections – a far tougher assignment than the elections just past – and replace the LDP in power.

In September, Abe resigned, and was replaced by Fukuda Yasuo, a more moderate figure.

---

[13] See e.g. Abe Shinzō, *Utsukushii kuni e* (Towards a Beautiful Country), Tokyo, Bunshun Shinsho, 2006.

Appendix I House of Representatives election results, 1946–1955

Party	Dates of successive elections					
	10 April 1946	25 April 1947	23 Jan. 1949	1 Oct. 1952	19 April 1953	27 Feb. 1955
Progressive	94 (20.3)[a] 10,351 (18.7)					
Democratic		121 (26.0) 6,840 (25.0)	69 (14.8) 4,798 (15.7)			185 (39.6) 13,536 (36.6)
Reformist				85 (18.2) 6,429 (18.2)	76 (16.3) 6,186 (17.9)	
Liberal	140 (30.2) 13,506 (24.4)	131 (28.1) 7,356 (26.9)		240 (51.5) 16,939 (47.9)		112 (24.0) 9,849 (26.6)
Democratic Liberal			264 (56.7) 13,420 (43.9)			
Hatoyama Liberal					35 (7.5) 3,055 (8.8)	
Yoshida Liberal					199 (42.7) 13,476 (39.0)	
Cooperative[b]	14 (3.0) 1,800 (3.2)	29 (6.2) 1,916 (7.0)	14 (3.0) 1,042 (3.4)			
Japan Socialist	92 (19.8) 9,858 (17.8)	143 (30.7) 7,176 (26.2)	48 (10.3) 4,130 (13.5)			

(Continued)

Appendix 1 *(Continued)*

Party	Dates of successive elections					
	10 April 1946	*25 April 1947*	*23 Jan. 1949*	*1 Oct. 1952*	*19 April 1953*	*27 Feb. 1955*
Left Socialist				54 (11.6) 3,399 (9.6)	72 (15.4) 4,517 (13.1)	89 (19.1) 5,683 (15.3)
Right Socialist				57 (12.2) 4,108 (11.6)	66 (14.2) 4,678 (11.6)	67 (14.3) 5,130 (13.9)
Labour–Farmer			7 (1.5) 607 (2.0)	4 (0.9) 261 (0.7)	5 (1.1) 359 (1.0)	4 (0.9) 358 (1.0)
Japan Communist	5 (1.1) 2,136 (3.8)	4 (0.8) 1,003 (3.7)	35 (7.5) 2,985 (9.7)	0 (0) 897 (2.6)	1 (0.2) 656 (1.9)	2 (0.4) 733 (2.0)
Independent	81 (17.4) 11,325 (20.4)	13 (2.8) 1,581 (5.8)	12 (2.6) 2,008 (6.6)	19 (4.1) 2,355 (6.7)	11 (2.4) 1,524 (4.4)	6 (1.3) 1,229 (3.3)
Others	38 (8.2) 6,473 (11.7)	25 (5.4) 1,490 (5.4)	17 (3.6) 1,602 (5.2)	7 (1.5) 949 (2.7)	1 (0.2) 152 (0.4)	2 (0.4) 497 (1.3)
Total	464 55,449c	466 27,362	466 30,593	466 35,337	466 34,602	467 37,015

aFor each entry: number of seats (% of total seats)
number of votes, in thousands (% of total votes)

bFrom 1947 election: People's Cooperative.

cThis figure is inflated, because voters had two votes in certain constituencies in the 1946 elections.

Source: Asahi Nenkan, various dates.

Appendix 2 House of Representatives election results, 1958–1972

Party[a]	Dates of successive elections					
	22 May 1958	20 Nov. 1960	21 Nov. 1963	29 Jan. 1967	27 Dec. 1969	10 Dec. 1972
LDP	287 (61.5)[b] 22,977 (57.8)	296 (63.4) 22,740 (57.6)	283 (60.7) 22,424 (54.7)	277 (57.0) 22,448 (48.8)	288 (59.2) 22,382 (47.6)	271 (55.2) 24,563 (46.8)
JSP	166 (35.5) 13,094 (32.9)	145 (31.0) 10,887 (27.6)	144 (30.8) 11,907 (29.0)	140 (28.8) 12,826 (27.9)	90 (18.5) 10,074 (21.4)	118 (24.0) 11,479 (21.9)
DSP		17 (3.7) 3,464 (8.8)	23 (4.9) 3,023 (7.4)	30 (6.2) 3,404 (7.4)	31 (6.4) 3,637 (7.7)	19 (3.9) 3,661 (7.0)
CGP				25 (5.1) 2,472 (5.4)	47 (9.7) 5,125 (10.9)	29 (5.9) 4,437 (8.5)
JCP	1 (0.2) 1,012 (2.6)	3 (0.6) 1,157 (2.9)	5 (1.1) 1,646 (4.0)	5 (1.0) 2,191 (4.8)	14 (2.9) 3,199 (6.8)	38 (7.7) 5,497 (10.5)
Independent	12 (2.6) 2,381 (6.0)	5 (1.1) 1,119 (2.8)	12 (2.6) 1,956 (4.8)	9 (1.9) 2,554 (5.5)	16 (3.3) 2,493 (5.3)	14 (2.9) 2,646 (5.0)
Others	1 (0.2) 288 (0.7)	1 (0.2) 142 (0.3)	0 (0.0) 60 (0.1)	0 (0.0) 101 (0.2)	0 (0.0) 81 (0.2)	2 (0.4) 143 (0.3)
Total	467 39,752	467 39,509	467 41,017	486 45,997	486 46,990	491 52,425

[a]LDP: Liberal Democratic Party; JSP: Japan Socialist Party; CGP: Clean Government Party; JCP: Japan Communist Party.
[b]For each entry: number of seats (% of total seats)
number of votes, in thousands (% of total votes)

Source: Asahi Nenkan, various dates.

Appendix 3   House of Representatives election results, 1976–1990

Party[a]	Dates of successive elections					
	5 Dec. 1976	7 Oct. 1979	22 June 1980	18 Dec. 1983	6 July 1986	18 Feb. 1990
LDP	249 (48.7)[b]	248 (48.6)	284 (55.6)	250 (48.9)	300 (58.6)	275 (53.7)
	23,654 (41.8)	24,084 (44.6)	28,262 (47.9)	25,983 (45.8)	29,875 (49.4)	30,315 (46.1)
NLC	17 (3.3)	4 (0.7)	12 (2.3)	8 (1.6)	6 (1.2)	
	2,364 (4.2)	1,632 (3.0)	1,766 (3.0)	1,341 (2.4)	1,115 (1.8)	
JSP	123 (24.1)	107 (20.9)	107 (20.9)	112 (21.9)	85 (16.6)	136 (26.6)
	11,713 (20.7)	10,643 (19.7)	11,401 (19.3)	11,065 (19.5)	10,412 (17.2)	16,025 (24.4)
DSP	29 (5.7)	35 (6.3)	32 (6.3)	38 (7.4)	26 (5.1)	14 (2.7)
	3,554 (6.3)	3,664 (6.8)	3,897 (6.6)	4,130 (7.3)	3,896 (6.4)	3,179 (4.8)
CGP	55 (10.8)	57 (11.2)	33 (6.5)	58 (11.3)	56 (10.9)	45 (8.8)
	6,177 (10.9)	5,283 (9.8)	5,330 (9.0)	5,746 (10.1)	5,701 (9.4)	5,243 (8.0)
JCP	17 (3.3)	39 (7.6)	29 (5.7)	26 (5.1)	26 (5.1)	16 (3.1)
	5,878 (10.4)	5,626 (10.4)	5,804 (9.8)	5,302 (9.3)	5,313 (8.8)	5,227 (8.0)

SDL		2 (0.4)	3 (0.5)	3 (0.6)	4 (0.8)	4 (0.8)
		368 (0.7)	402 (0.7)	381 (0.7)	500 (0.8)	567 (0.9)
Independent	21 (4.1)	19 (3.7)	11 (2.1)	16 (3.1)	9 (1.7)	21 (4.1)
	3,227 (5.7)	2,641 (4.9)	2,057 (3.5)	2,769 (4.9)	3,515 (9.8)	4,807 (7.3)
Others	0 (0.0)	0 (0.0)	0 (0.0)	0 (0.0)	0 (0.0)	0 (0.0)
	45 (0.1)	69 (0.1)	109 (0.2)	62 (0.1)	121 (0.2)	58 (0.1)
Total	511	511	511	511	512	512
	56,613	54,010	59,029	56,780	60,449	65,704

[a]LDP: Liberal Democratic Party; NLC: New Liberal Club; JSP: Japan Socialist Party; DSP: Democratic Socialist Party; CGP: Clean Government Party; JCP: Japan Communist Party; SDL: Social Democratic League.

[b]For each entry: number of seats (% of total seats) number of votes, in thousands (% of total votes)

Source: Asahi Nenkan, various dates.

Appendix 4 House of Representatives election results, 1993–2005

Party[a]	Dates of successive elections				
	18 July 1993[b]	20 Oct. 1996[c]	25 June 2000[c]	9 Nov. 2003[c]	11 Sept. 2005[c]
LDP	223 (43.6) 23,000 (36.6)	239 (47.8) 21,836 (38.6) 18,206 (32.8)	233 (48.5) 24,946 (40.97) 16,943 (28,31)	237 (49.4) 26,089 (37.51) 20,660 (34.96)	296 (61.66) 32,518 (47.77) 25,888 (38.18)
JSP/SDP	70 (13.7) 9,687 (15.4)	15 (3.0) 1,241 (2.2) 3,547 (6.4)	19 (3.9) 2,311 (3.80) 5,603 (9.36)	6 (1.25) 1,709 (2.87) 3,027 (5.12)	7 (1.45) 996 (1.46) 3,719 (5.49)
DSP	15 (2.9) 2,206 (3.5)				
CGP	51 (10.0) 5,114 (8.1)	[in merger with NFP]	31 (6.4) 1,232 (2.02) 7,762 (12.97)	34 (7.08) 886 (1.49) 8,733 (14.78)	31 (6.4) 981 (1.44) 8,988 (13.25)
JCP	15 (2.9) 4,835 (7.7)	26 (5.2) 7,097 (12.6) 7,269 (13.1)	20 (4.2) 7,353 (12.08) 6,719 (11.23)	9 (1.9) 4,838 (8.13) 4,586 (7.76)	9 (1.9) 4,937 (7.25) 4,919 (7.25)
SDL	4 (0.8) 461 (0.7)				
JRP	55 (10.8) 6,341 (10.1)				
NPH	13 (2.5) 1,658 (2.6)	2 (0.4) 728 (13)			
JNP	35 (6.8) 5,054 (8.0)				
NFP		156 (31.2) 15,812 (28.0) 15,580 (28.0)			

DPJ		52 (10.4) 6,002 (10.6) 8,949 (16.1)	127 (26.4) 16,812 (27,61) 15,068 (25,18)	177 (36.9) 21,814 (36.7) 22,096 (37.39)	113 (23.5) 24,805 (36.44) 21,036 (31.02)
LP			22 (4.6) 2,054 (3.37) 6,589 (11.01)		
CP			7 (1.4) 1,231 (2,02) 247 (0,41)	4 (0.83) 791 (1.33) –	
PNP					4 (0.83) 433 (0.64) 1,163 (1.74)
Independents[d]		9 (1.9) 2,509 (4.4)	15 (3.1) 2,967 (4,87)	11 (2.29) 2,728 (4.58)	18 (3.75) 3,240 (4.76)
Others		1 (0.2) 1,304 (2.3) 1,436 (2.6)	6 (1.2) 1,974 (3.3) 812 (1.3)	2 (0.41) 646 (1.09) –	2 (0.42) 155 (0.23) 2,077 (3.06)
Total	*511* *62,804*	*500* *56,528* *55,569*	*480* *59,769* *59,745*	*480* *59,103* *59,103*	*480* *68,067* *67,811*

[a]LDP: Liberal Democratic Party; JSP/SDP: Japan Socialist Party (to 1996); DSP: Democratic Socialist Party; CGP: Clean Government Party; JCP: Japan Communist Party; SDL: Social Democratic League; JRP: Japan Renewal Party; NPH: New Party Harbinger; JNP: Japan New Party; NFP: New Frontier Party; DPJ: Democratic Party (of Japan); LP: Liberal Party; CP: Conservative Party; PNP: People's New Party.

[b]For each entry: number of seats (% of total seats) / number of votes, in thousands (% of total votes).

[c]For each entry: number of seats (% of total seats) / number of votes, in thousands, in single member constituencies (% of total seats) / number of votes, in thousands, PR regional blocs (% of total votes).

[d]Note that Independents could stand for election only in single-member constituencies, since candidacy in PR regional blocs requires affiliation to a party or grouping).

Sources: For 1993 and 1996 elections, *Asahi Nenkan*, 1994 and 1997. For subsequent elections, *Yomiuri Nenkan*, 2001, 2004 and 2006.

Appendix 5 House of Councillors election results, 11 July 2004

Party[a]	Seats won in prefectural constituencies	Seats won in PR constituency	Total seats for this election	Grand total of seats[b]
LDP	34	15	49	115
DPJ	31	19	50	82
CGP	3	8	11	24
JCP	0	4	4	9
SDP	0	2	2	5
Independent	5	–	5	6
Total	73	48	121	242

[a]LDP: Liberal Democratic Party; DPJ: Democratic Party (of Japan); CGP: Clean Government Party; JCP: Japan Communist Party; SDP: Social Democratic Party.

[b]Members of the House of Councillors are elected for a six-year term, but only half the seats are renewed every three years (fixed term). The numbers in the far right-hand column are thus based on the total of those elected in July 2001 and those elected in July 2004.

Source: Yomiuri Nenkan, 2005. For annotated data on House of Councillors elections between 1947 and 2001, see J. A. A. Stockwin, *Dictionary of the Modern Politics of Japan*, London and New York, RoutledgeCurzon, 2003, pp. 60–70.

Appendix 6 House of Councillors election results, 29 July 2007

Party[a]	Seats won in prefectural constituencies	Seats won in PR constituency	Total seats for this election	Grand total of seats[b]
LDP	23	14	37	83
DPJ	40	20	60	109
CGP	2	7	9	20
JCP	0	3	3	7
SDP	0	2	2	5
PNP	1	1	2	4
NPJ	–	1	1	1
Minor party	0	0	0	1
Independents	7	–	7	12
Total	73	48	121	240[c]

[a] LDP: Liberal Democratic Party; DPJ: Democratic Party (of Japan); CGP: Clean Government Party; JCP: Japan Communist Party; SDP: Social Democratic Party; PNP: People's New Party, founded in 2005 by Kamei Shizuka and Watanuki Tamisuke; NPJ: New Party Japan, founded in 2005 by Tanaka Yasuo.
[b] The numbers in the far right hand column are based on the total of those elected in July 2004 and those elected in July 2007.
[c] Plus two vacancies.

Source: Asahi Shinbun, 31 July 2007.

Further Reading

General Reading on Japan and Japanese Politics

For general reference about various aspects of Japan, see Marius B. Jansen, *The Making of Modern Japan* (Harvard University Press, 2002); Duncan McCargo, *Contemporary Japan* (Palgrave Macmillan, 2nd edn, 2004); Paul J. Bailey, *Postwar Japan: 1945 to the Present* (Blackwell, 1996). Useful texts on politics include Bradley Richardson, *Japanese Democracy* (Yale University Press, 1997); Purnendra Jain and Takashi Inoguchi (eds), *Japanese Politics Today: Beyond Karaoke Democracy* (Macmillan Education Australia, 1997); T. J. Pempel, *Regime Shift: Comparative Dynamics of the Japanese Political Economy* (Cornell University Press, 1998); Gerald L. Curtis, *The Logic of Japanese Politics* (Columbia University Press, 1999); Ian Neary, *The State and Politics in Japan* (Polity Press, 2002); J. A. A. Stockwin, *Dictionary of the Modern Politics of Japan* (RoutledgeCurzon, 2003); Louis D. Hayes, *Introduction to Japanese Politics* (M. E. Sharpe, 2005); Takashi Inoguchi, *Japanese Politics: An Introduction* (Trans Pacific Press, 2005).

Historical Background

The most comprehensive recent history of Japan in English is *The Cambridge History of Japan* (Cambridge University Press, various years, in six volumes). For modern history, see vol. 5 (*The Nineteenth Century*), edited by Marius Jansen, 1989, and vol. 6 (*The Twentieth Century*), edited by Peter Duus, 1988. A single-volume history that has stood the test of time is Richard Storry, *A History of Modern Japan* (Penguin, 1960 and later editions). Another is W. G. Beasley, *The Modern History of Japan* (Weidenfeld & Nicolson, 1963 and later editions). An excellent history focusing on social aspects is Ann Waswo, *Japanese Society, 1868–1994* (Oxford University Press, 1996).

A recent political history is Richard Sims, *Japanese Political History since the Meiji Renovation* (Hurst, 2001). Another fascinating study is Carol Gluck, *Japan's Modern Myths: Ideology in the Late Meiji Period* (Princeton University Press, 1985). For detailed accounts of the formative period of the Meiji Constitution (broadly the 1890s), see Junji Banno, *The Establishment of the Japanese Constitutional System* (Routledge, 1992), and Andrew Fraser, R. H. P Mason and Philip Mitchell, *Japan's Early Parliaments, 1890–1905* (Routledge, 1995).

Japanese Society

A most useful introductory text on Japanese society is Joy Hendry, *Understanding Japanese Society* (RoutledgeCurzon, 3rd edn, 2003). A more specialized but intriguing study is Joy Hendry and Massimo Raveri, *Japan at Play: The Ludic and the Logic of Power* (Routledge, 2002). The changing social class structure is analysed in Hiroshi Ishida, *Social Mobility in Contemporary Japan* (Macmillan, 1993). A critical view of social patterns is given in Yoshio Sugimoto, *An Introduction to Japanese Society* (Cambridge University Press, 1997). For studies of marginality in Japanese society, see Carolyn Stevens, *On the Margins of Japanese Society* (Routledge, 1997), and Roger Goodman, *Children of the Japanese State* (Oxford University Press, 2000). A fascinating social history of housing is given in Ann Waswo, *Housing in Postwar Japan: A Social History* (RoutledgeCurzon, 2002).

The Economy

A useful text is David Flath, *The Japanese Economy* (Oxford University Press, 2000, 2003). See also Hiromitsu Ishi, *Making Fiscal Policy in Japan: Economic Effects and Institutional Settings* (Oxford University Press, 2000).

The Allied Occupation and Political History since 1945

The best book on the Occupation is John Dower, *Embracing Defeat: Japan in the Aftermath of World War II* (Penguin, 1999). See also Takemae Eiji, *Inside GHQ: The Allied Occupation and its Legacy* (Continuum, 2002). For a contemporary 'official' account, see Supreme Commander for the Allied Powers, *Political Reorientation of Japan, September 1945 to September 1948*, 2 vols (Greenwood Press, 1970; repr. of original 1949 edn published by US Government Printing Office). For post-war political histories, see Masumi Junnosuke (trans. Lonny E. Carlile), *Postwar Politics in Japan, 1945–1955* (Institute of East Asian Studies, University of California, Berkeley: Japan Research Monograph No. 6, 1985); Masumi Junnosuke, *Contemporary Politics in Japan* (University of California Press, 1995); Andrew Gordon (ed.), *Postwar Japan as History* (University of California Press, 1993).

The *Tennō* and Politics

Stephen S. Large, *Emperor Hirohito and Shōwa Japan: A Political Biography* (Routledge, 1992); Ben-Ami Shillony, *Enigma of the Emperors: Sacred Subservience in Japanese History* (Global Oriental, 2005).

The Government Bureaucracy

Contrasting views of the nature, role and effectiveness of the government bureaucracy are to be found in the following books: Chalmers Johnson, *MITI and the Japanese Miracle: The Growth of Industrial Policy, 1925–1975* (Stanford University Press, 1982); Daniel Okimoto, *Between MITI and the Market: Japanese Industrial Policy for High Technology* (Stanford University Press, 1989); Aurelia George Mulgan, *Japan's Failed Revolution: Koizumi and the Politics of Economic Reform* (Asia Pacific Press, 2002); Jennifer Amyx, *Japan's Financial Crisis: Institutional Rigidity and Reluctant Change* (Princeton University Press, 2004); Harumi Hori, *The Changing Japanese Political System: The Liberal Democratic Party and the Ministry of Finance* (Routledge, 2005); Aurelia George Mulgan, *Japan's Interventionist State: The Role of the MAFF* (RoutledgeCurzon, 2005).

Decision-Making, Public Policy and Interest Groups

The following is a selection of the fairly extensive literature on public policy, interest groups and decision-making in Japan: Kent E. Calder, *Crisis and Compensation: Public Policy and Political Stability in Japan, 1949–1986* (Princeton University Press, 1988); John C. Campbell, *How Policies Change: The Japanese Government and the Aging Society* (Princeton University Press, 1992); Junko Katō, *The Problem of Bureaucratic Rationality: Tax Politics in Japan* (Princeton University Press, 1995); Minoru Nakano, *The Policy-Making Process in Contemporary Japan* (Macmillan and St Martin's Press, 1997); Steven K. Vogel, *Japan Remodeled: How Government and Industry are Reforming Japanese Capitalism* (Cornell University Press, 2006).

Governance

Jennifer Amyx and Peter Drysdale (eds), *Japanese Governance: Beyond Japan Inc.* (RoutledgeCurzon, 2003); Glenn D. Hook (ed.), *Contested Governance in Japan: Sites and Issues* (RoutledgeCurzon, 2005).

The Electoral System and Voting Behaviour

The classic work on voting behaviour is Scott C. Flanagan et al., *The Japanese Voter* (Yale University Press, 1991). The successive electoral systems for the House of Representatives, and the ongoing system for the House of Councillors, are described in most textbooks. For useful analyses, see Bernard Grofman et al., *Elections in Japan, Korea, and Taiwan under the Single Non-Transferable Vote* (University of Michigan Press, 1999); Steven R. Reed (ed.), *Japanese Electoral Politics: Creating a New Party System* (RoutledgeCurzon, 2003); Yusaku Horiuchi, *Institutions, Incentives and Electoral Participation* (Routledge, 2005).

Party Politics

There has been no monograph on the LDP since Haruhiro Fukui, *Party in Power: The Japanese Liberal-Democrats and Policy-Making* (Australian National University Press, 1970), though some writers have tended to extract the LDP from party politics and treat it rather as part of government. For general accounts, see Masaru Kohno, *Japan's Postwar Party Politics* (Princeton University Press, 1997); Ronald J. Hrebenar, *Japan's New Party System* (Westview, 2000). On parties out of power, see Stephen Johnson, *Opposition Party Politics in Japan: Strategies under a One-Party Dominant Regime* (Routledge, 2000); Ethan Scheiner, *Democracy without Competition in Japan: Opposition Failure in a One-Party Dominant State* (Cambridge University Press, 2006); Sarah Hyde, *From Old Socialists to New Democrats: The Realignment of the Japanese Left* (Routledge, 2008); Inge Engel-Christensen, *New Party Success and Failure in Japan* (University of Oxford D. Phil. thesis).

The Constitution

There is an abundant literature on the 1946 Constitution. The following is a selection: John M. Maki, *Court and Constitution in Japan: Selected Supreme Court Decisions, 1948–1960* (University of Washington Press, 1964); Robert E. Ward, 'The Commission on the Constitution and Prospects for Constitutional Change in Japan', *Journal of Asian Studies*, vol. 24, no. 3 (May 1965); Hiroshi Itoh and Lawrence W. Beer, *The Constitutional Case Law of Japan: Selected Supreme Court Decisions, 1961–70* (University of Washington Press, 1978); John M. Maki (trans. and ed.), *Japan's Commission on the Constitution: The Final Report* (University of Washington Press, 1980); Koseki Shōichi (ed. and trans. Ray E. Moore), *The Birth of Japan's Postwar Constitution* (Westview, 1997); Ray A. Moore and Donald L. Robinson, *Partners for Democracy: Crafting the New Japanese State under MacArthur* (Oxford University Press, 2002); Glenn D. Hook and Gavan McCormack, *Japan's Contested Constitution: Documents and Analysis* (Routledge, 2001).

Local Politics and Government

The classic text in this area is Kurt Steiner, *Local Government in Japan* (Stanford University Press, 1965). Most general books have a relevant section, but the following are more specialist works: Richard J. Samuels, *The Politics of Regional Policy in Japan: Localities Incorporated?* (Princeton University Press, 1983); Purnendra Jain, *Local Politics and Policy-Making in Japan* (Commonwealth Publishers [New Delhi], 1989); Michio Muramatsu, *Local Power in the Japanese State* (University of California Press, 1997); Purnendra Jain, *Japan's Subnational Governments in International Affairs* (Routledge, 2005).

Labour and Employment

For recent books on labour and employment, see Mari Sako and Hiroki Sato (eds), *Japanese Labour and Management in Transition: Diversity, Flexibility and Participation* (Routledge, 1997); Ikuo Kume, *Disparaged Success: Labor Problems in Postwar Japan* (Cornell University Press, 1998); Peter C. D. Matanle, *Japanese Capitalism and Modernity in a Global Era: Re-Fabricating Lifetime Employment Relations* (Routledge, 2003); Marcus Rebick, *The Japanese Employment System: Adapting to a New Economic Environment* (Oxford University Press, 2005); John Crump, *Nikkeiren and Japanese Capitalism* (RoutledgeCurzon, 2003).

Civil Society and the Voluntary Sector

This is an area of increasing interest and significance. See the following works: Robin M. Leblanc, *Bicycle Citizens: The Political World of the Japanese Housewife* (University of California Press, 1999); Frank J. Schwartz and Susan J. Pharr, *The State of Civil Society in Japan* (Cambridge University Press, 2003); Stephen P. Osborne (ed.), *The Voluntary and Non-Profit Sector in Japan: The Challenge of Change* (RoutledgeCurzon, 2003).

The Politics of Agriculture

See especially the following works by Aurelia George Mulgan: *The Politics of Agriculture in Japan* (Routledge, 2000); *Japan's Interventionist State: The Role of the MAFF* (Routledge, 2005); *Japan's Agricultural Policy Regime* (Routledge, 2006); *Power and Pork: A Japanese Political Life* (ANU E Press and Asia Pacific Press, 2006).

The Politics of the Environment

The following works in this increasingly important area of concern are of interest: Timothy S. George, *Minamata: Pollution and the Struggle for Democracy in Postwar Japan* (Harvard University Asia Center, 2001); Isao Miyaoka, *Legitimacy in International Society: Japan's Reaction to Global Wildlife Preservation* (Palgrave Macmillan, 2004).

The Politics of Education

The following books approach the subject from differing perspectives: Leonard J. Schoppa, *Education Reform in Japan: A Case of Immobilist Politics* (Routledge, 1991); Shoko Yoneyama, *The Japanese High School* (Routledge, 1999); Christopher P. Hood, *Japanese Education Reform: Nakasone's Legacy* (Routledge, 2001); Robert W. Aspinall, *Teachers' Unions and the Politics of Education in Japan* (State University of New York Press, 2001); Roger Goodman and David Phillips, *Can the Japanese Change their Education System?* (Symposium Books, 2003).

The Politics of Social Welfare

The following are of interest: Gregory Kasza, *One World of Welfare: Japan in Comparative Perspective* (Cornell University Press, 2006); Leonard Schoppa, *Race for the Exit: The Unraveling of Japan's System of Social Protection* (Cornell University Press, 2006).

Foreign and Defence Policy

There is a huge literature here, from which the following is a brief selection: Inoguchi Takashi and Purnendra Jain, *Japanese Foreign Policy Today* (Palgrave Macmillan, 2000); Michael J. Green, *Japan's Reluctant Realism* (Palgrave Macmillan, 2003); Glenn D. Hook and Richard Siddle (eds), *Japan and Okinawa: Structure and Subjectivity* (Routledge, 2003); Hugo Dobson, *Japan and United Nations Peacekeeping: New Pressures, New Responses* (Routledge, 2003); Hugo Dobson, *Japan and the G7/G8* (Routledge, 2004); Glenn D. Hook, Julie Gilson, Christopher W. Hughes and Hugo Dobson, *Japan's International Relations: Politics, Economics and Security* (Routledge, 2nd edn, 2005); Christopher W. Hughes, *Japan's Re-emergence as a 'Normal' Military Power* (Routledge: Adelphi Paper 368–9, 2005); Caroline Rose, *Sino-Japanese Relations: Facing the Past, Looking to the Future?* (RoutledgeCurzon, 2005); Kazuhiko Togo, *Japan's Foreign Policy 1945–2003: The Quest for a Proactive Policy* (Brill, 2005).

Websites

See for instance the websites of the major newspapers:

http://www.asahi.com.english/
http://www.yomiuri.co.jp
http://www.mainichi.co.jp
http://www.nni.nikkei.co.jp
http://www.japantimes.co.jp

General websites include:

Japan Focus Newsletter: http://japanfocus.org/
The Japan Information Network: http://jin.jcic.or.jp
The Prime Minister's Office: http://www.kantei.go.jp

All other ministries, nearly all political parties, many other political organizations and interest groups, as well as a high proportion of national (and some local) politicians, have their own websites. Not all are in English, but many at national level are.

Index